The analysis of action

Recent theoretical and empirical advances

Edited by

Mario von Cranach
Professor of Psychology, University of Berne

and

Rom Harré
Lecturer in the Philosophy of Science,
University of Oxford

Cambridge University Press

Cambridge
London   New York   New Rochelle
Melbourne   Sydney

Editions de la Maison des Sciences de l'Homme
Paris

Published by the Press Syndicate of the University of Cambridge
The Pitt Building, Trumpington Street, Cambridge CB2 1RP
32 East 57th Street, New York, NY 10022, USA
296 Beaconsfield Parade, Middle Park, Melbourne 3206, Australia

© Cambridge University Press 1982

First published 1982

Printed in Great Britain at the Pitman Press, Bath

Library of Congress catalogue card number: 81–12304

British Library Cataloguing in Publication Data
The analysis of action.—(European studies in social
  psychology)
  1. Man—Congresses 2. Act (Philosophy)—Congresses
  I. Cranach, Mario von II. Harré, Rom
  III. Series
  128'.4 BD450

ISBN 0 521 24229 0 hard covers
ISBN 0 521 28644 1 paperback
ISBN 2 901725 48 1 hard covers France only
ISBN 2 901725 50 3 paperback France only

European Studies in Social Psychology

The analysis of action

European studies in social psychology

Editorial Board: J. M. F. JASPARS, University of Oxford; WILLEM DOISE, Université de Genève; COLIN FRASER, University of Cambridge; SERGE MOSCOVICI, Ecole des Hautes Etudes en Sciences Sociales; KLAUS R. SCHERER, Justus-Liebig-Universität Giessen; HENRI TAJFEL, University of Bristol; MARIO VON CRANACH, Universität Bern.

The series is jointly published by the Cambridge University Press and the Editions de la Maison des Sciences de l'Homme, in close collaboration with the Laboratoire Européen de Psychologie Sociale of the Maison, as part of the joint publishing agreement established in 1977 between the Fondation de la Maison des Sciences de l'Homme and the Syndics of the Cambridge University Press.

It consists mainly of specially commissioned volumes on specific themes, particularly those linking work in social psychology with other disciplines. It will also include occasional volumes of 'Current Research'.

Cette collection est publiée en co-édition par Cambridge University Press et les Editions de la Maison des Sciences de l'Homme en collaboration étroite avec le Laboratoire Européen de Psychologie Sociale de la Maison. Elle s'intègre dans le programme de co-édition établi en 1977 par la Fondation de la Maison des Sciences de l'Homme et les Syndics de Cambridge University Press.

La collection comprend essentiellement des ouvrages sur des thèmes spécifiques permettant de mettre en rapport la psychologie sociale et d'autres disciplines, avec à l'occasion des volumes consacrés à des 'recherches en cours'.

Already published:

Social markers in speech, edited by Klaus R. Scherer and Howard Giles

Advances in the social psychology of language, edited by Colin Fraser and Klaus R. Scherer

Forthcoming:

Social identity and intergroup relations, edited by Henri Tajfel

Contents

Contributors

M. BRENNER
Department of Social Studies, Oxford Polytechnic, Headington, Oxford OX3 0PB, U.K.

J. BRUNER
Department of Psychology, Harvard University, Cambridge, Mass. U.S.A.

D. CLARKE
Department of Experimental Psychology, University of Oxford, South Parks Road, Oxford OX1 3UD, U.K.

P. COLLETT
Department of Experimental Psychology, University of Oxford, South Parks Road, Oxford OX1 3UD, U.K.

M. VON CRANACH
Psychologies Institut, Universität Bern, Gesellschaftsstrasse 49, 3012 Bern, Switzerland

W. HACKER
Brabschützer Strasse 18, 8039 Dresden, G.D.R.

R. HARRÉ
Sub-Faculty of Philosophy, University of Oxford, 10 Merton Street, Oxford OX1 4JJ, U.K.

U. KALBERMATTEN
Psychologies Institut, Universität Bern, Gesellschaftsstrasse 49, 3012 Bern, Switzerland

G. KAMINSKI
Psychologies Institut, Universität Tübingen, Friedrichstrasse 21, 7400 Tübingen, G.F.R.

M. KRECKEL
Am Rednitzhang 2, 8500 Nuremberg/Eibach, G.F.R.

R. LAMB
Department of Experimental Psychology, University of Oxford, South Parks Road, Oxford OX1 3UD, U.K.

T. LUCKMANN

Fachbereich Psychologie und Soziologie, Universität Konstanz, 7750 Konstanz, Postfach 7733, G.F.R.

P. MARSH

Department of Social Studies, Oxford Polytechnic, Headington, Oxford OX3 0PB, U.K.

P. C. REYNOLDS

1660 N. LaSalle Street, Apt 3910, Chicago, Ill. U.S.A.

V. REYNOLDS

Department of Biological Anthropology, University of Oxford, 58 Banbury Road, Oxford OX2 6QS, U.K.

Preface and Introduction

MARIO VON CRANACH AND R. HARRÉ

This book concentrates on the topic of goal-directed action (henceforth to be abbreviated to GDA). It emerged from a conference on 'The Organization of Action' which was organized by the first editor in the Laboratoire de Psychologie Sociale of the Maison des Sciences de l'Homme at Paris. The conference was put on with the help of the Werner-Reimers-Stiftung of Bad Homburg, and was held in January 1979.

There were about thirty participants from various disciplines, including psychology, sociology, philosophy, linguistics and law and from several different countries. About twenty papers were presented concerning various fundamental methodological and empirical aspects of the topic. Although the organizer, with the aid of the planning committee (E. Goffman, R. Harré, G. Kaminski and V. Reynolds) had tried to compose a coherent programme and to define some basic common viewpoints, the discussion developed its own momentum. The meeting produced some pearls of clarity and insight, as well as moments of confusion and even despair. At the end most participants not only agreed that they had learned something, but also felt that there was a convergence of theoretical and empirical work from which a definitive field of research was emerging. Since this was, to our knowledge, the first interdisciplinary meeting addressing itself directly and exclusively to the topic of GDA, publication of some of the papers was felt to be desirable.

GDA is perhaps the most pervasive and important aspect of human behaviour. Try to imagine what you did yesterday and today, and what you will do tomorrow. You will find it difficult to think of any activity of importance which is not somehow related to goals and projects. 'To do' means to act rather than to be acted upon, or merely to react. The operation of GDA concerns nearly every aspect of individual and social life. Its understanding should, therefore, clearly affect all of the social and behavioural sciences. Understanding how we bring about our deliberate actions can hardly fail to have great practical value as well as intrinsic scientific interest.

For these obvious reasons, we should expect the study of GDA to contribute one of the central aspects of the social and behavioural sciences; and yet we know that this has not been the case. It is true that the picture varies from discipline to discipline, but even where GDA does contribute an essential category, as in sociology, it is mainly theoretically treated. In fact, there is an abundance of action theories, but it strikes us that empirical research, except from some specific schools such as Marxist psychology of activity, is extremely rare. This finding, if properly considered, is so incredible that it seems worthwhile looking briefly into its causes. It will be helpful for this purpose to examine the status of the concept of GDA in some of the sciences of man.

Let us begin with the most fundamental: philosophy. There has been a great deal of discussion of the concept of action in philosophical psychology. Three main lines of development have emerged, none of which has yet had much influence on the kinds of questions that are pursued in experimental psychology. In order to identify actions, to individuate and classify them and to study their sequential structure in human productions, some system of concepts is required. Considerable work on the critical analysis of action concepts has been done, summed up, for instance in the work of Goldman (1970). The upshot of this sort of study has been the realization that the question of whether a human performance should be properly considered to be an action, and if so what action, depends on hypotheses about actors' intentions and the categories of interpretation available to interactors. Parallel to and connected with philosophical analysis of action concepts has gone an investigation into the proper kinds of explanatory framework to be deployed in understanding how an action is produced by an actor. A good summary of the state of development of that field can be found in Aune (1977). Again it seems that wants, beliefs and intentions must play an indispensable role in formulating explanations. These are mental states and their deployment is largely in the course of cognitive processes. The third strand of recent philosophical psychology has concerned itself with the refinement of systems of concepts for handling the attribution of mental states and cognitive processes to oneself and others. Alston (1975) has set out the major alternatives and examined their relative merits.

With the backing of philosophical analysis the theoretical psychology of action has been pushed far in advance of the possibilities for empirical testing available in the existing experimental techniques. These are still dominated by assumptions left over from the behaviourist period. The situation is reminiscent of biology before molecular genetics. The work reported in this volume represents a conscious effort to remedy the disparity, by setting out exemplars of more advanced empirical techniques and starting to look for ways of grounding psychological theory in experimental exploration of action and its genesis.

In sociology, the category of action has always been considered important. One of the most popular definitions of action has been provided by Max Weber (see V. Reynolds, this volume); and Talcott Parsons developed a famous theory of action. These endeavours, for several reasons, did not result in a serious empirical treatment of GDA. The most important obstacle may be found in the difficulty of studying actions on a purely sociological level. Obviously, it is the individual who acts, and it is individual cognitions which exert immediate control over action, though a social dimension of mediated action must never be lost sight of. Before General Systems Theory had really developed, sociologists perhaps lacked an appropriate intellectual tool for the empirical treatment of social systems. At the borderline between sociology and psychology, researchers who worked within various branches of symbolic interactionism and phenomenological sociology (e.g. ethnomethodology) have provided ideas which serve just this task. Their work is based (at least partly) on the concept of a hierarchy of control from society to self to act. Unfortunately they have developed their own idiosyncrasies, which make it difficult for them to adjust even to those standards of empirical work which would be generally acceptable. It is only in the last decade that their ideas have become translated into reliable empirical studies.

In psychology the development has been complicated by the existence of several different ways of partitioning human behaviour. GDA fell somehow between stools. Western European and Anglo-American psychology was dominated by the disciplines of psychoanalysis and behaviourism for decades. Both approaches inhibited the development of a proper psychology of GDA, despite many promising beginnings. Psychoanalysis does not at all deny the existence of GDA, but it places the weight on unconscious motivational conflict, and conscious cognitive steering of action is considered relatively unimportant. And, of course, the dominant brand of classical Freudian psychoanalysis is basically unsocial. Behaviourism, at least in its rigorous form, denies a steering function for cognition in the genesis of behaviour and over-stresses stimulus dependency. This general attitude has deeply affected the style of thinking of psychologists, even if they do not consider themselves behaviourists. 'Reaction' and 'interaction' are commonly used without noticing that these concepts presuppose a concept of action *per se*. There have always been exceptions, diverging or different lines of thought, but in many cases they were peacefully absorbed by the mainstream of behaviourist thought and were lost to the study of GDA. For instance, the original Lewinian theory, largely an environmentally-oriented action theory, had little real impact in this regard. Heider's exposition of naive psychology was essentially a naive psychology of action. But it has been transformed and alienated into a quite restricted psychology of attribution. And even cognitive psychology, the latest and most influential achievement of psychological science, tends to deal with cognitive processes in isolation rather than relating them to their behavioural consequences. If action-related cognitions are considered, as in the field of artificial intelligence, the basis is an unreflective naive psychology. Most cognitive psychologists are wary of touching the dangerous topic of consciousness, following the silent maxim: only what a computer can simulate should be studied in man.

A further factor can be found in the methodological aspirations of psychologists. In experimental psychology statistical methods have been highly refined. These are generally based on probabilistic assumptions and favour inference rather than description. Their usefulness for the analysis of GDA is severely limited, since action analysis must depend on developing a conceptual system which can match the precision of naive psychology in the identification of the nuances of conduct. Few psychologists have, as yet, been willing to elaborate the tedious descriptions of goal-directed actions which are necessary before more analytical and explanatory work can begin. All these factors, and there are probably more, have continued to keep GDA out of the focus of Western psychological thinking.

In contrast to these main streams of Western psychology, Marxist psychology in Western Europe and especially in the socialist countries has favoured the study of GDA. At the outset psychologists were not hindered by the body–mind problem, quite the contrary. The Marxist theory of reflection (*Widerspiegelung*) and many action theoretical re-marks in the works of Marx and Engels encouraged the study of GDA, once purely Pavlovian approaches had been overcome. These ideas were developed in the research of Vigotsky, Rubinstein, Leontjew and many others in the Soviet Union, and by Tomaszewski and his school in Poland. A well-integrated theory of action emerged which focussed mainly on labour activities in an industrial setting. Participation in socially organized labour is seen as a major condition of personality development. Here the work also finds its limitations. Since labour concerns the execution of well-defined tasks in highly structured settings, there is little concern with individual conflicts, values and norms. And ironically the research tends to be restricted to the individual. The methods used in these studies are more or less traditional.

Finally we should like to point out that it is our impression that the situation is no better in those disciplines which might be expected to be immediately and practically interested in GDA. The distinction between intended and unintended infractions is essential to criminal law, and should obviously be based on an empirical GDA theory. But to what extent has this in fact been tried?

So much for our overview. We have reached the conclusion that the underdevelopment of GDA research could be linked to several factors. First, in spite of some advances, there exists a basic theoretical ignorance and prejudice which is reinforced by a lack of empirical and methodological imagination. Western psychologists generally just cannot see how GDA could be decently studied. Second, even those who do research on GDA are largely unaware of what goes on in the field and find it difficult to overcome interdisciplinary and international boundaries.

From such considerations we derived the aims of the conference. It was intended to aid in comparing the treatment of GDA in various disciplines and to develop a common theoretical framework. At the same time we hoped to illustrate research possibilities by examples and thus to encourage future empirical work. Finally we thought it vital to promote personal relations between the various participants and research groups. We were glad to observe that to an extent, although not completely, our expectations have been fulfilled.

The structure of the book, as it has finally emerged, is different from that of the conference. Some important topics unfortunately had to be abandoned, since their authors were not able, for one reason or another, to contribute. Thus there is only Hacker's paper left to represent the viewpoint of the Marxist psychology of activity. One paper was invited after the conference (Marsh) to complete a certain aspect of the work reported in this volume. Nearly all the papers have been elaborated and changed in response to critical discussion in Paris. Although the book in its present form is neither a complete nor a fully integrated representation of the field, its chapters still fit together and provide an overview of the actual problems of GDA research, as can be seen in the following outline.

The editors have provided a short introduction for each chapter. The two papers in Chapter 1 serve an introductory purpose. For this reason our Preface and Introduction refrains from a profound treatment of theoretical issues. In the first chapter we provide some basic theoretical and methodological ideas pertinent to the whole field, from the viewpoints of both philosophy and psychology, with the aim of providing a framework for the ordering and understanding of the other papers in the book.

Chapter 2 contains contributions which are all based on the first great line of thought in action theory, namely systems theory. Within this approach they treat problems of the two-dimensional (sequential and hierarchical) organization of GDA, but concern different topics and deal with different methods.

The contributions of Chapters 3 and 4 represent the second major approach to action theory, based on the ideas of symbolic interactionism and phenomenological sociology. (The third major theoretical source of GDA theory, naive psychology, is missing from the book as an explicit topic of concern, but constitutes the implicit basis of many of the papers.) The papers in Chapter 3 concern problems of the 'role–rule' approach, those in Chapter 4 treat the related but distinct problems of the impact of knowledge on action.

The papers in Chapter 5 are concerned with two more special but in no way less important questions. How is the capacity for GDA developed in ontogenesis? Whether and how can we analyse analogues of GDA in animals, especially in non-human primates? These papers promote deeper understanding also of many of the other topics.

Finally the editors present their conclusions, an evaluation of the present state of the field, as presented in the papers of the book, and a consideration of emerging trends.

Several fields for the possible application of a psychology of action are not represented here. In the hands of theoreticians of law such as Hart and Honoré (1959) and social psychologists such as Backman (1976) there have been theoretical and empirical developments in the study of the psychologies of action presumed in legal proceedings and processes, which have gone more or less hand in hand. But in the field of economics it is not easy to see any corresponding trend. The psychological element in economics has been represented by the highly schematized formal operations of decision theory. There has been a most useful burst of theorizing recently (see Hollis and Hahn 1979) but so far as we know this has met with little positive response from empirically-minded economists. Finally we are conscious of the absence of any work on the psychology of political action. This area should perhaps be the next to be cultivated with advantage. Some preliminary studies do exist, such as Wilson's study of conservatism (1973) but it concerns itself with attitudes rather than with action. Andre's (1979) psychopolitics has a well-developed theory, but lacks well-grounded empirical connections. We can only hope that this volume of coordinated theoretical and empirical studies will point the way to advances in the fields we have identified, similar to those we feel we are recording in the study of practical and social action as forms of GDA.

To sum up, our book does not represent the state of a mature problem area, but one of the first steps in its development. We are deeply obliged to many institutions and individuals for their aid in this pursuit, above all to the Maison des Sciences de l'Homme (Clemens Heller) and the Werner-Reimers-Stiftung (and its late director Konrad Müller). The British Social Science Research Council and the Australian Academy of Sciences contributed to the travel expenses. Finally we are grateful to Adriana Touraine and the personnel of the Maison des Sciences de l'Homme and to Agnes von Cranach for their aid in the organization of the conference.

References

Alston, W. (1975) 'Traits, consistency and conceptual alternatives for personality theory.' *Journal for the Theory of Social Behaviour* **5**, 17–48.

André, J. (1979) Privately circulated papers; reported in R. Harré, *Social being*, ch. 14. Blackwell, Oxford.

Aune, B. (1977) *Reason and action*. Reidel, Dordrecht.

Backman, C. (1976) 'Explorations in psycho-ethics: the warranting of judgements.' In R. Harré (ed.), *Life sentences*, ch. 12. Wiley, London.

Goldman, A. (1970) *A theory of human action*. Prentice Hall, Englewood Cliffs, N.J.

Hart, H. L. A. and A. M. Honoré (1959) *Causation in the law*. Clarendon Press, Oxford.

Hollis, M. and F. Hahn (eds.) (1979) *Philosophy and economic theory*. Oxford University Press, Oxford.

Wilson, G. (ed.) (1973) *The psychology of conservatism*, chs 4 and 17. Academic Press, London.

1. Theory and method

Introduction

To develop a programme of scientific research in any field, it is necessary to begin by building up a system of analytical and theoretical concepts and an associated methodology. Ideally these should derive from a critical examination of the rudimentary ideas and techniques that first suggested the possibility of the existence of an area of scientific interest. In our first chapter we offer a preliminary formulation of a system of concepts and a tentative description of the essentials of a methodology for the study of action. As the development of the field progresses both aspects will come to be revised and perhaps even radically modified. But without these preliminaries a scientific research programme cannot even properly begin.

Any study that purports to be scientific must include two systems of concepts. An analytical scheme is required to identify and classify the phenomena in the field of interest. Then an explanatory scheme is needed to develop hypotheses about the causal and productive mechanisms and processes at work to generate the regularities which the analytical scheme enables one to identify. In an advanced science these schemes are coordinate.

The classification scheme required for human action needs to be located on three levels. There is the level of mere movement; then there is the level of action, when the performance is conceived as intended by the actor; and finally there is the level of act, where actions are interpreted as having social and practical effects, outcomes, meanings and consequences. To develop an associated and coordinate explanatory scheme two important features of the analytic scheme need to be noticed. The scheme entails that actors should be thought of as acting in accordance with their intentions (plans, wants and so on). What they do has to be seen in terms of the realization of those intentions. Taken together these requirements impose a general *means–end* format on explanations.

1

But since we have identified three levels or networks of relations in which a human performance can be embedded, in each of which there could be means–end structures, the explanatory scheme must be hierarchical. Two possibilities for explanatory schemes meeting these requirements can be thought of, but only the full Aristotelian scheme ensures that all the relevant questions are asked, and that an ultimate human agency is preserved. Since actor's intentions and interactor's interpretations (based partly on hypotheses as to actor's intentions) are proposed as empirical realities, and in general, are available to conscious monitoring by people involved, the use of actor's capacities to attend to their intentions is an essential part of the methodology.

In the second part of the chapter the basic notion of Part 1, that action is goal-directed behaviour, is elaborated in such a way that the hierarchical and multidimensional structure both of cognitive operations and of action sequences is brought out. The analysis is pursued into sufficient detail to develop definite empirical hypotheses, *within the framework of the theory*, on the basis of which empirical studies can be organized.

The basic system that emerges involves specific concepts of three generic categories; manifest behaviour, cognition (possibly conscious) and social meaning. Within these broad categories each more specific concept is examined and more precisely defined for the purpose at hand. For example 'goal-directed behaviour' is carefully distinguished from 'planned behaviour', and 'normative' from 'conventional' strategies. Von Cranach shows how the concept classes are integrated into a total coherent system of analysis, description and explanation. Investigation of the processes, etc, picked out by each category of concepts involves its own appropriate methods, and we notice that these processes form a system and interact with one another, in ways which the study of concept integration makes intelligible. Only by looking at the whole system could a complete research programme be achieved. As a consequence the basic analytical unit is the act – the action as socially meaningful.

The idea that action is organized in a two-dimensional structure rather than sequentially involves hierarchy, as has been pointed out. But it also admits of the appearance of feedback links between levels of organization, so that goal-setting in terms of acts affects choice of means, for example, and resetting of goals involves new choices of means.

Most radical of all the proposals that are brought out by taking GDA seriously is the suggestion that consciousness should form an intimate part of the theory of action, and of the principles of research design. Conscious attention, monitoring and control of action become central topics of concern. Von Cranach explores the methodological consequences of the radical shift in empirical method required by the admission of these new objects of research attention. He shows that, contrary to tradition, there are no irremediable technical difficulties in the approach.

Theoretical preliminaries to the study of action

R. HARRÉ

Anticipatory summary

1. Introduction.
    1.1. A scientific approach to a field of phenomena requires two conceptual schemes.
        1.1.1. An analytical scheme for classifying the phenomena (expressed in terms of nominal essences).
        1.1.2. An explanatory scheme for accounting for the phenomena (expressed in terms of real essences).
    1.2. Ideally these schemes are coordinated.
        1.2.1. Failure to develop the explanatory dimensions can lead to a positivistic retreat to mere classification.
        1.2.2. In this condition men seem like automata.
2. Classification schemes and principles of analysis.
    2.1. Distinctions are complex.
        2.1.1. The practical order of life-sustaining work (Marx) v. the expressive order of the search for honour (Veblen).
        2.1.2. Both call for a means–end format in explanations.
        2.1.3. Each performance should be seen as behaviour–action–act, that is as embedded in three networks of relations.
    2.2. Actions and non-actions; boundaries of the field.
        2.2.1. Some non-actions are automatisms.
        2.2.2. Some non-actions are forced actions.
        2.2.3. Doing nothing is sometimes a kind of action.
    2.3 Framework of an action-taxonomy.
        2.3.1. Movement and action.
            2.3.1.1. Some movements can never become actions, though many can be, by being endowed with meaning, that is embedded in a relational net.

5

2.3.1.2. Actions become acts only when related to local social orders with local conventions. Hence there is no universal 1 : 1 correspondence between action-taxonomies and act-taxonomies.

2.3.2. Successful social action requires that the interpretation made by others of an actor's actions (via implicit assumptions of intentions) should be coordinate with those intentions.

2.3.2.1. *The* act is constituted by the 'intersection' of actor's intentions and interactor's interpretations.

2.3.2.2. Neither has absolute priority.

2.4. The above considerations require a social scientist to use two basic schemes: the actor's, associated with the antecedents of action, and the interactor's, associated with the consequences of action, which interact.

2.4.1. Categorizing by consequences can involve both physical and social outcomes.

2.4.2. Categorizing by antecedents involves actor's anticipations of consequences. This introduces the possibility of hierarchies of consequences.

2.4.3. Problems with intentions.

2.4.3.1. If intentions are ascribed via identifications of acts and acts are identified via presumed intentions the scheme is circular; but intentions may be avowed.

2.4.3.2. Sometimes an actor fulfills the intentions of another.

2.5 The boundaries of this conceptual scheme.

2.5.1. Behavioural unit segmentations are dependent on social classifications. In consequence there can be no fixed category of basic actions.

2.5.2 Interactor's beliefs about actor are always revisable, but this does not license wholesale scepticism.

3. Explanation schemata for actions; theories do not derive from induction from particulars, but through the development of models and analogies.

3.1. The 'want–belief' scheme. This is a plausible development and refinement of one commonsense explanatory mode as source model.

3.1.1. As the scheme is developed it assumes that wants (and perhaps even beliefs) could be efficient causes.

3.1.1.1. But want–belief conditions may be fulfilled without action occurring.

3.1.1.2. People can act when there are equally balanced alternative wants and beliefs.

3.1.1.3. The best solution is to suppose that people are agents.

3.1.2. But it is not clear how beliefs should be treated.

3.1.2.1. Perhaps beliefs are 'propositions in the mind', but the fact that beliefs can be avowed propositionally does not show that that is how they exist.

3.1.2.2. Perhaps beliefs are dispositions, but dispositions must be grounded in occurrent states.

3.1.3. Avowals of beliefs may be merely rhetorical devices to demonstrate publicly one's qualities as a person.

3.2. The Aristotelian schema can be construed as posing four questions, each of which must be answered for a complete explanation.

3.2.1. Efficient causes as sources of power to act may be private or public relative to the actor. If private and personal, then public and impersonal facts are not stimuli, but releasing conditions for action. This implies that people can be simple agents.

3.2.2. Final causes can be identified with the actor's prior representations of intentional acts, and formal causes with the local rules and conventions for realizing them, so they can be interpreted coordinately by interactor.

3.2.3. Material causes identify the media in which actor realizes his intentions.

4. Methodological consequences; the arguments of this chapter suggest a realist rather than a positivist form of action theory, i.e. psychological mechanisms must be treated as possibly real, and capable of being examined empirically, cf. this chapter, Part 2.

4.1. Conscious monitoring can yield information about acts attempted and the social knowledge and beliefs drawn upon in choosing appropriate actions to realize act-intentions.

4.2. But another step may be required, since the way a piece of social knowledge is represented in consciousness, say as an image or as a proposition, even as a feeling, may be a poor guide to its way of being in reality, when not so represented.

1. Introduction

A scientific approach in the understanding of a field of phenomena, no matter what it may be, involves the construction both of a classificatory and analytical scheme, and an explanatory scheme. A classificatory scheme is required to partition the field of phenomena into distinct types, to order those types into a taxonomy, and to predetermine, though never in an absolute and final fashion, the boundaries of that field. The explanatory scheme must provide the concepts in terms of which explanations of the phenomena as partitioned, ordered and bounded by the classificatory scheme, are to be constructed. Frequently explanatory schemes will be causal, but not always. Ideally, the schemes should be coordinate, that is there should be a thorough-going interaction between the way a field of phenomena is classified and the way it is explained. In the physical sciences the coordination of schemes has been brought to a high degree of perfection through the use of what, in philosophical parlance, could be called concepts of nominal and real essences. Nominal essences are the sets of characteristics which particulars in the field to be classified must meet to belong to categories, subcategories, and so on. These may be based on superficial appearances which can sometimes be sufficiently stable to be useful in the classification process. Real essences are the inner structures and underlying properties of the particulars and may sometimes include reference to the causal processes by which those particulars are brought into existence. Real essence, then, is in some measure part of an explanatory scheme, since the real essences of particulars explain why they appear the way they do. In chemistry and biology the classificatory and explanatory schemes, formulations of nominal and real essences, have become highly refined. Chemical elements are classified by their physical properties and chemical dispositions (nominal essences), and these are explained by the similar electron constitution of individual atoms of each element (real essences). Similar sorts of schemes have been produced for biology involving genetics as the mediating science between the properties of plants and animals which are used in external taxonomies and the underlying theory which explains the appearance and reappearance of these characteristics generation by generation.

The history of chemistry and biology suggests that there may be a long, hard struggle to bring about the coordination of the classificatory and explanatory schemes appropriate to a field of phenomena. In part, the difficulty lies in demarcating the field of phenomena itself, which may depend upon the development of the classificatory and explanatory schemes themselves. From time to time confidence in the general method of procedure which I have just outlined fails and the science is swept by a positivist reaction in which all reference to explanatory concepts, all attempts to identify and prove hypotheses about real essences, are abandoned for the time being. These periods are short-lived, but may at the time have severe consequences. The studies in this volume represent some of the first attempts to break through a hardened, positivistic shell which has surrounded the empirical study of action in the last forty or fifty years.

Positivist reactions in the physical sciences, though sometimes seriously delaying development, can be looked at with a measure of historical detachment. But in the human sciences such reactions involve assumptions about human nature which have moral and political consequences. There is a tendency during positivistic periods in the human sciences to retreat to a conception of men as automata and to an 'experimental' method of investigating their behaviour commensurate with that conception. It is not difficult to pass from despairing of penetrating to the core of human psychological functioning to an effective denial that it exists. The studies in this volume represent a serious attempt to develop positive doctrines and methods, working in general on the assumption that the positivistic period is, at least from the historical point of view, over.

2. Classification schemes and principles of analysis

2.1. Distinctions

It will turn out to be advisable to begin our discussion by identifying a number of important distinctions which cut across one another in the analysis of action and the identification of particulars in that field. We shall find throughout this discussion that the study of action is bedevilled by the necessity to use cross-cutting classifications. It is as if, having identified the plant kingdom and distinguished it from the animal kingdom, we found ourselves having to identify conscious plants as well as conscious animals.

2.1.1. The practical and the expressive orders. Looked at in the broadest possible way, human life seems to involve two main kinds of activities – those devoted to acquiring the means of life and maintaining organic existence, and those directed towards creating and sustaining public reputation, honour, dignity and so on. Now it is not at all my intention to suggest that these primary activity forms are reflected in distinctive kinds of actions. On the contrary, the very same action – for example, purchasing a bicycle in order conveniently to reach one's work-place – though clearly an event in the practical order, may also be seen as an act in the expressive order, since the choice of the ten-speed racer hints at a different sort of self-image than a comfortable Raleigh three-speed. More seriously, going on strike may be both an attempt to improve one's position in the practical order, perhaps enhancing one's wages relative to other workers', and a claim to advancement in the expressive order illustrating one's importance to society, demanding restoration of one's dignity, and so on. These orders, distinctive though they be, are usually to be recognized only analytically. They do not, generally, demarcate particulars in the world of action. The same action particular can be located in both orders. I shall be developing below a further set of distinctions which enable the phenomena of dual location to be adequately expressed. The recognition of these orders goes back far into the history of social analysis; its most recent and perhaps most vivid evocation is in the contrast between the analysis of bourgeois society proposed by Marx, built upon a base of the practical order, and the analysis by Veblen (1899) emphasizing the expressive order. The virtue of Veblen's work has been to identify the way these orders interact with one another, the practical order generating differences of wealth which may then be reflected in the symbols and practices of the expressive order, and the expressive order generating differences of value which may then be reflected in the practical order. Looked at from the standpoint of the variety of societies which human ingenuity has succeeded in constructing, it would be unwise to attempt to assign any unconditioned priority between these orders in the genesis of social forms and I shall certainly not do so.

2.1.2. *Means–end formats*. The studies in this volume, without exception, depend upon the use of a single, overriding principle, namely that action should be seen in terms of a basic means–end format. Every action points beyond itself, and, it seems, must be regarded for scientific purposes as a means towards some end. The imposition of this basic format on all the analyses, together with the distinction between the practical and expressive order which I have just been emphasizing, leads to a second point of importance. If one is classifying actions by reference to the means–end format then one must have some way of identifying ends, since it is only with respect to ends that actions are means. I shall be returning to elaborate this point in detail, but there are two general consequences which must be noticed now. Sociologists and psychologists, particularly perhaps Marx and Freud, have introduced the idea that the end for which a category of actions are the means may not be the end intended by the actor. Whether this point can be sustained or not, one must recognize the distinction between those actions for which the actor is the accepted authority as to ends and whose avowal of intentions can be taken as scientifically acceptable, and those where, for some reason or another, actors' views have to be called in question. The second point of importance is the distinction which must be made between the principles which an analyst would use to link means to ends in the practical and in the expressive orders. When one assumes that an action is embedded in the practical order, then its relation to ends is likely to be mediated by some principle or law of the natural world, for example in choosing to use an explosive charge to shift a lump of rock; whereas if an action is taken to be embedded in the expressive order, then an interpretative procedure must be used since the relationship between the action and the end is conventional. For example, using an explosive charge to make a political point requires the anonymous telephone call and the claiming of responsibility by a particular political group. The physical consequences of the explosion are not relevant as the end for which the use of the device was a means.

2.1.3. *The behaviour/action/act distinction*: it is upon this basic distinction that the whole of the action theory in this volume ultimately depends. Considered as a behaviour an event is nothing but a phenomenon in the physical world, related by physical chains of causality through a physiological system as far as it may be traced. But phenomena, generated by human beings, cannot be usefully demarcated into kinds and partitioned into elements by reference only to the criteria which one would develop on the basis of their physical/physiological properties alone. Events produced by human beings can also be embedded in a network of relations which depend upon an actor's intentions in producing the actions. Looked at with respect to this system of connections, the phenomena produced by human beings may be divided in ways and classified into categories quite distinct from those which would be used for analysing human events considered simply as behaviour. Finally, human phenomena can also be embedded in a larger-scale system of the social and practical world which human beings inhabit. A network of relations of a quite different sort now ramifies from the phenomenon in question. Considered with respect to that network, the particulars of the human field are acts. I shall be returning to the further refinement of the distinction between behaviour or movements, actions and acts, in a later section. At this point it is enough to identify the difference.

2.2. Actions and non-actions: boundaries of the field

Before attempting to apply a scheme to classify actions it is advisable tentatively to mark the limits of what sorts of phenomena are to count as actions. This marking can only be tentative since, as the analysis develops, refinements in the taxonomy of actions will come to bear upon what are taken to be non-actions. Three distinctions seem to be reasonable demarcations prior to any further refinement.

I begin with the most general idea, that action is what people do as opposed to what happens to them. Then within that broad category further distinctions can be made.

2.2.1. *Automatic functioning.* We could begin by marking off doings caused by the functioning of automatic machinery from all other doings. This would put shivering when cold, breathing, digesting, and so on, in the category of non-actions. It is not clear whether such non-actions should be put among the things that happen to a person, like falling ill, slipping, and so on, since there seems to be an implication in these cases that the causal influence is external. But what about the way in which falling in love is said to be something that happens to one? Is this a piece of monodrama perhaps? There have been some interesting psychological studies exploring the way this distinction is used. How what happens is construed seems to depend to some extent on whether the person talked about is oneself or someone else. This affects the exact location where the boundary between acting and being acted upon is drawn. A further distinction can be made between non-actions which can be brought under conscious control, such as breathing, and those which cannot. There is evidence that this distinction is drawn in different ways in different societies. More interesting are those cases where non-actions are convertible into actions by mere redescriptions. Sometimes to avoid responsibility we are able to achieve the contrary movement by redescribing actions as non-actions, removing the event from the moral order.

2.2.2. *Compulsion.* In some cases the dividing line between actions and non-actions seems to be represented by the distinction between unforced doings and forced doings, a further refinement of the distinction between those things that people do under internal or personal and those that are brought into being by external or public influence. (It is not a good idea, I think, to identify too closely the distinction between private and public matters with that between internal and external location of happenings, since there may be occasions when I make something private external, such as scribbling a note as a reminder for myself alone.) Sometimes a moral criterion can be imposed on this distinction, the device employed by Hart (1949). This would lead to a criterion based on assigned responsibility. Those events for which responsibility cannot be located would be what White (1968) calls 'human happenings'. But this move will not do as a general way of dealing with the distinction between action and non-action. Tennis commentators make great play with the distinction between a forced and an unforced error. A forced error is a miss-hit brought about by the placement or spin, etc, of the opponent's shot. In tennis commentary much greater censure devolves upon the unforced rather than the forced error, and yet it would be incorrect to claim that in the case of a miss-hit the shot was not an action of the player. He shaped up, he intended a volley, he played at the ball, but failed to execute the shot correctly. All this, as we shall see, fulfills some very powerful criteria for the ascription of the performance to the category of action.

2.2.3. *Deliberate inaction is action.* In such phrases as 'taking action' we seem to hear the echoes of another distinction, in which action is opposed to inaction or inactivity. But this will certainly not do as a general criterion for separating actions from non-actions. Daveney (1974) and others have pointed out that there are many contexts and occasions where one can be said actively or intentionally or deliberately to be refraining from acting (see also Luckman, this volume). 'Doing nothing' is not a uniform category of human happenings which stands over against 'doing something' in the way actions stand over against non-actions.

These preliminary distinctions are clearly not yet adequate as the source of a general system for the categorization of action.

2.3. Framework of an action taxonomy

I have already introduced the distinction between mere behaviour, intentional human action and social and practical acts. As I introduced the distinction it did not involve ontologically distinct entities but rather causally distinct networks of relations. The basic idea is that there is a central core (a happening) which is related through at least three distinct networks of influences to other core entities entailing three different but completely complementary modes of description of human activities. Human organic behaviour is related through causal networks, human action is related through teleological, intentional and means–end networks, and social and practical acts are related through their socially mediated consequences. Now it is crucial to setting up an action taxonomy to describe accurately the relationships between these networks at the nodal points. At the points of coincidence of the relational networks there is some ontologically unique 'something' which serves to anchor the three systems of relations at a particular point in space and time with reference to a particular human being. So, I wave my hand, and there are physiological antecedents and physical consequences. I do it as an action with some deliberate intention, with some aim or other, and in carrying on the social performance of farewelling I create and maintain relations of civility with you, sustain your impressions of my character, and so on.

2.3.1. *Movement and action.* Consider first the relation between behaviour as movement, and behaviour as action. It seems apparent that the following principles are uncontroversial.

2.3.1.1. Not all forms of physiologically mediated behaviour count as actions. There are a variety of such categories, tics, intestinal movements, and so on that are routinely excluded from the action network. Further, some physiological criteria which enabled one to partition a sequence of behavioural movements into elements would fail to pick out the physical bearers of actions. For instance, it would be quite plausible to claim that there are a variety of distinct movements involved in the single action of waving if one looked only at the musculature involved. The classification of events as actions must, then, refer to a presumed intention and a cognitively based conception of what counts as an element enabling an identification of movements relative to a 'top–down' partition. An extreme form of this is to be found in the phenomenon of hysterical paralysis in which conceptual units of the body fail to function, physically.

2.3.1.2. The relation between actions and acts is in some ways simpler in that it is a necessary condition for there to be a public performance of an act that some recognizable action should have been performed. However, the most elementary investigations of the relation between actions and acts shows quite clearly that even in communities related quite closely in space or time, actions and acts are not in 1 : 1 correspondence. The investigation of the gestural systems of Europe (Morris *et al.* 1979) illustrates this point quite clearly since iconically identical actions, i.e. intended sequences of movements having a conceptual unity, such as the forming of an 'O' with thumb and forefinger, have widely different social meanings in different European subcultures. So the social consequences of making an 'O' will be radically different, depending on whether they are related to the action by the network of conventions operative in, say, Greece, or by the network of conventions in, say, Denmark. Even in the same culture the same social act can be performed through a variety of intended actions, while the same intended actions can be used to perform a variety of social acts.

2.3.2. *Coordination requirements between intentions and interpretations.* However, there is a further complication. As I have described the matter so far I have taken for granted that the interactor has interpreted the action of the actor in the same terms as the actor has intended his creation, i.e. that the act as meant and the act as interpreted are the same. We need a further conceptual distinction to deal with the possibility that in real interactions this assumption may not be realized.

2.3.2.1. Icheisser (1970) made the requisite distinction by calling the performance of the actor, in so far as it generates an act as meant by him, *expression*, while the interpretations by interactor, in so far as they lead the interactor to suppose that an act has been performed, are *impressions*. The terminology is unfortunate since it runs counter to the use of 'expression' to make the public presentations of self. However, I shall follow Icheisser in construing the 'act' as the intersection between what is intended by an actor and the interpretation given to his actions by interactor. Most of the time, in close-knit communities, the possibility of misinterpretation creates little difficulty. Either misinterpretations do not matter or, for the most part, they do not occur, and even if they do, they are readily corrected. *Very* refined knowledge of the actions required to generate distinctive acts is routinely deployed by ordinary folk in the control of incidents in everyday life (see Kreckel, this volume).

2.3.2.2. One might now raise the question of the relative priority of the interpretative schemata of actor and interactor in classifying what has occurred in a social event. This is important for third parties to the interaction, such as social psychologists, or sociologists. As we shall see in the next section, there is no *a priori* way of determining priority. At this point in the discussion I should like to leave the issue unresolved, pointing out, however, that in practice, among engaged performers, priorities are negotiated and renegotiated from time to time. The outcome of such negotiations is often uncertain and they may form part of the game-framework of daily life in close-knit communities, such as families and work-places (see Lyman and Scott's (1970) study of such negotiations).

2.4. Two basic schemes

The discussions in the last section raised the issue of the relative priority of actors' intentions and actors' interpretations as categorizing criteria. Given that in daily life there are negotiations as to which of these schemes should be taken as definitive, say in the apportionment of blame, we must be prepared for the outcome of some negotiations to be uncertain. Necessarily, then, a social scientist approaching the social world must have amongst his resources two basic schemes of categorization. He will need to be able to categorize events from the point of view of the interactor, and that might be to categorize them with respect to consequences, for instance commitments, but he might also be able to categorize events from the point of view of actor, and that is to categorize them with respect to antecedents, for instance intentions. It should be noticed, and I shall emphasize this, that amongst the antecedents are actors' conceptions of consequences. And amongst the consequences are interactors' conceptions of antecedents.

2.4.1. Categorization with respect to consequences. Taking for the moment a third-party stance, one may be able to distinguish between those consequences of a human action which are physically or physiologically mediated, for example, the consequence that two boards are fixed together, as a way of identifying a particular sequence of physical movements as the action of nailing. This will provide us with a taxonomy based upon a presumed understanding both of the laws of nature and of the practical tasks in which men are engaged. The second range of consequences needed for categorization – and these, of course, may be categorizing the same action – is to look upon the action as having socially or conventionally mediated consequences. As Daveney (1974) has pointed out, the action of hammering may be located in a network of relations, one consequence of which is the construction of a stool, but the very same action of hammering may be located in another network of relations in which it is seen as a gesture of independence by a hen-pecked husband. To categorize an action of hammering as a gesture of independence is to provide it with an interpretation derived from a particular understanding of the micro-world in which it has occurred. There are more generic understandings where the conventions mediating the consequence of an action conceived as an act, are more generally viable, such as, for example, the kind of commitment entered into by the signing of one's name on a particular class of document. And there are innumerable other such examples. It is worth pointing out that the variety of conventionally mediated acts any given action can be used to perform at any given moment is virtually unlimited. By that I mean that different people from slightly different standpoints in the social world in which the action occurred may be inclined to give non-exclusive redescriptions of the event considered as an act and that there are indefinitely many standpoints. The point has been made by Anscombe (1957) in the context of the problem of definitively identifying intentions, but it is equally useful in categorizing with respect to consequences.

2.4.2. *Categorization with respect to antecedents.* For most purposes a social scientist can ignore the network of physical and physiological relations which form the material antecedents to the movement which is the substance of an action. But if we follow the previous account of actions as intended or meant performances, and acts as the social and practical consequences or outcomes of those performances, then one of the things an actor may intend are those very consequences. There may be many other consequences, of course, which he does not intend. It follows that the categorization of actions with respect to antecedents cannot be independent of their categorization with respect to presumed consequences. However, those consequences need not be the consequences that interactor creates by his interpretations, since in the actor's perspective the interpretations are presumed coordinate with actors' intentions unless *later* actors discover they are not.

This, unfortunately, is more complex than it might seem, since the expressive dimension, though it introduces centrally the moment-by-moment intentions of the actor, cannot be analytically separated from other aspects of the social world within which that actor is embedded. There is, for example, the situation he takes to exist, the setting he believes himself to be in, the life-course he supposes himself to be living, and so on. These matters become important when attention is paid to the hierarchization of actions, since momentary intentions may themselves have to be categorized with respect to overarching projects which a third party may perceive only dimly, but which may, in the cognitive processes leading to action, sharply differentiate actions for the actor himself. However, to preserve a systematic order in these remarks, I want to separate momentary intentions from what I shall call projects. A somewhat similar hierarchical structure is to be observed in the empirical studies by Hacker and von Cranach (this volume).

2.4.3. *Problems with intentions.* There are certain classical philosophical problems with respect to the concept of an intention, which must be noticed in offering an account of categorization of actions and acts with respect to their antecedents.

2.4.3.1. It has been pointed out by many commentators that there is a close relation between the identification of an action/act as being of a certain kind, and the attribution to the actor who produced it of an intention to produce that very action/act. If a third party, say, a social scientist, proposes to categorize actions/acts by reference to the intentions of actors, and it seems as if the intentions of actors can only be publicly known by the actions/acts they produce, then it seems as if the categorization with respect to antecedents is logically dependent upon categorization with respect to consequences and hence empty of empirical content. However, so to generalize the common occurrence which is described in the objection is to forget that our knowledge of the intentions of others is derived from two distinct and empirically independent sources. We infer intentions from actions, of course, but we may also know about intentions immediately by the avowals of actors. There is no particular reason to suppose that actors systematically lie about their intentions. There are complications with the concept of intention, which derive from the duality of intentional language. It is used for making public commitments independent of cognitive antecedents, and for revealing publicly, private cognitive antecedents. I propose to set aside this complication in this paper (cf. my analysis, Harré 1979).

2.4.3.2. The second philosophical problem arises through the fact of influence of one human being upon another. A simple case might be the use of a socially defined position of authority to issue an order to a subordinate for the carrying out of an action. Categorizing actions, then, with respect to their antecedents, if those antecedents are supposed to include intentions, must involve the identification of the source, as one might put it, of the action, which may lie in an actor at one or more removes from the person who actually carries out the performance. The obvious notion to employ here is that of responsibility or accountability. Considerable conceptual sophistication has been developed in the law, and more particularly in the philosophy of law, with respect to the attribution of responsibility (cf. Hart 1949). These considerations suggest that an initial microsociological analysis of events is required before a taxonomy based on the identification of intentions as antecedents and commitments, etc, as various kinds of consequences could be developed. The first classificatory divide would separate actions for which the immediate actor was held responsible from those in which he was merely an instrument of the intentions of others, or sometimes even the 'intentions' of an organization. Put in another way, it would be an important preliminary to decide whether the productive chain of the action terminates for all practical (moral) purposes 'in' the immediate actor, or ramifies beyond him to other persons, institutions, and perhaps even social structures.

2.5. The boundaries of this conceptual system

2.5.1. *Behavioural unit segmentations are dependent on social classifications.* In the previous section a number of ways have been proposed by which action types can be identified and action sequences segmented into elements. We have noticed that segmentation depends upon our prior capacity to identify social acts and the actions which in that locale are their means of realization. I have also established, I believe, the disconnection between natural taxonomies of movements as pieces of human behaviour and sociocultural taxonomies of actions as the performances of acts. Nevertheless, actions must be realized, somehow, in movements. My solution to that problem is firm and unequivocal, namely behavioural units are only relevant to the categorization of actions in so far as they are identified as the movement-complex conventionally assigned, in a culture, for the realization of an action type. On this view it would be improper to propose physical or physiologically-based criteria for basic actions. However, the question of basic actions remains, since if we admit a process of segmentation to be applicable to all flows of human activity, should we expect that the determined application of categories and classifications such as I have proposed would lead in the end to segmentation into units which were basic relative to all cultural conventions and practical activities? Various writers have proposed that a universal category of basic actions can be identified as the termination of categorization (for example, Goldman 1970), but they have based their universal category upon behaviour. Now in so far as it has been presumed that physical/physiological criteria would yield elements that could constitute the material basis of basic actions, such arguments are defective. We have already noticed that the complex of elements that constitutes the substance of an action is defined with respect to what is conventionally taken to be required to produce the action, and this of course, is not dependent upon the realization of any particular physical criteria. Furthermore, it has been pointed out by Enc (1975) that, in general, taxonomies depend upon a prior choice of theoretical position and the aim that the taxonomist has in making the demarcations that he does. Not even in the physical sciences is there an unambiguous physical criterion by means of which the elements of a classificatory scheme can be defined.

2.5.2. *Interactors' beliefs about actor are always revisable.* We have noticed the interaction between classification by antecedents and classification by actor's intentions which form part of the criteria by which interactor identifies those actions. Now it is clear that we must construe the cognitive status of interactors' mental states with respect to actor's intentions as beliefs or hypotheses. These beliefs are grounded in a variety of matters, including previous knowledge of the actor, a conception of what sort of action is afoot, the avowals of actor as to his intentions, and so on. Should we be intimidated by the possibility of an indefinite philosophical scepticism as to the possibility of identifying actor's actions for sure? Since every route we have to actor's intentions depends upon some ambiguation of his actions, we might be tempted to lose confidence in the scheme, since relative to any absolute demands for proof its offerings are weak.

At least two responses suggest themselves. One might simply dismiss the philosophers' scepticism as empty, since in the end the doubt that infects an interactor on a real occasion may be reduced to minuscule proportions. The responsibility of absolute certainty could be admitted in principle, since it would have little or no bearing on practical life. On the other hand, one might attempt an in-principle resolution by claiming that as far as social life is concerned, there comes a point at which actors' intentions are strictly irrelevant to the event. On this construal, one would insist that for most purposes it is the public reading of the action as act that is consequential in the world. The point was made by Austin, with respect to the alleged mental acts or states of mind which one might be tempted to attribute to a speaker when he says things such as 'I promise'. Austin (1965) insisted that even the existence of sincere intentions had no bearing whatever on the social force of the utterance of such performative formulae. He was, of course, making a philosophical point about meaning. It seems to me not too extravagant to follow him in making an empirical point about classification – namely that in the end the public criteria and public understandings of actions as acts have absolute priority over the personal and private intentions with which those actions are performed.

3. Explanation schemata for actions

It is worth perhaps beginning this section with the reminder that theories are not produced by induction from particulars. Rather, they are the product of the creation, in the active imagination of scientists, of hypothetical pictures or models as representations of the initially unobservable processes that generate observable patterns, which adherence to those very theories allows us to identify. There is an ineliminable complex of *a priori* elements in any theorizing. For the purposes of this study, I need not detain the reader by rehearsing the shortcomings of the view that the explanation of human action is to be achieved by reference to the environmental contingencies which are supposed to bring it about. In one way or another some form of a cognitive theory for the explanation of action must be sought. The reminder from the philosophical theory of theories is called for since in most cases the first form that a theory takes is a description, not of the real mechanisms and processes that generate non-random patterns, but of models or analogues of such mechanisms which are imagined to generate simulacra of the real patterns. The explanatory adequacy of a theory, i.e. its capacity to generate analogues of empirically-based descriptions of reality, is only one of the criteria on which the plausibility of such a theory might depend. There is also the question of the reality of the entities, properties, processes and relations which constitute the content of the theory. In the first instance, then, I shall be describing rival models of the productive processes that generate action. In the last section of this chapter I shall be considering the methodological issues that are reached by our attempts to identify such processes, structures and relations in the real world, and so to test which of our models is the best representation of the actual productive processes.

3.1. The first alternative: the want–belief schema

Turning to the forms of commonsense explanations of action for a source-model to guide the construction of an explanatory theory, one is immediately struck by the ubiquity of the citation of a combination of wants (needs, aims), and beliefs as to how these are to be achieved in everyday accounts. I shall call the want–belief combination a 'format of explanation' because explanations of particular actions are achieved simply by specifying the wants and beliefs that constituted their necessary and sufficient conditions of realization on a particular occasion. Generalizing the everyday format to a theory of action has several attractive features: it locates the explanation of action in attributes of individuals, and it provides an accessible psychological phenomenon – namely the entertaining or experiencing of a want, belief, need, aim, etc, together with a cognitive feature which is often not attended to explicitly in the course of the genesis of the action, namely the system of beliefs. Further, though some wants, needs and aims might be thought to be universal in mankind, incorporating the belief component in explanation-format allows explanations to be sited in particular cultures, since beliefs as to how certain wants should be realized may be of local significance only. Such a scheme can be made more sophisticated by introducing higher levels of wants and beliefs, with respect to which lower levels can be monitored, censored and generally controlled. Such a scheme has been developed by Alston (1977) and Taylor (1977). Though there are superficial differences between their ways of setting out this form of explanation, I believe their theories are essentially the same.

In the end, I shall be trying to preserve much of the Alston–Taylor point of view. However, there are some serious problems with that point of view as a way of exhaustively prescribing the form of explanation. These difficulties turn on the kind of causation which is supposed to obtain in the realm of action.

3.1.1. *A problem with efficient cause.* Considered with respect to the Aristotelian requirements for an explanation, the want–belief format seems to deal only with final and formal causes. It may be that the omission of an efficient cause component from the format is to be explained by an assumption that in the end there will be environmental contingencies which supply the deficiency. It seems unlikely that either Alston or Taylor would accept such a view. Alternatively, it may be – and I think this more likely – that Alston, Taylor and others who have adopted various versions of this theory have assumed that within the want–belief format itself an adequate causal account can be found. This might be because wants, since they seem to be directed and often to be emotionally charged, could themselves count as efficient causes. I would regard the suggestion that beliefs are efficient causes as extremely implausible. The upshot of the workings of the 'mental machinery' would be a kind of vector sum of wants whose resultant would, with the help of the required beliefs, generate action. One might note in passing that there is another version of a theory of the genesis of action which altogether burkes the issue of the sources of action by assuming a blanket Humean rather than Aristotelian view of causation. This is particularly associated with Davidson's (1963) theory of action in which mere committance of a type of cognitive element with a species of action is enough to provide a causal explanation since the lawfulness of the production is analysed in Humean terms.

I want to examine briefly the more interesting view that wants and beliefs do provide the material for an efficient cause explanation. Difficulties with this view can be summarized as follows:

3.1.1.1. It seems clear that in some cases want–belief conditions may be fulfilled and no action may follow. Philosophers have discussed the phenomenon of *akrasia*, weakness of will, in these terms. It seems generally agreed that the establishment of the existence of appropriate wants and beliefs does not exhaust the conditions sufficient to generate action. Just what is to fill the gap between the specifiable necessary conditions and the totality of sufficient conditions is not wholly clear.

3.1.1.2. In the Leibniz–Clarke correspondence, the protagonists engage in a lengthy debate on the nature of choice. Leibniz holds, roughly, the vector-sum theory that seems to be assumed by Alston and Taylor – namely that equally attractive wants and beliefs may be present to an actor, but in that circumstance no action will follow. The actor will have no sufficient reason for choosing one alternative course of action rather than the other. Clarke claims that this is psychologically implausible. Contrary to the vector-sum theory, he holds that human beings have a residual capacity to make a choice just in those conditions that the choice is not determined by an imbalance between the want–belief vectors on either side of the alternative. Such a view is consistent with the existentialist claim of the possibility – indeed the necessity – of making arbitrary choices in particular in committing oneself to moral or political positions. I do not think that philosophical analysis can take the argument very much further, but there are various solutions which we would have to distinguish empirically.

The solution which I find most attractive is to admit that persons are agents and can act contrary to any principle or rule to which they have previously been adhering. They would, in so acting, I suppose, act in accordance with some other principle or rule. There are complications about this, since in important cases the principle which is abrogated lies in the practical order, while the principle which replaces it as a guide to action lies in the system of beliefs associated with expressive acts (cf. Martin Hollis's (1977) treatment of Machiavelli's doctrine of the Prince as Lion and the Prince as Fox). Having admitted persons as agents and allowing for the possibility of a person moving from action according to one principle to action according to another, a mode of deliberation, with or without benefit of an overarching principle, we might want to admit, and this would be consonant with Alston's and Taylor's views, a hierarchical structure to the want–belief system. Human agency would consist, then, in the capacity to move from principle to principle at any given level of the hierarchy of principles, in accordance with differential adherence to various principles at higher levels, no matter what the principle to which adherence had previously been given. Such a solution provides the outline of a theory for formulating hypotheses about real processes in real people. I believe the methods developed by Hacker, von Cranach and others go some way towards testing hypotheses of this sort, but I shall return to this point in a later section.

3.1.2. *The problematic nature of beliefs.* In the foregoing I have assumed that there is no difficulty in giving an account of the mental attributes of human beings, that wants and beliefs are unproblematic entities with which we are all wholly familiar. That assumption would be quite unwarranted. I want to raise some difficulties, without any clear idea as to how they could be settled. In the context of this volume the problem that concerns me most is the characterization of beliefs. I have already pointed out that whereas it is part of the concept of a want that it should, at least in principle, be accessible to conscious attention, there is no such requirement on a belief. It seems clear that many of our beliefs are evinced or demonstrated only in action or public discourse. Some of them may never appear as consciously attended, allegedly real, mental existents. There are alternative accounts.

3.1.2.1. We might suppose that beliefs are to be understood as propositional attitudes expressed in sentences such as 'I believe that Evans Pritchard wrote *The Nuer.*' The content of the belief is represented in the 'that' clause and its belief-ishness by the propositional attitude-operator which introduces the whole sentence. Philosophers are familiar with the point that the truth of the whole sentence is independent of the truth of the clause under the propositional-operator. Notoriously it can be true of me that I believe propositions which are false. Were we to pass directly from the structure of the linguistic representation of beliefs to a theory about the mode of existence of such beliefs, we might be inclined to say that somehow there were corresponding sentences in the mind. But it seems to me – and this is a general point I want to emphasize – that there are no grounds whatever for supposing that the way beliefs are represented in consciousness or in the form of public speech is metaphysically consonant with how they exist when not so represented.

3.1.2.2. This can be made clearer still by reference to another account of the mental existence, the dispositional theory. Understood as dispositions, beliefs are to be attributed to people in the form of conditional assertions as what someone would do, would think, would say, etc, under appropriate circumstances, *ceteris paribus*. A dispositional theory of mind will not do in the form in which I have just expressed it, since to be justified in attributing dispositions in the basis of occasional behaviour one must be prepared to give an account of the grounding of those dispositions in some permanent feature of the individual to whom they are attributed (Armstrong 1968). I am inclined to think that many mental dispositions must be grounded in non-mental properties of a person, for instance properties of his nervous system. Such a doctrine does not require the reducing of mental attributes to the physiological properties. The mentalistic terms in many dispositions are ineliminable, representing as they do relational properties between a person and the things upon which he works, the actions he performs, and so on. But when beliefs come to be represented in consciousness, for example when I am running over the route I believe is the shortest way to Cambridge, my beliefs about the route could be manifested in any of a wide variety of forms, propositional, iconic, and so on. Most of the time my topographical beliefs are not so represented: I have only a disposition or tendency to form such representations. Though my beliefs are identified in terms of the content of such representations the content informs only the consequent clauses of the conditionals which attribute beliefs to me, leaving the issue of the grounding of those beliefs in permanent properties, of mind or brain, unsettled. So the fact that when I contemplate, or publicly reveal my beliefs, they appear in this or that form *can* say nothing about the form they have when not so revealed, i.e. what their permanent groundings might be.

3.1.3. *'Beliefs' as part of the rhetoric of public presentation of oneself as rational.*
In general, it seems to me, most of what we want to say about the role of beliefs and wants in social life can be said by reference to the part these play in public talk and the social construction of mind, i.e. in giving an account to others in acceptable terms to demonstrate our self-control, rationality and virtue. This practice, the practice of socially constructing a mental world for the benefit of the impression we make upon others, can be seized upon, I shall argue, to generate hypotheses as to the nature of the productive mechanisms which do, in the end, produce actions. Long ago, Vigotsky pointed out that during the process of individual development the public, social use of speech for instance, of performative utterances prefixed by 'I want', 'I believe', 'I think', etc, becomes a part of the private performances of individuals, and subjectivity is thereby born. This observation from developmental psychology suggests how serious an error it would be to identify the extent of the mental realm with the limits of the subjective.

One might argue, generalizing Vigotsky's observation, that the 'inner' or personal subjective cognitive processes by which action is generated are identical, or at least coordinate, with the public forms of speech in which, at least among adults, action is justified to others. If private cooperation takes the form of the practical syllogism this is because it is the form of public discussion of action. I must leave this thought undeveloped here, but it suggests various possibilities of empirical research.

3.2. The second alternative: the Aristotelian schema

The Aristotelian format, rather than identifying in advance the kinds of elements that must go into a 'mechanism' capable of generating action, is I believe more properly to be understood as specifying the questions which must be answered to constitute an explanatory account of a phenomenon. Four such questions can be posed. They can be stated separately, but they are interwoven in various complicated ways.

(i) What is responsible for the existence of the phenomenon in question?

(ii) What is responsible for the properties of the phenomenon in question?

(iii) What is the point of the production of the phenomenon? And here we impose a means–end schema on the phenomenon.

(iv) In what medium is the phenomenon realized?

In human action-theory answers to (iii) are an ineliminable part of the structure of explanation. In answering (iii), for human affairs, one is likely to offer the act, outcome or upshot as an answer. 'What is he raising his glass and drinking that wine for?' The answer might be: 'To congratulate someone.' I have already pointed out that to interpret wine-drinking, for example, as congratulation, requires the use of the local and, in the end, arbitrary conventions, which link acts with actions, in particular cultural settings. By the use of these conventions the relevant property of the action phenomenon is selected from all the possible features that could be germane to the question and so determine the answer to the second question. Answers to the fourth question will include, among other things, say, that it is the drink being wine, rather than water, that is the indispensable ceremonial element, social conventions determine that the drinking is a *wine*-drinking. Answers to the first question, why does the phenomenon come to be here and now, involve the answers to both (iii) and (ii), in that the phenomenon of congratulatory wine-drinking, i.e. the act/action, comes into existence at that moment through a complex of personal interpretations, individual intentions, and the social sense of the other actors involved (with the residual notion of pure agency to fall back upon in hard cases). Traditionally, we are accustomed to say that answers to the first question describe efficient causes, answers to the second question describe formal causes, answers to the third question final causes, and answers to the fourth question material causes. This sense of 'cause' is not identical with that of contemporary English.

I propose to consider each category of answer separately.

3.2.1. *Efficient cause theory*. If we fail to find a source of activity or power commensurate with the effect produced in the system whose behaviour we are studying, we may work with the assumption that, with respect to the effect in question, the system is passive. This requires that the energy for its transformations and productions must be presumed to come from without. Under these conditions the external element in the causal nexus will be an active stimulus which not only sets the system 'in motion' but provides it with the energy to proceed. For example, the moving ball *scatters* the stationary balls in a game of pool, being the only external source of energy. On the other hand, in many sorts of system, the system itself is supposed to have stored the energy for realizing the action, which is pent up, so to speak. In this case the external element in a causal nexus unblocks the release of the energy stored in the system. The removal of the block is a releasing condition. Whether such an event should properly be called an efficient cause of the coming into being of the phenomenon at that time is not important since it is the common alternative to external impetus. I would want to propose that we work with the assumption that it is as releasing conditions that causally relevant events are related to the causal nexus, until proved otherwise. Human action is then to be conceived on the model of a body which manifests its tendency to fall when a support is removed, rather than on that of a billiard ball which moves only when struck by another billiard ball.

If external causality is reduced to releasing conditions, our attention must turn to the internal properties of the system under consideration. If a human being produces actions appropriate to a certain environment and we hold it to be the case that the production of those actions was brought about by the removal at that moment of constraints to a pre-existing tendency to action, then we are required, it seems, to look for 'internal' determination in the search for explanations.

Commonsense explanations are happy to vacillate between two different kinds of terminations to the causal regresses this move opens up.

(i) Taking the asseverations of the actor *à pied de lettre*, causal regresses are supposed sometimes to terminate in motives, wants, needs, desires, etc. In commonsense explanations these are assigned vicarious causal power, and all that is required to complete the explanation is to give an account of the occasion which leads to the realization of a motive, need, want, etc, in action.

(ii) But the manifest inadequacy of this sort of explanatory regress, to

which we have already alluded in criticizing the use of an unsup-
plemented hierarchy of want–belief schemata, requires a theoretician of
human action to license another termination, the closure of a regress in a
pure human act: 'I just wanted to', 'I just did it', and so on. I propose to
adopt the principle that in human affairs explanations which terminate
in mental acts are to be preferred to those which terminate in unconscious motives, wants, etc, until proved otherwise.

Some consequences follow from the adoption of this principle. The
idea that causal regresses can terminate in mental acts involves
the introduction into the system of the idea of the person as a pure or
simple agent, an idea with which we have already been toying in
considering the capacity of people to give up acting according to
one principle in favour of acting according to another even when that
decision may itself be unprincipled. It seems to me extraordinarily
difficult to offer even the outline sketch of the empirical proof that
people are simple agents. The test of such an idea is in its power
to control our development of adequate theories. But in preferring
mental act-terminations to unconscious motive-termination, we are
also tacitly adopting a view of the nature of motives and the causally
relevant mental states.

There is a sharp contrast between psychologists' and philosophers'
views as to the referents of motive-terms, and the views held by
sociologists. Under the influence of the work of Burke (1969), Blum and
McHugh (1971) and others, sociologists have become accustomed to
treating motives as elements in a public discourse constructed for
expressive purposes. On this view motive-talk is to be construed as a
form of rhetoric designed to assist others to interpret one's behaviour as
intended action. This would block off a personally demeaning interpretation of one's behaviour as passive response to the situation one
finds oneself in, or the product of purely automatic functioning. Motive-
talk, then, is a way of demonstrating one's agency, but only in rhetorical
terms. Only people, it might be said, have motives, i.e. are able to give
reasons for *their* performance of their actions. If we took a wholly
sociological view of motives, one might be inclined to add wants, needs
and intentions to the list of those terms whose main role is rhetorical and
whose interest lies in their use to illustrate that one is a certain kind of
being. The more such terms from the psychological vocabulary that are
construed in that fashion, the less is the temptation to theorize about
action in terms of the vector-sum theory of wants, needs, desires and so
on, the theory described in section 1.

3.2.2. *Final and formal cause theory*. Once such a treatment has been developed for efficient causes of action, there is little difficulty in fitting together the classificatory scheme proposed in the first part of this chapter with the Aristotelian framework proposed in this section. Analysis of action, it was suggested, must proceed via the interaction between hypotheses as to the expressive intentions of actor and hypotheses as to the impressions formed by interactor, as he interprets actor's performances. The major analytical categories with which we begin are categories of social acts. This can be generalized readily to skilled practical performance where, for 'social act' one reads 'intended practical outcomes'. In so far as the intention to perform an act or to realize a practical outcome is a prior representation of that act or outcome which enters into the control of the action, then we have an immediate application for a modest form of the notion of final case. (Again, in the chapters in this volume by Hacker and von Cranach in particular, strong empirical evidence for the existence of such representations will be presented and their role in the genesis and control of action shown to be central.)

However, as I have emphasized, and as is apparent in the way want–belief theories are formulated, experiencing a want, or formulating an intention to perform an act, or planning to complete a certain physical task in a certain way with a certain outcome, does not provide the guidance necessary for the choice of a particular path of action to realize the planned or intended outcome. We need to draw upon our beliefs as to how such aims should be realized. In the practical order these beliefs will be concerned with possibilities of physical manipulation of material; in the expressive order with the conventions by which the society within which one is acting links actions with acts. Rules, conventions, plans, even laws of nature, in so far as they function in the belief system of the actor, would be comprehended under the heading of formal cause in the analysis I am proposing. One might speak in a less antique and Aristotelian fashion by talking of templates, but the form of the explanation and the assumptions as to the productive mechanisms are much the same.

3.2.3. *Material cause theory*. I am inclined to think that the least important element in the fourfold explanation schema is that concerned with the medium in which acts are realized. Frequently the rules or conventions which determine with which actions a project is to be realized pre-empt a decision as to the material in which realization is permitted. There are obvious physical limitations which predetermine material realization of plans, while there are social restrictions – though of a more convention-al nature on the physical realization of acts. For instance, the act of greeting among men in Anglo-Saxon communities is not to be realized in actions of kissing, though that would be an acceptable medium of realization among Latin folk.

4. Methodological consequences

The explanatory scheme as I have set it out could be treated simply as a prescription of a way of speaking, a way of formulating satisfying accounts of events. I think the message of the papers collected in this volume is that the proposals I have put forward as to the explanatory format we should adopt for understanding actions is to be seen as a realistic sketch of the actual system by which actions are produced in the real world by real people. In short, it seems to me that the material presented here supports a case for a realist interpretation of action theory.

4.1. The use of conscious monitoring

The detailed presentation of research work shows a substantial agree-ment as to the methodological requirements of proper work in this field. A central innovation is the important role that conscious attention by actors plays in the methods adopted in a wide variety of studies. What is the justification for such an innovation? One might argue, negatively, that no good and sufficient reason was ever produced in the old psychology for excluding conscious reports. But I think a much more convincing case can be made than that. The first step is to ask what the role of conscious representation of processes or parts of processes might be in ordinary everyday control of action. The work done in a number of different fields, including linguistics, suggests that consciousness is a feature of human and even perhaps of some animal nervous systems, and that it naturally occurs because its role is to maximize efficiency in the processes of repair and restitution of a system which has gone, in some measure, awry. Consciousness seems to be brought into an active state either when there is some kind of uncertainty or confusion as to goals, or when though the goal is given, some trouble arises in the means. Consciousness, by representing aspects of the system which is at work producing the actions, allows efficient reprogramming of goals, the resetting of subgoals in cases of difficulty, and the deliberate search of the repertoire of rules and procedures in an attempt to provide improved performance. I shall call this process the 'natural accessing' of the system. If we were to study hundreds of thousands of similar people doing similar tasks, it seems likely that natural breakdowns would occur all over the common system, enabling us to access bits and pieces of it by paying attention to the natural processes of repair. Eventually, through 'brute force and bloody ignorance' we might be able to reconstruct in mosaic form the outline structure of the total system as a type. A major innovation in methodology reported at this meeting is the use of deliberate interference to artificially produce conscious accessing of the system. Fragmentary glimpses of the productive process can be gained, which, taken together and mapped on a single graph, as Hacker and von Cranach have done, enable us to get a vision of the total system.

4.2. Reservation: the form of something as consciously represented may not be its form in reality

However, one must be clear that the form which conscious representation of elements of the system takes may be a bad guide to the nature of those elements in the real world as they actually exist. We have already noticed the difficulties that arise in attempting to pass from the form in which beliefs are represented, particularly the propositional form when beliefs are stated, to the form in which beliefs exist in the real world, as properties of human beings. It seemed quite implausible to suggest that beliefs existed as sentences. Similarly, when Hacker's and von Cranach's workers consciously access their control systems by being forced to contemplate a repair and come up with images, rules and the like, we have yet to develop an adequate theory to pass from this material to the mode of existence of these items in the real world. So far as I know, only one serious attempt to tackle this problem has so far been made. Fodor has proposed in his *Language of thought* (1976) that one should schematize and abstract from some form of computer language to provide an 'as it were' language of the brain. I think there are serious difficulties with his proposal. On the other hand, there is the heroic excision of the question, represented most vividly by Gilbert Ryle's *Concept of Mind* (1949), in which the analysis of the forms of speech we use to create a public representation of mind are claimed to be adequate, so that no further question couched in mentalistic terms could be asked. In that case, Hacker and von Cranach, Kreckel, Brenner,

Collett *et al.* have reached the end of the line. As far as I can see we are not in the position at this point in the realization of the research programme to make a decision one way or the other about this important matter.

References

Alston, W. P. (1977) 'Self-intervention and the structure of motivation.' In T. Mischel (ed.), *The self.* Blackwell, Oxford.

Anscombe, G. E. M. (1957) *Intentions.* Blackwell, Oxford.

Armstrong, D. M. (1968) *A materialist theory of the mind.* Routledge & Kegan Paul, London.

Austin, J. L. (1965) *How to do things with words* (ed. J. O. Urmson). Clarendon Press, Oxford.

Blum, A. F. and P. McHugh (1971) 'The social ascription of motives.' *American Sociological Review* **36**, 98–109.

Burke, K. (1969) *A grammar of motives.* University of California Press, Berkeley.

Daveney, T. K. (1974) 'Intentional behaviour.' *Journal for the Theory of Social Behaviour* **4**, 111–29.

Davidson, A. (1963) 'Actions, reasons and causes.' *Journal of Philosophy* **60**, 685–70.

Enc, B. (1975) 'On the theory of action.' *Journal for the Theory of Social Behaviour* **5**, 145–67.

Fodor, J. A. (1976) *The language of thought.* Harvester Press, Brighton.

Goldman, A. (1970) *A theory of human action.* Prentice Hall, Englewood Cliffs, N. J.

Harré, R. (1979) *Social being.* Blackwell, Oxford.

Hart, H. L. A. (1949) 'The ascription of responsibility and rights.' *Proceedings of the Aristotelian Society* **49**, 171–94.

Hollis, M. (1977) *Models of Man.* Cambridge University Press, Cambridge.

Icheisser, G. (1970) *Appearances and realities.* Jossey-Bass, San Francisco.

Lyman, S. M. and M. B. Scott (1970) *A sociology of the absurd.* Appleton-Century-Crofts, New York.

Morris, D., P. Collett, P. Marsh and M. O'Shaughnessy (1979) *Gestures: their origins and distribution.* Cape, London.

Ryle, G. (1949) *The concept of Mind.* Hutchinson, London.

Taylor, C. (1977) 'What is human agency?' In T. Mischel (ed.), *The self.* Blackwell, Oxford.

Veblen, T. (1899) *The theory of the leisure class.* Macmillan, New York.

White, A. R. (1968) *The philosophy of action.* Clarendon Press, Oxford.

The psychological study of goal-directed action: basic issues[1,2]

MARIO VON CRANACH

1. Introduction

Scientific interest in the problem of goal-directed action (henceforward to be abbreviated as GDA) has a long history and has resulted in a considerable body of literature. A survey of this literature reveals, however, two characteristics: the research is almost exclusively of a theoretical nature, so that we possess a tremendous number of 'action theories'; and it comes from many disciplines except empirical psychology (the Marxist psychology of activity is an exception to both of these statements). GDA did not fit into the preferred schemata of psychological thinking, whether they were behaviouristic or psychoanalytical: nor could it very easily be approached by the traditional 'hard' methods of test or experiment. These preconditions seem to be changing now; the advance of cognitive psychology has prepared the ground for a cognitively oriented theory of GDA (see Aebli 1980), and appropriate methods of data assessment such as systematic observation, content analysis of accounts and others have been developed which merit no less confidence than the more traditional ones. Furthermore, especially in applied fields like clinical (Semmer and Frese 1979, Grawe 1980) and industrial psychology (Hacker 1978), the practical value of the concept of GDA has been more and more readily accepted. For all these reasons we can observe an increasing number of empirical attempts to get a hold on these problems. It is my impression that we are just now experiencing the advent of an empirical psychology of GDA; a branch which certainly constitutes a new approach since it attacks new problems, and may lead

[1] Dedicated to Richard Meili, the founder of the Bernese Institute of Psychology, for his eightieth birthday.
[2] The research on which this article is based was funded by the Swiss National Foundation. I am grateful to Agnes von Cranach for her improvements of the English text and to Urs Kalbermatten for drawing the figures.

35

to a considerable change of the discipline's picture of man; but is still at least partly in line with theoretical and methodological traditions which have proved successful in the history of psychology.

In this article, I shall outline some of the major theoretical and methodological problems in this field. Related examples can be found in some of this volume's contributions and in other investigations to be cited; many of my considerations are based on a recently published book (von Cranach *et al.* 1980). My first intention in this paper is to state the issues clearly, my second to provide an order to locate diverging opinions. (Of course, in this pursuit I cannot conceal my own bias.) Limitations of space force me to be selective, but I shall still try to give a systematic treatment. Finally, I should like to emphasize that I owe many of these ideas to my co-workers and students.

The term 'action' is often used as just another name for 'behaviour'. My discussion here refers especially to GDA, with the accent on *goal-directed*, since GDA and behaviour are not the same; I shall not offer a schema for the treatment of behaviour theory in general. Although GDA, from the conceptual point of view, seems to constitute the more specific case, I am convinced that it constitutes the more common form of human conduct; and that mere behaviour can be found only in rare cases.

GDA is sometimes referred to by the use of rather vague expressions, like 'the intentionality of human behaviour'. The fully developed concept of GDA comprises several characteristics which imply some of its major scientific problems. In my discussion I shall proceed by unfolding the definitions' characteristics to dimensions of theoretical and methodological discussion. To provide an overview, I shall develop a complete and idealized definition first.

2. A definition of GDA

A partially complete definition of GDA, comprising the major viewpoints contained in the most prominent treatments, could read as follows:

[1] *GDA refers to an actor's goal-directed, planned, intended and conscious behaviour, which is socially directed (or controlled).*[3, 4]

---

[3] Let me just mention that the characteristics 'intended' and 'conscious' are often theoretically denied or deliberately or silently neglected, because they are erroneously thought to constitute a menace to the 'scientific' causalistic concept of man, since they presuppose assumptions of conscious steering and free will. This omission amounts to a

For practical purposes, additional information has to be appended:

[2] *An 'act' is a unit of (goal-directed) action, which is located in a specific social setting ('situatedness') and can be characterized by its directedness towards a distinct goal.*

Finally, a basic assumption of GDA theory and research should be explicitly stated:

[3] *GDA is a complex behavioural system.*

These statements imply a number of subordinate propositions. [1] defines GDA in terms of six characters; one of these is behaviour which is further qualified by the other five terms; it also introduces the figure of the actor. [2] provides us with the distinction between (goal-directed) *act* and *action*; it further emphasizes the situatedness of the act. [3] has important theoretical and methodological consequences. All of these are recurrent and interrelated themes, showing up again at various stages of our explications. For our preliminary inspection, it will be practical to begin with actor, action, act and social behaviour, to proceed to the defining characters of GDA and to end up by treating some general aspects of systems as related to GDA.

2.1. The actor

This concept signifies of course the acting subject. As far as the psychological literature on GDA is concerned, the actor is a human being.[5] To my knowledge, all action theories go beyond this specification and represent the actor as a *person*.[6] But theories of GDA differ in the importance they award to personality, the intensity of theoretical treatment and the number of dimensions they actually consider. Sometimes they seem to use 'personality' in the sense of differential or trait psychology; Miller, Galanter and Pribram (1960) for instance concentrate

castration of the concept which, as a usual consequence of this kind of an operation, leaves its victim innocent and manageable, but greatly diminishes its creative and innovative power.

[4] With numbers in square brackets I shall emphasize statements which I consider of general importance. Since this is not a formal theory, these sentences vary in their nature; they are definitions, postulates and hypotheses as well as methodological or factual claims. Sometimes, these statements are super- and subordinated by logic or content (as indicated by decimal numbers).

[5] See, however, the papers by Peter Reynolds and Vernon Reynolds in this volume, considering possibilities of GDA in apes; and studies of organizational action (various papers in Mayntz 1971, Silverman 1970).

[6] In this attribution of personal qualities action theory deviates from many other psychological theories whose subject could as well be a beetle or a cuckoo clock.

on 'planning' as a point of departure for assessing personality differences. But in most theories of GDA personality is considered as a
precondition for agency (for example the role of 'autonomy' and
'reflexivity' in Harré (1979)). Such qualities are considered to be based on
a broad range of integrated cognitive and moral capacities and psychological structures; besides the general capacity of abstract cognition and
symbolic interaction, cognitive structures like the self and the value
system are of particular importance. These are qualities acquired in
socialization and participation in social life. A special conception of the
actor's personality has been developed in the culture-historical school of
Soviet psychology, where the interdependence between personality and
labour activity is elaborated in detail; personality (in a very comprehensive sense) is seen as the basis of action, and as developing mainly
through participation in collective labour activities (Wertsch 1978).

2.2. Act–action

This distinction has been emphasized by Harré (for example 1972; Harré
and Secord 1972) and is now widely accepted. The term *action* refers to
the goal-directed behaviour as such. An *act* is a socially defined unit of
action, dividing the stream of action into meaningful sections. Most acts
are characterized by a specific goal. The specific pattern of an episode in
terms of acts and actions is called its act–action structure (Harré 1972).

2.3. Social situation

The term *social situation* refers to a temporal–spatial unity, whose
meaning is at least partially related to the meaning of the act it
comprises; acts, as socially meaningful units, are embedded in social
situations. This idea is generally accepted, but in fact leads to widely
differing theoretical and methodological consequences. To understand
these variations, we have to recognize that social situations can at least
differ in regard to three dimensions:
  (i) the spatial dimension, including arrangements of physical objects
      (the 'setting' in Harré's (1979) terms),
  (ii) the temporal aspects (episodes as segments of orders of nested time
      spans),
  (iii) the participants (interacting social subjects).
Closer inspection reveals that it is impossible, both in theory and in
empirical work, to include all possible sources of variation in these

dimensions in practical research. Each dimension allows for different assumptions and classifications; theories and research strategies determine what is to be included; basic theoretical preferences largely determine the outcome (the rule-stressing approach: the situation lends meaning to the action; the goal-stressing approach: situational characters influence the course of action, but the action generates and structures the situation). Different approaches are justified in their selection according to their specific aims; whatever their choice, they should, however, take into consideration the following requirements.

(i) The specific chosen aspect of the situation should be theoretically justified.

(ii) The theory should specify the proposed dynamic relation between act and situation.

(iii) In empirical research, the situation's social meaning and its impact on action should be assessed and evaluated according to these principles.

2.4. GDA as a qualified behaviour

Let us now turn to the details of the definition of GDA and consider its characters as provided in statement [1]. Since all the qualifying characters refer to behaviour, it will be convenient to begin with this term.

2.4.1. *Behaviour.* Like many key terms in the sciences, 'behaviour' resists exact definition.[7] For our purpose, it will be sufficient to state that the concept comprises all of the manifest activities of the human body. These are always related to internal psychophysiological principles of organization; it is a specific set of such principles, referred to in the

---

[7] To arrive at clear ideas we have to strive for clear definitions. We should not neglect, however, the basic difference between a verbal definition and its application to real (natural and cultural) events. Especially a definition in the Aristotelian sense (*definitio fit et genus proprium et differentia specifica*) signifies an entity of meaning with sharp boundaries, the latter provided by the *differentia specifica*. In nature, qualitative changes tend to be gradual and, if there are several qualities involved, overlapping, so that sharp borderlines are rare. This difference given, how could we proceed to equate defined concepts with natural entities (operationalization)? The solution is easier in the case where we can produce our own reality, as in the experiment. If this is excluded, as is the case in social research or at least in its necessary descriptive phase, our proceeding must be less elegant: we shall identify typical or ideal cases, where all the definition's characteristics can clearly be found; but we shall also accept the majority of cases, which contain only some of the characters in a less clear form. Methodological prescriptions and definitions of categories in systematic observation and content analysis regulate this proceeding in detail. So we act a little bit like parachutists, airborne in our approach but pedestrian in empirical combat.

specification of [1], which characterizes behaviour as action. But given what we have said about definitions, action is not a well-defined subclass of behaviour; instead, its attributes vary in degree and follow each other in (non-random) sequential distribution and levels of organization of the behavioural stream. (This principle will be further specified in the following sections.)

2.4.2. *Goal-directed.* The term *goal-directed* emphasizes the fact that GDA is directed towards a goal, which term should also be defined:

[1.1] *A goal is the imagined state aspired to as the outcome of an action.*

This definition makes it clear that the term goal refers to a cognition, the content of which is placed in the future (the end of the action), and is aspired to. The term goal-directed therefore implies the assumption that (at least in this case) *cognition directs behaviour*. Action theory is therefore cognitive theory. The goal's behaviour-directing capacity is contained in two of its components: that it is a representation of the future (*imagined*), and that this future is *aspired* to. This aspired-to future is represented as a concrete and specific *state*; this distinguishes the goal from other behaviour-directing desiderata, for example *values*.

2.4.3. *Planned.* The term *planned* refers to the fact that a behaviour is guided by a *plan*.[8] We propose the definition:

[1.2] *A plan is the design of the action, consisting of an anticipating representation of certain characteristics of its means of execution.*

This definition is preliminary in so far as a more exact description of what is represented, namely the means of execution, is missing. We note that we have to develop a terminology for the executive side of the action. But apart from this problem, we can note two important implications for our understanding of GDA: first, the plan is again an anticipating representation, stressing the cognitive nature of action theory; second, for a GDA a plan, at least in a rudimentary form and on some level of organization, is a necessary requirement. Even routine actions will be subconsciously monitored by latent plans of which the actor becomes aware in the moment of deviation.

2.4.4. *Intended.* The term *intended* signifies that the actor *voluntarily* transforms goal and plan into behaviour.[9] We have many goals in mind

[8] Western psychology owes this concept, of course, largely to Miller, Galanter and Pribram (1960).

[9] In our restriction of the term *intention* to the volitional qualities of GDA, we may differ somewhat from the common use of the term. We feel, however, that this is justified,

and constantly develop plans for their realization; but in fact we execute only a few of these. Obviously it is not enough that goals are desirable and plans are designs of action; to realize them, specific exercises of the will are necessary. So we need a specific command, a *'resolution'* to start the execution of the act, and further continuous efforts to maintain it. We can therefore state:

[1.3] *A GDA is intended if it is voluntarily executed by the actor.*

Note that the volition required in [1.3.] refers to the execution, not necessarily to goal and plan.

2.4.5. *Conscious.* The term *conscious* qualifies the preceding characters: goal, plan and intention are considered to be *conscious* cognitions. The term refers to a specific mode of psychological activity. It might be preferable not to define consciousness in general, but only in relation to our specific problems:

[1.4] *An action-related cognition is conscious if the actor is subjectively aware of it.*

Subjective awareness means that the actor, within the given limitations of his capacity of language and memory, can report on a conscious cognition. This is the point of departure of assessment methods. To be verbally reported, any subjective experience, for example also an emotion, has to be transformed into a conscious cognition.

Conscious cognitions of GDA may vary along several dimensions, the most important of which may be: *comprehensiveness* (how many and which of the goal and plan cognitions are conscious?); *clarity; form* (verbal representation or imagery); *time* and *time span* of appearance and other characteristics. To predict when a cognition will be conscious, an *attention theory* is required.[10]

2.4.6. *Socially directed (or controlled).* These terms refer to the social nature of action. In an elaborated form, the concept implies a twofold relationship: society controls (and directs) GDA; and in performing socially directed, meaningful acts, the actor (partially) constructs society. The terms *directs* versus *controls* refer to degrees and qualities of influence; assumptions about the impact of social control (for example: goal-

since the distinction between the cognitive and volitional aspect of GDA is necessary, and since the term *intentionality* in its usual wide and ambiguous sense is empirically useless.

[10] The term *conscious* is henceforth put in parentheses to indicate that not all cognitions are always conscious.

achievement versus rule-following) constitute a major source of variation in GDA theories.

Theories of social control are mainly focussed on two kinds of operating mechanisms: first, *external* control by influencing the course of action through environmental devices and exercise of power. Second, *internal* control by implanting into the individual (in the course of socialization) cognitive and motivational/emotional structures (for example scripts, rules, knowledge, values, needs, etc), which guide his action. Theoretical emphasis is on internal control; both forms cannot, however, be always clearly distinguished (for example, is there any purely external control?) and should be conceived as operating jointly. The notion that internal control influences the actor's cognitions (for example: socially implanted goals) corresponds to the conception of a *hierarchy of control mechanisms*. To summarize:

[1.5] *Social control (internal and external) operates through the actor's (conscious) cognition.*

GDA is a system[11] because it is behaviour. In view of the present state of most of the behavioural and their neighbouring sciences (for example ethology, neurophysiology, linguistics, and many psychological disciplines), the equation of behaviour and system hardly needs justification. Today, any non-systemic treatment of behaviour is obsolete; if it is in a particular case still considered necessary, this strategy should be justified.

If statement [3] is therefore self-evident, it is not trivial, because it leads us to apply our general knowledge of behavioural systems to the case of GDA. Of the many generally accepted assumptions about the nature of behavioural systems, I want to consider three, namely twofold structure, two-dimensional organization and bidirectional adaptation.

2.5.1. *Twofold structure.* Complex behavioural systems are commonly analysed on the basis of the assumption that they possess a twofold, namely a manifest and a latent, structure; both are considered to be interrelated. This assumption, although rarely stated, is implicit in most empirical treatments of behaviour. Thus, we distinguish in psychology between behaviour on the one side, and cognition and various forms of disposition on the other, in linguistics between surface structure and deep structure; in genetics (including behavioural genetics) between phenotype and genotype. In most cases, it is assumed that the two

---

[11] In our use of the term *system*, we presuppose the assumptions of General Systems Theory (von Bertalanffy 1956, Buckley 1968, Ackoff and Emery 1972).

structures are (in certain respects and to a degree) isomorphic, and that they interact; concerning their interaction, it is often assumed that the latent structure (in interaction with the system's environment) *produces* (triggers off) the manifest one, while the latter's operation *induces changes* in the first one. (Thus, eating is produced by the physiological drive of hunger and consequently changes this drive.) According to the statement [3.1] GDA has a twofold structure; *behaviour* constitutes its manifest side; *(conscious) cognition* (with the qualities of goal-directedness, planfulness, and intentionality) constitutes the latent side of the structure. To sum up, we may state:

[3.1] *GDA is characterized by a twofold structure, namely a manifest structure (behaviour) and a latent structure ((conscious) cognition): both are interrelated.*

2.5.2. *Two-dimensional organization.* Behaviour is organized along two interrelated dimensions, sequence and hierarchy. *Sequence* refers to the temporal pattern of behavioural units on a given level of organization; under normal conditions, behavioural units appear in an ordered and well-adapted sequence (simultaneous occurrence of course not excluded). *Hierarchy* refers to the pattern of super- and subordination. Higher-order elements normally differ from lower-order ones by extension (a higher-order element is related to several lower-order ones) and function. For the sake of simplicity elements of similar hierarchical position and function can be conceived as located on qualitatively different levels of organization (or regulation); this kind of abstraction is useful if not taken too literally. Levels of organization are conceived as interrelated by specific mechanisms, for example feedback loops.

The principle of two-dimensional organization of behaviour is generally accepted in the behavioural sciences. Sequential organization is self-evident, and is also compatible with a probabilistic viewpoint. Hierarchical organization, the systemic viewpoint, is ultimately based on the assumption that a structure of super- and subordination is the simplest way to achieve coordination and cooperation within a system. This principle forms a basis of modern neurophysiology (since the Hixon symposium, Jefress 1951); of ethology (since Tinbergen 1951; compare Dawkins 1976; Eibl-Eibesfeldt 1978, Lorenz 1978) and many fields of psychology (for example memory, artificial intelligence and cognitive psychology in general). Two-dimensional organization is also one of the most important principles in most psychological action theories; it has been especially elaborated in Marxist psychology of activity and consequently in industrial psychology (Hacker 1978). To explain goal-directedness, these theories tend to combine the concepts of levels of regulation and of a hierarchy of control mechanisms. For our present purpose, we may state:

[3.2] *GDA is organized along two dimensions, sequence and hierarchy.*

2.5.3. *Bidirectional adaptation.* In order to survive, any system operates under two constraints: those imposed by its environment and those originating from its own internal organization. This notion applies primarily to system–environment relationships, but should also be considered in studying levels of organization. The principle forms a necessary basis of systemic thinking but is rarely explicitly acknowledged. In biology it is generally inherent in functional thinking (for example Remane 1952; compare von Cranach 1976); in systems theory it has been formulated by Ackoff and Emery (1972). Action can be considered as functioning in the service of adaptation,[12] hence of both kinds of adaptation; thus we can state:

[3.3] *The function of GDA is bidirectional adaptation: outward-directed adaptation meets the necessities of the actor's relations to his environment, inward-directed adaptation considers the actor's internal needs.*[13]

We assume that outward and inward-directed adaptation in action normally operate jointly. The relation of statement [3.3] to statement [3.1] has to be considered.

3. General strategies of GDA assessment[14]

On the basis of my GDA definition, I shall now deal with some of the problems occurring in empirical GDA research. Since theory and method go hand in hand (theory bearing methodological consequences)

---

[12] The term *adaptation* is used here in a positive sense, as in biology; it designates the organism's constant and active striving to cope with the challenge of given conditions and carries no negative connotation (as it is often the case in social sciences).

[13] Harré (this volume) has proposed the distinction between private–public, personal–social and individual–collective. These dimensions might coincide with our distinction of inner-directed and outer-directed adaptation. Since I have not yet investigated this idea thoroughly, and my distinction is meaningful in systems theory and has been useful in research I prefer here to preserve my terminology.

[14] I am using the term *assessment* (in the sense of the German *Erhebung* or *Feststellung*) to designate the operations used to derive GDA data. I am avoiding the term *measurement* because of my conviction that the methods used in GDA research (and perhaps in social science in general), even if reliable and valid, do not constitute true measurement in the sense of measurement theory; for the major reason that the performance of both actor and scientist is partly based on common knowledge of social meaning, and therefore cannot be considered as independent.

I shall discuss these topics jointly. I cannot possibly aim at completeness, but shall try to concentrate on important problems.

In any empirical study of GDA it must be assessed in its details: this trivial truth applies to all kinds of studies, whether they aim at investigating processes of industrial labour, problem-solving in cognitive psychology, or communicative episodes; whether they test specific hypotheses in an experimental procedure or proceed in a more descriptive way. In this paragraph I am treating some very general problems which refer to all methods of GDA assessment; these are related to the traits of GDA theory which have already become visible in our discussion of the GDA concept.

3.1. Key-variable assessment versus detailed description of ongoing processes

Action theories offer a very rich repertoire of concepts for the description and analysis of ongoing processes, cognitive and behavioural, in GDA. (It is just in this attention to interrelated details, and not in rigorous restriction, that their superiority in regard to 'general behaviour theories' is based.) Since most of its concepts can be correlated with empirical operations, it would seem appropriate to make use of them in empirical research. This is however rarely the case. In most empirical studies, researchers do not make full use of their theoretical insights; instead they prefer traditional research strategies and restrict their assessment to a few input and outcome variables. But the classical experimental approach, concentrating on the interrelation of independent and dependent variables, is of limited value in GDA research. The neglect of theoretical information in empirical research on GDA is particularly conspicuous in regard to its cognitive side: goal-related cognitions are rarely assessed.

3.2. Appropriate analytic models

Methods of data assessment and analysis (like behaviour observation systems and statistical methods) are normally based on inherent analytical models which contain assumptions about the nature of the analysed behaviour. It is sometimes overlooked that these should correspond to the theoretically assumed nature of GDA. Thus, since GDA theory is basically non-probabilistic, methods based on probabilistic assumptions should be applied with care. Probabilistic sampling of units, for example, or Markow chain analysis would contradict the inherent assumptions of GDA theory.

The considerations stated in [3.1] and [3.2] can be summarized:

[4] *GDA-related processes should be investigated in detail and by use of appropriate analytic models.*

3.3. Classes of constructs

3.3.1. Behaviour, cognition and meaning. The terms of our GDA definition point to three broad, qualitatively different classes of constructs: behaviour, (conscious) cognition and social meaning.

Behaviour (class I)[15] comprises various kinds of concepts which refer to characteristics of the manifest course of action (starting and end points, action steps, nodes and their characteristics, environmental factors, levels of organization, etc).

(Conscious) cognition (class II) comprises constructs referring to functionally and/or qualitatively different (conscious) action-related cognitions (like goals, plans, strategies, values, norms, decisions, emotions, etc).

Social meaning (class III) comprises action-related social representations[16] (norms, rules, conventions, knowledge) which refer to individual cognitions (like goals or values) and/or behaviour (like action steps or levels of organization).

It is assumed that social meaning operates through social cognition (*social control*); this presupposes that the concepts of (conscious) cognition are at least partly socially represented and vice versa.

One or more of these classes of concepts are contained in every action theory; a complete theory of GDA should contain all of them. The degree of differentiation within classes varies between theories. For example, if the 'goal' is defined as an 'executed self-instruction' (Werbik 1976), the concept of an execution is included; if it is defined as above [1.1], a separate concept of 'deliberation' must be introduced.

Each of these concept classes poses its own theoretical and empirical problems. In empirical research, data of the three types should therefore be separately assessed and analysed before their integration is tried. So we can state:

[5] *GDA-related concepts refer to manifest behaviour, (conscious) cogni-*

---

15 The roman numerals designating classes will henceforth be added to concepts to indicate their class membership.

16 For a treatment of the concept of social representation, see Moscovici and Farr, in press.

tion and social meaning. According to the differences between these classes of concepts, their operationalizations are also different.

3.3.2. Integration of concept classes

Conceptual integration

Concepts in the three classes tend to be interrelated in a twofold way: any particular concept in a class is related to one or more concepts of its own class and/or to one or more concepts in one or both of the other classes.

Here are some examples:

According to [1.1], the concept of *goal* (II) refers to the imagined and aspired to *state at the end of the action*, namely the *action result* (I), which, if reached, corresponds to *goal attainment* (II) in performance of an act. Goals can also be based on *social conventions* (III).

According to [1.2], the *plan* (II) consists of an anticipating representation of certain characteristics of its execution; the latter part of the definition refers to the concept of *course of action* (I). A *strategy* (II) may be defined as a hierarchical preference order of plans. Plans and strategies can be *normative* or *conventional* (III).

The concept of *decision* (II) refers to a situation in the *course of action* (I) where two or more action possibilities branch off: the concept of *node* (I).

The concept of *rule* refers to a *social convention* (III) which is *consciously represented* and *considered as an obligation* (II) by the actor. It is a typical example of a concept which is both a member of classes II and III.

Levels of *hierarchical behaviour organization* (I) correspond to *levels* of *cognitive regulation* and *steering* (II), which are distinguished by degrees of conscious awareness mediated by *attention* (II).

Many other examples could be provided to demonstrate in more detail how conceptual integration leads to a conceptual network which unifies our given conceptual classes into one theory.

Empirical integration

The conceptual network derived from conceptual integration leads to two kinds of empirical operations, its descriptive and its predictive validation.

Descriptive validation. Our conceptual network, even if convincingly formulated, could be completely fictitious. Before going into more speculative empirical research, we must prove that it is based in reality. This calls for a twofold empirical confirmation: first, we must ensure that the theoretical terms correspond in fact to a configuration in the data (for example: That there exist in fact (conscious) cognitions which correspond to the concept of 'strategy', in whatever way it may be defined). Second, the correlation of data of different classes has to be proved (for example: does the cognitive 'strategy' correspond to a behavioural regularity?). In a field where the overwhelming majority of studies are not only purely theoretical, but also violate the explicit or implicit spirit of most empirical work done in the behavioural and social sciences, the value of this descriptive approach is obvious. It has the additional effect of giving us insight into empirical properties, distributions and relations of variables, and thus forms a basis for more directed empirical research (for example, see von Cranach *et al.* 1980, and pp. 115ff. of this volume).

Predictive validation. Like other social science theories, GDA theory guides the derivation of empirical hypotheses, both within and between concept classes. Again, we illustrate this principle by examples:

If a *node* (I) in the *course of action* (I) is *attended* to (II), *decisions* (II) are necessary which *slow* down *behaviour* (I).

A *decision* (II) at a *node* (I) which is distant from the *end point* (I) of *course of action* (I) is resolved rather by reference to a *value* (II, III) than to a *goal* (II).

Perceived *levels* of *cognitive regulation* (II) determine the *attribution of moral responsibility* (II, III).

If *cognitive conflict* (II) is not resolved by a *decision* (II), it will influence behaviour at a *lower level* of *organization* (I) by *subconscious self-regulation* (I, II).

Note that only the proposed conceptualization and operationalization of the three classes make the empirical investigation of basic postulates of symbolic interactionism possible. (For example: social meaning ·····➤ handed to actor ·····➤ integrated into cognitive system ·····➤ social control of behaviour.)

The considerations of 3.3.2 can be summarized in the statement:

[6] *GDA theory is derived by conceptual and empirical integration of concepts from the three classes and by descriptive and predictive validation of the resulting statements.*

3.3.3. *The conceptual triangle and its realization in research.* These considerations on concept classes and their integration into theory, as well as their methodological consequences, can be summarized in schematic form (Fig. 1). In the inside of our triangle we have indicated our concept

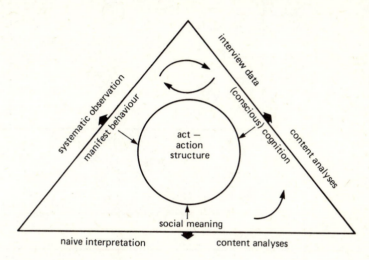

Fig. 1. The triangle of concepts in GDA theory

classes: manifest behaviour, (conscious) cognition and social meaning. Arrows between these classes symbolize the mainstream of theoretical ideas: social meaning exerts social control by influence on cognition, cognition directs, regulates and monitors behaviour, behaviour (as monitored) acts back on cognition. The integration of these concepts results in the construction of the total act–action structure in GDA, as indicated by the circle in the centre.

Each class of concepts is related to its own empirical methods; examples of these have been indicated outside of the triangle. (Some of the problems inherent in these methods will be discussed later in this paper.) Their empirical integration leads again to a reconstruction of the act–action structure.

The realization of this model presupposes a complete research situation (Fig. 2), which allows for the performance of all of these operations in relation to the same GDA.

Complete studies of this type have, to our knowledge, not yet been published. It should be noted that this type of study, as depicted in Figs.

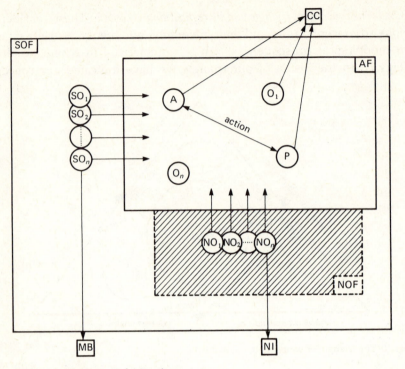

Fig. 2. The complete research situation

Fields	Participants	Data
AF Action field	A Actor P Partner O_1 – O_n Others	CC Conscious cognitions
SOF Scientific observation field	SO_1 – SO_n Scientific observers	MB Manifest behaviour
NOF Naive observation field	NO_1 – NO_n Naive observers	NI Naive interpretation

1 and 2, can in principle be posited in a natural or laboratory situation and performed as descriptive, quasi-experimental or experimental research. We are however convinced that descriptive research is preferable at our present state of knowledge; if experiments are performed, they should rather manipulate the total situation, since it would be premature to experiment on single GDA variables taken out of their act–action context.

3.4. The act as a minimal frame of analysis[17]

Goal-directedness and social meaning are particularly important aspects of GDA. On each level of analysis, the goal not only directs the behaviour, but also shapes it into its specific form (selective function of goal instrumentality). This could still result in more or less isolated, idiosyncratic activities; it is the social meaning of the goal which links it to the actor's system of socially meaningful cognitions (culminating in his 'self'), and gives to GDA its social quality (which again reinforces its individual significance). Socially meaningful goals define the GDA unit of the *act*.

From these considerations it follows that the act should normally constitute the minimal frame of analysis in studies of GDA, even if the immediate focus of the research may be directed at a lower level. For example, our studies of the detailed organization of GDA on the lowest level, as well as of its interlevel coherence (von Cranach *et al.* 1980, ch. 8) were only possible by placing the behaviour within the frame of 'acts'. On the other hand, studies on 'decision-making', as well as decision theory itself, often fail to situate the investigated choice-behaviour in the frame of acts: it is only the particular node, not its place in the course of action, which is studied as a decision situation; and the relation of the 'decision consequences' to the actor's goals tend to be neglected. So we can state:

[2.1] *The act constitutes the minimal frame of analysis in studies of GDA.*

3.5. Appropriate situations for the study of GDA

Aside from theoretical assumptions, the organization of GDA is still hardly known. In view of the very rich arsenal of concepts offered by GDA theories, the question arises whether it is in fact possible to assess equally differentiated corresponding data, how these are interrelated and what is their interplay. These questions refer to all of the three variable classes developed in 3.1.3. Therefore, our research should at present rather be descriptive than analytic.

The manifestation of GDA variable classes can only be expected in situations which correspond to certain standards. These may be characterized by the demand:

[7] *GDA should be investigated in real and natural situations.*

---

[17] The term *frame of analysis* is here used to designate the scope of the study: the more comprehensive frame of theoretical considerations and/or empirical findings into which the aspired-to detailed analysis is to be posed in order to make full sense.

In this statement, 'real' is meant to indicate that the action-related situational conditions are not just fictitious but exist in reality; 'natural' means that from the actor's viewpoint they are neither artificial nor alienated and could be part of his everyday life in his culture.

There are many reasons for our demand. The full richness of GDA-related behaviour and cognitions only develops in real situations. A real situation consists of a pattern of environmental circumstances which do really exist at the time and place of the action and are not just fictitious; their inherent meanings and prescriptions are therefore true. Such a situation contains the actual circumstances which lead to the GDA under study, and induce the actor to full goal-directed behaviour. A situation is real if the actor could say (in fact he will not think of it because it seems self-evident): 'This is life.' A situation is not real, if circumstances, partner, task and the actor's own behaviour are only imagined. Why should this be important? The actor should take situations seriously, and the situation should bring into operation the full impact of external situational cues and internal cognitive standards. Under these conditions the actor is more likely to use his full repertoire; and only the demand characteristics of a real situation will trigger off the true interplay of inner-directed and outer-directed adaptation processes on the various levels of organization.

Let us now consider our second qualification. In view of the variability of life conditions in modern civilization it seems difficult to determine what is a natural situation; this question cannot be decided in general, but only in view of our research purpose. GDA research demands that the actor follows true goals under circumstances he can take seriously. In an artificial situation, even if it is realistic, the actor may still feel that this could never happen in real life, and consequently cut off some of his cognitions and feelings; he takes a stance which differs from what the situation (and the researcher) silently presupposes, and which he himself would take if it was everyday life. Since the impact of situational detail is intricately mediated by the actor's cognition, nobody could easily predict the effect of such an alienation.

Action theory allows for a determination of the conditions of natural situations: the actor should pursue genuine and internalized goals. He should experience his action as intended and autonomously guided, at least to the extent he would expect in everyday life. He should not perform under the impression of acting towards an artificial goal adopted only for the sake of the investigation. In the planning and execution of the action he should be as free as in everyday life; therefore he should not feel restricted by the particular research conditions; restrictions as they are common in daily performance, for example by conventions, rules and norms are, however, natural conditions. The actor should be free of anxiety of the research situation, to be observed and evaluated, and should not experience the situation as alienated. A final point: the action and its situation should be meaningful in the cultural context. This in turn will normally mean that the situation could occur in everyday life; that it is an object of social conventions and could be interpreted by naive observers.

To sum up, we should prefer real life situations at the work-place, in the home, at school, etc. With great care, it is possible to arrange such situations for the purpose of the study. A laboratory task is real and natural if it is studied as such and in its own right. It tends to be unnatural if it stands for something else. Role-playing can be anything between real–natural and fictitious–artificial; its validity as a situation for GDA should be investigated in every particular case.

In short, we advocate the position that we should take the situation seriously, more seriously than is normally the case in psychological research. I am afraid this will only be possible at the cost of a loss of 'experimental control'.

4. Manifest behaviour

Although the integration of construct classes into act–action structures should be considered the ultimate goal, each of these classes (manifest behaviour, (conscious) cognition and social meaning) alone poses its own special difficulties. In the remaining sections of this chapter, I shall discuss theoretical and methodological problems as they are met in empirical psychological research on manifest behaviour and conscious cognition. Limitations of space do not allow one to treat the problems of social meaning as a separate class of constructs (see however the papers by Kreckel and Luckmann in this volume); but as far as it influences GDA organization, it should be reflected in conscious cognition.

In my discussion of manifest behaviour, I shall restrict myself to two problems which arise from its systemic character: two-dimensional organization and bidirectional adaptation.

4.1. Two-dimensional organization

Statement [3.2] introduces the notion of two-dimensional organization in GDA. In this paragraph we shall go into more detail; particularly, we shall justify the principle and point to some of its difficulties and consequences.

Let us first introduce a few further concepts (see also the papers by Hacker, von Cranach and Kalbermatten, and Kaminski in this volume). At a given *level* of *organization*, a *course of action* consisting of *action steps* extends from *starting point* to an *end point*. The joint representation of a sample of many different courses of action (extending between the same starting and end points) results in a *network*; action steps are demarcated by *nodes* where alternative courses of action branch off. Such nodes may be distinguished by specific environmental cues, their *characters*. This *sequential organization* is illustrated in Fig. 3, which represents a realistic example from a study of children fighting for toys (von Cranach *et al.* 1980). Behaviour in GDA is however organized at various levels. 'Fighting for toys' is only one of the many acts these children perform in their daily kindergarten routine; there are other acts like playing, eating, resting, etc. These can be observed and their sequence depicted in a quite similar manner. This then constitutes a higher level of organization, the units of which are acts instead of action steps. The activities at such a level may again function as subunits in the service of a still higher goal, as in labour activities, where practically all the activity concentrates on social production; or the activities may rather be uncoordinated, as in our kindergarten, where the 'goal level' seems to constitute the highest level of intrinsic order, still higher-order structures being mainly created by external conditions. In any case, however, the single act (on the goal level) also constitutes a link in a chain of acts; and a set of chains will constitute a network, just as we have shown for the 'strategic' level above.

On the other hand, within a given act each action step can be dissolved into its component movements on the next lower level (termed 'operational level' in our own studies). Thus, the same action step in a sequence can be differently structured; in addition to variation in sequential movements, action steps may differ along dimensions like *speed* or *force* which are rated as qualities, although the latter can be finally reduced to structural differences.

This *inclusive order* is however but one characteristic of the hierarchical organization of GDA. As a second aspect we find that hierarchical levels tend to be *qualitatively different*. Here we are referring to differences in the non-formal aspects of the organization, the material and content side of processes which characterize the interaction of components on a

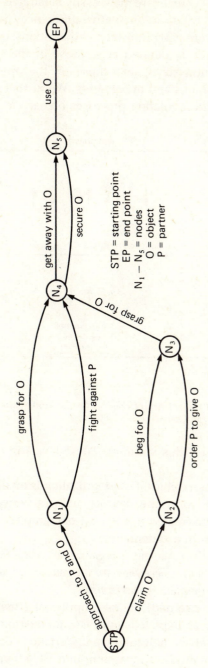

Fig. 3. The network of the act: fighting for a toy in the kindergarten (from von Cranach *et al.* 1980)

given level. Qualities, of course, are more easily illustrated than defined. In our study of fighting children, qualitative differences in the assumed levels of organization were part of the latter's definitions: the units of the goal level constitute *socially* defined acts, those of the strategic level *functionally* defined action steps, and those on the operational level *structurally* defined positions and movements. We further assumed that cognitive organizing and regulating processes on each level differed in

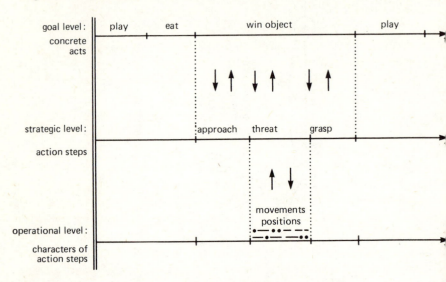

Fig. 4. Hierarchical order in the activity of children in the kindergarten, as a basis for observational studies (from von Cranach *et al.* 1980)

their quality (see Hacker, this volume). These levels in our study are depicted in Fig. 4.

A third character of hierarchic GDA organization is finally constituted by the *processes* which form the *dynamic linkages* between levels of organization; this will be treated in the next paragraph.

To summarize all this in a statement:

[3.2.1.] *In GDA, sequential behaviour is organized on levels (levels of regulation or organization). These show an inclusive order, differ in quality and are linked by mediating mechanisms.*

As far as theory is concerned, the assumption of a two-dimensional organization of action, as depicted here, is a marked advance. In the end, however, it will only be helpful if we undertake to develop equally structured research methods: the assumption of a two-dimensional organization asks for two-dimensional assessment. The latter should reflect the former's characteristics. There is first the distinction of sequential steps on certain levels.[18] The *inclusive order* of units can for example be reflected in *nested observation systems*, where a *unit* (that means an item) in an observation system for a given level constitutes the *object of analysis* (to be broken down into several lower order items) on the next lower level. Second, theoretically assumed qualitative differences between levels should be reflected in the unit definitions on the various levels. Third, the validity of these definitional properties should be separately investigated; thus socially defined goals can be validated by investigations of the social definitions given by a reference group; the functions which are assumed in functional definitions can be empirically tested by other means (for a detailed methodological treatment, see Kalbermatten and von Cranach 1980).

In short:

[3.2.2] *The study of hierarchically organized behaviour requires nested assessment methods.*

Finally, we should not overlook the point that the assumption of levels is a heuristic simplification of hierarchic nesting, which may sometimes be useful, sometimes misleading. In most cases we begin our analysis on a level which we determine on the basis of the observed sequential order of its units. We cannot take it for granted that events which are (by hierarchical subordination) equally distant from two of these sequential units are themselves organized in a similar sequential relationship.

The matter is further complicated by the fact that in most cases actors do more than one thing at the same time. *Multiple* (interlaced and simultaneous) acts and action steps can be related to the same goal, to related or unrelated goals. In their analysis, we have to proceed from higher to lower levels and finally refer to the goal structure, a pattern of (conscious) cognition. (We cannot thoroughly discuss the matter here; see however Kaminski, this volume.)

4.2. Feedback loops as links between levels

The distinction of levels is only the first step in the investigation of hierarchical organization; the establishment of coherence between levels constitutes a further, perhaps the most important problem. Quite

---

[18] Here we have to beware of the reductionistic pitfall of assuming that some levels are more 'real' than others. There is for example no reason to assume that lower-order units possess more reality than higher-order ones.

generally, the notion of a system's hierarchical organization is useful only to the extent that we can also establish interrelations between the assumed levels of hierarchy: otherwise the conceived system falls apart. What are the mechanisms which mediate between organization levels of GDA? Following the lead of Miller, Galanter and Pribram (1960) as well as of the proponents of Marxist psychology of activity, it is now generally assumed that this function is served by feedback mechanisms: higher-level events provide the superordinate goals (and that is why we speak of hierarchical super- and subordination), but they are regulated by lower-level variations in the service of better goal achievement (see Hacker, this volume). In terms of our operationalization, observed variations of behaviour on lower levels account for outcomes of behaviour on higher levels. This is seen as a cybernetic cycle, in which the achievement of goals (or subgoals) on the various levels serves as a desired value; behaviour is regulated so that the deviation from these is as small as possible. This then constitutes a rather clear case of outward-directed adaptation. On the other hand, we should expect that inward-directed adaptation also plays its role. Behaviour in GDA should for example reflect the impact of inner constraints like motives, values and attitudes, which can equally operate as standards in cybernetic cycles; and the resulting behaviour pattern may represent a compromise between competing external and internal standards (see von Cranach and Kalbermatten, this volume).

This then leads to the statement:

[3.3.1] *Feedback loops interrelating levels of organization operate according to external and internal standards.*

Obviously these are problems of cognition (the latent action-steering mechanism) as well as of behaviour. Our discussion within the boundaries of these realms creates clarity, but also results in a somewhat artificial division.

5. Conscious cognition

5.1. States of consciousness

In this section we are treating selected problems concerning the role of conscious cognition in GDA research. First, we shall turn to the conscious appearance and function of distinct types of action-related cognitions. Second, we shall discuss their structure and content, and third, problems of their assessment.

For this purpose we need a classification and terminology for basic states of consciousness, even if still preliminary and rough. In our discussion, we shall use the following distinctions:

Conscious cognitions, as we have defined them in [1.4], are those of which the actor is aware and about which he can report.

Non-conscious cognitions are cognitive processes to which the actor has no access; he cannot report on them, but they can be (partly and very imperfectly) inferred from other behavioural effects.

Unconscious cognitions are a specific class of non-conscious cognitions: those which have been (according to psychoanalytical theory) repressed from consciousness by defence mechanisms. In our present discussion, we are not directly concerned with this class.

Subconscious cognitions finally constitute a borderline case between the conscious and the non-conscious ones: cognitions which are at the very fringe of consciousness, so that the actor is just a little bit aware of them, so that they can become conscious very easily. (We should however not forget that there are many borderline and mixed cases between our rough classes of cognitions.)

This distinction of different states of consciousness is essential, because GDA theories assume that action cognitions, as related to different organization levels, may be differently represented in consciousness (Hacker 1973 and this volume, von Cranach *et al.* 1980); and the attention theorem which will be developed in statement [11] predicts the distribution of conscious cognitions over sequence and levels on the basis of functional assumptions. This is reflected in our statement:

[8] *GDA-related cognitions differ in their conscious representation: the distribution of differently represented cognitions is systematically related to patterns of sequential and hierarchical GDA organization.*

The distinction of states of consciousness is also of methodological importance.

5.2. Attention

Up to now when speaking about cognition we have put the word *conscious* in parentheses, indicating a problem which we shall now try to resolve. The essence of our argument will be that the term cognition can only serve its task as a defining part of GDA, if it is treated as conscious. It is therefore necessary to understand its appearance in consciousness. For this purpose, we propose an *attention theorem* which predicts consciousness on the basis of its organizing functions in relation to GDA.

5.2.1. *Reasons for and against the consideration of consciousness.* Various reasons let us insist that in GDA theory cognitions should be treated as conscious.

 (i) Consciousness is the most obvious and pervasive character of human mental life. It is the conspicuous quality of our existence from (shortly after) birth to death and from dawn to dusk. It is very unlikely that it would be a good research strategy to neglect it!

 (ii) In general, our representations of cognition, especially of a major part of its structure and content, are modelled after conscious cognition. We tend to treat non-conscious cognitions like a friend who has left the room: although we can no longer see him, we are pretty sure how he looks. Similarly, we often conceive of non-conscious cognition as if it resembles its conscious form in every respect but conscious awareness. In respect to this assumption there are three points to be made: first, without this notion only very meagre and abstract schemata of cognitive processes would be possible, rather like those we have to restrict ourselves to in animal psychology; second, this attitude contains a silent postulate of isomorphy which should be clearly stated and justified; third, this assumption can in no way justify the other attitude held by so many psychologists, that just the conscious quality is unimportant.

(iii) Naive psychology constitutes one of our most important sources of knowledge about the content, form and function of GDA-related cognitions, and most of naive knowledge stems from our (the actors') conscious cognitions.

(iv) These arguments lead to a further one: conscious cognition, as we know and experience it, possesses unique qualities. It represents and recreates reality in the form of images and symbols, and equally reflects the actor's own state. Thus it builds its own systems, which can function (to a degree) according to their own laws and independently from the real world of physical objects and forces and the constraints of space and time. These are the qualities of conscious cognition which make it such a unique tool for problem-solving and acting. We do not know to what degree non-conscious cognition shares these properties.

Since these arguments seem quite reasonable, we may ask ourselves why most psychologists remain so reluctant to acknowledge them; or, if they do acknowledge them, why they still avoid drawing the obvious consequence that they should include conscious cognition in their research. And here again we find a very good reason: conscious cognition seems to evade control. Up to now, psychological theory does not predict what cognition should be consciously experienced and when and in what form this should happen: the transition from the non-conscious seems arbitrary. For this reason (and possibly because of some unreflected prejudice) most psychologists avoid thinking about con-scious cognition; they consider it a 'tricky business' (but so is be-haviour!), and leave it at that.

To sum up, there is only one way out: trying to make consciousness of cognition predictable. When should we expect that a cognition enters consciousness? As far as GDA-related cognitions are concerned, an answer to this question is attempted in our attention theorem.

5.2.2. *Attention processes.* In order to predict consciousness of cognition in GDA, I propose to begin with two basic assumptions. The first one defines attention by its function:

[9] *Non-conscious cognitions become conscious by the operation of atten-tion processes.*

This postulate contains the notion that conscious and non-conscious cognitions are essentially similar in content and structure. It further stresses the fact that attention is considered a *process* the result of which is the cognitive state of consciousness. Attention can be further specified by two subordinated notions:

[9.1] *The focus of attention is relatively narrow.*

[9.2] *Attention is either voluntarily or involuntarily directed at parts of the system of ongoing cognitions.*

Statement [9.1] stresses the fact that only a relatively small part of cognition is conscious at a given time; [9.2] underlines that attending can, but need not be, a goal-directed activity itself. (These assumptions are quite in line with traditional ways of thinking about properties of attention, so that it seems unnecessary to back them up by arguments and citations.)

The second basic postulate assumes that conscious cognition serves a *function*:

[10] *Conscious cognition directs and regulates action.*

This postulate, which is in line with our definition of consciousness as a property of GDA [1], is based on the assumption that conscious cognition constitutes an information processing system of higher order, which is in some respects superior to similar systems, especially non-conscious cognitions, and serves specific tasks in GDA.

From these two postulates, we can now derive a theorem which predicts the operation of attention processes in GDA.

> [11] *The attention of the actor is directed towards where it is needed or stimulated.*

This general statement can now be decomposed into hypotheses concerning specific circumstances of operation of attention processes in GDA, for example:

> [11.1] *GDA-related cognitions become conscious if required in the organization of action.*

> [11.2] *Attention is directed to those action steps and levels of organization, which meet specific difficulties (for example resolutions, evaluation, decisions, etc).*

This theorem can be elaborated much further. It is corroborated, although in a preliminary way, by our research (von Cranach *et al.* 1980).[19]

Finally I should like to add two comments:

(i) Note, that the proposed attention theorem is restricted to GDA-related cognitions (for application to other cognitions, additional assumptions should be added).

(ii) The functional advantage of attention for GDA operations is based on its symbolic and depicting nature; the price we pay for this is *narrowness* (see [9.1]). Thus attention may be disadvantageous for tasks which demand a broad perspective (for example creativity).

5.3. Conscious cognition and action: functional and temporal relationships

On the basis of their conscious mode, we have distinguished between classes of cognitions (3.2.2); their relationship to action allows for further distinctions.

5.3.1. *Functional classification.* First, we can take our departure from the assumed functional relationship between a conscious cognition and a given action.

---

[19] The reader should note that this principle is in line with ideas concerning the 'prise de conscience' as formulated by Claparède (1968) and Piaget (1923); and with basic ideas of Marxist psychology ('All psychological processes, since they mirror reality, possess steering functions concerning movements, actions or behaviour. Consciousness also has this function.' Rubinstein 1971, p. 50; my translation). Similar ideas have also been developed by Thomas and Tolman (compare Graumann 1966, pp. 100–5).

Action-related (in contrast to *non-related*) *cognitions* are least specific in this respect: what is assumed is a relationship in content or form between cognition and action, without any further specification of the relationship's function. This class can be further divided into the subclasses of action-monitoring and action-steering cognitions.

Action-monitoring cognitions are those in which the ongoing activity is noticed and monitored, a precondition for concomitant or subsequent correction and some other cognitive and behavioural consequences (for example action-specific learning). But to cause effects, these consequences must be represented in additional consecutive action-steering cognitions: the influence of action-monitoring cognitions on the course of action is indirect rather than direct.

Action-steering cognitions are more specific; they exert a direct guiding influence on action.

Action-evaluating cognitions can exert influence on consecutive parts of the action.

5.3.2. *Temporal classification.* The complete research situation depicted in Fig. 2 silently presupposes a close temporal relationship between cognition and action. But closer consideration results in the conclusion that this can only be part of the story. The unique quality of cognition, especially conscious cognition, as a higher-order information processing system (5.2) has been assumed to be based just on the fact that it operates relatively independently from space and time. Thus, we can here and now plan acts which will be executed at a distant place tomorrow. On the basis of temporal relation to behaviour, we can again distinguish several action-related cognition classes: *action-preceding, action-accompanying* and *action-following cognitions.* (A further definition of these classes seems unnecessary.)

5.3.3. *Interclass relations.* So far we have established classifications of cognitions as to their state of consciousness (5.1) and of their function and temporal relation to action. These classes are neither independent nor of equal importance, as expressed in the following statements:

    [12] *In GDA research, we are mainly interested in action steering and monitoring, preceding and accompanying conscious (or subconscious) cognitions.*

  [12.1] *Only action-preceding and action-accompanying cognitions are action-steering. In case of non-routine actions, and if action-steering is problematic, these should be conscious.*

(Action-following cognitions can of course be action-steering in regard to other, future actions.)

[12.2] *Only action-accompanying and (less frequently and only if the time lapse is small) action-following cognitions are action-monitoring. We expect that action-accompanying monitoring cognitions are subconscious or conscious respectively (according to the specifications of [11]ff), and that action-following monitoring cognitions will in general be conscious.*

We have seen that classes of action cognitions are related. The inspection of an example reveals further properties of GDA-related cognitions. In statement [1.1], we have defined a *goal* as the imagined and aspired-to state at the end of an action.[20] We assume that goals *direct* action; they are *action-steering* cognitions. Goals can serve their steering task if they are conceived before or at the beginning of the action: in this (most important) function, goals are action-preceding cognitions. There are of course also occasions during the ongoing action where action-steering is needed: decisions at nodes, for example, can demand for the consideration of goals (as familiar in chess-playing).[21] Here, goal cognitions appear as action-accompanying. A specific instance is the case where the actor considers whether or not the goal should be abandoned in view of difficulties. Finally, if the goal is reached, it might be necessary to check the achieved state against the initial expectation. In all these cases of goals as *action-accompanying*, the original action-preceding cognition is so to speak reanimated, and action-monitoring functions are subsidiary to action-steering functions. It is now easy to imagine how the given classifications of GDA-related cognitions can be combined with our attention theorem to derive a more specific hypothesis concerning the appearance of action-related cognitions.

5.4. Content and structure of GDA-related cognitions

Our example nicely illustrates yet another, quite important point: it is the specific *content* of the goal cognition, as a (figurative or symbolic) image of the end state combined with a feeling of aspiration, which is

---

[20] This definition refers to the goal at the act level, not to subgoals at the action level; and to the most important type of goals, namely 'goal as a result'; there are other types, for example 'clarification' and 'process' goals (Steiner 1980).

[21] It should however be noted that in ordinary action people rarely seem to construct their way back and forth from the goal to the present decision situation, as a chess player would. Very frequently, they resort to a less demanding strategy and use a general standard, in most cases a value or a norm, as a criterion for the decision (see von Cranach *et al.* 1980, ch. 8).

the basis of its function. Psychology has traditionally placed much weight on the formal characteristics of processes; in GDA research the content of cognitions is of primary importance, because it explains the cognitions' specific action-related function. Classifications of GDA-related cognitions therefore involve a rich repertoire of differentiated categories (compare for example the systems of content analysis by Morgenthaler and Lang, in von Cranach *et al.* 1980).

Let us also shortly attend to a structural aspect of GDA-related cognitions: to their hierarchical order. A goal, as we have seen, tends to constitute a *unit* of cognition, although a differentiated one: a holistic Gestalt, which appears within a limited time period and is normally expressed in distinct formulations like 'I wish . . .; in order to . . .', etc. In its compact form, it can become part of superordinated cognitions. Morgenthaler (1979) has demonstrated that higher-order GDA cognitions can consist of ordered sequences of various (lower-order) single GDA cognitions; a decision for example is a higher-order cognitive process which integrates various single cognitions (among them goals) in a highly stereotyped sequence to perform its GDA-related function. Other typical higher-order GDA-related cognitions are plans, strategies and attitudes. Our recent research has shown that beside these superordinated cognitive processes there exists a second form of superordinated cognitions, the common *focus* or *object* which typically interrelates sequences of single cognitions. So we find that GDA-related cognition exposes its own highly complex hierarchical order. Up to now, we failed to really understand the nature of this order and its relation to the order of manifest behaviour. Yet we can state:

[13] *GDA-related cognitions are hierarchically ordered.*

5.5. Problems of assessment

It is not only theoretical preassumption and lack of predictive control which hinders psychologists from including ongoing conscious cognition in their research, but also the conviction that there is less security in the assessment of thoughts[22] than of behaviour.[23] In fact, in order to work with GDA-related cognitions we should assess them with adequate reliability and validity. Unfortunately, to our knowledge research

---

[22] Compare for example Nisbett and Wilson (1977) and the related discussion (Smith and Miller 1978, Shotter 1978, von Cranach *et al.* 1980, ch. 8, etc).

[23] Of course, many psychologists refer to rather restricted *reactions* when speaking about behaviour; the assessment of freely ongoing behaviour poses very difficult methodological problems, too.

on these aspects is lacking; we are just beginning to understand the basic methodological questions. In this paragraph, I shall very shortly review some of the general properties of the methods in use.[24]

First, let us remember statement [3.1]: the purpose of our research on GDA as a system is to reconstruct its latent structure, and we can only do so by way of inference from some kind of data. In this regard, the reconstruction of conscious cognition from verbal report does not differ from other research on latent structures. What does make a difference is the role of consciousness in the generation of data: the circumstance that some (if not all) other psychological data seem to be processed, on their complicated way to the protocol, only or preponderantly through the consciousness of the researcher, while our data first and additionally stem from and pass through the conscious cognition of the reporting actor.[25] So we shall concentrate here primarily on the research processes underlying and eliciting the actor's reports[26] – reports on his action-preceding and action-accompanying cognitions.

Before inspecting the methods themselves it will be appropriate to consider the specific difficulties we have to deal with: why are reports on conscious cognitions unreliable? We can classify the sources of error into recall and distortion problems. In addition to these, we must consider the danger of interference of the assessment procedures with the GDA-related cognition under study.

Recall problems arise from the fact that the content of consciousness undergoes rapid changes. The function of GDA-related conscious cognitions, as assumed in our attention theorem [11], would lead us to expect that they vanish as soon as they are no longer needed, to give room to those which become useful under the new circumstances of the rapidly changing situations. Using some of the general assumptions of memory psychology (even if in a very rough and unsophisticated way) we would expect that action-related cognitions are stored in short-term memory (STM) as long as and immediately after they have been conscious, because STM is conceived as a working store and at least partly corresponding to consciousness (Atkinson and Shiffrin 1971).[27] We

---

[24] For discussion of methodology, see Klinger (1978) and Singer (1978).

[25] In general, interview and questionnaire methods do not differ from our proceedings in this respect. The difference is mainly in the content of the questions.

[26] We should not overlook, however, that the further transformation of the report once it has been elicited, for example recording, transcription, analysis, etc, are of equal importance for the end result. These problems are more often treated in methodological discussions and therefore are here omitted.

[27] This assumption refers originally to the verbal memory, and its application to other forms of memory is questionable. This illuminates our difficulties in the practical

should therefore assume that immediate recall of conscious cognitions will be relatively easy and veridical.

On the other hand, once more time has passed between the conscious cognition and its report, recall will be from long-term memory (LTM), which involves recoding (for example from an acoustic to a semantic code in the case of verbal material; see Baddeley 1979) and reordering; recall will be more difficult and less veridical. The distortion of conscious cognition in recall from LTM leads already to our second point.

Distortion problems. Beyond the distortion which goes along with sheer storing and recall processes, there are other forms of adulteration. Here I refer to the large diversity of processes which happen as functions of self-evaluation and defence (cases of assimilation in the service of inward-directed adaptation, to use the language of [3.3]), without actually constituting conscious lies: selection, reorganization, rationalization and the creation and changes of meaning. It is difficult to estimate their true importance, but no doubt they exist. Although the modus and the time characteristics of their operation are hardly known, it seems justified to assume that their effects increase with time.

Interference. It is a general insight that measurement procedures tend to interfere with their object. This effect may be tolerable when we try to determine the outcome of a process, but becomes vital when we are interested in the process itself. Conscious cognition processes are very fragile, and the slightest intrusion (by instruction, diverted or directed attention, interruption, etc) may not only influence their content and quality, but also alter their course and results. The subject's remark: 'I noticed it, but I do not think it influenced what I did' is in fact the proof that the event influenced what he *thought*. In our methodological decisions, we have to weigh interference against other advantages and dangers.

5.6. Assessment methods

On the basis of these considerations, I propose to distinguish, according to the reporting actor's performance involved, between two types of

application of the psychology of memory: in spite of its tremendous progress during the last decades, its answers are difficult to use because of lack of integration. What should we do with the results referring specifically either to verbal or to visual or to acoustical memory, when our situations usually do contain an integrated mixture of multimodal stimulation? What are the mutual influences of these stimuli in relation to qualities of storage and reproduction? And the notion that the two-store model is too simple and to be replaced by a hierarchy of interacting stores (Baddeley 1979) is illuminating, but not immediately helpful. Forced to use these findings as a rule of thumb, we act like a layman.

report: immediate report and recall. As to the immediate report, the way of its elicitation determines the reporting actor's task; these methods can therefore be further subdivided, depending on whether they are based on continuous monitoring or interrupting and answer on the spot. Recall methods can be further classified according to the time between action-related cognition and report.

5.6.1. *Immediate report.* Immediate report methods have in common that *the actor reports during or immediately after the occurrence of his action-related cognitions.* He therefore reports directly from consciousness or STM respectively. We can therefore expect relatively high veridicality and little distortion. The disadvantage of these methods lies in the fact that reporting is an action itself which may interfere with the GDA under study; reporting action-related cognitions might influence the ongoing or following action and its related cognitions. The use of these methods in interactive situations is excluded for obvious reasons.

Ongoing continuous report

In this case, the actor is instructed to report continuously about his ongoing conscious cognitions (for example the different techniques of 'thinking aloud' or 'self-talk'; compare Pope 1978).[28] The advantage of these methods has already been mentioned. They involve, however, several difficulties: the cognitive activity demanded for reporting can interfere with GDA-related cognitions. In order to minimize this influence, extensive training (one week in one of our studies; Engeli 1979) may be useful. This training also relieves the subject from feelings of alienation and helps to accustom him to a kind of behaviour which is normally negatively defined by society. Another and more severe difficulty is based in the difference between cognitive and speech activities. To simplify, cognitive activity is multidimensional (more than one cognition at a time) and can be very fast, whereas speech is sequentially organized and relatively slow; in thinking aloud, cognition must be adapted to the constraints of speech. This may mean that the report will be continuous, but fractional and selected.

---

[28] The reader should notice that the methods described here are methods for the study of conscious cognition in general (for example the papers from the book by Pope and Singer 1978); their application to the study of GDA-related cognitions constitutes a special case.

Interruption methods

In this case, the actor is somehow interrupted in his cognitive and behavioural activity and asked to report what he has (or had) just now in his consciousness (for example 'thought sampling', Klinger 1978). This technique has several advantages: it allows the use of representative samples, and the subject can be instructed to give detailed (non-selective) reports. Technical refinements and standardization of the method as well as a combination with other methods of assessment are possible. The disadvantage (especially for GDA research) is in the interruption which destroys the flow of ongoing GDA-related cognitions and the activity itself. Sample size may become a critical problem, because many fresh subjects are needed: repetitive interruption creates expectations in subjects which again interfere with ongoing cognitive processes.

5.6.2. *Recall techniques.* Here the actor is requested to report on his GDA-related cognitions *after the action has been finished.* Recall is practically always from LTM. If one actor serves only once, there will be no interference with the action under study. Standardization of the assessment method (whether interview or questionnaire) is possible. The disadvantage of the method lies in the possible impact of recall and distortion errors. These effects may depend on the time interval between GDA and assessment. This is of course a continuum; for the sake of clarification, let us discuss two extreme types.

Report at the end of the act

In this case, the actor is requested to report immediately after the act has been finished, so that interference is no longer possible. (In our own studies, we combined an interview with a self-confrontation method; see von Cranach *et al.* 1980, ch. 8). The advantage of these methods is that recall and distortion problems are minimized (although not completely eliminated). Sometimes, for example, the method will make a cognition fully conscious which was originally only subconscious (this refers especially to reported perceptions). Disadvantages may be seen in the restriction to certain action types: the advantages of immediacy get lost with long complicated acts, and the need to assess after the act restricts the range of practical possibilities and creates considerable effort and expense.

Delayed report

Here the actor's report is elicited at any convenient time after the act has been performed. Advantages of this method are its general applicability and the relative ease to gain delayed data by interview or questionnaire: it is easier to find an opportunity if the exact moment is unimportant. The disadvantage is of course the great risk of unreliability, due to problems of recall (especially as far as the details are concerned) and distortion.

In addition, in these studies, there will often be no behaviour records available, so that no comparison with manifest behaviour data can be made. In general, this method will remain *ultima ratio* where assessment at the end of the act is impossible.

5.6.3. *Conclusion*. Because of the different advantages and disadvantages, appropriate methods have to be selected according to the specific demands and constraints of the particular research. In any case, standardization and investigation of the chosen method, although costly, seems desirable.

In GDA research, we are mainly interested in action-preceding and action-accompanying conscious cognitions; let us now shortly evaluate the listed methodological alternatives under this viewpoint. *Ongoing continuous report* can be used, if sufficient training can be provided to minimize interference effects, to study *individual action* in *non-communicative situations*. *Interruption methods* may be useful for *survey studies*, where we investigate for example the distribution of GDA cognition classes; they can hardly be used to study the systems characteristics of act–action structures. Among the *recall techniques* the *elicited and controlled report at the end of the act* will be the preferred method in case of *short concrete* and *interactive actions*; it will produce data on *action-accompanying cognitions* of a decent quality.

Action-preceding cognitions (as far as their effect on ongoing action is concerned) can only be studied by *delayed recall*. It is this point where we meet the greatest difficulties, but these cognitions are so important that we cannot do without them. At a closer look, the situation can be seen to be not without hope; so we can develop distinctions of what should be more and what should be less trustworthy. I would for example propose that delayed reports on cognitions which are by their very nature enduring should deserve more confidence than report on short-lived cognitive processes; and reports from stable standard situations more confidence than reports from situations which involve insecurity and defence. Values, for example, are generally considered as persistent parts of cognitive personality structure; under favourable circumstances and with due caution, it should be possible to assess value cognitions some time after they originally occurred. Long-term goals are persistent by their very function (for example 'At that time I had decided to become a medical doctor') and can be reproduced with delay. On the other hand, I would hesitate to investigate the cognitive details of strategies and decisions processes with too much delay, and generally distrust the delayed report of these short-lived cognitive processes which might be especially susceptible to distortion (for example the conscious cognition during an intense marital conflict).[29] From such considerations, I would suggest the development of two methodological aids: first, we should establish, in analogy to the historians' 'source critique' and to some methods of forensic psychology (Trankell 1971), a system of rules for the evaluation of cognitions reported with delay; second, we should construct and investigate standardized interviews assessing both more immediate and more distant GDA-related cognitions. Let us summarize all these points very shortly:

> [14] *In the assessment of GDA-related cognitions, we must avoid interference with ongoing GDA and overcome recall and distortion problems; different methods are indicated for different purposes.*

6. Epilogue

Although selective, this paper became longer than intended, and so I shall be short in my concluding remarks. Rereading the statements in square brackets will provide a summary. Let me therefore just emphasize a few points of special importance:

(i) GDA is an important (if not the most important) kind of human behaviour.

(ii) GDA is no longer an object of exclusively philosophical and sociological study, but a field of psychological research, which comprises theoretical, methodological and empirical investigation.

(iii) The psychological concept of GDA integrates cognitive, behavioural and social viewpoints, and so must its theory and research.

(iv) It is possible today to develop adequate and empirically useful psychological theories of GDA; some have already been proposed.

---

[29] Unfortunately, it is just this type of cognition which is so important in the criminal trial.

These are greatly influenced by General Systems Theory and the new developments of cognitive psychology.

(v) GDA methodology has to proceed beyond what is now usual, without violating existing standards of quality. These developments will have to depart from the existing, already highly sophisticated social science methodology.

References

Ackoff, R. L. and F. E. Emery (1972) *On purposeful systems.* Aldine, Chicago.
Aebli, H. (1980) *Denken: Das Ordnen des Tuns. I: Kognitive Aspekte der Handlungstheorie.* Klett-Cotta, Stuttgart.
Atkinson, R. C. and R. M. Shiffrin (1971) 'The control of short-term memory.' *Scientific American* **225**, 82–90.
Baddeley, A. D. (1979) *Die Psychologie des Gedächtnisses.* Klett-Cotta, Stuttgart.
Bertalanffy, L. von (1956) 'General systems theory.' *General Systems* **1**, 1–10.
Buckley, W. (ed.) (1968). *Modern systems research for the behavioral scientist.* Aldine, Chicago.
Claparède, E. (1968) *L'Éducation fonctionelle.* Delachaux-Niestlé, Neuchâtel.
Cranach, M. von (1976) 'Conclusions.' In M. von Cranach (ed.) *Methods of Inference from animal to human behaviour.* Aldine, Chicago.
Cranach, M. von, U. Kalbermatten, K. Indermühle and B. Gugler (1980) *Zielgerichtetes Handeln.* Huber, Bern.
Dawkins, R. (1976) 'Hierarchical organization: a candidate principle for ethology.' In P. P. G. Bateson and R. A. Hinde (eds.), *Growing points in ethology.* Cambridge University Press, Cambridge.
Eibl-Eibesfeldt, I. (1978) *Grundriss der vergleichenden Verhaltensforschung,* 5th edn. R. Piper, München.
Engeli, M. (1979) 'Theorie der handlungsbegleitenden lauten Selbstgespräche.' Unpublished thesis, University of Berne.
Graumann, C. F. (1966) 'Bewusstsein und Bewusstheit: Probleme und Befunde der psychologischen Bewusstseinsforschung.' In W. Metzger (ed.), *Handbuch der Psychologie. I: Allgemeine Psychologie.* Verlag für Psychologie, C. J. Hogrefe, Göttingen.
Grawe, K. (ed.) (1980) *Verhaltenstherapie in Gruppen.* Urban & Schwarzenberg, München.
Hacker, W. (1978) *Allgemeine Arbeits- und Ingenieurpsychologie,* 2nd edn. Huber, Bern.
Harré, R. (1972) 'The analysis of episodes.' In J. Israel and H. Tajfel (eds.), *The Context of Social Psychology: a critical assessment.* Academic Press, London.
— (1979) *Social being.* Blackwell, Oxford.
Harré, R. and P. F. Secord (1972) *The explanation of social behaviour.* Blackwell, Oxford.
Jefress, E. L. (ed.) (1951) *Cerebral mechanisms in behavior: the Hixon symposium.* Wiley, New York.
Kalbermatten, U. and M. von Cranach (1981) 'Hierarchisch aufgebaute Beobachtungssysteme zur Handlungsanalyse.' In P. Winkler (ed.), *Methoden zur Analyse von Face-to-Face Situationen.* Metzler, Stuttgart.

Klinger, E. (1978) 'Modes of normal conscious flow.' In K. S. Pope and J. L. Singer (eds.), *The stream of consciousness*. Plenum Press, New York.

Lorenz, K. (1978) *Vergleichende Verhaltensforschung: Grundlagen der Ethologie*. Springer, Wien.

Luhmann, N. (1971) 'Zweck-Herrschaft-System. Grundbegriffe und Prämissen Max Webers.' In R. Maynz (ed.), *Bürokratische Organisation*. Kiepenheuer & Witsch, Köln.

Mayntz, R. (ed.) (1971) *Bürokratische Organisation*. Kiepenheuer & Witsch, Köln.

Miller, G. A., E. Galanter and K. H. Pribram (1960) *Plans and the structure of behavior*. Holt, New York.

Morgenthaler, Chr. (1979) 'Zur subjektiven Perspektive handelnder Personen.' Unpublished thesis, University of Berne.

Moscovici, S. and R. M. Farr (in press) *Social representations*. Cambridge University Press, Cambridge.

Nisbett, R. E. and T. D. Wilson (1977) 'Telling more than we can know: verbal reports on mental processes.' *Psychological Review* **84**, 231–59.

Piaget, J. (1923) *Le langage et la pensée chez l'enfant*. Delachaux-Niestlé, Neuchâtel.

Pope, K. S. (1978) 'How gender, solitude and posture influence the stream of consciousness.' In K. S. Pope and J. L. Singer (eds.), *The stream of consciousness*. Plenum Press, New York.

Pope, K. S. and J. L. Singer (1978) *The stream of consciousness*. Plenum Press, New York.

Remane, A. (1952) *Die Grundlagen des natürlichen Systems, der vergleichenden Anatomie und der Phylogenetik*. Geest & Port, Leipzig.

Rubinstein, S. L. (1971) 'Grundthesen der Bewusstseintheorie.' In T. Kussmann (ed.), *Bewusstsein und Handlung. Probleme und Ergebnisse der sowjetischen Psychologie*. Huber, Bern.

Semmer, N. and M. Frese (1979) 'Handlungstheoretische Implikationen für kognitive Therapie.' In N. Hoffmann (ed.), *Grundlagen kognitiver Therapie*. Huber, Bern.

Shotter, J. (1978) 'In criticism of attribution theory: prospective and retrospective functions of self-description.' Paper at British Psychological Society, December 1978, London.

Silverman, D. (1970) *The theory of organization*. Heinemann, London.

Singer, J. L. (1978) 'Experimental studies of daydreaming and the stream of thought.' In K. S. Pope and J. L. Singer (eds.), *The stream of consciousness*. Plenum Press, New York.

Smith, E. R. and F. D. Miller (1978) 'Limits on perception of cognitive processes: a reply to Nisbett and Wilson.' *Psychological Review* **85**, no. 4, 355–62.

Steiner, V. (1980) 'Zielstrukturen in konkreten interaktiven Handlungen.' Unpublished thesis, University of Berne.

Tinbergen, N. (1951) *The study of instinct*. Oxford University Press, Oxford.

Trankell, A. (1971) *Der Realitätsgehalt von Zeugenaussagen: Methodik der Aussagepsychologie*. Vanderhoek & Ruprecht, Göttingen.

Werbik, H. (1976) 'Grundlagen einer Theorie sozialen Handelns.' *Zeitschrift für Sozialpsychologie* **7**, 246–61 and 310–26.

Wertsch, J. V. (ed.) (1978) *Recent trends in Soviet psycholinguistics*. Sharpe, New York.

2. Practical and interactive action

Introduction

The three papers by Hacker, Kaminski, and von Cranach and Kalber-matten are dealing with practical action aiming at practical ends, although 'interactive action' as investigated in some of the research reported by von Cranach and Kalbermatten certainly constitutes a borderline case. The authors also have very similar viewpoints at least in regard to three central concepts of action theory:

(i) The definition of action as a goal-directed, planned, intended, and (partly) consciously directed activity.

(ii) The assumption of a two-dimensional organization of action.

(iii) The emphasis on cognitive steering reflected in concepts like perception of the environment, goal, mental representation, plan and strategy, and control by means of regulation and feedback.

Within this general agreement, there is still room enough for consider-able differences. Hacker's presentation is a perfect example of an investigation of action in industrial and engineering psychology (in fact, the author has written one of the outstanding modern textbooks in this field). This research is rooted in the German tradition (for instance Werner Straub) but also in the Marxist psychology of labour activity. The preferred methodology is largely that of experimental psychology, and so is the dominant way of thinking; this is reflected in the way in which purely experimental laboratory studies are used to prove or illustrate action theoretical propositions. Still, Hacker and his co-workers acknow-ledge the value of descriptive research. At the beginning of his paper, Hacker points to the particularities of labour activity, as for instance prescribed task, dependency on machines and the constraints of pro-ductive co-operation; in this system, the actions' degrees of freedom are limited and predetermined by the task. Against this background, Hacker discusses the relationship between the actions' surface and deep structures. An action structure exposes three sides: a behavioural, a logical, and a psychological structure, the latter one constituting the deep structure which is the final target of this research. Following Tomaszewski, Hacker enumerates five essential psychological aspects: *re-definition* of a *task* as a *goal; orientation* to the conditions of the activity in regard to *environment* and *memory data;* designing of *strategies* (as *memory representations*); decision for a *program* variant (again based on *memory representations*); and finally *control* by feedback. (This is seen as instrumental and regulated by goals as standards.) Note the importance of memory representations in these principles; memory representations are therefore treated in detail, in regard to goals and to the design and testing of programs. Finally, Hacker goes into some details of the characteristics of internal representations, treating problems of task-dependence, type of coding and the reduction of effort by redefinition of the prescribed task. In general, action is treated in this article as an activity exclusively determined by its instrumental functions in the service of the task in the labour environment. Hacker carefully avoids transgressing the borders of labour activity; but in fact he develops a coherent model of GDA, firmly supported by data.

Although Kaminski shares many of Hacker's assumptions, his arguments call the achieved model into question, at least to some degree. So he asks at the beginning of his paper: 'Does it really make sense to use "action" as a fundamental theoretical unit in psychology? Is *the* action possibly the wrong starting point (or at least not the most fruitful one) if we want to study actions? Would it perhaps be better if we first, or at least simultaneously, asked about generic and differential features of systems of more or less interconnected and interwoven actions and then (again) about generic and differential features of single actions?' Behind this quotation stands the doubt whether single actions do often occur in everyday life. Kaminski's central interest is 'multiple action', the 'simultaneous performance and control of several component actions, partly independent of each other, some of which were hierarchically organized'; he encountered this type of action in his studies of the behaviour of beginner skiers. Kaminski's background is the theory of motor skills, especially as applied in sports psychology, and the paradigm of 'problem-solving' which 'may be viewed as a special kind of acting which is slowed down by barriers. Therefore, it lends itself well to detailed analysis via observation and thinking aloud. This is why the theory of problem-solving processes may be used (although tentatively) as a paradigmatic conception for the structural and functional interpretation of different kinds of complex action in everyday life, where details in the course of action are less accessible. However, this paradigm needs some modification and extension. The question is in what respects the theory of problem-solving has to be differentiated to become useful for the description and explanation of complex actions'.

In multiple action, the actor is likely to be overcharged, and one of Kaminski's concerns is to find out how the actor can cope with 'psychological overload'. In the pilot study underlying his report (which is in fact an extensive and comprehensive descriptive study), Kaminski has investigated the behaviour of several groups of beginner skiers for several weeks. (This type of action differs, of course, from that investigated by Hacker; for example, Kaminski stresses the occurrence of 'maintenance goals' rather than 'attainment goals'.) In addition to the observations, the skiers have been asked to report their thoughts, immediately after action, and the instructions and verbal comments of the instructors have been analysed. From these data, it becomes obvious that the skiers find themselves under the pressure of *multiple information input* and are thus forced to act in a multiple way. For the investigator, these findings give rise to conceptual and methodological questions. For example, what is an action, what are its components, and what criteria can be used to answer these questions? The shifting and unstable focus of conscious steering and monitoring seems unsuited to serve as a proper criterion. From here, Kaminski proceeds to analyse the 'functional context' of single actions in terms of hierarchical organization and multiple acting and to the discussion of the consequences of these constraints for the actor's processing capacity. He concludes that the 'basic unit of action' must be changed, and proposes a 'list of generic features of action' including the following notions:
An action
- does not exist singly, but rather always occurs together with other actions;
- consumes processing capacity;
- is susceptible to impairment by the consequences of capacity shortages;
- is open to the balancing of different regulations necessary within an action hierarchy;
- is open to being coordinated with other actions;
- is open to being modified by strategies of complexity reduction.

These features apply, so Kaminski argues, to other kinds of multiple action in everyday life as well. In order to understand how the actor economizes his limited information-processing capacity Kaminski proposes a model of successive stages of complexity generation and reduction. Other solutions are indicated, but in general more questions are raised than answered in this paper.

Von Cranach and Kalbermatten aim at a comprehensive psychology of goal-directed action which also applies to ordinary and interactive action as we encounter these in everyday life. The authors take as a starting point the research on labour activity as it has been presented by Hacker, but go beyond it in three respects:

(i) The theory of labour activity is extended by taking into account the social nature of goal-directed action. To do so, the labour activity model is put into a framework of a theory of *social steering and control of action* following ideas from symbolic interactionism and phenomenological sociology. The basic proposition is that society controls individual behaviour by implanting socially shared cognitions (*social conventions* which convey *social meaning*) into the *individual cognitive system* which in turn controls the individuals' *manifest behaviour*.

Thus the theory integrates three classes of theoretical concepts referring to manifest behaviour, (conscious) cognition, and social meaning (cf. von Cranach, this volume).

(ii) The manifold concepts of this theory (partly already contained in the labour activity model) are elaborated in detail and used in research. This requires for example descriptive investigations into the microstructures and microfunctions of movements and cognitions and mutual coherence of their variations. Researchers should take their own theoretical assumptions seriously, for example by trying to directly investigate the processes of conscious action-related cognitions.

(iii) For this purpose, research methods are developed which take the specific qualities of action-related cognitions into account and are suited to describe and analyse the manifold relationships of action theoretical concepts. Traditional experimental methods are useful, but not sufficient for this type of study.

In the presentation of their empirical work, the authors concentrate on the two variable classes of manifest behaviour and conscious cognition; with their research examples they try to demonstrate that the kind of research which they advocate is possible. They briefly describe new methods like nested observation systems for the assessment of hierarchically ordered behaviour, and the self-confrontation interview to assess conscious action-related cognitions. Their results document the intrinsic social nature of goal-directed action as it appears for example in the documented functions of social norms as desired values in regulation processes.

Objective and subjective organization of work activities

WINFRIED HACKER

1. Some features of the approach

During the last ten years, the psychological group of the Dresden Technological University has dealt with the structure and regulation of actions. Our motivation is very specific: we assume that the approach of a 'psychology of action' will be the most suitable means for a human-centred psychological analysis for the evaluation and design of jobs. Thus, our experience is limited to actions which are part of working activities.

Some mental processes, representations, states and traits manifest themselves in actions. They serve for orientation as the basis of the regulation of activity.

Every action performs an order or accomplishes a task. Thus, order and task are indispensable concepts of a psychological analysis of actions. Therefore, we assume that all mental processes and representations are organized in such a way that they permit a successful and efficient accomplishment of tasks. We suppose that the task-dependent structure and code of the regulating mental processes and representations is one of the main characteristics of actions. In our opinion, the action is something like the psychological unit or 'molecule' of activity. Unfortunately, this unit seems to be definable only by means of goals, which is a difficult concept because of problems with the methods for the identification of goals.

Actions are goal-oriented and, therefore, people are conscious of them. Normally, actions are regulated by the anticipation of their results. This anticipation together with the intention of implementation is the goal. More complex goals are achieved via partial results, which are anticipated in the form of subgoals. Together with the necessary procedures, these subgoals may form programmes or plans of actions.

81

The programmes are organized simultaneously in a sequential and hierarchic mode (for details see Hacker 1978). Although these statements of our approach seem to be compelling, some of them are more or less hypothetical. So far, to my mind, the existence of motor programmes in addition to the anticipation of results has not been verified experimentally (Heuer 1978). On the other hand, some further components of this approach are adequately verified. This holds, for instance, for regulation by anticipation.

The determination of the organization of actions by anticipation should be valid for every type of action, including simple ones, regulated on the sensorimotor level. We investigated this question. I will try to outline some of our research topics. The first example: the disputed 'law of constant movement time' by von Weizsäcker (1947) states that the tracing of one and the same figure of different size requires the same time, i.e. the figure is drawn with different speeds, dependent on size.

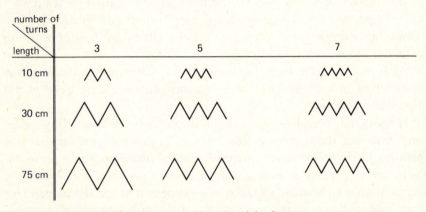

Fig. 1. Variation of the complication and lengths of the figures

Similarly, with positioning movements, the time required – when the distance to the target is increased – will grow less than the distance between the targets grows (Schmidtke 1960, Hacker 1967). These findings are due to visual *anticipation* of the figural path, or the distance to the target, for the effect disappears if anticipation is impossible. On the other hand, an exact constancy of time has never been proved.

Therefore, we tried to vary the complexity of figures more exactly. For this reason reversal points, for example of zig-zag figures, were used (Fig. 1). Moreover, the tolerances for tracing precision and the length of

Table 1. *Experimental design with zig-zag-shaped figures*

	Length (L)	L_1 10 cm			L_2 30 cm			L_3 75 cm		
	Number of turns (NT)	3	5	7	3	5	7	3	5	7
Tolerances (T)										
T_1											
T_2											
T_3											

length tolerance	L_1 10 cm	L_2 30 cm	L_3 75 cm
T_1	0.5 mm	1.5 mm	3.75 mm
T_2	1.0 mm	3.0 mm	7.50 mm
T_3	2.0 mm	6.0 mm	15.00 mm

Fig. 2. Variation of the tolerances

paths were varied (Fig. 2). Thus, the experimental design shown in Table 1 was used.

A three-way analysis of variance has shown significant differences for the time required between the path lengths, the demands on precision and the levels of figure complexity (Fig. 3). Obviously, the law of constant movement time only describes the special condition, that lengthening the path is accompanied by a reduction of precision, which compensates for the increase of time required due to the lengthening. For the subjects with lowest precision in the case of the largest tolerances, Fig. 4 shows the approximation to constancy of time in spite of the path being lengthened.

We conclude that the subjective tendency concerning precision systematically covaries with the requirements made by a figure on regulation.

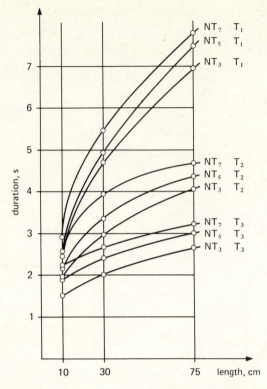

Fig. 3. Mean duration of tracing in relation to length, complication (NT_3 . . . NT_7) and tolerances (T_1 . . . T_3)

Thus, the law of constant movement time is due to the anticipated regulation requirements as a whole, not only to the anticipated length. Obviously, anticipation is a key feature in the organization even of simple actions.

2. What are the peculiarities of work activities?

Since our experience is limited to work activities, it would be fair to point out the peculiarities of work actions. But we assume that these peculiarities highlight common features of actions in their original form:

(i) Work actions *perform prescribed tasks*. They can be *redefined* into subjective tasks, if degrees of freedom are given.

(ii) Work actions accomplish *meaningful* tasks only *by means of cooperation*. Division of labour will generate tasks that are often *per se* meaningless.

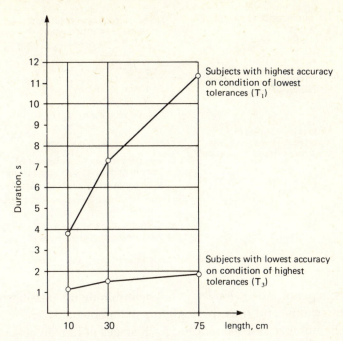

Fig. 4. Duration and accuracy of tracing, contrasted for two groups of subjects with greatest differences in accuracy

(iii) Work actions are *evaluated* in advance and their organization is modified due to this predictive evaluation. The most important evaluation criterion is efficiency. Efficiency is a ratio of effort and result. Working people are mostly interested in effective not in elegant solutions.

(iv) In industry, work actions are *dependent parts* of the technological process. Their organization is determined by these objective technological conditions.

The determination of the organization of actions by their conditions, in our case by socioeconomic conditions, including technology

In modern semi-automatic or even automatic production, human actions are only necessary at special stages of the production process. The characteristics of these technological stages determine the requirements made on the operator and thus the possible organization of human actions. In Fig. 5, the white boxes labelled *a, b,* and so on illustrate these stages with human components. Some of them may offer various possibilities of suitable operations on degrees of freedom of actions,

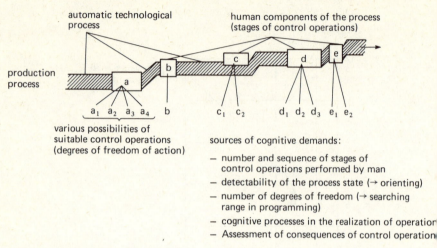

Fig. 5. Main sources of cognitive job demands in man–machine systems

others may not. Their characteristics determining the possible organization of actions, and thus the cognitive requirements, are:

(i)   the number and sequence of such stages of human actions

(ii) the detectibility and discriminability of those process stages that are critical for actions

(iii) the number of possible actions, i.e. of the degrees of freedom, indicating the difficulty of decision-making and of programme development

(iv) the cognitive operations in carrying out the programmes

(v)   the predictive evaluation of possible consequences.

The influence of *perceived or subjective degrees of freedom* on the organization of action is essential. With the number of different ways to achieve a goal, the requirements made on decision processes are increasing. And different decisions will generate different mental regulation processes. Therefore, an analysis of the organization of actions must start with the analysis of the conditions of actions including the objective degree of freedom. In field studies it could be shown that the best workers identify the objective degrees of freedom of their jobs more adequately and cope with them more effectively than the others do.

Degrees of freedom in a real work situation

In extended field studies we were interested in the real degrees of freedom of workers in carrying out their jobs. By means of work studies

with a flow-diagram technique we tried to find out what are these degrees of freedom that determine the possible goal-setting. We found the following scale (Rothe 1978):
  (i) jobs without any degree of freedom for individual decision-making and goal-setting
  (ii) jobs with degrees of freedom, which allow goals concerning the *speed* of action
  (iii) jobs with goals concerning the *sequence* of operations
  (iv) jobs with goals concerning *means and procedures*
  (v) jobs with goals concerning the *characteristics of the result*.

If degrees of freedom are given as to means and procedures of the action or the characteristics of the desired results, problem-solving demands might arise. In this case goal-setting will become a part of the problem-solving steps of the preparation phase of the action.

Recently, Rothe (1978) demonstrated that with increasing number and complexity of degrees of freedom an activity also becomes more complex in terms of the number of different operations. This coincides with decreasing perceived fatigue, monotony and saturation but increasing work satisfaction.

The second peculiarity which I would like to discuss briefly is the determination of the organization of actions by their expected effort.

If a presented task offers degrees of freedom, it will be redefined as a task suitable for the individual. In the industrial working process this redefinition leads to tasks with an acceptable ratio of effort and result. The redefinitions reducing the perceived effort were experimentally analysed in information integration and assembly tasks. We found (Matern 1976, Hacker 1977, Kasvio 1978):
  (i) Subjects avoid strategies including complex logical or mathematical rules even if they are highly skilled in their use. Instead, they prefer very simple rules, categorizations, or even rough ratings.
  (ii) The preferred strategies show less perceived fatigue and activation, measured by means of the heart period time (Kasvio 1978).
  (iii) The reduction of effort seems to result especially from the lower load of the short-term memory in the case of the preferred strategies.

Thus, the regulative deep structure of actions is determined to a decisive extent by the predictive evaluation of effort.

Hierarchically organized rules: some experimental research

Many processes consist of units generated one from another by transformational rules. A branching hierarchy of transformational rules should produce an effective mode of storage. Restle and Brown (1970) found that in the prediction of rule-generated sequences of items the hierarchically organized rules are discovered and used in the function of hypotheses; the difficulty of these rules has no effect on the performance, depending only on the overall hierarchical deep structure; the difficulty of the prediction is a monotonic function of the level of the hierarchy; the detection of the hierarchical structure starts on the lowest level and stops on the highest one.

These results oppose the expectation of context-dependent programmes of information processing in the control of actions. Therefore, we looked for the validity of the cited results in a more natural task. (Further details of the experiments are given in Hacker 1977.)

Method. 16 rows, each with 5 overlapping building elements, were displayed visually. 36 subjects were asked to discover the sequences required for assemblage and to note them on sheets (Fig. 6). There were 4 different sequences which could be transformed one into the other by rules of differing difficulty (repetition; inversion; change of the type of sequence). These rules were used on four hierarchical levels, thus generating 16 rows (Fig. 7). For quick transmission, memory storage and thus reduction of visual scanning in the display is required. In a $6 \times 3 \times 7$ factorial design, the degree of regularity of the item sequences, the instructions and the number of repetitions are varied. Dependent measures are the number and the duration of scanning movements to the display, regarded as a symptom of storage, the required time, the errors and the rated self-reports of regularity and difficulty of the item sequences and of effort.

Results.

(i) The hierarchical structures were only partially discovered and used in tasks that did not require the detection of the deep structure for correct execution.

(ii) Contrary to prediction experiments, the accuracy of detection of the hierarchical rules was not a monotonic function of the level of hierarchy, but depended on the position of rules of different difficulty. The detection of rules started with the simplest rule.

(iii) There was no general kind of internal representation of the hie-

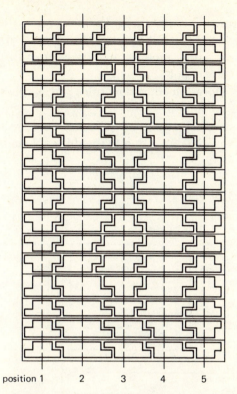

position 1   2   3   4   5

Fig. 6. Model of an assembly task. The elements ('building stones') are to fit on sticks, represented by the broken lines, in the possible sequences. Here the sequence in the bottom two rows is 1–2–3–4–5, in the third row up 1–2–5–4–3, and so on

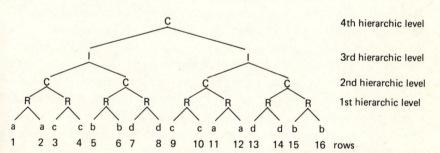

Fig. 7. Examples of a hierarchy used in the experiments: $(C(I(C(R\{a\}))))$. C = change of the type of sequence, I = inversion, R = repetitions

rarchy of rules. Depending on the position of the simplest rule, a representation of different parts of the overall structure resulted.

(iv) A systematic application of higher-order rules to hierarchically inferior ones was not observed.

(v) In all cases, storage mediated by rules and simple storage of isolated items were combined.

We think these results cannot confirm the findings of experiments in predicting sequences. This is due to the different cognitive demands of

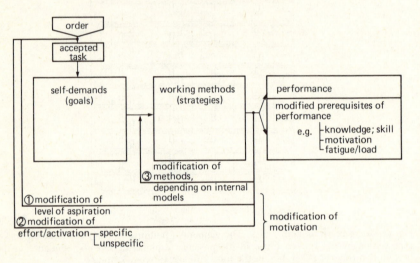

Fig. 8. Interrelations between motivation, methods of work and fatigue

our independent variables, including the role of the difficulty of rules. The results hint at a context-dependent principle of processing hierarchical sequences of information. By means of the combination of a rule-governed hierarchical organization and the associative storage of item sequences, not only the cognitive effort and short-term memory load but also the long-term storage of isolated items were reduced.

We conclude: men never bear load passively. Working people anticipate load. Consciously or unconsciously, they modify their goals or their strategies to cope with load. Expected load does not, therefore, change only the surface structure of an action, but also – and primarily – the generating and regulating deep structure. The flow diagram illustrates these modifications of the organization of action (Fig. 8).

3. The problem of surface v. deep structure of action

The following three aspects have to be distinguished in the analysis of industrial work operations (Fig. 9). Only the sequence of movements is

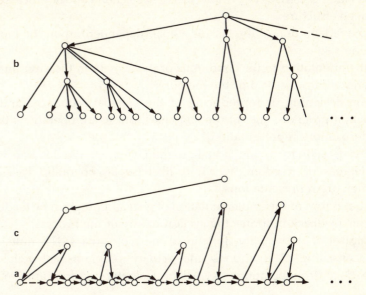

Fig. 9. Aspects of the analysis of work activities
a = sequence of movements (– – – →), b = logical structure of the presented task, c = hierarchical sequence of cognitive activities: psychological structure (——→)

immediately visible. The classical time-and-motion studies describe only this surface structure of the work operations. The logical structure of the task to be solved may be represented above this sequence of movements. It subdivides the task to be solved into partial tasks, considering thereby not only motor elements but also cognitive components within the meaning of the testing and modification steps of algorithm descriptions. However, the psychological or deep structure proper that is of interest here is not identical with this logical structure. The nodes are symbols of the hierarchy of the subgoals in representing it as a graph. The arrows correspond to cognitive processes that further break down or recode the superordinate parts of the task.

A new action firstly demands an analysis of *orientation* for the purpose of *programming*. The required steps of this program must be *stored*. Then they have to be *recalled* in the necessary *sequence*. Finally, they must be arranged into the *super*ordinate program in such a way that they are *its dependent components*.

The question as to mental regulation leads to this deep structure that is simultaneously hierarchic and sequential.

Reverting to Tomaszewski (1964), we assume that the following five aspects are necessary for the analysis of the action control processes by this deep structure:

(i) the redefinition of the task as a goal, dependent upon the motivation

(ii) the orientation to the conditions of the activity in the environment and within the data of the memory

(iii) the designing or reproducing of the subgoal sequences and the action programs, i.e. of the strategies. These are operations based on memory representations

(iv) the decision for an individual program variant in the case of existing degrees of freedom, which is likewise an operation based on memory representations

(v) the control of the implementation of goal and program by feedback; this feedback indicates the cyclical nature of the process.

For control of the activity, functional units (i.e. the TOTE units) will form consisting of intentions and activity programs as well as of feedback control operations (see Miller, Galanter and Pribram 1960).

4. Functions of the memory representations

The decisive links of mental control of the actions are the internal or memory representations. All phases of action are guided by them. It is useful to classify these representations into three types:

(i) the goals or the desired values

(ii) the representations of the conditions of implementation

(iii) the representations of actions themselves, i.e. of the required operations, transforming the given state into the desired one.

The goal as the essential kind of internal representation, i.e. the anticipated result of the action, is the indispensable constant of every goal-directed process, as Ashby and Conant (1970), Bernstein (1967) and Anochin (1967) have demonstrated. The goals are relatively stable memory representations that act as the necessary desired values in the comparison between the actual and the desired state during the implementation of an action. In the feedback processes mentioned, the actual state attained at every time is compared with the goal as the required state.

Memory representations have an irreplaceable function in the preparation of actions. This holds first for the *designing and testing of action programs*.

Internal representations of properties of the technological process, the means of production, or the raw materials enable internal program-testing to be carried out before their implementation in practice. Furthermore, internal representations represent the base for the selection of action programs as far as degrees of freedom for a differentiated approach exist. They serve for the prognostic evaluation of the consequences of possible steps and the decision on the path to be taken. Thus, internal representations are the 'material' on which the decisive steps of information processing in the organization of goal-oriented actions are performed.

The *orientation*, too, is influenced by the quality of the internal representations. Different memory representations will result in different hypotheses on the present state of a technological process, thus inducing other search strategies, and the selection of other sources of information.

In the sense of a multilevel regulation approach, at least three levels of internal representations (including the programs) may be distinguished: the unconscious preprogrammed sensorimotor level, the conscious conceptual level, and the level of intellectual problem-solving and planning. As a matter of fact, not only the productivity aspect of psychological job design, but also the personality aspect are related to these levels of regulation. The higher the level in the hierarchic scale, the greater is the possibility of discovering more variety of operations, more autonomy, more possibilities of intrinsic motivation, and even more effective working strategies.

In our field research it was shown that the more elaborated these representations are, the more effective is the performance. For example:
  (i) the most effective workers developed a more sophisticated network of goals and subgoals
 (ii) they use more effective signals, that inform about future states of the technological process
(iii) they know better the probability of important events, e.g. faults, thus using more effective strategies of fault-finding
 (iv) they predict the future course of processes more accurately
  (v) they predict a wider range of possible steps of a program including their consequences and alternatives.

Thus, on the basis of a more elaborated system of representations, a planned (as opposed to momentary) type of the organization of action may take place, that will enable higher efficiency without increasing work-load.

5. Some characteristics of internal representations controlling actions

Internal or memory representations are characterized by specific features, determined by their functions in controlling actions. The most important features are:

(i) task-dependence or compatibility, consequently
(ii) the type of coding and
(iii) the already-mentioned reduction of effort by the redefinition of prescribed tasks.

I would like to outline an example of our research concerning the problems of task-dependence. It is well known that the regulation of actions by memory representations is more effective than regulation by momentary input-processing. However, different representations in memory are possible with different consequences for the efficiency of actions.

Hypothesis 1. The memory model represents the untransformed input. Transformations between input and representations are preserved.

Hypothesis 2. By means of feedback, the internal representation represents the information necessary for response organization. Transformations between internal representations and response organization are preserved. This is the point of task-dependent memory representations.

Hypothesis 3. The memory model represents the information in a memory-specific code, i.e. a code suitable for rehearsal.

We studied a simple type of assembly-task, common in the production of electronic equipment. The main independent variable is a different presentation of the necessary information for the required task, e.g. in the form of a completed product, a compatible or incompatible scheme, a typed or tape-recorded list of instructions (for details see Hacker and Clauss 1976, Cavallo 1978).

Some results. Before memory representations are established, the assembly time per element is a monotonically increasing function of the number of cognitive operations required (this is shown by the upper curve of Fig. 10). In the last repetition of the training procedure, a memory representation was developed. This was verified by free recall. In this case, the dependence of time on cognitive complexity disappears more and more (lower curve of Fig. 10).

This reduction of time is due to the saving of those cognitive processes

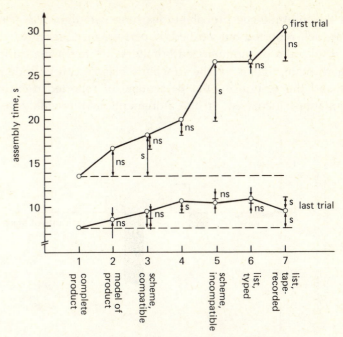

Fig. 10. Assembly time as a function of cognitive requirements and repetitions (cognitive requirements, number of cognitive operations required); for details see Hacker and Clauss (1976).

which initially produced the high differences. Therefore, the learning rate increases with the number of cognitive transformations between memory and response, which become superfluous after the development of compatible memory representations.

For further verification we asked whether, on the contrary, an identical information presentation may produce *different* memory representations in the case of different strategies of task accomplishment. Cavallo (1978) verified this hypothesis in her experimental study, which also used assembly tasks. Thus, the task-dependent structure of memory representations which regulate actions seems to be verified. However, a number of more analytic questions about the nature of that effect remain unanswered.

A further issue of our research concerns the *code* of memory representations which control actions. The earlier research of Matern (1976) showed significant relations between the modality of information presentation, difficulty of task and the prevailing type of the reported code, i.e. iconic, verbal or dual (iconic and verbal). For simulation, a modification of the multiple-cue probability learning paradigm was used. The codes are self-reported but verified by performance measures.

The results can be summarized briefly. With increasing difficulty of task (here manipulated by the functions between three independent signals and the response), the percentage of reported dual memory representations increased. In the aforementioned assembly task, too,

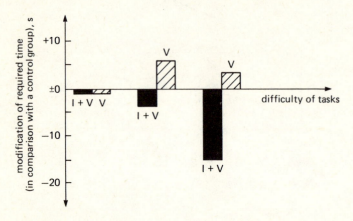

Fig. 11. Modification of required assembly time, in comparison with a control group without any instruction.
I + V = iconic and verbal instruction, V = verbal instruction. For details of experimental design see Hacker (1977)

the dual and the iconic representations prevailed not only in the case of a pictorial information presentation, but also in that of an alphabetical list.

We interpret the prevalence of dual representations as due to the simplification and facilitation of task accomplishment. This is verified by self-reports of perceived difficulty and fatigue, by a psychophysiological analysis of effort and by performance measures (Kasvio 1978).

Figure 11 illustrates the reduction of required time in the assembly task with a hierarchic design already mentioned (Hacker 1977), in comparison with a control group. The more difficult the hierarchic task structure, the greater is the reduction of working time in the case of dual information presentation in contrast to verbal presentation.

Thus the content, structure, and code of the memory representations, which control actions really seem to be of central interest for the organization of the type of actions we have discussed.

References

Anochin, P. K. (1967) *Das funktionelle System als Grundlage der physiologischen Architektur des Verhaltensaktes.* Fischer, Jena.

Ashby, W. R. and R. C. Conant (1970) 'Every good regulator of a system is a model of that system.' *International Journal of Systems Science* 1, 89–97.

Bernstein, N. A. (1967) *The coordination and regulation of movements.* Pergamon Press, Oxford.

Cavallo, V. (1978) 'Leistungs- und beanspruchungsbestimmende Eigenschaften operativer Abbilder – untersucht an Montagetätigkeiten.' *Informationen der Technischen Universität Dresden,* no. 22–16–78.

Hacker, W. (1967) *Grundlagen der Regulation von Arbeitsbewegungen.* Supplementary volume 1 of *Probleme und Ergebnisse der Psychologie.*

— (1977) 'Zur Anforderungsabhängigkeit der Nutzung von hierarchischer Ordnung in Sequenzen.' *Zeitschrift für Psychologie* 185, 1–33.

— (1978) *Allgemeine Arbeits- und Ingenieurpsychologie,* 2nd edn. Huber, Bern.

Hacker, W. and A. Clauss (1976) 'Kognitive Operationen, inneres Modell und Leistung bei einer Montagetätigkeit.' In W. Hacker (ed.), *Psychische Regulation von Arbeitstätigkeiten.* Deutscher Verlag der Wissenschaften, Berlin.

Heuer, H. (1978) 'Über Bewegungsprogramme bei willkürlichen Bewegungen.' Unpublished thesis, Marburg University.

Kasvio, L. (1978) 'Strategien beim Erlernen funktioneller Beziehungen.' *Informationen der Technischen Universität Dresden,* no. 22–9–78.

Matern, B. (1976) 'Zum Einfluss der Art der Signaldarbietung auf das Erlernen funktioneller Beziehungen.' In W. Hacker (ed.), *Psychische Regulation von Arbeitstätigkeiten.* Deutscher Verlag der Wissenschaften, Berlin.

Miller, G. A., E. Galanter and K. H. Pribram (1960) *Plans and the structure of behavior.* Holt, New York.

Restle, F. and E. Brown (1970) 'Organization of serial pattern learning.' In *Psychology of learning and motivation* vol. 4.

Rothe, S. (1978) 'Arbeitsinhalt und Möglichkeiten zur selbständigen Zielsetzung.' *Informationen der Technischen Universität Dresden,* no. 22–17–78.

Schmidtke, H. (1960) 'Über die Struktur willkürlicher Bewegungen.' *Psychologische Beiträge* 5, 428–39.

Tomaszewski, T. (1964) 'Die Struktur der menschlichen Tätigkeiten.' *Psychologie und Praxis* 8, 245–55.

Weizsäcker, V. von (1947) *Der Gestaltkreis – Theorie der Einheit von Wahrnehmen und Bewegen.* Enke, Stuttgart.

What beginner skiers can teach us about actions

G. KAMINSKI

1. Fundamental features of the approach

The main accent of this contribution is on theoretical argument. Although it is based upon certain empirical investigations with skiing novices, these studies cannot be described here *in extenso* (cf. Kaminski 1972, 1973). Experiences gained in these investigations are called upon merely for elucidation and exemplification.

The basic questions here are: Does it really make sense to use 'action' as a fundamental theoretical unit in psychology? Is *the* action possibly the wrong starting point (or at least not the most fruitful one) if we want to study actions? Would it perhaps be better if we first, or at least simultaneously, asked about generic and differential features of systems of more or less interconnected and interwoven actions and then (again) about generic and differential features of single actions?

Much evidence seems to support positive answers to these last questions.

2. Some information about the empirical basis of the argument

2.1. Short report on the investigations with beginner skiers[1]

Why choose beginner skiers as the objects of investigations? I had the opportunity to make observations on myself when I learned to ski. These made me expect that by starting investigations with very complicated forms of acting (contrary to the usual procedure) it would be possible to uncover both general and fundamental aspects of actions. The basic idea was the following: if we succeeded in finding out certain fundamental features of these complicated actions, this should then facilitate analysis of relatively simpler ones. These simpler actions can be

[1] This investigation was supported by grants from the Bundes–institut für Sportwissenschaft, Köln.

99

conceived of as reduced variants of a general prototype, this being the maximally complicated action. Proceeding in the opposite direction did not seem to promise any success. For if we started with the thorough analysis of isolated, relatively simple actions we never would arrive at a theoretical synthesis of the functioning of maximally complicated actions. (Nevertheless, the analysis of simpler actions is undoubtedly useful in itself.) And some day we hope to reach an understanding of our most complicated actions. If we do not keep these complicated forms of acting in mind, we are constantly in danger of interpreting simpler actions in an all too simple way, that means in a fundamentally too simple way.

In close co-operation with sports psychologists and physical education experts, 25 beginners in downhill skiing were investigated during four skiing courses, each of which lasted one week. All verbal instructions given by the trainers were tape-recorded (and subsequently transcribed). Portions of the skiing were filmed, and after each action (i.e. realization of a single more or less complex task) the skiers gave accounts (also recorded and transcribed in full) of their experiences to interviewers in the field, in the manner sometimes employed in problem-solving research (e.g. Newell and Simon 1972) and lately in other research fields as well. The tasks that the skiers had to do proved to be 'multiple actions' in the sense that they principally required simultaneous performance and control of several component actions, partly independent of each other, some of which were hierarchically organized. Thus, the skiers were nearly continuously 'overloaded' and produced many deficient responses, which may yield information on intentions and shortcomings of orientation and controlling mechanisms. Skiers apparently apply specific strategies to reduce the overload conditions in a more or less useful (and purposeful?) way (J. G. Miller 1960) and they try to make optimal use of their limited capacity for action control.

2.2. Some comments on how these investigations are related to theoretical concepts

The investigation had been planned on the basis of theoretical concepts suggested by preliminary observations (Kaminski 1972, 1973). Thereby, we drew on paradigmatic presuppositions developed and confirmed empirically in the problem-solving domain (Kaminski 1970, Lüer 1973, Dörner 1974, 1976, Wickelgren 1974).

Problem-solving may be viewed as a special kind of acting which is slowed down by barriers. Therefore, it lends itself well to detailed analysis via observation and thinking aloud. This is why the theory of problem-solving processes may be used (although tentatively) as a paradigmatic concept for the structural and functional interpretation of different kinds of complex action in everyday life, where details in the course of action are less accessible. However, this paradigm needs some modification and extension. The question is in what respects the theory of problem-solving has to be differentiated to become useful for the description and explanation of complex actions.

The main aim of the investigations was to gather different kinds of data (especially verbalizations of the ski instructors, self-reports of the skiing novices, film records of a great variety of task performances) about a relatively complex type of acting and its changes caused by learning, and all this, as far as possible, under naturalistic conditions (cf. Willems and Raush 1969). Even a rather rough content-analytical evaluation of the data should suffice to show to what extent those paradigmatic presuppositions proved useful and where they needed expansion and/or modification.

A further aim of the investigation was to gain hypotheses about the regulation of actions of high complexity and about personal and ecological conditions influencing performance and its cognitive representation.

The task programme of the skiing courses contained some systematic variations so that, at least to a limited extent, testing of some special hypotheses was possible.

3. Some further characterization of the approach

In order to facilitate the localization and comprehension of the theoretical argumentation to follow, the investigations on which they are based should be characterized more closely.

Carrying out the investigations under 'naturalistic' conditions obliged us to take into account the practical aspects of the skiing courses and the interests of the participants. Therefore, our studies could hardly be considered a purely psychological field experiment. Rather they should be conceived of as an interdisciplinary pilot study.

In its psychological perspectives the investigation has, as mentioned before, its theoretical and methodological basis in problem-solving research. To understand movement tasks as 'problems' would be quite unusual in problem-solving psychology. There, one is used to dealing with single more or less complicated 'static' problem spaces and their cognitive treatment, rather than with tasks as complex and short-lived as those usually encountered in sports.

Within kinesiology of sports, however, the concept of 'problem' can be found referring to movement tasks. But there it is far from being bound up with theoretical aspirations as they are known from problem-solving research in psychology (Göhner 1979, Kaminski 1979). The concepts of 'action' and 'acting' as applied, for instance, to skiers may therefore be seen as an extension of the notion of 'problem-solving'.

Within psychology, movement issues traditionally are treated under headings like 'psychomotor processes', 'motor behaviour', 'human performance', 'sensorimotor control', 'motor learning', 'psycho-motor skills', etc (Welford 1968, Singer 1972, 1975, Rüssel 1976). The execution of relatively simple movement tasks is being investigated in minute detail with the help of extremely precise measurement procedures. Correspondingly detailed and precise are the theoretical models (Pew 1974, Schmidt 1975).

In this context the concept of 'action' would appear far too vague. Not until recently have perspectives with a coarser grain been used, whereby the notion of 'action' turns up, referring to everyday behaviour (Neisser 1976, Fowler and Turvey 1978, K. M. Newell 1978). Action processes as complicated as skiing, however, are still left out of consideration.

Even the experimental investigation of 'multiple acting' ('dual tasks'; 'concurrent activity') has been confined to very simple sorts of behaviour (compared with skiing) up to now (Welford 1968, p. 132, Elliott and Connolly 1974, p. 145).

The analysis of acting and multiple acting under more naturalistic conditions is an essential feature of some investigations of Bruner's (1970, 1973; Bruner and Bruner 1968). They apply in part to very early stages in infancy and aim at tracing the beginnings of acting and its organization in ontogenesis. Piaget's observational studies should also be mentioned here (1936, 1937).

In principle, the investigations with beginner skiers were guided by similar intentions. Their methodological approach, however, differed essentially insofar as the acting of adults was being induced through verbal instructions and as reports about the action processes were being demanded from the actors (Kaminski 1973).

The TOTE model (Miller, Galanter and Pribram 1960) was intended to

provide a general conceptual basis for the interpretation of the functioning of everyday acting. However, its theoretical propositions remain too
sketchy to guide the theoretical and empirical analysis of actions as
complicated as skiing.

The application of the 'action' concept in microsociology (Lofland
1976) as well as in pragmalinguistics (Heringer 1974) and in language
philosophy (Searle 1969) is usually confined to the structural presuppositions of certain kinds of social interaction. The details of processing
and regulating actions during their course in time seem to be of minor
interest there, whereas just that is of central importance in the case of
the skiers.

4. Essential features of the acting of skiing novices

The theoretical argument to follow will refer repeatedly to certain
aspects of the skiing of beginners. Therefore the most essential features
of this kind of acting should be listed in advance:

4.1. As can be shown by content-analysing the instructors' verbalizations, the instructions according to which the beginner skier acts always
contain a multiplicity of partial tasks. There are not only partial tasks
which have to be carried out sequentially, but the essential point is that
there are always several partial tasks which must be worked on
simultaneously and which can be more or less independent of each
other.

The reason for this is that the whole system 'skier' has mechanical
contact with its environment at several points (two skis, two poles; in
the most unfavourable case it has even more points of contact, which
however should be avoided) and that within this system there exist
many degrees of freedom for change in the several parts of the body,
their relation to each other and to the equipment. The whole system is
very unstable once it has been set in motion in relation to the environment. It then no longer has complete control over the input, but rather
has input imposed on it, often in a very surprising way. In order to keep
from falling, however, the skier has to act in such a way that all inputs
are processed, at least as far as is necessary to maintain his balance.
Besides this, goals set by the instructions have to be attained (e.g.
certain positions in space, changes of direction, etc).

The communications from the ski instructor cannot fall short of a
certain degree of complication because the pupil has to be provided with

acting directions for several simultaneously relevant input channels and action sectors.

4.2. The events the beginner skier has to deal with often come in very rapid succession, so that he often finds himself under severe time pressure. (This is documented by the self-reports of the skiers and it can be inferred from film analysis.)

4.3. The circumstances of action are 'dynamic' (Dörner 1976, p. 19) in the sense that new and goal-related occurrences are continuously emerging, even – or particularly – when the actor is inactive. Therefore, inactivity inevitably leads to catastrophe, to a fall. (This also can be evidenced by self-reports and by film records.)

4.4. This breakdown of the system, the fall, is a greatly feared event, which one tries to avoid if ever possible (as again is shown by self-reports). Because very many errors in all kinds of action sectors can lead to this catastrophe (as can be evidenced by analysing the antecedents of such incidents in films) errors in any sector have to be avoided.

4.5. In the investigation mentioned, the subjects, college students, had no specific previous experience with actions of this kind; they were absolute beginners and selected as such for the investigation.

Now it should be pointed out that characterizing the skiing of novices this way has important consequences for 'the action' conceived of as a basic theoretical unit.

What is an action? Which general features do we want to ascribe to actions? With the help of which criteria do we want to distinguish different kinds of actions? What theoretical components do we need to explain the genesis and functioning of actions?

The first argument to be presented in reference to these questions is not a new one: some events produced at different times by the organism may look the same when seen from the outside, but under certain circumstances they allow or even require differing interpretations; the stemming out of a ski, for instance, may be performed in such a way that the actor is able to report on it, it may be goal-oriented, intended, planned, accomplished through active aspiration – always presupposed that we agree sufficiently on what we mean by these attributes and how we intend to apply them.

Under certain circumstances, it could be that only a few of these attributes apply to the same event as seen from the outside, perhaps even none of them do (depending on the definition of the attributes). The latter might occur, for instance, if attention is directed to a different partial action within the whole system, or if the stem has been mastered completely through extensive practice.

It would be less fruitful to ask now whether this event would still be an action or not; it seems rather more important to ask:
(i) under which conditions does the one or the other feature apply to those events? And
(ii) what are the consequences when this or that variant is realized?
These questions point beyond the single action to the functional context in which it occurs.

5. The functional context of a single action

5.1. The hierarchical organization of action systems

What is the functional context? What does it consist of? How far does it reach? Where does it end?

A first answer could be that the stem is part of a hierarchical action system (cf. Miller, Galanter and Pribram 1960, Powers, Clark and McFarland 1960, Goldman 1970, Hacker 1973, Elliott and Connolly 1974, Fowler and Turvey 1978, K. M. Newell 1978). It could firstly be part of a simple swing, which then could be part of the action unit 'passing through one particular gate', and this again could be part of an action 'a descent'.

If an action is something that is 'regulated' and is controlled from somewhere, then we have to ask how the regulation of this single stem (which remains necessary in any case) and the regulation of this swing and the regulation of the passing of this gate, etc, are related to each other. This is one example of a question that can only be raised when we include the functional interrelations between several actions in our considerations.

5.2 Multiple acting

This hierarchical system would be just one kind of functional context for the stem. Simultaneously, some different partial actions which in part overlap with it temporally are realized: shifting the weight of the body, rotating the trunk, a certain positioning of the poles, etc (Kaminski

1973). We could say that these partial actions occur in a more or less coordinated fashion.

But here again questions arise which lead beyond the consideration of a single action: what are the preconditions of coordination? In what way is this kind of synchronizing of different partial actions functionally accomplished in detail? Should we understand this coordination of several actions in itself as an action? Or as what else? (Kaminski 1976).

5.3. The minimal total context and limited processing capacity

What else must be taken into consideration as a functional context of a single action? We can observe that the system 'beginner skier', being in motion, experiences catastrophes relatively often, meaning that it falls down a lot. One possible explanation for this could be that a downhill skier is confronted with a certain ensemble of objective partial demands by which especially the beginner is often overtaxed. That means we suppose that the actor has only a limited total acting capacity at his disposal, whatever that may involve in detail (Underwood 1978).

The functional context of any single action therefore seems to have a certain total extension which is determined by this ensemble of objective demands on the downhill skier. The action capacity of the beginner does not always suffice for the realization of this total functional context. It seems that the beginning skier, overtaxed as he is, seeks and finds possibilities for reducing the total functional context in its complexity. Many kinds of behavioural characteristics (roughly speaking, simplifications of behaviour) can best be explained by the assumption that the skiing pupil thereby tries to avoid or escape being overtaxed. Not infrequently, however, this leads all the sooner to catastrophe.

The film records give evidence of characteristic differences in the task fulfilment of the novices compared with that of the instructors. Seemingly they can be traced back to the beginners' applying specific strategies of overload reduction (cf. J. G. Miller 1960). To give a few examples:

Two (or even more) executive systems (e.g. limbs) are being 'linked', steered jointly, although they ought to remain disjoined.

Degrees of freedom of the body are eliminated by 'freezing', stiffening certain joints.

Certain partial movements (subordinate actions, subroutines) are temporally displaced, i.e. they are staged either prematurely or too late, at a point in time when the momentary load for regulation is relatively low.

Again, such strategies for reducing complexity can only be discovered within a perspective that greatly transcends the single action and which tries to encompass the actional totality of the organism at a certain moment, particularly when it is being challenged in an almost maximally complicated way.

6. Consequences for the conception of the basic unit, 'action'

The functional properties of systems composed of actions have consequences for the single action and codetermine its functional properties. Therefore we could enlarge the list of generic features of single actions to include the following:

An action

– does not exist singly, but rather always occurs together with other actions;
– consumes processing capacity;
– is susceptible to impairment by the consequences of capacity shortages;
– is open to the balancing of different regulations necessary within an action hierarchy;
– is open to being coordinated with other actions;
– is open to being modified by strategies of complexity reduction.

7. Multiple acting and multiple orientation; some tentative generalizations

7.1. Multiple acting in everyday life

We shall now attempt to generalize, cautiously, the considerations which have been developed primarily with reference to the beginner skier.

Let us assume that the strategies and techniques that the beginner skier applies to reduce the complication of his acting are nothing unusual. In other words, let us assume that something like this also occurs elsewhere, perhaps even constantly. Then we could expect that certain characteristics of everyday acting might be understood as results of similar endeavours of complexity-reduction. When we can, we arrange our acting in such a way as to allow the most comfortable acting possible.

It could be objected that we usually are not confronted with demands of that degree of complication in everyday life and thus are not forced into such multiple acting as the beginner skier is.

A first reply would be that it is true that in everyday life we are usually engaged in multiple acting, but that we are not aware of many of our partial actions, or we no longer consider them to be actions. This can become evident when we observe everyday actions in slow motion or when we analyse speech utterances in detail; or take the case of driving a car, which in many respects resembles the multiple acting of the skier.

7.2. Orientational contexts

Secondly, it should be pointed out that the context of determination of a single action is open to a much greater extent than has been revealed so far. This can be elucidated by taking up the example of beginner skiers once again.

If one analyses the verbalizations of the ski instructors completely, then it is interesting to note that they by no means refer only to the movement tasks and their immediate circumstances. The ski instructors spontaneously offer quite a lot of more or less encompassing orientational contexts to which a single action may be put in reference: a task worked on previously, future tasks, an action performed by themselves, and so forth.

Likewise, the utterances of the skiing pupils show that they can refer a single action to many different orientational contexts respectively and that, in fact, they occasionally do just this. To put it differently, one and the same action can mean a goal-related positional change in many different 'action spaces' (Kaminski 1974) and may, under certain circumstances, be intended as such (cf. Goldman 1970). Possible goals for the stem could be for instance:
– to do it better than the last time,
– to do it as much like the skiing instructor as possible,
– to do it differently from another pupil,
– to make progress in learning the simple swing,
– to enjoy the consciousness of one's own dexterity, and so on.

Because the processing of orientational contexts implies functional costs, the beginner skier is not free to choose any of the many possible orientations at any point in time. Sometimes he cannot afford too much of this kind of processing. Nevertheless, all of these contexts are relevant for him and each of them is applied under certain conditions. This leads to questions like: under which conditions is which orientational context used and what consequences does this have? (At this point attention should be drawn to the problems dealt with by attribution theory; e.g. Jones *et al.* 1971, Harvey, Ickes and Kidd 1976.)

In everyday life, too, we are able to localize any actions in many different orientational contexts or action spaces. The question here is also: which orientation do we in fact use under which conditions, and with what consequences and effects? The tendency toward complexity-reduction would lead the actor to reduce his orientation to a minimum. With the reduction to too few or too narrow orientational frames he would take risks, under certain circumstances, that could only be predicted by using broader orientational contexts.

7.3. The implications of maintenance goals

Relevant to the question of capacity consumption, as caused by the inclusion of a larger or smaller number of orientational frames, is still another problem that has not been mentioned before. When we consider generic features of actions and when we speak of goal-directedness and goal-orientedness in that connection, we generally think at first of goals one sets for one-self (or which are set by others) and which one strives for and which one seeks to attain: these will be called *'attainment goals'*.

Again, in the case of the skier, but not just in his case, one can demonstrate that there is at least one more kind of goal, which might be called a *maintenance goal*. Over longer or shorter periods of time a skier has to maintain a certain body posture, or a certain position of one pole, or the alignment of his skis, or his balance against the force of gravity. In their consequences for the total load on the actor, attainment goals are probably more propitious because their range of relevance can be kept within limits more easily. When subgoals have been attained, they can then be forgotten. Maintenance goals can be permanently relevant. Somebody who operates with many orientational contexts and at the same time with many maintenance goals is acting under particularly complicated conditions. He is probably under extraordinary pressure to reduce complexity.

8. Some further generalizations

8.1. Orientation in a relatively new situation

What can we expect with relation to the functioning of everyday acting when we conceive of man as principally performing multiple actions and as having limited action capacity? We could expect that at the beginning of a new set of circumstances he starts with something like 'complexity-generation': he should let himself be stimulated by presently perceptible cues which actualize potentially relevant orientational contexts, and then by means of a rough appraisal should find out which ones are in fact relevant at that moment. Then, in a series of decision processes, he has to restrict himself to relatively few contexts, until it appears that he can cope with them through adequate acting. In this entire phase, the actor, in order to minimize risk, should produce as little externally evident acting as possible because no orientational context has been sufficiently confirmed as yet to allow reliable preparation and regulation of acting. After the beginning of specific acting within the contexts chosen, the actor must continue with a minimum of orientational activity with respect to the contexts eliminated previously in order to avoid risks. It must repeatedly be tested whether the elimination was justified.

Evidence for this kind of assumption is easily found by observing everyday social behaviour. Furthermore, some of these considerations seem to agree with several aspects of Goffman's frame analysis (1974).

8.2. Degrees of cognitive and linguistic differentiation

Let us assume that an individual's acting systems function approximately as has been sketched. Then certain characteristics of our cognitive equipment would seem to fit into these conceptions of acting very well. This refers to the fact that we can handle our orientational contexts or parts of them on many levels of differentiation, that is with a more or less coarse or fine grain, and that we process them with more or less global algorithms (Dörner 1976). Also, language seems to have adapted to these functional necessities (Rosch 1978). When there is limited time at our disposal for orientation and acting, we can think or express something in a rough or preliminary manner. If more time is available, and furthermore if acting requires it, we can differentiate the same thing more and more: we can recode (G. A. Miller 1956).

Here again, the skiing pupils offer some evidence of this phenomenon. One can observe in their utterances that they often express their experiences primarily in a very global manner: 'It went a lot better this time', 'That was very difficult', etc, before they explicate these statements and shift to reporting details.

In the knowledge upon which the actual constitution of orientational contexts is based, we should find prerequisites for dealing with different coding levels (Jörg and Hörmann 1978, Aebli 1979).

9. Specialities of social and linguistic actions

Until now, the argument has concentrated mainly on the functional context of an action and repeatedly asked what it implies for the concept of action. For the most part, the complex motor actions of the beginner skiers were used as a prototype of acting. Now it must be asked how far this particular type of acting can really be generalized. There certainly are kinds of actions which introduce fundamentally new features; these are social actions and in particular linguistic actions (along with the special kinds of knowledge which must be utilized for their realization). There is surely much to be said in this connection, but at this point a few remarks will do.

Without doubt, the beginner skier is confronted with rather complicated circumstances which change rapidly and often unforseeably. Someone who is confronted with another person and who has to deal with him possibly receives very rich and rapidly changing input. He has to orient himself to this input in order to be able to act adequately. Besides that, he knows that the other person also operates with orientational contexts, and that all of his own acting can be interpreted by the other person, that means it can be localized within the other's orientational contexts; this again is goal-relevant within his own orientation contexts. Therefore the additional task arises, in principle and inevitably, of using one's own acting to steer or at least to codetermine the orientation of the other person toward oneself with regard to certain goals of one's own (Goffman 1959).

The conception of acting outlined here (that is acting systems and orientational contexts) suggests that many characteristics of human social life are to be understood as means of reducing the complexity which can otherwise lead to overload. This idea is not a new one (compare e.g. Luhmann 1973), but it offers itself here again. Social concepts, stereotypes, social schemata, etc facilitate orientation; conventions, social rules, etc restrict the variety of possible actions to a manageable range. A special case would be the communicational conventions within language such as lexical categories (Rosch 1978) and syntactic and other morphological rule systems. Linguistic and non-linguistic communication are also forms of multiple acting. Here as well the questions which have been raised with respect to other kinds of multiple action are relevant.

Interesting and perhaps even fruitful as those questions may be which evolve out of the transfer of the concept of multiple action to other areas of acting, they of course represent only a fraction of the total spectrum of problems that are raised by the functioning and the structural background of social and particularly of linguistic actions.

10. Some further aspects of skiing neglected here

It must be stressed that some other aspects of actions which are of great importance particularly for the beginner skier have not been touched on here, for instance the relations between actions or action systems and emotional processes, furthermore the relations between motor actions and anatomical, physiological and especially neurophysiological aspects of organismic functioning. Also, the relations between momentarily occurring action and the modification of the bases of action through learning have been excluded (cf. Fowler and Turvey 1978). It is well known that by reorganizing his knowledge and his operational units, the actor is able to change the functional properties of his acting in the sense that he saves on the amount of capacity needed for regulation.

References

Aebli, H. (1979) 'Zur Darstellung von Handlungen und Begriffserklärungen mit Baumdiagrammen und Netzen.' In H. Ueckert and D. Rhenius (eds.), *Komplexe menschliche Informationsverarbeitung*. Huber, Bern.

Bruner, J. S. (1970) 'The growth and structure of skill.' In K. Connolly (ed.), *Mechanisms of motor skill development*. Academic Press, London.

— (1973) 'Organization of early skilled action.' *Child development* **44**, 1–11.

Bruner, J. S. and B. M. Bruner (1968) 'On voluntary action and its hierarchical structure.' *International Journal of Psychology* **3**, 239–55.

Dörner, D. (1974) *Die kognitive Organisation beim Problemlösen*. Huber, Bern.

— (1976) *Problemlösen als Informationsverarbeitung*. Kohlhammer, Stuttgart.

Elliott, H. and K. Connolly (1974) 'Hierarchical structure in skill development.' In K. Connolly and J. Bruner (eds.), *The growth of competence*. Academic Press, London.

Fowler, C. A. and M. T. Turvey (1978) 'Skill acquisition: an event approach with special reference to searching for the optimum of a function of several variables.' In G. E. Stelmach (ed.), *Information processing in motor control and learning*. Academic Press, London.

Goffman, E. (1959) *The presentation of self in everyday life.* Doubleday, Garden City, N.Y.

— (1974) *Frame analysis.* Harper & Row, New York.

Göhner, U. (1979) *Bewegungsanalyse im Sport.* Hofmann, Schorndorf.

Goldman, A. J. (1970) *A theory of human action.* Prentice-Hall, Englewood Cliffs, N.J.

Hacker, W. (1973) *Allgemeine Arbeits- und Ingenieurpsychologie*, 2nd edn. Deutscher Verlag der Wissenschaften, Berlin.

Harvey, J. H., W. J. Ickes, and R. F. Kidd (eds.) (1976) *New directions in attribution research*, vol. 1. Lawrence Erlbaum, Hillsdale, N.J.

Heringer, H. J. (1974) *Praktische Semantik.* Klett-Cotta, Stuttgart.

Jones, E. E., D. E. Kanouse, H. H. Kelly, R. E. Nisbett, S. Valins and B. Weiner (1971) *Attribution: perceiving the causes of behavior.* General Learning Press, Morristown, N.J.

Jörg, S. and H. Hörmann (1978) 'The influence of general and specific verbal labels on the recognition of labeled and unlabeled parts of pictures.' *Journal of Verbal Learning and Verbal Behavior* **17**, 445–54.

Kaminski, G. (1970) *Verhaltenstheorie und Verhaltensmodifikation.* Klett-Cotta, Stuttgart.

— (1972) 'Bewegung – von aussen und von innen gesehen.' *Sportwissenschaft* **2**, 51–63.

— (1973) 'Bewegungshandlungen als Bewältigung von Mehrfachaufgaben.' *Sportwissenschaft* **3**, 233–50.

— (1974) 'Studieren als Handeln und als Trauern.' *Psychologische Beiträge* **16**, 310–37.

— (1976) Theoretische Komponenten handlungspsychologischer Ansätze.' In A. Thomas (ed.), *Psychologie der Handlung und Bewegung.* Hain, Meisenheim.

— (1979) 'Die Bedeutung von Handlungskonzepten für die Interpretation sportpädagogischer Prozesse.' *Sportwissenschaft* **9**, 9–28.

Lofland, J. (1976) *Doing social life.* Wiley, New York.

Lüer, G. (1973) *Gesetzmässige Denkabläufe beim Problemlösen.* Beltz, Basel.

Luhmann, U. (1973) *Vertrauen: Ein Mechanismus zur Reduktion sozialer Komplexität.* Enke, Stuttgart.

Miller, G. A. (1956) 'The magical number seven plus or minus two. Some limits on our capacity for processing information.' *Psychological Review* **63**, 81–97.

Miller, G. A., E. Galanter and K. H. Pribram (1960) *Plans and the structure of behavior.* Holt, New York.

Miller, J. G. (1960) 'Information input overload and psychopathology.' *American Journal of Psychiatry* **116**, 695–704.

Neisser, U. (1976) *Cognition and reality.* Freeman, San Francisco.

Newell, A. and H. A. Simon (1972) *Human problem solving.* Prentice Hall, Englewood Cliffs, N.J.

Newell, K. M. (1978) 'Some issues on action plans.' In G. E. Stelmach (ed.), *Information processing in motor control and learning.* Academic Press, London.

Pew, R. W. (1974) 'Human perceptual – motor performance.' In B. H. Kantowitz (ed.), *Human information-processing: tutorials in performance and cognition.* Lawrence Erlbaum, Hillsdale, N.J.

Piaget, J. (1936) *La naissance de l'intelligence chez l'enfant.* Delachaux-Niestlé, Neuchâtel.

— (1937) *La construction du réel chez l'enfant.* Delachaux-Niestlé, Neuchâtel.

Powers, W. T., R. K. Clark, and R. L. McFarland (1960) 'A general feedback theory of human behaviour.' *Perceptual and motor skills* **11**, 71–88 and 309–23.

Rosch, E. (1978) 'Principles of categorization.' In E. Rosch and B. B. Lloyd (eds.), *Cognition and categorization.* Lawrence Erlbaum, Hillsdale, N.J.

Rüssel, A. (1976) *Psychomotorik.* Steinkopff, Darmstadt.

Schmidt, R. A. (1975) A schema theory of discrete motor skill learning. *Psychological Review* **82**, 225–60.

Searle, J. R. (1969) *Speech acts.* Cambridge University Press, Cambridge.

Singer, R. N. (1972) *The psychomotor domain: movement behavior.* Lea & Febiger, Philadelphia.

— (1975) *Motor learning and human performance.* Macmillan, New York.

Underwood, G. (1978) 'Concepts in information processing theory.' In G. Underwood (ed.), *Strategies of information processing.* Academic Press, London.

Welford, A. T. (1968) *Fundamentals of skill.* Methuen, London.

Wickelgren, W. A. (1974) *How to solve problems.* W. H. Freeman, San Francisco.

Willems, E. P. and H. L. Rausch (1969) *Naturalistic viewpoints in psychological research.* Holt, New York.

Ordinary interactive action: theory, methods and some empirical findings[1]

MARIO VON CRANACH and URS KALBERMATTEN

1. Aims and structure of this paper

Our topic is goal-directed action (GDA) as it forms a pervasive aspect of everyday life. Our treatment is partially based on the concept of GDA and related general considerations, as presented by von Cranach, and presupposes some of the theoretical and empirical investigations by Hacker and Kaminski (all this volume). In order to develop the typical aspects of ordinary interactive action, we shall begin by comparing it with labour activity as it has been the object of so much detailed investigation (see Hacker 1978). We shall then discuss some of our theoretical assumptions and finally present detailed examples of our research methods (namely systematic observation, interview and self-confrontation techniques and content analysis), and empirical findings. (Most of this research has been presented in detail in von Cranach *et al.* 1980.)

2. Some characteristics of ordinary interactive action

In order to elaborate its specific characteristics, we want to compare, in this paragraph, ordinary (concrete) interactive action with labour activity (henceforth to be abbreviated as OA and LA respectively) in regard to their preconditions, their organization and their results. 'OA' refers to everyday activities like cooking a meal, going to the movies, shopping or debating with a friend, 'LA' refers to stereotyped acts of a routine

[1] The research here reported was supported by the Swiss National Foundation. It is the product of the joint efforts of the participants of our research project, namely Vincenz Brunner and Katrin Indermühle, and of Josef Lang, Christoph Morgenthaler, Vera Steiner and other student members of our standing study group on the organization of goal-directed action. We are grateful to Agnes von Cranach for her help in improving our English text.

character as they are typically performed in factories, in the context of man–machine systems, in order to achieve a material output of general social value. Both OA and LA constitute important types of GDA, and their comparison can clarify many aspects of general importance; we should not, however, overlook the fact that other frequent and important forms of GDA, like teaching in school or counselling, are intermediate forms.

Why should we pay so much attention to LA research? There are some good reasons: LA theory is the most advanced branch of action theory, and among the scarce and scattered empirical studies of GDA, the research into the organization of labour activities stands out like a solid block.[2] So it constitutes a nucleus of important action-theoretical knowledge and principles, to which other aspects can be added to constitute a more general theory of action. This becomes obvious if we consider the characteristics of ordinary interactive action against this background.

OA and LA have in common that they both refer to *concrete* activities aiming at the inducement of change in the environment by use of *manifest behaviour* (in contrast to *abstract* action, like problem-solving, aiming at cognitive achievements). But in LA, the aspired change is exclusively material (if we neglect for a moment Harré's 'expressive order'), while OA can involve influencing persons (as in *interactive* action). In their definition, both OA and LA seem to be in line with the general trend in the literature to define GDA as 'goal-directed, planned, intended and conscious behaviour, which is socially directed' (von Cranach, this volume). Within this general frame, LA research has elaborated some of the most important aspects of GDA organization in general (see Hacker, this volume):

(i) the notion of two-dimensional (sequential and hierarchical) organization

(ii) the idea of the feedback loop as a mediator between hierarchical levels (Hacker's 'Veränderungs-Vergleichs-Rückkoppelungs-Einheit' (VVR), an elaborated version of Miller, Galanter and Pribram's (1960) TOTE unit)

(iii) the concept of an internal (cognitive) model (Hacker's 'operatives

---

[2] It is therefore easy to understand why the general trend is to transfer this model to all types of GDA, as for instance in the recent application of Hacker's action concept to psychotherapy (e.g. Schmidtchen 1978, Semmer and Frese 1979). And yet closer inspection reveals that this type of action research is a very specific rather than a general model: due to its tradition, aims and preferred research situations, it is restricted in theoretical and methodological aspects.

Abbild-System' (OAS) as an elaborated version of Miller, Galanter and Pribram's 'image' which integrates essential aspects of task, situation, goal structure, and plan)

(iv) the coordination of hierarchical behaviour levels with levels of cognitive control, which are qualitatively different in respect to conscious representation.

In all these (and some more) respects, LA research represents enormous progress. Its restrictions can be explained from two factors: its preference of a traditional experimental methodology, inadequate to some of the requirements of GDA research; and its specific research object and interest, namely, organized productive labour. Let us briefly discuss these points.

In contrast to its very progressive theory, LA research, as far as we can see, has not yet advanced to a methodology adequate for the study of GDA in general. It seems to proceed mainly in clean investigations following the traditions of experimental psychology.[3] This is of course a 'variable approach' which mainly considers antecedents and consequences of acts, while ongoing action processes are rarely studied in detail (compare statement [4] in von Cranach, this volume); methods useful for such a purpose (like systematic observation) are rarely used.

But there is another default which weighs even heavier in its consequences: in spite of the eminent role of cognition, and especially *conscious cognition*, in the underlying theory, cognition is often inferred from behaviour or circumstances, sometimes assessed in a more general way (by application of questionnaires, for example), but to our knowledge no one has ever tried to assess ongoing conscious cognition. In short, empirical research does not quite live up to its own theory; progress beyond a certain point is therefore not likely to occur.

Our second point concerns the impact of *research interest*, and the research situation and type of GDA which has been chosen in consequence, on LA theory. In modern industrial societies, labour activities proceed within highly structured organizations and at least partially determined by machines. This context determines this form of GDA (*and its investigation*) in a very basic way; its influence operates mainly in the direction of a *decrease of the actor's freedom*, of an *accentuation of the action's instrumental character* and all the *processes which are apt to enhance its*

---

[3] See for instance the studies by Hacker and his colleagues, cited in Hacker (1976); studies performed in the context of the Soviet psychology of activity (Kussmann 1971) or the Warsaw school (Tomaszewski 1978); as well as research performed in Western Europe (Volpert 1980).

instrumental purpose; and a *repression or omission of processes which interfere* with it. In many instances this concerns just the individual's social representations, the conflicts arising from contradictory values and motives and the immediate influence of social interaction: in spite of its impressive humanistic motivation, LA research could not completely avoid treating man as a machine and although LA theory stresses the social nature of labour, it has to some extent desocialized the concept of GDA.

These now are the tendencies on which many of the differences between LA and OA are based. A few examples will help to understand how they come about:

Course of action. In LA, there exists an ideal model of execution for each specific task; particular acts can be described in terms of deviation from this standard and, for this reason, will be more or less similar. In OA, individual actors tend to develop their own courses of action. In interactive OA, the course of action must be kept highly variable in order to cope with the partner's unforeseen actions, but the individual may develop differentiated preference orders for various possibilities.

Goals. In LA, individual goals are derived from the prescribed task; in OA, we find at least partial freedom of goal determination and cognitive processes like choice between different goals, of changing or giving up goals during the act consequently play a major role. In interactive OA, goals will in addition be negotiated between partners, and *multiple goals*, instrumental and social, will normally codetermine the course of action.

Internal models. In structured LA, the internal model governing the action sequence and hierarchy will be prescribed to a high degree. Within a structure of predetermined external cues and internal goals and plans, only few points of intervention (*Eingriffspunkte*, Hacker 1978) where true degrees of freedom exist are left. It is the actor's first duty *to know and to accept* this predetermined structure and his own possibilities. In OA, and especially non-routine and interactive OA, the actor must invent and constantly reconstruct his internal model to adapt to situational demands. The application of prefabricated plans and strategies is therefore restricted.

Decisions and values. Since LA is task-oriented, decisions between alternative courses of action are largely determined by the possibilities of goal attainment. From the social institution's point of view, it is not desirable that the individual introduces personal criteria into the working process, and the action is structured accordingly. In OA, nearly every decision, even of a seemingly trivial character, is value-relevant, and in order to decide the actor will resort to his value system.

Regulation and feedback. Similarly, in LA prescribed higher-order goals determine lower-order ones, so that we can truly speak of 'regulation processes'. In the feedback loops which regulate performances and link the 'levels of regulation', theoretical values are considered to be exclusively determined by external, instrumental task-related standards. In OA, internal standards like motives, emotions and values also constitute theoretical values, and the finally executed action seems to be a compromise between competing theoretical values.[4]

There are many more examples of this kind. We have summarized some of the differences between types of GDA in Table 1. These lead however to consequences in research. While research in LA has been mainly based on elaborated ideas from systems theory, general psychology and neurophysiology, the study of OA cannot do without insights from naive behaviour theory (e.g. Heider 1958, Laucken 1974) and symbolic interactionism or phenomenological sociology respectively (e.g. Harré 1972, Schutz and Luckmann 1975). This led to the introduction of additional concepts, whose translation into operations necessitated the use of other and new methods (as summarized in Table 2). In the following section, we shall elaborate some of the particularities of OA in more detail.

3. Basic theoretical assumptions

The work here reported is based on a reasonably comprehensive 'theory of concrete action' which we developed in the beginning of our studies of GDA (von Cranach 1975); it was based on our knowledge of naive behaviour theory (Heider 1958, Laucken 1974), the systems approach to GDA (Miller, Galanter and Pribram 1960) and ideas from symbolic interactionism (as contained e.g. in Harré and Secord 1972); if we had known at that time of the Marxist study of LA, we would have

---

[4] Since we find degrees of freedom and organizational processes on each level, we have, in our own research, preferred to speak of *organization* (levels of organization) rather than *regulation*.

Table 1. *Types of concrete GDA*

	Labour activity	Ordinary action	Ordinary interactive action
Course of action	Predetermined, follows ideal model	Task-oriented, but idiosyncratic variations	Variable; differential strategies to cope with partner and situation
Goals	Task-dependent, prescribed, institutionalized; to be accepted and internalized Instrumental goals.	Task-oriented, but at least partially chosen; change and giving up possible through Instrumental goals	To be negotiated and/or carried through Multiple (instrumental and interactive) goals and subgoals
Motivation and resolution	Motivation at least partly extrinsic; motivation by material reward, ideology, convention, sanctions Resolution and constant effort partly facilitated by prestructured situations	Motivation more intrinsic; more self-control by internalized standards Resolution and constant effort necessary	Intrinsic and extrinsic (stimulation from interaction and partner) Intervention of social motives (e.g. competition). Resolution and effort socially influenced (facilitated or inhibited)
Internal models	Partly prescribed or known Few degrees of freedom Medium-level strategies Low-level routines desirable	Partly prescribed, more degrees of freedom, depending on degree of habituation and routine	Constant invention and reconstruction Little routine Impact of social norms
Regulation and feedback	Levels of regulation Externally determined theoretical values. Automatized regulation	Internal and external standards Levels of organization	Internal and external standards Differentiated organization on levels
Decisions, values, rules and norms	Decisions related to goal attainment Little concern with values and rules Conflict avoided by labour organization (institution) and training	Value relevant for goal determination and decisions	Constant concern of values, rules and norms ('social control') Frequent conflict

Table 2. *Research on types of GDA*

	Labour activity	Ordinary/interactive action
Prevalent theory	Neurophysiology; experimental psychology; systems theory (based on naive behaviour theory)	As for LA. *In addition* naive behaviour theory; linguistics; systems theory; communication theory; symbolic interactionism
Concepts	Sequential and hierarchical organization Internal representation (goal, internal model, motive, etc) Regulation by feedback Institutional and task conditions	As for LA. *In addition* more differentiated cognitive constructs, and concepts related to social control (types of knowledge, value, norm, rule, decision, perception of partner and task, attribution) Inward- and outward-directed adaptation; regulation and organization
Methods	1. Experiment (field and laboratory) 2. Measurement of output 2. Observation 4. Questionnaire	1–4, as for LA. *In addition* systematic observation on various levels; self-confrontation techniques; interviews and content analysis ('accounts') 'Thinking-aloud' techniques Assessment of 'naive interpretations'

progressed faster. This theory corresponds to some of the principles discussed in von Cranach (this volume), namely, the definition of GDA referring to goal-directed, partly consciously guided, planned and intended behaviour; the principles of twofold structure, two-dimensional organization, bidirectional adaptation and social control; and the interrelation of the three concept classes of manifest behaviour, conscious cognition and social meaning (our 'conceptual triangle', see von Cranach, this volume, section 3.3.3). For a complete presentation the reader must be referred to von Cranach *et al.* (1980); in this paper we shall only elaborate those details which are immediately necessary for an understanding of the presented empirical examples. Here, these are mainly the principles of sequential and hierarchical organization as related to cognitive steering, subconscious self-regulation and social control.

3.1. Course of action

The function of sequential organization is based on the principle that preceding action steps determine the following, but are also executed in their service. Our concepts concerning the *course of action* which comprises *action step, starting point, end point, node, characters of node*, and *network of pathways* have already been described (von Cranach, this volume, section 4.1 and Fig. 3). As an example we cite two statements from our theory:

[1.3] *Action steps are the smallest elements of the course of action on the strategic level of organization; they are marked off by nodes.*

[1.4] *At a node, alternative courses of action branch off. (Cited from von Cranach* et al. *ch. 4).*

Note that these definitions allow for an operationalization of the concepts; using the two characters given here for the concept of node, namely 'boundary for action steps' and 'ramification', we can locate nodes in observation data. The concepts of the course of action, as described here, apply especially to the medium level of our theory, the *strategic level*; in this case, the course of action determines the *structure of the act on the next lower level*. These concepts refer to manifest behaviour, but are related to concepts of conscious cognition concerning the cognitive steering of action; and to concepts of social meaning concerning social control (see von Cranach, this volume, section 3.3.2). Similar concepts can be applied to other levels.

3.2. Levels of organization

This problem is also discussed in von Cranach (this volume, section 4.1 and Fig. 4). We conceive OA as organized and controlled on coordinated levels. In general, higher levels are assumed to be characterized by choice of goals, plans and strategies and to be organized mainly by cognitive and emotional processes (*cognitive steering*); lower levels are organized by more subconsciously regulated neurophysiological mechanisms. As in sequential organization, the *act* constitutes the basic organizing unit of the various processes running at the various levels, and also the basic *frame of analysis*.

We consider three levels, organized in time and space; but above our highest level, still higher ones are occasionally introduced if necessary. These levels are assumed to be founded in properties of the organization of GDA and therefore designated as *levels of organization*; they serve to coordinate variables of cognition as well as of behaviour as they are explained in our theory. The highest level is the *act level* (I), characterized by conscious representations of goal-related cognitions referring to molar behavioural units which are often socially meaningful. The second level (II) is the *strategic level* which relates to cognitive steering and control functions *within the act* which are presumed to be preponderantly conscious; the lowest level (III), the *operational level*, refers to preponderantly subconscious regulation processes *within the action steps* (the units of level II). As far as organization in time is concerned, levels II and III follow the delimitations of level I, level III also those of level II. The manifold relationships between the levels of organization and the environment are described in Fig. 1. Let us now describe in more detail the assumed variables and processes which operate at these levels.

Act level. On level I, the actor structures the stream of behaviour into actions; he does so by means of *goal determination*. A goal is the imagined and aspired-to state at the end of an act. According to the particular choice of acts by the various participating actors, the *goal structure* of an episode emerges. Research into goal structures has resulted in the differentiation of an empirically valid classification of goal constructs which we can but outline here.

(i) Goals can be distinguished according to their *relational characteristics*: for example, within goals we can again establish hierarchical orders of *supergoals* and *subgoals*, and more than two goals may be

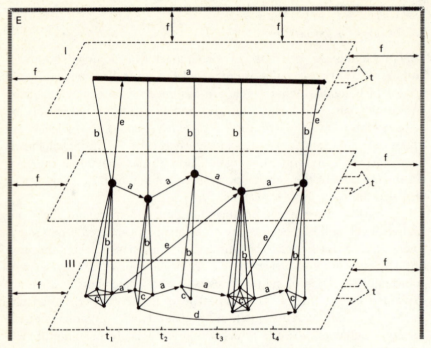

Fig. 1. Dynamic relations between hierarchical levels of organization (= LO)
I, II, III = the three levels of organization
t, t_1 . . . t_4 = time
E = environment (broken line)
a, b, c, d, e, f = different kinds of dynamic relations
    a = Arrows within an LO in time direction: *sequential* organization
    b = Lines between LOs: the dynamic of these lines flows in both directions as *steering*
        (downwards) and *regulation* (upwards)
    c = Lines between simultaneous units of an LO: for example of LO III simultaneous
        movements
    d = Arrows between units of the same LO which do not stand in a direct sequence (later
        consequence)
    e = Arrows between LOs and units of LOs which do not stand in direct sequence (later
        influence on a higher LO)
    f = Arrows between LOs and the environment: interaction between all LOs and the
        environment (at any moment)

pursued by one actor at the same time (*parallel or multiple goals*),
thus constituting a preference order (*main goal or subsidiary goal*).

(ii) Another classification derives from the goals' content
characteristics; thus we can distinguish between goals referring to
the act's product (*result goals*) or to the quality of the performance
itself (*process goal*). Another case is the *group goal* or *shared goal*, an
individual cognition of course which contains however the knowledge of sharing.

(iii) Other goal constructs refer to goal-related cognitive processes. In the case of competing goals, for example, goal determination will appear as a *choice* between goals (before the execution of the act begins) or a *change* of goals during the act; concerning a given goal, decisions to either *maintain* it or *to give up* may occur.

Under normal conditions, goals are assumed to be consciously conceived. That does not mean that they should constantly remain in the focus of attention; instead, they should become conscious if this is necessary for purposes of steering or motivation (see von Cranach, this volume, section 5.2).

Strategic level. On level II, the course of action is directed at the goal by means of *cognitive steering* and *control*, exerted through plans and strategies. A *plan* is the design of an act at the strategic level; it consists in the cognitive anticipation of the course of action in its details (action steps, nodes, etc). A *strategy* is a preference order of plans (concerning one particular goal), considering different possible circumstances. In order to execute a plan, a *resolution* is necessary which is conceived as a specific process with cognitive, motivational and emotional qualities. A *decision* finally is the choice between alternative courses of action.

We assume that cognitive processes on level II are conscious (at least in general), although not necessarily permanently, instantaneously or with equal and constant quality. Variations are partly predicted by the attention theorem (see von Cranach, this volume, section 5.2.2).

Operational level. On level III, the detailed execution of the course of action, as represented in action steps, is adapted to the actor's internal states (an instance of inward-directed adaptation) and to changing environmental conditions (outward-directed adaptation), preponderantly by means of *subconscious self-regulation*; occasionally self-regulation becomes conscious (the well-known example of learning a new skill: transition from conscious to subconscious).

Adaptation to internal conditions (motives, values, norms, etc) facilitates or inhibits the execution of the action steps, and additional and/or conflicting movements may be produced. Prototypes of facilitation are motor habits or fixed action patterns which enhance speed, force or directionality of execution. A prototype of inhibition is internal conflict, leading to a decrease in these qualities.

In adaptation to the environment, action steps are in their very details organized towards their subgoals; thus, the attainment of the final goal of the act is also promoted. This is achieved mainly by feedback mechanisms.

Finally, it should be noted that all these levels are equally real and manifest and therefore equally suited for assessment (as to this term, see von Cranach, this volume, n. 14 on p. 44). GDA is an integrated organization of behaviour on all levels, and its effects (internal and environmental) are produced on all levels; it seems therefore inevitable that assessment and analysis also must proceed on all levels simultaneously.

Bidirectional adaptation by means of hierarchical behaviour organization (an example). In human behaviour, OA is a standard mode of adaptation (see von Cranach, this volume n. 12 on p. 44) to the constraints of the environment (outward-directed adaptation); at the same time, it is a means to serve the actor's internal needs (inward-directed adaptation; see von Cranach, this volume, section 2.5.3). Outward- and inward-directed adaptation can be in conflict. Adaptation is achieved by multilevel activity (on the described level of organization). We want to illustrate this complicated matter by an example.

Let us assume that A is hungry and wants to go to a restaurant (goal). Leaving his house he notices that it is raining (perception of external condition, barrier), and A is afraid of catching a cold (emotion-related cognition). There are many different modes of adaptation on all levels of organization; let us just consider a few simple possibilities:

Level I: (a) Staying home and eating a cold meal (maintaining *super-goal*, changing *goal*).

(b) Still going to the restaurant (maintaining *goal*).

In case of I (b), the execution of the act must consider the environmental circumstances (rain) and the internal condition (fear of cold); this can happen by adaptation on levels II or III:

Level II: (a) Taking a taxi instead of walking (change of *plan*, choice of an *alternative action step* in the course of action). If this possibility is often practised and already premeditated, we may speak of a *strategy*.

(b) Walking in spite of rain (maintaining *plan* and *subgoal*).

In the case of II (b), we expect adaptation on level III. There are many possibilities:

Level III: (a) Stepping out of the house hesitatingly (exposition of *conflict* between goal and plan on the one side and emotion-related cognition on the other).

(b) Walking very fast or running.

(c) Drawing the head between shoulders while walking.

These changes on the operational level may occur in case A's internal condition (i.e. goal and plan conflicting with emotion-related cognition) remains unchanged. Of course, A can also adapt by changing his internal state (e.g. by telling himself he should not care so much about a little bit of rain). In this case, we might perhaps observe quite a different performance on level III:

(d) Holding head up straight, expressing the disregard of rain in the manner of walking.

This attitude may be kept up until a new criterion of the situation's characteristics makes itself felt (water running down the neck) and enforces a new adaptation.

3.3. Perception of external and internal events

Perception and constant monitoring of the environment and the actor's own internal states provides the basis of bidirectional adaptation. Perception is an ongoing process, which relates to the course of action on all levels of organization and results in conscious, subconscious and non-conscious cognitions (cf. von Cranach, this volume, section 5.1).

4. Manifest behaviour in ordinary action

4.1. Behaviour assessment by means of a hierarchically ordered observation system

4.1.1. *Levels of analysis.* Our hierarchical behaviour analysis is based on an observation system consisting of hierarchically ordered *levels of analysis;*[5] these reflect the order of levels of organization described. Their characteristics are:

(i) Hierarchical dissolution: each higher order unit is dissolved into a system of lower order units (of the next lower level).

(ii) Qualitative differences between levels, which are mainly brought about by the differences in the theoretical and operational definitions of the observation units constituting the various levels.[6]

The highest level of analysis (I) is the *goal level,* where the stream of behaviour is segmented into socially meaningful acts; this is mainly

[5] For a detailed description of this methodology, see Kalbermatten and von Cranach 1981.
[6] See the Appendix to this chapter, pp. 156–8.

done by use of goal constructs, which are *socially* defined. Level II is the *functional level* analysed in terms of (preponderantly) *functionally defined* action steps and corresponding behavioural and cognitive constructs. Level III is the *structural level* where the analysis proceeds in terms of movements and positions; these are *structurally conceived* and *physically defined*. The relationship of these levels of analysis to the assumed

	levels of organization	levels of analysis ⟶	observation units
I	ACT LEVEL	GOAL LEVEL	SOCIALLY MEANINGFUL
	conscious representations of goals	goal constructs	molar, 'natural', socially defined
II	STRATEGIC LEVEL	FUNCTIONAL LEVEL	FUNCTIONAL
	cognitive steering and control	action step, etc	socially meaningful, 'natural', functionally defined
III	OPERATIONAL LEVEL	STRUCTURAL LEVEL	STRUCTURAL
	subconscious self-regulation	elements of action steps	molecular, physically and structurally defined

Fig. 2. The interrelationship between (theoretical) levels of organization, levels of analysis and observational units in the hierarchical model

levels of organization is depicted in Fig. 2; the two constitute, so to speak, two sides of the same coin.

4.1.2 *Construction of a hierarchically ordered observation system.* This example and the following results come from our investigation of a very specific OA: the fight of children in the kindergarten for toys ('possession fight' = PF). In several studies, we have investigated over 300 PF (a more extensive presentation of these studies and their results is given in von Cranach *et al.* 1980). Most of these studies were performed in the kindergarten of our institute, which contains video and observation equipment; other studies were performed in a public kindergarten in Berne. The children in our own kindergarten were between 2½ and 5 years old and played in groups of seven to nine children; in the public kindergarten, the age was about 5–6 years, and the classes were larger. Video-films were taken unnoticed, or without creating much disturbance; analysis was done from the video-tapes.

Demarcation of 'possession fight' on the goal level

Instead of structuring the whole stream of action into different kinds of acts, we restricted ourselves to determination of all acts of the type under study, PF, during the observation period. Only two-person conflicts were included.

A PF is a naturally and frequently occurring, well-discriminable, interactive and socially defined OA. The actor's (= A) goal consists in carrying through his claim to an object (= O) against another child (partner = P), who pursues the same goal. According to their own definition of the situation, only one of the two can win. We have determined the PF on the basis of our social knowledge, which is what helps us to 'see' when two children fight for a toy; in order to derive a more exact determination, several researchers have independently defined its main criteria; these constitute the core of our operational definition:

(i) Both the involved children *claim possession of the same object.*
(ii) The claims occur *simultaneously (they overlap in time).*
(iii) At least one of the children does not accept the partner's claim and wants to *exclude him from the use of the object.*

Using these criteria, it is possible to identify PF in the stream of behaviour of our kindergarten children with high confidence. To fix the beginning and end of PF, some additional rules have to be established. Note that the chosen criteria correspond to general social knowledge, and that the given operational definition constitutes, in its essential parts, a *social definition.* To confirm this assumption, we asked a group of 38 naive judges (students), who did not know our definition, to select all PF from two video-taped episodes (each of 12 minutes' length). With an agreement between 95–100 %, they identified all the eight fights we had selected on the basis of our definition; and they did not name any PF we had not found ourselves.

Observation units at the functional level: action steps

Here, we investigate the course of action, nodes, network of pathways and other concepts related to manifest behaviour at the strategic level in a way which conforms to our theoretical assumptions related to (conscious) cognitive steering and control. This is mainly done by identifying action steps and using them to reconstruct the course of action. (In this paragraph we shall concentrate on the first operation.)

Our operational definitions of action steps are in essential parts functional; action steps are defined in regard of their function for achieving the act's goal,[7] which constitutes the reason why they are

---

[7] This is in line with the definition of function in systems theory, according to which functional units produce effects on a higher level (cf. Ackoff and Emery 1972, ch. 1, pt. 2).

Table 3. *A catalogue for the observation of possession fights on the functional level (from Kalbermatten 1977)*

Categories of non-verbal behaviour	Categories of verbal behaviour
1. Turn towards (TT)	24. Claim (C)
2. Turn to partner (TTP)	25. Request (RQ)
3. Turn to object (TTO)	26. Command (CO)
4. Turn away (TA)	27. Protest (PR)
5. Turn away from partner (TAP)	28. Threaten (TH)
6. Turn away from object (TAO)	29. Accept a claim (A)
7. Watching (WA)	30. Justify (J)
8. To be turned off (TB)	31. Propose a compromise (PC)
9. Approach (AP)	32. Offer an alternative (OA)
10. Approach to partner (APP)	33. Change the topic (CT)
11. Approach to object (APO)	34. Verbalization (V)
12. Withdraw (WI) (go away)	
13. Withdraw from partner (WIP)	
14. Withdraw from object (WIO)	
15. Withdraw with object (WWO)	
16. Give ground (GG)	
17. Grasp/take away (GT)	
18. Use (U)	
19. Release (R)	
20. Secure (S)	
21. Fight against partner (FP)	
22. Fight for object (FO)	
23. Threaten (T)	

included in the system. Since these functions are socially meaningful, they also tend to be subjects of social definition. The definitions are also structural in so far as the behaviour is depicted which makes up the action step.

As an example, let us consider the 'Approach'; this is a frequent and important action step, regularly appearing at the beginning of the PF.

'Approach': (1) A increases his possibility to make P and/or O a target of consecutive action by (2) actively decreasing his distance, under general body orientation towards A and/or O. (3) The manner of approach (walking, running, crawling) is unimportant.

The functional part of this definition (1) describes its function to achieve the goal (which is the justification to include it into our category system); the structural part (2) serves to identify the behaviour related to the function and to demarcate the activities at the beginning and end; (3) indicates which structural characters are unimportant (but possible objects of differentiation on the structural level of analysis).

We cannot expect however all the action steps of our catalogue to possess equally distinct functions. To describe the course of action, it can be necessary to include action steps which are not unequivocally related to goal attainment. In some cases, as in 'Approach', functions seem to be strongly and *positively related* to the obtaining of the object and the winning of the PF; in some cases the function is *negative*, as in 'Turning away from object and/or partner', a behaviour which will produce failure; and sometimes a behaviour may serve *several different functions*, or constitute an *involuntary reaction*, as in the case of 'Release', which may either mean that the actor gives up or that he frees his hands for a new, more severe attack.

Functional catalogues of PF have been developed in our different studies by different researchers; although they vary in number of categories and details of the definitions, they tend to contain an essentially identical common core of categories which seem to constitute the basic repertoire of action steps used by our children in PF. The catalogue developed by Kalbermatten (1977) may serve as an example (Table 3).

Various objectivity checks of the interobserver and test–retest type, between and within trained and naive observers, resulted in all cases in agreement of over 80 %, and in higher scores in some cases.

Observation units on the structural level: details of body movements

Functionally defined units can be executed in various ways; it is therefore necessary to study their structures in more detail. This is performed on the next lower, the *structural* level of analysis. Here we try to describe an action step in its spatial and temporal course.

Our catalogues on this level contain: body movements and body positions, temporal descriptions (in 0.1 s periods), spatial relations and orientations towards the environment, relations to objects, body contacts, interactions, accompanying verbal utterances (if they do not make up their own functional category) and paralinguistic phenomena and environmental conditions; in short, we attempt to give a very complete picture of the action steps and the circumstances of their occurrence. Therefore, these systems have to be rather comprehensive. And in addition to this difficulty, they have to consider the fact that our subjects move freely in space.

Categories on this level are very often physically defined; body movements, for example, are often described within a three-dimensional space model. The catalogues are specific for different functional units and contain in some cases literally hundreds of items; still, because of the physical descriptions used, interobserver agreement is very high (for details see Kalbermatten and von Cranach, 1981).

Because of the great expenses in labour and time (at least half a researcher's year for each action step), we have up to now analysed no more than eight action steps ('Approach', 'Grasp/take away', 'Use', 'Release', 'Secure', 'Fight against partner', 'Fight against object', 'Threaten') in detail.

To illustrate the way in which we proceed, here are some of the items of the catalogue for the action step 'Grasp/take away' (total size of the catalogue: ca. 500 items).

Grasp/take away:

Hand position in relation to body:

   height:
   – hand over head
   – hand level to head
   – hand level shoulders
   – hand level trunk
   – etc.
   horizontal position:
   – hand before body
   – hand behind body
   – hand right side of body
   – hand left side of body
   – etc.
   movement of hand:
   – upwards
   – downwards
   – forward
   – backward
   – etc.

4.2. Selected results

In this section, we restrict ourselves to the presentation of examples which demonstrate the assumed particularities of OA (in comparison to LA). Our hierarchical observation methods are based on our assumptions about multi-level organization. The resulting data can be regarded separately for each level, and in their hierarchical integration. (Most of the data presented in this section come from a subsample of 62 fights, and therefore contain 124 different courses of action.)

4.2.1 *Differential efficiency of action steps.* LA tends to be the product of prolonged social experience. For this reason, there exists a body of social knowledge concerning the relative efficiency (instrumental power) of action steps in achievement of the goal, which gets transformed into rules and organizational features of the institution within which the LA takes place; the actor acquires this knowledge in his professional socialization, and once on the job, he is supposed to apply it to his task and act in the most efficient way. In OA, the actor is far less informed about the relative efficiencies of the various action steps at his disposal; and in interactive action, an additional difficulty arises: A's freedom to choose the appropriate action steps is restricted by the moves of his partner. If the interaction is competitive and antagonistic, as in our PF, the availability of an action step is even more restricted (by the opponent's prior and simultaneous behaviour). So we can expect to find that the efficiency of action steps contained in the observed courses of action is very different; and these differences should be related to chances of winning or losing the fight.

Winners and losers of PF make in fact different use of the categories of the repertoire, as shown in Fig. 3; this difference is significant ($p = 0.04$,

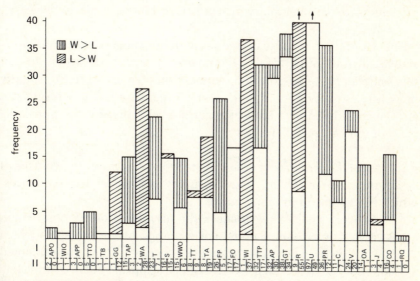

Fig. 3. The use of categories of action steps by winners (W) and losers (L) (from von Cranach *et al.* 1980)
Line I: abbreviations of categories (see Table 3)
Line II: number of instances for W on left, L on right

Wilcoxon). Some categories are more frequently used by winners, others by losers.

What does this difference mean? Independently from this distribution, we have classified the categories according to the function of the behaviours for the outcome of the PF. For this purpose, we have distinguished between the classes:

(i) *Positively or negatively functional action steps (F+, F−)*
These have a distinct and unequivocal (positive or negative) function for goal attainment (e.g. 'Grasp/take away' or 'Accept claim' respectively).

(ii) *Multifunctional action steps (MF)*
These can stand in the service of goal attainment, but also serve other functions (like 'Turn towards', which is essential for producing further positive action steps, but is also used in many other connections).

(iii) *Action steps of alternative function (AF)*
These stand in service of another goal, but are frequently inserted into the sequences of our courses of action ('Use' of the object in most cases is linked with *playing*).

(iv) *Functional or reactive behaviours (F/R)*
These can be used for goal attainment, but may also constitute an enforced or involuntary reaction (see our example of 'Release', p. 131).

The distribution of these categories in the action of winners and losers shows a distinct pattern (Table 4; note that there are no F− action steps in this sample). As to be expected, winners show much more F+, slightly more MF, as many AF and much less F/R than losers. These results can also be considered as a kind of construct validation for the functional parts of our category definition.

4.2.2. *Networks of courses of action.* A network depicts all the courses of action in a sample. Thus, we get a survey of the observed sequences, which can be useful in many ways:

– A network enables us to check the usefulness of the observation system's repertoire of units. For example, two action steps which always occur in the same sequence should eventually be combined into one; an action step which regularly appears in two completely different connections might eventually serve two different functions, etc.

– Networks constitute valuable descriptions of the act; they show the

Table 4. *Frequency of functionally different action steps in the courses of actions of winners and losers*

Positive functional (F+)		T, FP, GT, PR, C, CO, TH, J, RQ, OA		
Multifunctional (MF)ˆ		AP, TTP, TA, TT, WWO, WA, TAP, TTO, APP, WIO, APO, V		
Alternative functional (AF)		WI, U, TB		
Functional or reactive (F/R)		GG, R, S, FO		
		(For the meaning of the abbreviations, see table 3.)		
	Winners	Losers	Total	$\chi^2 = 70.36$
F+	173	74	247	$\varrho < 0.0005$
MF	147	133	280	
AF	85	86	171	
F/R	23	82	105	
Total	428	375	803	

relative importance of particular action steps and nodes as well as the existence of typical pathways. Thus, they enable us to formulate more specific questions e.g. about decisions, plans and strategies, and facilitate the interpretation of particular results in the context of the act.

- The comparison of networks from different samples helps to develop hypotheses concerning various aspects of the differences.
- On the basis of networks, formal qualities of pathways can be analysed.

The concept of network plays an important role in the study of artificial intelligence, in theories of action-related cognitive processes and the storage of action-related knowledge, and action theories in general (see Aebli 1980). Still we have rarely found accounts of networks which are really based on empirical observation of actions (for an exception, see Brenner 1980). The reader might therefore be interested to see how such networks look. Our examples are selected to emphasize the particular character of OA as compared to LA. These cases have not been formally treated nor transformed; they represent simple arrays of the raw data.

Figure 4 shows the central part of the network of the *losers* of our subsample ($n = 62$). As to be expected for an interactive OA, these networks are quite complicated; still only a few of the possible pathways have been used, some of them frequently. There are two conspicuous starting points: in the case of 'Approach' the actor is actively beginning the fight; in the case of 'Use', he is attacked by another child, while playing more or less peacefully.

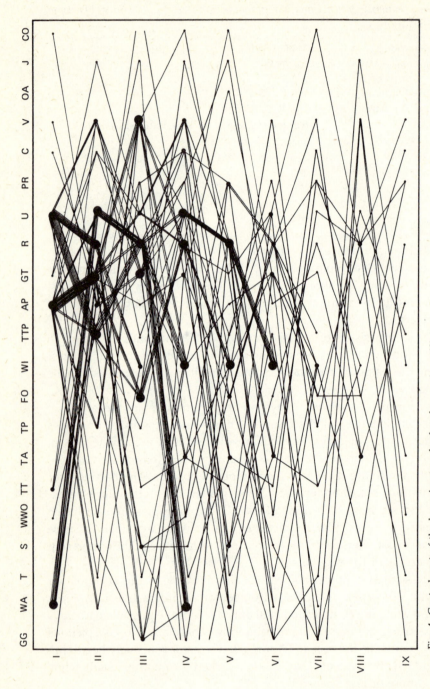

Fig. 4. Central part of the losers' network of pathways ($n = 62$)
Top, abbreviations of categories (see Table 3); Roman numerals in left margin indicate the sequence of action steps.
● node with 1 or 2 pathways

Individual networks

As discussed in section 2, we should expect that in OA individual strategies are developed. We can illustrate this by comparing the courses of action of two children from our sample, Fabia and Trommler, who are similar in respect to number of fights ($n = 17$ each), and mean length and variation of the sequences (Fabia: $X = 6.76$; $S_D = 2.88$, Trommler: $X = 7.06$; $S_D = 2.76$). Their networks are depicted in Fig. 5.[8] Fabia (F) seems to expose a greater variation in the first two action steps; Trommler (T) makes more use of the verbal categories (at the right side of Fig. 5b). The ratio of verbal categories is F : T = 10 : 32.

In Fig. 6, we have depicted the strategies of the two children in a more schematic way. Both Fabia and Trommler either participate in PF in a more passive way (starting from the 'Use'), depicted as F_1 or T_1 respectively; or they begin the PF with an active approach (F_2 or T_2). In F_1, Fabia wins if she dares to threaten or fight her partner; in other cases, she gives up rather soon ('Let go') and loses the fight. In F_2, she wins when grasping for the object immediately after the fight. Trommler wins mostly when he is user (T_1); he uses many verbal categories like 'Protest' or 'Offer an alternative', sometimes fighting before arguing. In T_2, he loses in most cases after 'Let go'.

On the basis of frequencies of combinations of action steps, Gugler (1977) constructed a measure of similarity between courses of action. He found, that within samples of individual courses of action, there was significantly more similarity than within chance samples of equal size, but only if the partner was kept constant. This suggests the existence of partner-specific interactive strategies even in small children.

4.2.3. *Hierarchical organization as a function of bidirectional adaptation.* After having coded and hierarchically ordered our data, we can analyse them according to the assumptions expressed in Fig. 1. For this purpose we take the action step (functional category) to be analysed as the temporal reference unit, and relate it to events before, during and after this time span on all three levels. We shall now demonstrate this procedure for the example of the action step 'Grasp/take away', in order to provide data concerning *the operation of bidirectional adaptation in the organization of OA*.

---

[8] Note that these are *individual* networks, which result however from an *interactive* situation. To attribute the observed particularities to individual properties therefore is to treat the partner's influence as constant or random.

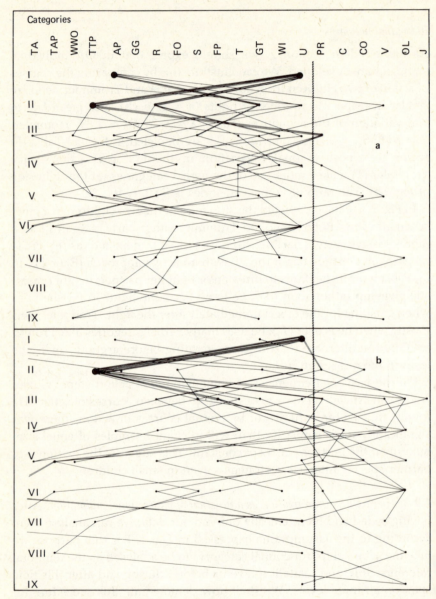

Fig. 5. Networks of pathways of two children, Fabia (**a**) and Trommler (**b**). Roman numerals in left margin indicate the sequence of action steps; wavy line separates non-verbal (left) from verbal (right) categories (see Table 3).

- • node with 1 or 2 pathways
- ● node with 3 or 4 pathways
- ● node with 5 or more pathways

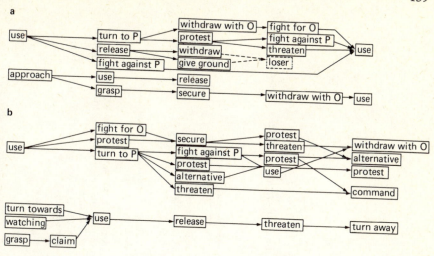

Fig. 6. Schematic presentation of the preferred strategies of Fabia (**a**) and Trommler (**b**)

'Grasp/take away' serves the function of obtaining possession of the object; Fig. 4, as well as our discussion of individual strategies, shows that it plays an important role in PF. Closer inspection reveals that 'Grasp/take away' can be very differently executed. Kalbermatten (1977) compared two forms of 'Grasp/take away' which tend to be executed under very different conditions: the secret, stealthy grasping of an object to which P does not attend for a moment, and the forceful taking in a kind of raid. We shall henceforth talk about 'Secret grasp/take away' and 'Forcible grasp/take away'. Among 60 cases of 'Grasp/take away', Kalbermatten found 8 of 'Secret grasp/take away' and 17 of 'Forcible grasp/take away'. He developed an observation system which gives a detailed description of the action step and the circumstances of its occurrence on the operational level, and also comprises preceding action steps and the situation of departure. In its main part, the system analyses the movements of 'Grasp/take away' in 46 items, each comprising ca. 10 subitems; the consequences of the action step are analysed in 7 items comprising 41 subitems. On the basis of these data, 'Secret grasp/take away' and 'Forcible grasp/take away' are compared with each other as well as also to other forms of 'Grasp/take away'. Table 5 summarizes the most important results; only very significant relations have been included; in 'Secret grasp/take away', these characteristics apply to all 8 cases. Fig. 7 shows the multilevel process.

A short synopsis may help the reader to interpret these results (numbers in parentheses refer to the items of Table 5). Although both

Table 5. Comparison of 'Secret grasp/take away' and 'Forcible grasp/take away' in their structural details (two-dimensional analysis)

Time, condition, variable	No.	Secret grasp/take away (SGT)	No.	Forcible grasp/take away (FGT)
Conditions of departure:				
Persons	1	A is non-possessor	↓ 31 →	A is possessor and/or
	2	P is dominant	↓ 32 →	A is dominant
Object	3	O is small/middle sized	↓ 33 →	O is big
Before GT				
A	4	No particular activity	34	A shows various activities, unrelated to P and O
	5	If A carries another O with himself, he does not use it	35	A does not talk
	6	A observes the play of P	↓ 36 →	A plays alone, no attention to P
	7	Orientation towards P and O, and near to P and O (longer than 7 s)	↓ 37 →	Immediately after orienting towards P and O, FGT is started
P → O / ↘ A	8	P has no body contact to O (or finishes body contact to O)	↓ 38 →	P holds O in one or both hands, or has also body contact
	9	P in grasping distance to O (about 50 cm)		
	10	P turns away from O and A (no visible control) (also during SGT)	↓ 39 →	P looks at O
	11	P sits, lies or kneels (also during SGT)		
A → P	12	A grasps for O immediately after P turns	40	A orients suddenly to P, then FGT

	14	...orientated towards P: visual control of P, not of O
	15	Knees bent (A is near the floor, kneels or crouches)
Pattern of Execution (A)	16	FT by bending trunk
	17	GT from stand still
	18	Grasping from distance (arm and body movement)
	19	No use of feet to shorten distance
	20	Grasping with one hand only
	21	Only fingertips in contact with O
	22	Lifting O from the ground
	23	Pulling O nearer
After GT	24	A secures O
	25	A loses PF
	26	A does not fight (no FP or FO)
	27	A lets O go, withdraws
	28	P reacts immediately after noticing A's SGT (eventually during SGT)
	29	P shows verbal reaction (e.g. protest) first
	30	P undertakes active countermeasures (pursuit, FGT)

← 43 →	Orientation towards O
↓ 44 ↑	Body upright, feet moving
↓ 45 ←	Grasping out of approach movement
← 46 →	Grasping with both coordinated hands
← 47 →	Whole hand and ball of thumb contact O
48	Fast grasping movement (short duration)
← 49 →	A often wins (11 : 6); loses if P is possessor
← 50 →	A fights for O
51	A uses O in an unspecific way

Note: Numbers refer to the text. Corresponding or contrasting terms in the columns SGT and FGT are indicated by arrows.

A = Actor, P = Partner, O = Object.

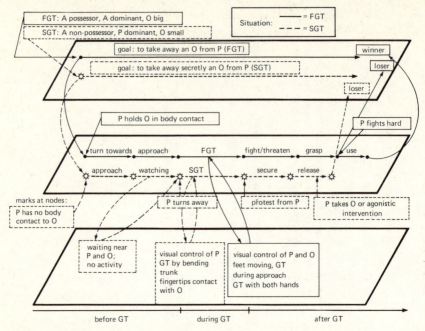

Fig. 7. The two-dimensional organization of the action step 'Grasp/take away': comparison of 'forcible' (FGT) and 'secret' (SGT) grasping (data from Kalbermatten 1977)

'Secret grasp/take away' and 'Forcible grasp/take away' serve the same function, the context within which they are applied is different, especially in regard to possession and dominance.[9]

Secret grasp/take away

(*Situation of departure*) A wants to get O (*goal level*), but is neither possessor nor dominant (1, 2). In this weak position, and if O is rather small than big (3), he chooses, instead of other possible action steps (e.g. 'Request') to take it secretly (*strategic level*). The 'Secret grasp/take away' can only be realized if favourable conditions exist *before* the execution of the *action step* is started (8, 10, 11); anyhow, A prepares to be able to seize an opportunity (4, 5, 6, 7); and he acts immediately when the favourable moment arrives (12). The execution of this action step (items *during the*

---

[9] *Possession* and *dominance* are important conditions of departure. In the Berne kindergarten, possession seems to constitute the more important predictor for the outcome of PF (in contrast to territorial or purely antagonistic fights). By interrogation of children and teacher, and analysis of the children's utterances during fights, we have reconstructed the system of their possession norms, and we have scaled the children for dominance: in two of our three samples, including the source of the data presented here, possession predicts the outcome in more than 70 % of the fights.

action step) shows a characteristic and significant pattern (*operational level*) which seems to be shaped as well by outward- as by inward-directed adaptation: as far as the *given circumstances* are concerned, A has to watch P (13, 14) and to perform a smooth and fast grasp from a somewhat distant, crouching position (15, 16, 17, 22, 23); but A's internal conditions, namely his *conflict to grasp for the object in violation of a possession norm*, expresses itself in the *manner of grasping* (20, 21). *After* the 'Secret grasp/take away', A tries to secure O (24; *strategic level*), but is invariably detected (28) and attacked (28, 29, 30) by P. He gives up (26, 27; *strategic level*) and loses the PF (25; *goal level*).

'Forcible grasp/take away'

This form of 'Grasp/take away' is very different. As far as the *situation of departure* is concerned, A is dominant and/or possessor (31, 32) and the action step is also applied to gain possession of larger objects (33). *Before the action step*, A suddenly notices that P has taken O; although he does not need O at the moment (34; *goal level*), he decides to act immediately (35, 37, 40, 41) and without any consideration of P (38, 39; *strategic level*). The grasp itself (*during the action step*) is totally determined by its purpose (42, 48); there is a conspicuous difference to 'Secret grasp/take away' in the way the hands are used for grasping (46, 47). If necessary, A uses other action steps *after the grasp* (*strategic level*); he usually wins, unless P is possessor of O; but if winning the PF, he has no real use for O since he had no purpose in mind from the beginning (49, 51; *goal level*).

This example illustrates the complicated interaction between the adaptation to 'internal' and 'external' conditions in the organization of manifest behaviour. Of course, this is an interpretation of the data, and the reader may especially doubt our ascription of hand and finger movement in the 'Secret grasp/take away' to norm conflict. But our detailed studies of other action steps corroborate our assumptions. The analysis of the 'Approach' on the structural level has shown, for example, that possessors and non-possessors differ significantly in their execution of the movement, the latters showing more *signs of insecurity* (directionality of the approach, displacement activities, orienting behaviour, etc); and this insecurity also relates to *grasping movements at the end of the approach*. In spite of their complexity, human cognition and behaviour may in fact constitute a highly integrated system, so that social representations, like norms and values, may find expression in the movements of the little finger. The detailed, two-dimensional analysis of manifest behaviour can help to reveal these intricate and variable connections.

5. Action-related cognitions

5.1. The assessment[10] of action-accompanying cognitions by self-confrontation interviews and content analysis

The necessity to assess conscious cognitions has already been explained (this article, section 2; and von Cranach, this volume, sections 2.1. and 5); basic methodological issues have been discussed in von Cranach (this volume, section 5.6). In this paragraph, we report on action-related accompanying (and in some cases also preceding) cognitions; these have been assessed by means of elicited and controlled report at the end of the act. Our method involves the following steps:

(i) The actor executes an act under natural conditions.

(ii) A video-film of his action is taken, if possible without his know-ledge.

(iii) Immediately after the act, the film is played back at the actor; in a more or less standardized procedure, he is asked to report his thoughts and feelings during the act ('self-confrontation' inter-view).

(iv) The transcript of the report is investigated, by use of content analysis, for the appearance of action-related cognitions.

Let us now have a more detailed look at steps (iii) and (iv) of this procedure.

The self-confrontation interview. The term self-confrontation (Nielsen 1962) refers to a situation in which a person is confronted with his or her own behaviour. Studies on the phenomenon of 'objective self-awareness' (Duval and Wicklund 1972, Frey, Wicklund and Scheier 1978) let us assume that such a situation brings internal events and states into the focus of attention.[11] In our studies, subjects were confronted with the video-film of their own action. An interview which evokes the actor's immediate report in such a situation is likely to reproduce with a fair quality what the actor can remember about his cognitive conscious

---

10 The term 'assessment' is explained in von Cranach, this volume, n. 14 on p. 44.

11 Wicklund (1979) concludes from several studies that, under the condition of self-awareness, verbal self-reports and actual behaviours are in higher agreement. For several reasons however, we hesitate to use the published studies on 'objective self-awareness' to evaluate our self-confrontation method.

experience during the act. Methodological studies are necessary and under way.

In the studies here reported, the video-films were shown several times in consecutive trials; the actors were instructed to stop the tape whenever they remembered cognitions or feelings during the scene, and to report these as accurately as possible. Additional questions were used to separate cognitions which actually happened during the episode from afterthoughts, and to locate cognitions in the stream of events.

Of course, advantages and dangers of such a method have to be carefully considered (see von Cranach *et al.* 1980). A consideration of factors contributing to error should distinguish between processes related to the perception of the video-taped behaviour and those of the interview. In regard of the former, we have to deal with 'confrontation effects' (surprise and other emotions, self-evaluation, etc), which however constitute a separate research object; these factors can for example be controlled by showing the whole film in a first extra trial. Other desirable effects involve memory and localization errors, reorganization, rationalization and self-attribution. The interview itself, although constructed to disclose these errors, produces additional biases, the most important of which stems from the translation of cognitions, reflected emotions and images into language. In addition, the operation of other well-known interview errors like social desirability, self-presentation and justification must be considered (in fact, the content of our transcriptions seems to indicate that these factors did not exert a strong effect). By our specific methods of self-confrontation, interview and analysis we have tried to avoid or control these errors as far as possible (see Table 6), and we are fairly confident that this has been achieved to an extent.

Content analysis. The classical definition of content analysis as 'the objective, systematic and quantitative description of manifest content' of verbal material (Berelson 1952) assumes a distinction between manifest and latent meanings. We believe, on the contrary, that meaning is always latent insofar as it can only be ascribed on the basis of social experience (Lisch and Kriz 1978); it is therefore crucial that the researcher's decisions are clearly stated, so that he can control, follow or reject his ascription of meaning. For this purpose, we followed these rules:

(i) The system of content analysis, as well the definitions of categories as the related verbal indicators, were completely formulated.

Table 6. *The assessment of action-related conscious cognitions: sources of errors and our countermeasures*

Impact of error during/from	Kind of error	Countermeasures
Act	Reorganization, self-attribution and justification	Choice of suitable situation and action: natural, normal, medium involvement Avoidance of evaluation anxiety
	Forgetting	Self-confrontation
Video-camera	Distraction Enforced self-awareness and evaluation Enforced attention to rules and norms	Hidden camera Adaptation, involving activity and situation
Self-confrontation and interview	Self-evaluation, reorganization, rationalization Self-attribution Selection	Particular method of video-presentation and interview: preparation, fractioning, localization of answers, exact questions, control questions Particular categories of content analysis

(ii) Rules for categorization and interpretation were clearly stated.

(iii) The analysis of interview sections was performed in a very thorough, nearly idiographic way, stating also the preassumptions (knowledge, inferences) underlying the researcher's decisions.

Space does not allow for a detailed presentation. The categories were translations of our action theoretical terms, partly in great refinement; additionally, we considered other conspicuous features of our interviews. For the different studies, several different systems were developed which contained between 50 and 70 categories. A reliability check in one of the studies (repeated coding after 4 months) yielded a correlation of 0.89.

5.2. Selected results[12]

These examples come from three studies: Morgenthaler (1979) studied naturally-occurring interaction among students (Sekundarstufe) and teachers (five different lessons) in the normal course of instruction; the

---

[12] The data presented in this paragraph are based on three different studies (PhD and Licentiate theses) by Morgenthaler (1979), Lang (1979) and Steiner (1980); interview and content analysis methods are different in details, but similar in their basic features.

students co-operated in groups on various different free and unstructured tasks (e.g. interpreting a story or designing an illustration); both teachers and students were investigated. Lang (1979) also studied student interaction in religious instruction, but here the task (assorting cards, assigning terms to stories) was much more structured and led to typical patterns of co-operation. Steiner (1980) asked her subjects, who were co-operating in pairs, to cook a meal or make a parcel of a difficult object (a pram).

5.2.1. *The role of values and norms in decisions.* In OA and interactive OA, nodes in the course of action are only rarely consciously perceived by the actor (less than 10 % in our cases). If he does however experience the need to decide, decisions normally only involve two alternatives, and only the finally chosen alternative tends to be clearly conceived, as depicted in Fig. 8 (data from Morgenthaler 1979). These decisions are

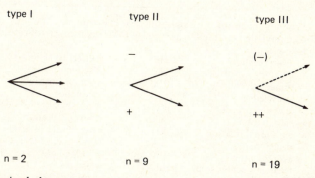

Fig. 8. Perceived alternatives in 30 decisions in teacher–student interaction (data from Morgenthaler 1979)
Type   I: reported perception of more than two alternatives
Type II: reported perception of a clearly excluded and a chosen and realized alternative
Type III: one alternative is clearly named and chosen, the other only indicated

rarely met by reconstructing the way to the goal, as a chess player would; even if the actor resorts to goals and plans, these are only shortly considered. More often, the actor uses as his criterion a general standard like a value or a norm. Even minute and trivial decisions, like how to make a knot in a cord while packing a parcel, are met by reference to values (decision to make a 'nice' knot) (Steiner 1980). Fig. 9 shows the detailed sequences of reported cognitions in the 28 cases of type II and type III decisions (as depicted in Fig. 8). Note the remarkable tendency, in the flow of cognitions, from upper left to lower right. Fig. 10 shows the same data in a more schematic form. We see that decision cognitions

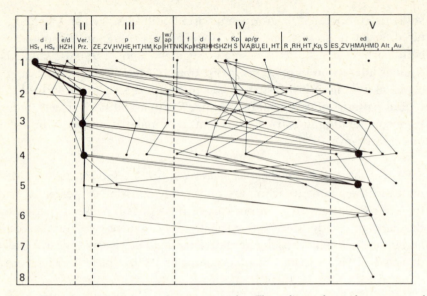

Fig. 9. Flow of cognitions during decisions at nodes. The ordinate shows the sequence of cognition. The abbreviations in the abscissa relate to German names of categories, to be translated as follows:

d	= interpretation	HE	= effect of action
e	= memory	HT	= action strategy
p	= projection	HM	= action possibility
w	= knowledge	S	= situation
ap	= attitude–process	Kp	= constellation of persons
f	= statement	NK	= no codification
gr	= emotional reaction	RH	= regularity of action
ed	= decision	VA	= valence
HS	= action step	BU	= judgement
HS$_f$	= partner's action step	EI	= estimation
HS$_e$	= own action step	R	= rule
HZH	= action context	ES	= decision
Ver. Prz.	= information processing	HMA	= exclusion of action possibility
ZE	= goal as result	HMD	= realisation of action possibility
ZV	= prosecution of goal	Alt	= alternative
HV	= intent	Au	= execution

tend to begin with perceptions (I), proceed to searching processes (II), resort to criteria (III and IV) and end by execution (V). Rules, values and (general) knowledge are more often referred to and used as criteria than plans and goal-related cognitions (35 : 13), and they are far more often processed back and forth in the final search for a deliberation (18 : 4).

Another important effect of values on GDA is based in their influence on the choice of goals and subgoals. We have found cases in which conflicting values led to internal goal conflict, and goal conflict in turn to distortions in the regulation of manifest behaviour.

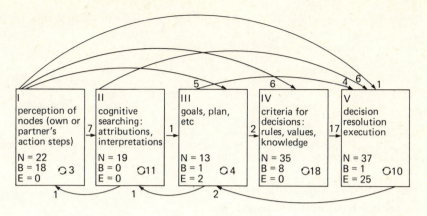

Key: N = total of cognitions within class
B = total of cognitions beginning in class
E = total of cognitions ending in class
○ = total of cognitions which are followed by cognitions within the same class
⟶ = total of cognitions between classes

Fig. 10. Flow of cognitions during decisions at nodes: schema

5.2.2. *Interrelations between cognitions of interacting group members.* As other action systems, interaction also possesses a twofold structure, the latent part of which consists of the interacting members' cognitions. To our knowledge, such structures have never been investigated in detail. Unfortunately, our own material is unsatisfactory in this respect; although we have investigated a few groups (a laborious task like all research of this kind), these differ in size, duration of interaction, topic and other features, and the methods applied are slightly different. We therefore restrict ourselves to examples, and the reader should regard these as exemplars of a yet unknown species, rather than as representative evidence.

Overlap of cognitions

To what extent do cognitions of the interacting group members in fact meet, how far do they relate to the same topic and consider the partner or group?

Some ideas may be derived from the reported cognitions of three 4-person groups working on different tasks.

Group 1 (Morgenthaler 1979). This group was involved in a discussion about the meaning of a short film, Polanski's *The fat and the thin one*: what can be done so that master and servant achieve a better understanding?

Table 7. *Idiosyncratic and shared cognitions (per cent) in three groups with different tasks*

| | Classes of cognition overlap* | | | | |
	I	II	III	IV	n
Group 1	50	32.1	10.7	7.1	56
Group 2	44.9	23.2	26.1	5.8	69
Group 3	12.6	4.8	44.3	38.3	167

* In class I the topic was mentioned by one group member, in class II by two members, class III three members and class IV four members.

This task was rather unstructured, as neither a concrete goal nor a procedure had been prescribed.

Group 2 (Morgenthaler 1979). In the context of the same lesson, this group had to present the outcome of their discussion to the plenum. Although this task seems better defined, the group had to improvise since they had discussed the subject with some levity, and had not prepared themselves for the presentation.

Group 3 (data from Lang 1979). This group had practised co-operation for 15 minutes on another task; they were then interrupted, and instructed. They received the text of two short stories (texts from the Bible) and a pile of cards on which concepts had been printed; these had to be assorted to the stories in their correct sequential order. This is a well-structured task, which was approached by all groups (there were three more than this one) in the same manner.

Results: Table 7 shows the percentage of situation- and task-related cognitions classified for number of actors reporting cognitions referring to the same topic. As can be seen, groups 1 and 2 show a preponderance of idiosyncratic, group 3 of shared cognitions. We tend to interpret this difference in terms of task structure and achieved co-operation, and we would expect even more sharing in a well-functioning team.

The *development* of shared and social considerations gives further insight. Here, we only present data from group 3. This group's course of interaction can be divided into five clear consecutive phases (Table 8).

Phase 1 is characterized by considerations, evaluations and emotions which are related to the preceding, interrupted task. All of these cognitions are idiosyncratic. In *phase 2*, the actors *individually* begin to accept the new task and to develop goals; there is quite an amount of cognitive overlap. In *phase 3*, a joint plan for the solution of the group problem is developed and executed (splitting the group into two subgroups, one for each story); and the work in these subgroups

Table 8. *Group 3: The development of topic-sharing in consecutive phases of co-operative interaction (group 3), per cent*

| Phase | Classes of cognition overlap* | | | | |
	I	II	III	IV	n
1	6.2	6.2	37.5	50.0	32
2	42.1	10.5	0.0	47.4	19
3	17.7	0.0	19.3	62.9	62
4	0.0	0.0	100.0	0.0	21
5	0.0	12.1	87.9	0.0	33
					167 Total

* For these classes, see Table 7.

Table 9. *The distributions (per cent) of self-related (S) and other-related (O) cognitions over consecutive phases of co-operative interaction (group 3)*

Phase	S, %	0, %	
1	100.0	0.0	
2	63.2	36.8	
3	30.7	69.3	
4	19.0	81.0	
5	18.2	81.0	
n	73	94	167

proceeds. Here we find a maximum of sharing. *Phases 4 and 5* are concerned with the comparison of the two subgroups' results, and consecutive corrections. Here we find much sharing, but we do not understand why there are no cognitions shared by *all* members.

These findings have their counterpart in the distribution (over sections) of the cognitions either concerned with *the own person* (self-related = S) or with *the group or partner* (other-related = O) as shown in Table 9: self-related cognitions decrease, other-related cognitions increase during the problem-solving interaction. Both tables together depict aspects of the *development of social thought* during successful solution of a group task. Hopefully, we shall soon be able to present more systematic and detailed data about these issues.

5.2.3. *Interactive goal structures.* Having looked at the development of social thought in interactive tasks *in globo*, it will be interesting to regard an important *specific* cognitive variable in particular. Steiner, in one of our first explorative studies,[13] asked two pairs of subjects to make a packet (to be mailed) of a pram and a complicated 'art object'; after the objects had been packed up, the actors were interviewed in a self-confrontation situation. In the subsequent content analysis, Steiner concentrated on a variety of 'goal cognitions': according to *content*, she distinguished *information goals* (goals to find something out), *process goals* (referring to the *way of performance* of the act) and *result goals* (referring to the aspired end state of the act); in regard to the goal's function, she distinguished between goal attainment, change, repetition (keeping up) and abandoning of goals. Fig. 11 depicts the sequence of goal-related cognitions during the first 7.25 minutes. We found considerable differences between the two pairs.

Beatrix and André had met only a few times before the trial. For the depicted sections, they reported 56 goals, 6 of them simultaneous goals of the two partners; in 5 cases these were corresponding, in 1 case opposed. The goal structure of the episode clearly exhibits the form of a stair, thus suggesting that normally one goal-related activity had been concluded before the next was undertaken. Only 5 goals had been maintained after others had been taken up, and these were superordinated ones in most cases. Beatrix and André developed a true pattern of *co-operation* and *labour division*, characterized by *turn-taking* in goal-related cognition. André's cognitions were more related to information and process goals, Beatrix's more to result goals, so that André appeared as planning and leading, Beatrix as executing. There was little conflict between the two; the scenes constituted the thematic units, and there were few conflicting, but many corresponding goals. This pattern of co-operation may have been a result of the fact that the partners' relationship was unproblematic, and that they were mainly interested in their task.

Quite in contrast, our second pair, Jeanne and Karl, were involved in a long and intensive relationship before the trial. Their goal structure offers a very different picture. For this first part of their work, they reported 72 goals; 11 of these were simultaneous, 3 opposed and the others corresponding. The stair pattern is less distinct, since in 17 cases goals were repeated, or different goals persecuted at the same time. Only 6 of these are instrumental supergoals, the other 11 interac-

13 This task proved far too complicated and also too long (ca. 45 minutes) for the beginning, and therefore had to be abandoned; still, the results of the pilot study seem very interesting.

tive and/or antagonistic goals (especially in the lower part of the diagram). The activity of this pair is rather *uncoordinated*; neither clear leadership nor division of labour is visible. Information and process goals are more related to *interaction* than to *task*. The two actors see the scenes quite differently, and their goals are frequently in contradiction or unrelated. How is this pattern to be explained? It is our impression that this couple has introduced their interpersonal conflicts into the task. For this reason, they are *occupied*, at the same time, with the *task and their relationship*, and their interactive goals are characterized by misunderstandings, distrust, fear of quarrelling and a certain task-related rivalry.

To sum up, it is our impression that goal structures are suitable means to depict essential features of task-related interaction, as co-operation, labour division, task orientation, etc. As other action-related cognitions, goal cognitions constitute the latent structure which we must try to assess and investigate, in order to explain manifest behaviour in ordinary interactive action.

6. The social nature of goal-directed action

In this article, we have compared ordinary interactive action to the more stereotyped forms of labour activity in order to illustrate some of its typical aspects;[14] we have found that these are pervaded by social factors. Instead of unnecessary repetitions, let us finally consider some of the scientific implications of this social side of goal-directed action.

A basic proposition underlying all of our research has been that *social control operates through the actor's (conscious) cognitions, which in turn play an important role in behaviour organization* (von Cranach, this volume, section 2.4.6). We have further argued (von Cranach et al. 1980) that this proposition should be broken down into the following three theorems:

(i) The *convention theorem* proposes that the members of social communities share certain representations concerning matters of functional importance; these are the *social conventions*. (A social convention is a social representation (see Moscovici and Farr, in press), or more often a part of it, which is shared by the members of a community.)

(ii) The *attribution theorem* assumes that social conventions influence the perception and judgement of one's own and of others' behaviour as

---

[14] We should like to stress that this comparison was not performed to blame industrial psychologists, from whom we learned so much, for errors and omissions.

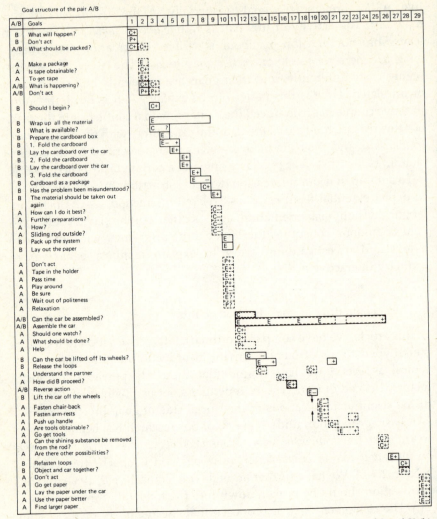

Goal structure of the pair A/B

Fig. 11. Interview data: goal structure of two pairs of actors, A and B (a) and J and K (b)

Ordinate: A, B, J, K in far left column are the abbreviations of the names of the actors; the second column contains the goals, which have been named in the self-confrontation interview or during the action. Abscissa: the numbers 1–29 designate time intervals of 15 s (from video-tape).

The individual boxes show the sequential localization of the goals, a 'goal' being defined as everything that an actor imagines and strives for:

☐ goals of actors B and J

⌞⌟ goals of actors A and K

There are three types of goals:

C = clarification goals: information is sought

E = result goals: an imagined state at the end of an activity is aspired to

P = process goals: what is aspired to is not a result, but rather a state of being, or way of execution, which extends over a shorter or longer period of the action

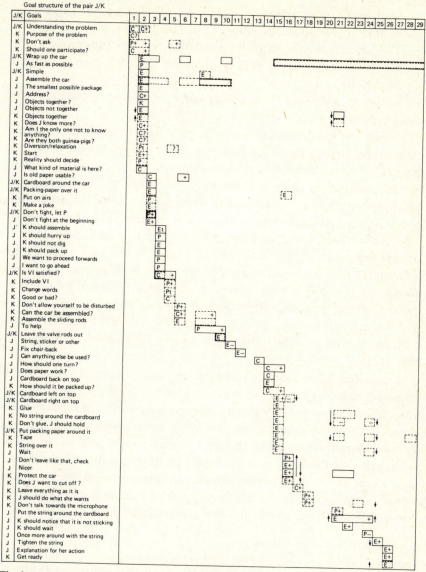

Goal structure of the pair J/K

The letter or signs in the boxes (at the right side) represent:

+ = the goal was reached

− = the goal was not reached

? = there is uncertainty as to whether the goal was reached

t = partially reached goal

empty = no indication with respect to the reaching of goals, but efforts were continued or were renewed in order to reach the goal.

When two actors are referred to on the left side of a line (e.g. J/K), a special goal constellation is indicated:

overlapping boxes: the goals of the partners were alike and simultaneous

arrows next to the boxes: the goals of the partners were opposed well as the definitions of situations. (This does not exclude, of course, the existence of idiosyncratic attributions.)

(iii) The *retroaction theorem* finally states that self-attributions (based on social conventions) act back on the actor's organization of his own behaviour.

It is easy to understand how the dynamic interplay of these principles should result in social control.

The full elaboration of these principles has inspired our research programme; it consists in a number of steps, only a few of which we have as yet undertaken (but not finished). In regard of the convention and the attribution theorems, we have elsewhere published research which shows that important action-related cognitions are attributed, under certain circumstances, with high agreement (von Cranach *et al.* 1980, Kalbermatten and von Cranach, in press). In fact, two kinds of attributions seem to exist: *idiosyncratic* ones (showing little interjudge agreement) and *conventional attributions* (with high interjudge agreement). What is still lacking is the link to society: it has to be demonstrated that conventional attributions are in fact rooted in social representations, and constitute ideas integrated into a context of social meaning which is widely shared in society because of its functional importance.

In regard to the retroaction theorem, we have illustrated in this article how both manifest behaviour and conscious cognition operate under the impact of factors which are social in content and quality. It remains to be shown that these actually are the very same cognitions which are socially shared. Research to this end is under way, and we are quite optimistic that the issue will (as usual) prove much more complicated than foreseen, but basically in agreement with our expectations. Since we all carry society in us, the prototype of human behaviour, goal-directed action, is intricately and pervasively social in origin and nature.

Appendix: units of observation

The methodology of systematic behaviour observation is today well established (Weick 1968, von Cranach and Frenz 1969, Hutt and Hutt 1970, Fassnacht 1979), so that we shall not treat it here in general; to understand how we construct our hierarchical observation system it will be necessary, however, to explain in brief the way in which our observation units are defined.

An essential operation in systematic observation is the theoretical and operational definition of *observation units* which the observer uses to divide the stream of behaviour into parts. The principles of unit construction can be classified in many ways (Bekoff 1979, Fassnacht 1979). Here, our most important distinctions refer to socially meaningful versus physically defined, and to functionally versus structurally defined units; the well-known distinctions between natural versus artificial, and molar versus molecular units are related to these. For the sake of clarity, we shall treat all of these as separate dichotomies, although in reality they tend to constitute interrelated dimensions.

Socially meaningful versus physically defined units

Society assigns social meaning to individual behaviour; this meaning depicts the behaviour's function for the operation of socially relevant processes. Therefore social meaning is (as far as OA is concerned) mainly related to molar acts, like 'making a present', 'mailing a letter', 'offending', etc. (We do not refer here to the fact that each symbol's or word's denotative meaning is socially based, but only to holistic functions in the social process.) The various social meanings are normally assigned to distinct sections of behaviour: behaviour units are thus *socially defined*. Concerning such definitions, more or less unanimity can be observed within communication communities; this is necessary for smoothly running social functioning.

In the construction of his observation system, the researcher can use such socially defined units if he thinks it essential to assess the social meaning of behaviour. Other research questions may justify the exclusion of social meaning from the observation system. In this case, meaning-free observation units will be constructed, in most cases by use of *physical definitions*. These refer to physical behaviour characteristics (which are more or less free of meaning) like detailed descriptions of angle, speed, distance, location and similar characteristics of the behaviour.

Let us add two further points: in so far as both the observer (in his assessment performance) and the actor (in his observed behaviour) act on the same premises of social meaning, the 'measuring instrument' is not independent from its object (see von Cranach, this volume n. 14 on p. 44). This circularity is not based in the method chosen, but in the fact that observer and observed are both members of the same communication community, whose definition of meaning at the same time determines the scientific question and the object of research. On the other hand, since the assumption of unanimity constitutes a basis for the assumption of social meaning and hence the observation unit, the latter can (and should) be validated by testing this very assumption.

Functional versus structural units

Behaviour (as a system) possesses structures and functions. The structure of a system may be considered as the totality of its subsystems and their relations; its function as the mutual influence between the system and its environment and its subsystems. Structure and function are interconnected, they constitute two sides of the same thing. Both viewpoints can be used to define observation units.

Functional observation units are conceived as dynamic and describe the effect of one unit upon another and on the total result of behaviour; the basis of their definition is a more or less hypothetical function. Thus, in the definition of the interactive observation unit 'Threat' (an action step in children's 'possession fight') it is assumed that threat leads to a change in the opponent's behaviour by indicating a future attack. (This assumed function can be validated, e.g. by looking whether quarrels which include threat contain in fact less fighting.) Functions are very often socially defined; they can be assessed with high security. *Structural units* are defined by configurations of certain structural characters. These characters can be physically defined.

The principles of functional and structural definition are not exclusive. The exact boundaries of a functional definition, for instance, often must be structurally defined.

Natural versus artificial units

We tend to consider perception as the interaction between a structured environment and an active (and therefore structuring) perceiver; for this reason we consider the famous debate about natural versus artificial observation units at least partially misleading. Anyhow, for most practical purposes natural units in social research seem to be 'natural' for the observer because they are socially defined.

Molar versus molecular units

Molar units are relatively large comprehensive units, molecular ones are small and approach the 'just noticeable' in the ideal case.

Unit syndromes and their use in hierarchically organized observation systems

The inherent logic of these unit types leads to typical unit syndromes: there is an affinity between the poles *social, functional, natural* and *molar* on the one hand versus *physical, structural, artificial* and *molecular* on the other. In our hierarchically organized observation systems, their inclusive character as well as qualitative differences of levels of analysis lead to their differentiation in regard to unit types: on higher levels of analysis, we tend to use socially defined ('natural') units of a functional and molar character; our lowest level of analysis contains physically and structurally ('artificial') defined molecular units.

A final question concerns the direction of analysis: Should we proceed 'upwards' or 'downwards'? There are good arguments for both opinions (e.g. van Hooff 1970, Lorenz 1978). From the perspective of systems theory, the latter viewpoint deserves preference; in regard to structure, the sequence of subunits does not necessarily correspond to that of the superunits (Miller, Galanter and Pribram 1960), so that nested systems can be better disentangled by proceeding downwards; and the functions can be deduced only from the system's relations to its supersystem. Anyhow, a pragmatic stance seems advisable in these matters.

References

Ackoff, R. L. and F. E. Emery, (1972) *On purposeful systems*. Aldine, Chicago.
Aebli, H. (1980) *Denken: Das Ordnen des Tuns. I. Kognitive Aspekte der Handlungstheorie*. Klett-Cotta, Stuttgart.
Bekoff, M. (1979) 'Behavioural acts: description, classification, ethogram analysis and measurement.' In R. B. Cairns (ed.), *The analysis of social interactions*. Lawrence Erlbaum, Hillsdale, N.J.

Berelson, B. (1952) *Content analysis in communication research.* The Free Press, Glencoe, Ill.

Brenner, M. (1980) 'Aspects of conversational structure in the research interview.' In P. Werth (ed.), *Conversation, speech and discourse.* Croom Helm, London.

Cranach, M. von (1975) 'Interaktive Verhaltensweisen als Bestandteile sozialer Handlungen.' In *Bericht über den 29. Kongress der Dt. Gesellschaft für Psychologie in Salzburg, 1974.* Hogrefe, Göttingen.

Cranach, M. von and H. Frenz (1969) 'Systematische Beobachtung.' In C. Graumann (ed.), *Handbuch der Psychologie, vol. 7. I: Sozialpsychologie.* Hogrefe, Göttingen.

Cranach, M. von, U. Kalbermatten, K. Indermühle and B. Gugler (1980) *Zielgerichtetes Handeln.* Huber, Bern.

Duval, S. and Wicklund, R. A. (1972) *A theory of objective self-awareness.* Academic Press, New York.

Fassnacht, G. (1979) *Systematische Verhaltensbeobachtung – eine Einführung in die Methodologie und Praxis.* Ernst Reinhard, München.

Frey, D., R. A. Wicklund and M. F. Scheier (1978) 'Die Theorie der objektiven Selbstaufmerksamkeit.' In D. Frey (ed.), *Theorien der Sozialpsychologie.* Huber, Bern.

Gugler, B. (1977) 'Zur Erfassung und sequentiellen Analyse des Streitgeschehens bei Vorschulkindern.' Unpublished dissertation, University of Berne.

Hacker, W. (1976) *Psychische Regulation von Arbeitstätigkeiten.* Deutscher Verlag der Wissenschaften, Berlin.

— (1978) *Allgemeine Arbeits- und Ingenieurpsychologie,* 2nd edn. Huber, Bern.

Harré, R. (1972) 'The analysis of episodes.' In J. Israel, H. Tajfel (eds); *The context of social psychology: a critical assessment.* Academic Press, London.

Harré, R. and P. F. Secord (1972) *The explanation of social behaviour.* Blackwell, Oxford.

Heider, F. (1958) *The psychology of interpersonal relations.* Wiley, New York. (German edn: *Psychologie der interpersonalen Beziehungen.* Klett-Cotta, Stuttgart, 1977.)

Hooff, J. A. van (1970) 'A component analysis of the structure of the social behaviour of a semi-captive chimpanzee group.' *Experientiae* **26**, 549–50.

Hutt, S. and C. Hutt (1970) *Direct observation and measurement of behaviour.* Thomas, Springfield, Ill.

Kalbermatten, U. (1977) 'Handlung: Theorie – Methode-Ergebnisse.' Unpublished dissertation, University of Berne.

Kalbermatten, U. and M. von. Cranach (1981) 'Hierarchisch aufgebaute Beobachtungssysteme zur Handlungsanalyse.' In P. Winkler (ed.), *Methoden zur Analyse von face-to-face Situationen.* Metzler, Stuttgart.

—, — (1981) 'Attribution of action-related cognitions.' In H. Hiebsch, H. Brandstätter and H. H. Kelley (eds.), *Social psychology* (Proceedings XXII International Congress of Psychology, Leipzig 1980). Deutscher Verlag der Wissenschaften, Berlin, and North-Holland, Amsterdam.

Kussmann, Th. (1971) *Bewusstsein und Handlung. Probleme und Ergebnisse der sowjetischen Psychologie.* Huber, Bern.

Lang, J. (1979) 'Gruppenarbeit in der Schule analysiert mit der Theorie konkreter Handlungen.' Unpublished thesis, University of Berne.

Laucken, U. (1974) *Naive Verhaltenstheorie*. Klett-Cotta, Stuttgart.

Lisch, R. and J. Kriz (1978) *Grundlagen und Modelle der Inhaltsanalyse*. Rowohlt, Reinbeck.

Lorenz, K. (1978) *Vergleichende Verhaltensforschung: Grundlagen der Ethologie*. Springer, Wien.

Miller, G. A., E. Galanter and K. H. Pribram (1960) *Plans and the structure of behavior*. Holt, New York. (German edn: *Strategien des Handelns (Pläne und Strukturen des Verhaltens)*. Klett-Cotta, Stuttgart, 1973.)

Morgenthaler, Ch. (1979) 'Zur subjektiven Perspektive handelnder Personen.' Unpublished dissertation, University of Berne.

Moscovici, S. and R. Farr (in press). *Social representations*. Cambridge University Press, Cambridge.

Nielsen, G. (1962) *Studies in self-confrontation*. Munksgaard, Copenhagen.

Schmidtchen, S. (1978) *Handeln in der Kinderpsychotherapie*. Kohlhammer, Stuttgart.

Schütz, A. and Th. Luckmann (1975) *Strukturen der Lebenswelt*. Soziologische Texte, Luchterhand.

Semmer, N. and M. Frese (1979) 'Handlungstheoretische Implikationen für kognitive Therapie.' In N. Hoffmann (ed.), *Grundlagen Kognitiver Therapie*. Huber, Bern.

Steiner, V. (1980) 'Zielstrukturen in konkreten interaktiven Handlungen.' Unpublished thesis, University of Berne.

Tomaszewski, T. (1978) *Tätigkeit und Bewusstsein. Beiträge zur Einführung in die polnische Tätigkeitspsychologie*. Beltz, Basel.

Volpert, W. (1980) *Beiträge zur Psychologischen Handlungstheorie*. Huber, Bern.

Weick, K. E. (1968) 'Systematic observational methods.' In G. Lindzey and E. Aronson (eds.), *Handbook of social psychology*, vol. 2. Addison-Wesley, Reading, Mass.

Wicklund, R. A. (1979) 'Die Aktualisierung von Selbstkonzepten in Handlungsvollzügen.' In Fillip Sigrun-Heide (ed.), *Selbstkonzeptforschung*. Klett-Cotta, Stuttgart.

Describing sequences of social interaction

PETER COLLETT AND ROGER LAMB

One of the enduring problems which arises in the study of social interaction is how to characterize the sequence of activities produced by interacting parties. There are many ways of characterizing or describing sequences of social behaviour, and it will be the purpose of this paper to explore the formal properties of some of these types of description. We shall try to show that different modes of description reflect different assumptions about the nature of individual activity and social interaction, that certain assumptions are more tenable than others, and that those descriptions which satisfy such assumptions are more likely to reveal the underlying patterns of social interaction.

The simplest conception of dyadic interaction is one which presupposes that individuals alternate in occupying the centre of the stage. Here the idea is that A makes a social move, which is followed by a move from B, which in turn is followed by a move from A, and so on

Fig. 1. Type One description

through the sequence. This conception, which for convenience we call a Type One description, is represented in Fig. 1.

A Type One description is best suited to those sequences where each person makes only one move before relinquishing his turn to the other person. Chess, for example, can be described with a Type One description, simply because the rules of the game require that players take turns and that they only make one move per turn. In chess the alternation rule and the single-move rule conspire to produce sequences which, for all

161

practical purposes, can be handled with a Type One description. We read in the newspaper that Fischer opened with Pawn to King's Four, that Spassky replied with Pawn to King's Four, that Fischer replied with Knight to King's Bishop Three, and so on, and we are perfectly satisfied that the account captures the essentials of the game.

It is sometimes said that social behaviour is like a chess game. This analogy is usually offered in order to draw attention to the rule-governed aspects of social behaviour rather than any chess-like properties of its sequential structure. Social interaction may bear some affinities to chess, but these do not include the ways in which it is produced in time. For one thing, social interaction is not governed by a single-move rule, with the result that individuals are usually allowed to make more than one move per turn. Under those circumstances where it is assumed that an alternation rule is in operation, and where it is also assumed the the numbers of moves per turn is optional, we may speak of a Type Two description (see Fig. 2).

Fig. 2. Type Two description

Type Two descriptions abound in psychology. Most applications of Bales's (1950) scheme to social behaviour are couched in terms of alternations between interactors who produce variable numbers of moves within each turn. Flanders's (1970) analyses of classroom interaction also have the form of a Type Two description. In these analyses the teacher and the students alternate their turns at talk and are allowed to perform more than one activity within each turn. At first glance a Type Two description seems perfectly suited to teacher–student interaction, but on closer inspection it can be seen to provide a parody of the classroom, in which students always remain silent while the teacher is talking, the teacher never interrupts students, and both teacher and students only react to what the other has said during their turn at talk.

Although Type One and Type Two descriptions differ with regard to the number of moves that they permit within each turn, they share the same attitudes towards time. In both cases time is seen as a left-to-right progression where events can be considered as having either uniform or variable temporal properties. When the duration of each action unit is ignored in a description we may speak of an 'event base', and where the duration of each unit is preserved we may speak of it as having a 'time base' (cf. Bakeman 1978). Both Type One and Type Two descriptions can accommodate an event base or a time base, so that each kind of description may be regarded as having two temporal formulations of the same action sequence. In the case of a Type Two description, for example, the same sequence might have the appearance shown in Fig. 3.

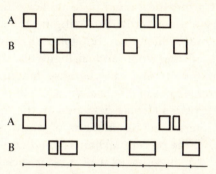

Fig. 3. Type Two description with event base and with time base

Event base formulations disregard real time. In an event base formulation each unit (in this case a square) represents an activity, and all units have the same size regardless of the durations of different activities. In a time base formulation the duration of each activity is taken into account and the units differ in size accordingly. Because time base formulations respect the duration of activities they necessarily contain more information than event base formulations. This means that event base formulations can be derived from time base formulations, but not the reverse. Time base formulations are more powerful than event base formulations simply because they do not allow questions relating to the duration of events to go begging. All sequence descriptions are concerned with the temporal order of events. When a sequence description accommodates a time base, it automatically permits an investigation of the relationship between the duration of events and their order. This cannot be done when a sequence description employs an event base, and that is why an event base is usually inferior to a time base.

Type One and Type Two descriptions both incorporate the assumption of alternation, namely that only one person is producing the action at any point in time. This idea, that social interaction can adequately be captured by considering the more active party to the exclusion of the less active party, can be traced to a naive model of conversation structure.

Conversation, it is commonly supposed, consists of turns at talk – one person holds the floor while another waits to assume the role of speaker. This model of conversation has been reinforced by theatrical and literary conventions. In the theatre the actor who, so to speak, holds the centre of the stage often dominates the action out of all proportion to what happens outside the theatre. This is necessitated by the fact that the theatre audience is always third party to what is happening on the stage, and the fact that a theatrical attempt to replicate the activities of real listeners would be unnecessarily distracting for the audience. A similar convention is found in literature, but for a slightly different reason. Literary accounts of interaction and dialogue also conform to a Type Two description, but in this case because language is ill-suited to represent concurrent states of affairs at the same time, and because even where it is done it places terrible demands on the reader.[1]

Theatrical and literary representations of social interaction need to make concessions to the perceptual limits of audiences and readers, and that is why they usually offer us a picture of social life which, while perfectly comprehensible, is quite unlike the world we inhabit. Of course the theatre and literature seldom lay claims to verisimilitude. As literary forms they can always plead exemption from the requirements that we might wish to impose on a science of human behaviour. The assumption of alternation which suffuses the theatre and literature is totally inappropriate for the study of social interaction. Even conversation, which appears, on the face to things, to be the prime candidate for a Type Two description is far more complicated than the description will allow. As Yngve (1969), Duncan (1972) and others have shown, the listener in a conversation is by no means inert. While the speaker is holding the floor the listener engages in a variety of activities which are geared to gaining the floor, denying any desire for the floor, showing he has understood, that he disagrees, or whatever. Some of the actions produced by the listener are linguistic, others non-linguistic. Whatever their modality, they are nonetheless activities which a Type Two description would totally ignore. Because a Type Two description overlooks the activities of the less active party it fails to offer a full account of what is happening between two people. Type Two descriptions assume that the

---

[1] The manner in which some modern writers seem to have attempted to break away from diachronic conventions in narrative has been a major topic of discussion in literary criticism, at least since Frank (1963) introduced the idea of 'spatial form'. He suggested that in reading such writers as Proust or Joyce one was meant 'to apprehend their work spatially, in a moment of time, rather than as a sequence' (p. 9).

less active party is, for all practical purposes, inert, and therefore that there is no overlap between the activities of what one might regard as the more active and the less active person. In both of these assumptions a Type Two description is usually incorrect, for as we have noted listeners are seldom inert, and their activities often overlap with those of speakers. In fact, if a Type Two description takes its inspiration from a conception of conversation structure, it is certainly a bad model to apply to the analysis of conversations.

A Type Three description, on the other hand, does not assume alternations of the interactors, and it therefore allows for simultaneous activity by both parties as well as overlap between their respective activities (see for example Condon and Ogston 1967, Jaffe and Feldstein 1970). Fig. 4 shows a Type Three description.

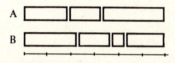

Fig. 4. Type Three description (time base)

Type Three descriptions may use either an event base or a time base, although they are more commonly associated with the latter. We have already noted that an event base description can be derived from a time base description, but that the reverse is not possible because a time base description always contains more information than an event base description. The derivation of an event base from a time base in the case of a Type Three description has the form depicted in Fig. 5.

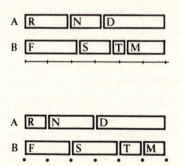

Fig. 5. Type Three description with time base and with event base

An event base description is derived from a time base description by locating the points in the time base description where a new activity is initiated *by either party*. The points in the time base description are arranged as an equal interval scale and the information concerning initiation of action units is then transposed to the event base record. It is invariably the case that the points in the time base description are unequally spaced, simply because the conjunction of some activities takes longer than others. An event base description overlooks the actual amount of time it takes before one or both parties switches to a new activity. Instead it registers the contiguity of activities without regard to their duration. This means that some activities which actually took longer than others, and which appear as such in the time base description, will appear to be shorter than those same activities in an event base description. This is as much the case within individuals as it is between individuals. In Fig. 5 we notice, within individuals, that activity R takes longer than activity N and activity F takes longer than activity S, but this does not seem to be the case in the event base description (here the letters R, N, etc, are symbols for different types of activities). Likewise, between individuals, we see that while action R actually takes longer than action S, it appears to be shorter in the event base description. An event base description will usually deceive the reader if it is read as a time base description. Although we normally associate scalar length with duration, no such implication is intended by an event base description. An event base description merely records the temporal order of conjunctions of activities, so that the dotted scale in Fig. 5 represents the order in which new activities are brought into play, rather than the time and order with which they enter the sequence.

All of the sequence descriptions that we have discussed so far permit analyses of the temporal order of activities produced by each person, as well as an analysis of the temporal order in which the activities were initiated by the dyad. It is possible, in other words, to identify the order of events for A, the order of events for B, and the order of events for A and B with a Type One, Type Two or a Type Three description. However this is the full extent of the information that can be extracted from Type One and Type Two descriptions because by their very nature they are series descriptions. A Type Three description, on the other hand, is a parallel description because it presupposes that when two people are interacting they are both active at the same time, and the activities of one person may overlap with those of the other person. This means that while a Type Three description can provide information about the temporal order of activities produced by each person, as well as the order in which the activities were initiated by the dyad, it can also provide information on what each person was doing in relation to what the other person was doing at that time. If we return to the last example we considered, namely the event base Type Three descriptions, this will become more clear (see Fig. 6).

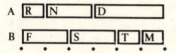

Fig. 6. Type Three description (event base)

When we examine each person separately we see that the order of A's activities was R–N–D, and the order of B's activities was F–S–T–M. We also notice that the temporal order of activities for the dyad, that is, the order of events considered without regard to who produced them, is R/F–N–S–D–T–M. But because a Type Three description is a parallel description we can also express the sequence produced by both individuals together as a *conjunction* of activities, while at the same time retaining the relevant information about who did what. A description of the conjunction of activities may be represented as (R,F)(N,F)(N,S)(D,S)(D,T)(D,M), where the number of double brackets indicates the number of occasions when an activity was initiated by either member of the dyad, and where the first symbol in each bracket records the activity of A, and the second symbol the activity of B which was produced within the same time segment. Because this kind of notation has two symbols in each bracket, and because the first symbol always refers to an activity of one person, the second to an activity of the other, it is obviously amenable to reformulation in a matrix where one person moves among the rows and the other among the columns. We call this technique Conjoint Analysis, and its format a Conjoint Matrix.

In the most simple form of Conjoint Analysis the activities produced by one person are arranged along the rows, while the activities of the other person are arranged along the columns of the same matrix. The Type Three description is then entered in the matrix by placing dots in all those cells which define the conjunction of activities produced by the two people, and then connecting the dots with a line which represents the order of the conjunctions. In this way the left-to-right Type Three description can be recast as a trajectory through an activity space. In producing a Conjoint Analysis it is necessary to consider, firstly, the dimensions of the matrix and, secondly, the orders of the rows and columns.

1. Dimensions of the matrix

There are basically two kinds of Conjoint Matrix – a 'minimal' matrix, where the numbers of rows and columns correspond to the numbers of separate activities performed by the respective parties, and an 'expanded' matrix where the number of rows and/or columns is greater than the number of separate activities performed by the two parties. The Type Three description which we considered earlier can be entered in either a minimal or an expanded matrix. It is entered in a minimal matrix by locating the separate activities of A along the columns and the separate activities of B along the rows. (Under those circumstances where A or B produces the same activity twice within the same sequence, that activity is still located only once in the rows or once in the columns. In other words, every row must have a different label, and every column must have a different label, but one of the rows may have the same label as one of the columns.) Once the rows and columns have been labelled, dots are placed in the cells which represent conjunctions of activities and these dots are then connected in series to indicate the progression of the sequence through the activity space. A minimal conjoint analysis of our Type Three description is presented by Fig. 7.

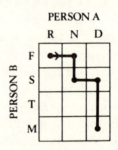

Fig. 7. Conjoint Analysis (minimal) of Type Three description

An expanded matrix can be produced when it is decided that it would be insufficient to trace the sequence through a space which is defined by only those activities performed by the respective parties. One may decide to use an expanded matrix when studying a single dyad, either because it is felt to be necessary to locate activities which were performed by A but not B, and vice versa, or to locate activities which were performed by neither A nor B beside those performed by A and/or B. Alternatively one may decide to use an expanded matrix when studying several dyads, if only because different dyads have produced different ranges of activities. There may also be reasons for selecting a minimal rather than an expanded matrix, one reason being that the same ranges of activities are not open to both parties in a dyad.

An expanded matrix can be produced either by entering all the activities performed by both parties in the rows and the columns, or by entering these as well as other activities which are deemed to be relevant to this dyad, or to this and other dyads. In the first case one might simply enter all the activities performed by A and all the activities performed by B along the rows, and then do the same for the columns. The resultant matrix and its trajectory would then have an appearance something like that shown in Fig. 8.

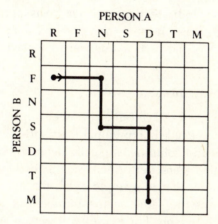

Fig. 8. Conjoint Analysis (expanded) of Type Three description

Expanded matrices always have rows and/or columns which are not visited by the trajectory because for each person they include activities which were not performed by that person. Expanded matrices are particularly useful when they have been designed to accommodate the records of more than one dyad. To the extent that different dyads engage in different activities, it may prove necessary to enlarge the matrix to include the full range of activities performed by the members of all the dyads being considered. It may also be necessary to employ an expanded matrix when no reasonable grounds can be found for assigning the members of a dyad to either the rows or the columns. In other words, when the members of several dyads can consistently be distinguished in terms of some criterion, such as sex, relative age, role or whatever, then those individuals who fall into one category should be assigned to the rows, and those who fall into the other category to the columns. However, when no workable criterion can be found to distinguish individuals across different dyads then it may be necessary to produce two Conjoint Matrices for each dyad – with an individual occupying the rows in one matrix and the columns in the other – in order to effect a proper comparison between dyads.

Finally it may be worth noting that when the rows and columns of an expanded matrix are located in the same order, then the matrix will contain a leading diagonal and it will be symmetrical about that diagonal. Entries in the leading diagonal indicate that the members of a dyad have performed the same activity concurrently, while entries in cells which mirror each other across the diagonal – what we call *corresponding* cells – indicate that the dyad has performed the same conjunction of activities on more than one occasion, but that on these occasions the roles of the participants were reversed.

2. Ordering the rows and columns

The way in which rows and columns are labelled partly depends on the type of matrix being used. In a minimal matrix the allocation of activity labels to the rows and columns is usually determined by the orders in which the activities were performed by the two parties. Because a minimal matrix is peculiar to a single dyad, the numbers of rows and columns are always the same as the numbers of separate activities performed by each person. For example, if person A had produced a sequence of activities R–N–D–N–R, and person B had produced a sequence of activities N–S–T–S–F, then A would be assigned three columns (i.e. R, N and D) and B would be assigned four rows (i.e. N, S, T and F). In an expanded matrix, on the other hand, the numbers of rows and columns always exceed the numbers of separate activities performed by each person, and the matrix always contains rows and/or columns which are not visited by the trajectory for that dyad.

An expanded matrix is defined by its possessing more columns than the number of separate activities performed by A and/or more rows than the number of separate activities performed by B. One way or another it is expanded, beyond the minimal matrix. In principle there are no constraints on the expansion of a matrix. The rows and columns may represent some or all the activities performed by the other party as well as activities that were not performed by either party. Furthermore, when several dyads are being compared in the same expanded matrix, the matrix may contain only the range of activities which was performed by members of the dyads or it may be extended to include activities that were not performed by any of the dyads.

There are several procedures for ordering the rows and columns of an expanded matrix. When the expanded matrix has been designed to include only the separate activities performed by two people, then the same order of activities is usually adopted for both rows and columns, and it usually follows the order in which the activities were initiated by the dyad. Of course this procedure cannot be used when the expanded matrix has been designed to include the separate activities performed by the members of several dyads. Under these circumstances the best idea is to calculate the average rank position of each activity across all the dyads and then to allocate activity labels to the rows and columns in accordance with the average rank position of the activities. These two procedures offer solutions to the problem of how to order rows and columns where it has been decided that only activities which *were* performed are to be included in the matrix. However, it may be felt that activities which were *not* performed should also be accommodated in the matrix. In this case it is usually necessary to appeal to some theoretical framework when ordering rows and columns. Suppose, for example, that the activities being studied are degrees of orientation to the other person. In this kind of study it may be discovered that certain orientations were not adopted by any members of the dyads being considered. But this would not present a problem because it would be possible to appeal to the compass as a basis for ordering the rows and columns. Rows and columns would be ordered according to the natural adjacency of different degrees of orientation even though some of these were not assumed by people in the dyads being studied.

The problem of ordering rows and columns is not simply a matter of ensuring that a matrix looks tidy. Admittedly, when rows and columns are ordered haphazardly then trajectories are likely to double back on themselves like a drunken spider's web, but what is more important is that a matrix which has not been organized on some principle will usually thwart any attempt to combine or collapse rows and columns in the search for superordinate patterns.

Studies of sequential structure have, to date, largely been concerned with the activities produced by one or more dyads. The tradition has been to focus exclusively on those activities which were performed rather than those which were not performed, with the result that there has been a tendency to overlook the relationship between what is and what is not done in social interaction. A left-to-right sequence description is always a description of the temporal structure of activities that were produced, and consequently it fails to accommodate the sequence within the context of other activities. This remains true even when a left-to-right sequence is located in a minimal matrix, but it is not the case when the sequence is located in an expanded matrix. By definition, an expanded matrix includes activities other than those that were separately performed by the members of a dyad. As such it allows activities which were performed to be contrasted with those that were not performed, and conjunctions of activities which did arise to be compared with those that did not.

So far we have demonstrated that there are at least three models for the description of sequences, and that the last of these, the Type Three description, can also be examined with Conjoint Analysis which involves either a minimal or some form of expanded matrix. We have also shown that Type One, Two and Three descriptions are predicated upon different assumptions about the nature of individual activity and dyadic interaction, and that these assumptions become more tenable as one progresses through the different models. The most sophisticated of these, the Type Three description, presumes that the members of a dyad are both engaged in some kind of activity or other, and, furthermore, that their activities can overlap. However it is possible to extend this model even further by supposing that just as two individuals can do the same or different things at the same time, so too each individual may perform several activities simultaneously, and these activities may overlap with each other and with those performed by the other person.

A sequence description which assumes that an individual's behaviour can adequately be described by considering a single variable or a single stream of activities is by nature *unimodal*, while a description which incorporates several variables or streams of activity is by nature *polymodal*. Type One, Two and Three descriptions are all unimodal insofar as they only provide for one variable or one stream of activities per person.[2] A Type Four description, on the other hand, presupposes that each individual is performing several activities concurrently. It assumes, in other words, that the model which holds for the dyad can also be

---

[2] A modality may be either a variable or a stream of activity. We distinguish between a variable and a stream of activity in the following way. The activities which comprise a variable are conceptually linked, but logically exclude each other. Talking and silence would be examples. A stream of activity comprises activities, some of which are neither conceptually linked nor logically exclusive. Eating, grooming and walking would be examples.

applied to individuals in the dyad. A Type Four description, which incorporates a time base, might look something like the picture in Fig. 9, where A and B are the two interactors, variable 1 is talking (T) versus remaining silent (S), and variable 2 is looking at the other person (O) versus looking away from the other person (W).

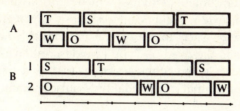

Fig. 9. Type Four description (time base)

A Type Four description is defined by its possessing at least two variables or streams of activity per person. In the illustration offered above the description records the left-to-right sequence of just two variables, namely talking and looking, for each interactor. It shows that A begins by talking while looking away, and that B begins by being silent while looking at A. Then A looks at B while he continues to talk and while B continues to be silent and look at A, and so on through the sequence. A Type Three description only includes one variable or one stream of activity per person, and it therefore only allows for an examination of conjunctions of activities between individuals. A Type Four description, on the other hand, permits an examination of conjunctions of activities both between and within individuals – in other words, it allows one to see what each person was doing while the other person was doing something, as well as what each person was doing while he or she was doing something else. Type Four descriptions have not been used very often. Those who have employed this type of description include Kendon (1967, 1976), Golani (1976) and Collett and Lamb (1980). The notation schemes of Laban (1956) and more especially Eshkol and Wachmann (1968) incorporate a Type Four description.

If we look at a Type Three description again we see that it may describe either a single variable or a single stream of activity. In the former case it may deal with, say, different types of gaze, in the latter with activities like eating, grooming, walking, etc. When a Type Three description deals with a stream of activity it necessarily engages in 'modality-hopping'. By this we mean it describes, in the same stream, activities which would be found in different modalities in a Type Four description where each modality represented a variable rather than a stream of activity (e.g. Fabricius and Jansson 1963). Of course a Type Four description may also contain modalities which describe streams of activity rather than variables. When it does it too will engage in modality-hopping. As the term suggests, modality-hopping is found wherever a stream contains activities which rightfully belong to different variables. To this extent sequence descriptions which engage in modality-hopping can be seen to do to the individual what a Type Two description does to the dyad. A Type Two description assumes that one person is inert while the other is active, just as a modality-hopping description assumes that one modality is out of commission while the other is in action.

A Type Four description can also be transformed from a time base to an event base formulation, but not the reverse. The principle for deriving an event base is similar to that used with a Type Three description, except that in the case of a Type Four description the initiation of *any* new activity, whether it occurs between or within individuals, constitutes another activity unit on the event base record. Fig. 10 shows what the Type Four description offered in Fig. 9 would look like once it had been given an event base.

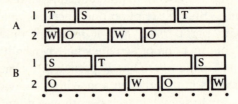

Fig. 10. Type Four description (event base)

Generally speaking, an event base formulation will tend to look more like a time base formulation in the case of a Type Four description than it will in the case of a Type Three description. This happens because there are usually more changes between streams in the former, and because the more changes there are between streams the more an event base will approximate to a time base. This notwithstanding, it is nevertheless worth noting that there are important differences between the event base record and the time base record for a Type Four description, such that certain activities, which actually take longer than others, will appear as being shorter in the event base record, and vice versa. This may occur within the same stream of activity for an individual, between the same streams for different individuals, or between different streams for different individuals.

In principle there is no limit to the number of variables or streams of activity that can be included in a Type Four description. Each new variable or stream of activity merely requires the addition of two new rows in the description, and the description should be able to tolerate a fairly large number of rows provided it remains easy to read. However, it is at the point at which a Type Four description is transformed into a Conjoint Matrix that the problem of number becomes most pressing. The introduction of new activities for consideration in a Type Three description increases the number of rows and columns that are needed in its Conjoint Matrix in an additive fashion. But the situation is a little more complicated when one comes to a Type Four description. A Type Four description is also concerned with the conjunction of activities *within* each individual, and that is why the addition of new activities for consideration in a Type Four description inflates the number of rows and columns that are needed in its conjoint representation multiplicatively. In a minimal matrix for a Type Four description all the conjunctions of all the activities performed by A are arrayed across the columns in such a way that the different activities of one stream are nested in the different activities of another stream, and so on depending on the number of streams being considered. The same applies to B and the organization of the rows. The total number of rows or columns is always equivalent to the product of the number of activity types in all the streams. In the example offered earlier there are four rows and four columns, that is $2(T + S) \times 2(O + W)$ in each case.

In deriving a Conjoint Matrix for a Type Four description it is necessary to begin by deciding on the order of importance of the variables or streams of activity. Suppose that one had decided that the question of whether or not someone is talking is more important than the question of whether or not they are looking at the other person, then one would nest the looking dichotomy within the talking dichotomy. If there were other variables, then their constituent activities might be nested under these. Having decided on the order of the variables one would arrange the combinations of activities along the rows and columns, and then proceed to trace the trajectory of the sequence through the activity space. Fig. 11 shows what the Conjoint Matrix for our Type Four description would look like.

The Conjoint Analysis presented in Fig. 11 shows the trajectory of the dyad through various conjunctions of activities involving talking and

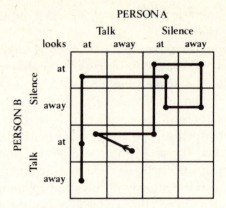

Fig. 11. Conjoint Analysis (minimal) of Type Four description

looking. The trajectory here consists of horizontal and vertical movements, where horizontal movements indicate that a new activity or activities have been performed by A, and vertical movements that a new activity or activities have been performed by B. It is possible to distinguish the introduction of one new activity from the introduction of two new activities by examining the relationship between the rows or columns connected by the trajectory. For example a change in one variable by A would appear as a shift between columns 1 and 3, or columns 2 and 4, whereas a simultaneous change in two variables by A would appear as a shift between columns 1 and 4, or columns 2 and 3. The same would apply for B's movements through the rows. When there are vertical or horizontal movements it means that there has been some change or changes on the part of one of the interactors, but when there are diagonal movements which cross rows and columns at the same time it means that there have been simultaneous changes on the part of both interactors. Again it is possible to distinguish diagonal movements which are due to a single change per person from those which are due to more than one change per person, and these in turn from diagonal movements which are due to a single change by one person and more than one change by the other person.

The Conjoint Analysis we have been considering has obvious advantages over the pair of matrices which could be extracted separately for the variables of talking and looking. Had we produced a Type Three description for talking and another Type Three description for looking, they would have had the appearance shown in Fig. 12.

The only way in which a Conjoint Matrix which contains two or more

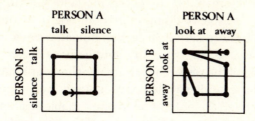

Fig. 12. Conjoint Analyses (minimal) of Type Three descriptions

variables can be recovered from Conjoint Matrices which consider these variables separately is by marking the time or order of each transition across the two matrices. However, it should be said that this is a rather cumbersome procedure because it is seldom easy to see how the variables presented in different matrices interrelate.

A Conjoint Matrix can be derived from a Type Three or a Type Four description which has either a time base or an event base. When the description has a time base then information about the duration of activities and their conjunctions can either be included in or excluded from the Conjoint Matrix. In the examples offered so far the Conjoint Matrices have all ignored the duration of events. We have shown how a Conjoint Matrix can be used to represent the trajectory of a sequence through various conjunctions of activities, but not how it can simultaneously be used to provide information about the duration of each conjunction. In order to produce a Conjoint Matrix which has a time base one can simply use the expedient of recording the duration of each conjunction beside (or inside) the dot which represents the stationary period of the trajectory through that cell. This would show how long the dyad had spent performing the conjunction of activities defined by that row and that column, and it would also be possible to recover the duration of each activity, simply by adding the time values of all the dots connected by a straight line through a row or column.

A Type Four description, and its corresponding Conjoint Matrix, is always more powerful than one or more Type Three descriptions because it contains information about the relationship between variables or streams of activity within individuals, as well as information about the relationship between variables or streams of activity across individuals. A Type Three description presupposes that a single variable or stream of activity can adequately capture the complexity of a sequence, but even the most cursory observation should be sufficient to indicate that behaviour is organized in several modalities simultaneously, and that people are capable of doing more than one thing at a time.[3]

It would not be necessary to insist that human behaviour is polymodal were it not the case that so many studies have regarded it as being otherwise. Most of the research on human behaviour has been unimodal in character: those studies which have ignored the temporal dimension have usually limited their attention to one variable at a time, while those which have been concerned with sequential organization have invariably looked at one stream of activity. There are two arguments that can be used to support a unimodal conception of behaviour, and both are rather weak. The first is that a unimodal conception renders a study more manageable by eliminating extraneous variables. This of course begs the question of what is meant by extraneous, and raises the possibility that those aspects of behaviour which have not been considered may throw light on those which have. The second argument is that where it can be shown that the operation of one variable adequately accounts for the operation of another variable, it can reasonably be assumed that extraneous variables are unimportant. The trouble with this argument is that variables which are thought to be extraneous may in fact offer a more convincing explanation than the variable being considered.

We have seen that there are at least four types of description of interaction sequences, and that they differ in the assumptions that they entertain about the nature of individual and social activity. We have also proposed that there is an underlying progression from the Type One description, which is the least acceptable, to a Type Four description, which is the most realistic of the four types. A Type One description, we have noticed, assumes that interactors take turns and that they only perform one activity per turn. A Type Two description also assumes that interactors take turns, but it allows that they may produce more than one activity per turn. A Type Three description parts company from a Type One and a Type Two description by accepting that individuals may be concurrently active, and that their activities may overlap with each other. A Type Four description takes a further step by assuming that

---

[3] As Bakeman (1978) has pointed out, a sequence description which contains several modalities can always be reduced to one which contains a single hypothetical modality. In other words, it is possible to collapse each individual's concurrent activities in the different modalities into categories of conjoint activity, such as looking-and-talking or looking-and-silence, and then to locate these categories in a Type Three description. A Type Three description can, in turn, be reduced to a single sequence of symbols which defines the conjunction of conjoint categories across two individuals.

each individual can be engaged in several activities at the same time, and these activities may overlap both between and within individuals. The assumptions inherent in these four types of sequence description are distilled and summarized in Fig. 13.

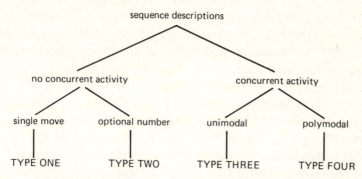

Fig. 13. Assumptions of the four types of sequence description

The tree diagram in Fig. 13 suggests that the first decision an investigator needs to make is whether or not he is going to regard the separate activities of two individuals as being organized concurrently. If he assumes that their activities are not organized concurrently, then he must decide whether these activities are to be arranged in terms of a single move (Type One) or several moves (Type Two) per turn. If, on the other hand, he assumes that interactors can be concurrently active, then he has a simple choice of deciding between a unimodal (Type Three) and a polymodal (Type Four) conception of individual activities.[4]

As one proceeds from a Type One to a Type Four description one notices not only a steady accumulation of more realistic assumptions about social and individual behaviour, but also a corresponding increase in the range of analyses available to each type of description. A Type One description, for example, assumes that each individual makes only one move per turn. This means that a Type One description cannot be used to examine the hierarchical organization of an individual's activities. A Type Two description, on the other hand, allows any number of activities per turn, with the result that it is possible to look at the way in

---

[4] The four descriptions that we have presented are all models of inter-individual rather than intra-individual processes. It is also possible, however, to identify two types of intra-individual description, one where the individual produces a single stream of activity, the other where the individual produces two or more streams of activity concurrently (cf. Dawkins and Dawkins 1976).

which the separate activities produced by an individual combine to form superordinate units. This is also true for a Type Three and a Type Four description, although, interestingly, the notion of a turn is not automatically evident in these types of description. In a Type One and a Type Two description a turn corresponds to some activity or sequence of activities produced by the individual; in other words, it is inherent in the definition of activity. But because Type Three and Type Four descriptions allow for concurrent activities it is never clear, short of applying some arbitrary definition, which activities are to form the basis of turn-taking. In other words, in a polymodal description individuals may 'take turns' in several modalities. Where this is the case it will be necessary to specify which modality or stream of activity is being used to identify turn-taking. This notwithstanding, it is fair to say that investigations of hierarchical organization seldom present any problem for a Type Three description, or for that matter a Type Two description. This is because the candidates for combination are all located in the same stream. However, in a Type Four description the candidate activities occur in different streams, and consequently it may be difficult to determine exactly which activities mark the onset, and which the termination, of superordinate categories of activity. Hierarchical organization necessarily implies subsumption, with some units being subsumed under others. The requirement of subsumption is invariably satisfied in a Type Two and a Type Three description, if only because there is no alternative. However in a Type Four description it often happens that an activity in one stream initiates a superordinate unit while an activity in another stream terminates it. It may even be the case that the activity which initiates the superordinate units actually terminates after the superordinate unit ends.

In our work on introductions, for example, we have used a time base Type Four description to record the speech and various motor activities (such as looking, orientation, smiling, touching, pointing, etc) which occur when someone introduces two people to each other (Collett and Lamb 1980). We have also identified the phases of each person's performance in terms of the function being fulfilled by their activities. The introducer, for example, can usually be seen to go through three phases, namely 'establishing' the parties by indicating that an introduction is about to take place, 'introducing' them to each other, and 'completing' the sequence. The introducee and the receiver can also be seen to go through three phases, in this case 'preparing', 'greeting', and then 'engaging' each other in conversation or 'disengaging' from each other. When the phases or function segments of each person are examined in relation to the various streams of activity that they have produced, it often emerges that a segment which starts with an activity in one stream is terminated with a different activity in another stream. For example, the introducer may begin the 'establishment' segment by extending his arm towards the person he is about to introduce, and then go on to terminate that segment and begin the 'introduction' segment with a verbal formula. All of this would be completely unproblematic were it not for the fact that hierarchy requires subsumption, and subsumption in turn that the units being combined occur in the same stream, or if in different streams, that they do not begin before or end after the superordinate unit.

One of the cardinal doctrines of action theorists is that behaviour is organized hierarchically. Small units of action, we are told, combine to form larger units, which in turn are subsumed under still larger ones. This idea appears to have been inspired by the successful application of hierarchical models to language, where phonemes combine into morphs and morphemes, and thence into sentences. Action theorists such as Birdwhistell (1970), Scheflen (1973) and Kendon (1972) have insisted that similar patterns can be detected in sequences of non-linguistic activity. Birdwhistell, for example, is quite explicit in his use of a linguistic analogy. He speaks of kinemorphs combining to form kinemorphic constructions, just as phonemes combine to form morphemes.

Basically there are three types of hierarchy. The first type, which we call a *rank hierarchy*, is defined by the principle of exclusion, where the members of subordinate categories are excluded from superior categories. This is exemplified by the army, where privates are subordinate to lance-corporals, who in turn are subordinate to corporals, and so on. Although subordinate categories are related to superior categories, they are not constituents of superior categories. Nelson (1973), for example, makes the point that the Curia is not a part of the Pope, and Dawkins (1976) remarks that the soldier is part of his platoon but not of his platoon commander.

There are two types of hierarchy which are organized on the principle of inclusion. These are the *aggregate hierarchy* and the *sequential hierarchy*, and they can further be divided into three sub-types in terms of the nature of their subordinate and superordinate categories. In an aggregate hierarchy subordinate categories are included in superordinate categories, and each type of category may be either *substantial* or *conceptual*. This means that substantial categories may be contained in other substantial categories, substantial categories may be contained in conceptual categories, or conceptual categories may be contained in other conceptual categories (but conceptual categories cannot be contained in substantial ones). When we say, for example, that walls are made of bricks and mortar, and a house of walls, we imply an aggregate hierarchy where certain substantial categories are contained within other substantial categories. Alternatively when we say that oranges and lemons are citrus fruit, we provide an aggregate hierarchy in which the subordinate categories are substantial and the superordinate categories conceptual. The superordinate categories are conceptual because it is impossible to point to a citrus fruit without pointing at an orange, a lemon, or whatever. This type of aggregate hierarchy is usually called a *taxonomy*. The third type of aggregate hierarchy is found whenever conceptual categories subsume other conceptual categories, as in the case of laws constituting a legal code.

Aggregate hierarchies have a static view of the world. Whether their subordinate and superordinate categories are substantial or conceptual, they all deal with synchronic organization. By contrast a sequential hierarchy is concerned with diachronic organization and the ways in which units that are arranged serially can be combined into categories which in turn can be combined into others. Sequential hierarchy also takes three forms, depending on the characteristics of the subordinate and superordinate categories. In the study of social interaction a category may be regarded as substantial when it is concerned with the *morphology* of behaviours, and conceptual when it is concerned with their *function*. This means that one can consider morphological categories which are contained in other morphological categories, morphological categories which are contained in functional categories, or functional categories which are contained in other functional categories.

A good example of a morphological–morphological sequential hierarchy may be found in the case of walking, where individual movements of the limbs combine in sequence to form steps. Here both the subordinate and superordinate categories are realized substantially. A morphological–functional hierarchy might appear in the coding of a greeting. If the separate movements of someone's hand back and forth through the air were labelled as a 'wave', then the relationship of movements to label would be one of morphology to function. If the 'wave' were then combined in series with other categories such as 'verbal greeting', then one would also have a functional–functional hierarchy. In both cases the 'wave' may be regarded as functional rather than morphological because it involves ascription of semantic rather than formal properties.[5]

Unimodal sequence descriptions need not present any problems for the investigator who is intent upon producing an hierarchical arrangement of his material. This is true whether the hierarchy he has in mind is morphological–morphological, morphological–functional or functional–functional. Small morphological units of speech can be combined into larger morphological units as readily as morphological units of movement can be combined to form functional categories, or functional categories to form other superordinate functional categories. But when an investigator attempts to construct any one of the three types of sequential hierarchy using polymodal material he will encounter serious problems of subsumption. The problem of subsumption is not peculiar to a particular type of sequential hierarchy, but rather to attempts to identify hierarchical arrangements in polymodal material.

It appears that the transposition of hierarchical notions from language to action has been rather hasty and uncritical. For one thing, speech is produced as a *single* stream of activity, whereas action is made up of *several* streams of concurrent activity. This means that while it is relatively easy to identify hierarchical arrangements in speech, it is not so easy to detect them in action. However, when one produces a Type Two or a Type Three description this does not present itself as a problem. In both cases activities are located in the same stream, and they can therefore be combined as readily as can the units of speech. But this is only because Type Two and Type Three descriptions obscure the problem of subsumption. A Type Four description, on the other hand, exposes the problem of subsumption. It provides a far more comprehensive account of people's performances, but in the process it calls into question the idea that subordinate units can neatly be subsumed within superordinate ones.

When an investigator commits himself to a Type Three or a Type Four description – that is, when he assumes that interactors can be concur-

---

[5] In their discussion of the relationship between 'acts' and 'actions', Harré and Secord (1972) speak of 'movements we wish to treat as actions', and actions in which 'we see acts performed'. 'All sorts of movements,' they suggest, 'can constitute the actions in the performance of which the act is carried out.' (p. 158.) The example they offer is marriage, which is an 'act' involving different 'actions' in different cultures, while the culturally accepted set of actions need not require identical movements in every case. In our scheme the relationship between movement and action would form part of a substantial–conceptual aggregate hierarchy because it is concerned with rules of equivalence. By contrast, the relationship between action and act would form part of a functional–functional sequential hierarchy because it is concerned with the combination of categories through time.

rently active – then he will also be able to cast his material in the form of a Conjoint Matrix. A Conjoint Matrix has several distinct advantages over the left-to-right sequence description from which it is derived:

(i) The most obvious virtue of the Conjoint Matrix is that it captures sequences in a form which is immediately visible and which forces one to think in terms of *conjunctions* of activities.

(ii) When a left-to-right description is transferred to a Conjoint Matrix it is much easier to determine the frequency of individual and joint activities, as well as the way in which the sequence iterates through combinations of activities. In a complex left-to-right description the same activity or combination of activities may occur on several occasions without it being obvious that this has happened. However, when this same sequence is placed in a Conjoint Matrix this kind of repetition should automatically be clear. These advantages may of course accrue without any loss of the information contained in a left-to-right description.[6]

(iii) A Conjoint Matrix depicts an interaction sequence in a space which can be expanded to include activities which were not performed by the parties being considered. This is especially useful when the sequences of several dyads are recorded in the same matrix. When the left-to-right descriptions of several dyads are placed side by side, it is often difficult to see exactly what they have in common, but when these same sequences are relocated in a single Conjoint Matrix the pattern of their similarities and differences can readily be detected.

(iv) A Conjoint Matrix can be analysed, either by disregarding time or by bearing time in mind. In the first type of analysis one can simply calculate the cell totals, the row and column totals or the variances for the rows and columns. In a sequence analysis one can examine the row transitions, the column transitions or the cell transitions. Furthermore, because a Conjoint Matrix retains all the information on the string of events which preceded a particular row, column or

---

[6] The closest methodological relative of the Conjoint Matrix is Coombs's 'conjunctive analysis' (Coombs 1964, Coombs and Smith 1973). This technique allows the binary entries in a matrix to be described in a set of overlapping sectors which express the combinations of the columns. Coombs and Smith have shown how this method can be used to trace the development of an individual, or a group of individuals, through several stages. It is possible to envisage this method being applied to social interaction data by assigning, say, half the columns to one person and half to the other person, although it would not be amenable to sequences which contained iterations of the same activities.

cell transition it can more readily be used to determine nth order transitions than other sequence analytic techniques.

There are various approaches to the study of social interaction. Some of these assume that it is quite in order to examine the relationship between behaviours without taking their temporal organization into account, but there are others which take the view that the proper study of social interaction should involve an investigation of its sequential properties. Those which fall into this second category require a method for describing sequences. We have outlined four of these methods for describing sequences and have demonstrated how each is founded upon different assumptions about the nature of social and individual action. Finally we have shown that the more advanced methods of sequence description entertain more realistic assumptions and that they also admit modes of analysis which promise to reveal the true complexity of social interaction.

References

Bakeman, R. (1978) 'Untangling streams of behavior: sequential analyses of observation data.' In G. P. Sackett (ed.), *Observing behavior. Vol. 2: Collection and analysis methods*. University Park Press, Baltimore.

Bales, R. F. (1950) *Interaction process analysis: a method for the study of small groups*. Addison-Wesley, Reading, Mass.

Birdwhistell, R. (1970) *Kinesics and context*. University of Pennsylvania Press, Philadelphia.

Collett, P. and R. Lamb (1980) 'Introductory manoeuvres.' (In preparation.)

Condon, W. A. and W. D. Ogston (1967) 'A segmentation of behaviour.' *Journal of Psychiatric Research* **5**, 221–35.

Coombs, C. H. (1964) *A theory of data*. Wiley, New York.

Coombs, C. H. and J. E. K. Smith (1973) 'On the detection of structure of attitudes and developmental processes.' *Psychological Review* **80**, 337–51.

Dawkins, R. (1976) 'Hierarchical organisation: a candidate principle for ethology.' In P. P. G. Bateson and R. A. Hinde (eds.), *Growing points in ethology*. Cambridge University Press, Cambridge.

Dawkins, R. and M. Dawkins (1976) 'Hierarchical organisation and postural facilitation: rules for grooming in flies.' *Animal Behaviour* **24**, 739–55.

Duncan, S. (1972) 'Some signals and rules for taking speaking turns in conversations.' *Journal of Personality and Social Psychology* **23**, 283–92.

Eshkol, N. and A. Wachmann (1968) *Movement notation*. Movement Notation Society, Tel Aviv.

Fabricius, E. and A.-M. Jansson (1963) 'Laboratory observation on the reproductive behaviour of the pigeon.' *Animal Behaviour* **11**, 534–47.

Flanders, N. A. (1970) *Analyzing teaching behavior*. Addison-Wesley, Reading, Mass.

Frank, J. (1963) *The widening gyre*. Rutgers University Press, New Brunswick, N.J.

Golani, I. (1976) 'Homeostatic motor processes in mammalian interactions: a choreography of display.' In P. P. G. Bateson and P. H. Klopfer (eds.), *Perspectives in ethology, vol. 2.* Plenum Press, London.

Harré, R. and P. F. Secord (1972) *The explanation of social behaviour.* Blackwell, Oxford.

Jaffe, J. and S. Feldstein (1970) *Rhythms of dialogue.* Academic Press, New York.

Kendon, A. (1967) 'Some functions of gaze direction in two-person conversation.' *Acta Psychologica* **26**, 22–63.

— (1972) 'Some relationships between body movement and speech: an analysis of an example.' In A. Siegman and B. Pope (eds.), *Studies in dyadic communication.* Pergamon Press, Elmsford, N.Y.

— (1976) 'Some functions of the face in a kissing round.' *Semiotica* **15**, 299–334.

Laban R. (1956) *Principles of dance and movement notation.* Macdonald & Evans, London.

Nelson, K. (1973) 'Does the holistic study of behaviour have a future?' In P. P. G. Bateson and P. H. Klopfer (eds.), *Perspectives in ethology.* Plenum Press, London.

Scheflen, A. E. (1973) *How behavior means.* Gordon & Breach, New York.

Yngve, V. H. (1969) 'On getting a word in edgewise.' In M. A. Campbell (ed.), *Papers from the 6th Regional Meeting, Chicago Linguistic Circle.* Chicago Linguistic Circle, Chicago.

3. Rules in the organization of action

Introduction

In Chapter 2 practical actions were subject to analysis. The work reported there shows that action sequences are ordered structures, taking just the means–end format we proposed hypothetically in Chapter 1. One is naturally prompted to ask whether perhaps social and expressive activity can be treated similarly, that is analysed as structured sequences of actions.

A strong research tradition has recently sprung up in social psychology based on the idea that the incidents and episodes within which people engage each other can be shown to be sequentially structured, if the activity is analysed in terms of intended actions meant as the performance of socially meaningful acts. In this chapter various consequences and limitations of the ideas behind the new tradition are discussed.

A central feature of this approach to action is the demand that actions should always be seen as 'coupled' to what Clarke calls 'incidents'. An incident is an episode of social interaction characterized by several features, including diachronic structure, means–end organization and hierarchy of goals, and by the fact that several persons contribute to its serial unfolding. Various models can be used to provide analytical and explanatory concepts for understanding incidents, including likening incidents to games and to dramatic performances. But the most pervasive analogy suggested by Clarke is with language production. This suggests that action studies ought to borrow from the linguists' use of 'rule' and to refine the means–end format to a rule-following process.

Adopting a general linguistic model has some immediate effects on methodology. One must begin with the analysis of concrete cases, that is use the intensive design, studying single cases as typical exemplars of kinds. By the application of generic act–action categories, corresponding to the use of generic grammatical categories, structure can be discerned, since there are sequences of types of acts; e.g. insults are followed by protests which are followed by apologies, more often than mere chance would allow. The upshot of this kind of study should be a 'grammar', that is a set of hypothetical rules from which the structure of an incident type exemplified in the cases studied intensively can be reconstructed. But actual grammars, as proposed by linguists, have proved not to be adequate as models for action genesis theories. The comparison of action with speech production offers an encouragement to use a certain kind of method, rather than specific and detailed analogues, which could be immediately transferred to social analysis.

By bringing in ideas from systems theory the development and unfolding of action sequences can be followed. All this can have quite direct application in the management of practical affairs, and, by using the techniques and practices already successful in therapy, management and so on, the researcher can borrow from already existing informal methods for analysing and understanding actions undertaken in pursuance of the performance of social acts.

As Clarke shows, the idea that much of human action is rule-governed has animated much recent research both theoretical and practical. The question now arises, is there any restriction to the kinds of episodes and incidents that are susceptible to the analytical use of the associated models? Just what incidents should be treated as analogues of rituals, games or dramatic performances? In his contribution Brenner points out that while these ideas work well for some categories of circumscribed situations and action sequences, there are many 'open' sequences where the situation of action is never fully or stably defined. In these kinds of social events even the rules of action are changeable, and may be deliberately changed. Instead of looking for standard forms, an investigator of open incidents may need to be on the look-out for processes of bargaining and negotiating, animated by an interplay of individual strategic considerations. In directing his research exclusively at the discovery of action types prescribed by pre-existing rules and local conventions, an investigator may overlook essential dynamic aspects of the mutual production of the action.

The fact that people sometimes deliberately leave their actions not fully defined, and that they may actively discuss, dispute and negotiate the rules as they go along, sets some limits to the proper field of application of the idea of a 'grammar' of action. In particular it suggests the necessity of keeping in mind the important distinction between 'closed' and 'open' episodes. Incidents in the latter category are not fully prescribed by the kind of rules that control the structure of the former.

In the third part of this chapter Peter Marsh reports on his empirical study of the ritualized 'fights' that form part of the way status and social hierarchy is determined among football fans. He shows that rules function in the control of the production of ritual action, ensuring that it is orderly and structured. But Marsh also demonstrates the role of rules in the way the events that have occurred among groups of rival fans are given meaning in later discussion and negotiation. It is the systematic ways that the 'fights' are interpreted that allows them to be used in the distribution of honour and reputation among the participants. There is a 'grammar' of action, in Clarke's sense, but the incidents, to use Brenner's term, are 'closed'.

The sequential analysis of action structure

DAVID D. CLARKE

Consider any human action and the chances are that you will find it occurs as part of a larger sequence, episode, project, scenario or incident, rather than in isolation from its context. It is almost inconceivable that a mode of conduct could exist in which people selected items *independently* from the repertoire of things they know how to do, and carried them out as a succession of unrelated events. That would be no more like a normal human activity than a random selection of words from a dictionary is like a sentence. In fact real sentences or activity sequences that have been 'scrambled' into the wrong order are often so clearly the disordered version of something sensible and familiar, that the original order can be recovered by people who have never seen it before (Clarke 1975). You can make 'anagrams' with action sequences, in other words, which show them to be orderly and rule-governed. If you do not believe that this indicates they have a special structure, try making an anagram of your telephone number and having someone rediscover the original from that.

Structure activity sequences exist on many levels of description from brief conversations through relationships, disputes, careers and life-stories, up to historical epochs or perhaps even the whole course of history itself, which although difficult to predict, could hardly be called random. Analyses may be done in a similar way on many different scales, treating any given event as an object whose subcomponents are of interest, or as a single part in a larger whole. No matter what the scale might be I will call these structures by the general name of *incidents*. The style of analysis to be described here will be called *incident dynamics* in order to acknowledge the influence of Forrester's system dynamics method (e.g. Forrester 1972) on the way the problem is conceived and tackled.

The anatomy of an incident

Incidents as a whole do not share any single defining feature or property. Instead they have a family resemblance in which a number of features are usually found, but with different exceptions in different cases. They may involve the practical order of action (Harré, this volume) or the expressive order or both, but the following properties tend on the whole to recur.

1. *Complex structure*. Each incident is a thing of many parts, where the parts are generally actions or acts, and the relations between them may include causality, similarity, facilitation, inhibition, means–ends, and many others.

2. *Boundaries*. Incidents have a beginning and an end, at least in the sense that systems have boundaries. These may reflect the purpose of the study more than the nature of the phenomenon, may be imposed by the analyst and may change from one occasion to another. Nonetheless it remains feasible and useful to treat some objects, events and relations as being within the immediate domain of enquiry, while other entities constitute an environment, separated by a boundary, and in some cases at least in transaction or mutual influence with the system itself, depending on whether it is 'open' or 'closed'. It does not matter that for one study the system may be a cell in the environment of the body, and in another the whole body interacting with its surroundings. In the same way an argument, on one occasion, is seen in the context of a relationship, and on another occasion the whole relationship can be seen in the context of a person's life-story.

3. *Hierarchical structure*. Incidents are hierarchically structured. Small pieces make up the larger pieces and so on. That much is obvious and true for most things from a beetle to a housing estate. There is a more interesting sense, though, in which hierarchical structure can play an important part. This is seen most clearly in the organization of words (or more properly morphemes) into sentences, but is probably important in many other cases as well. At first sight the succession of words (or actions) might appear to be built up from beginning to end, earliest to latest, so that each item is chosen in the light of those that went before. This is what linguists call a *left-to-right* construction. In the alternative hierarchical or *top-to-bottom* construction it is actually the hierarchical

structure that organizes things, so that sentences are not so much built up as broken down, starting not with the first item and then the second and so on, but with a general notion or symbol standing for the whole thing, which is then subdivided over and over again to produce more and more specific versions of the sequence that will finally result. Of course the end result is *produced* from left to right, with the first item being spoken first and so on. It may even be planned and constructed that way in the head of the speaker, but as a way of writing abstract formulae of sentence constitution for the purpose of specifying a language, the top-to-bottom approach has distinct technical advantages. Chief amongst these is the capacity to produce sequences within sequences, digression, nestings or embeddings as they are variously called. For instance it is easy enough to write formulae to produce sentences like

'The company the people favoured prospered'
provided you treat
'The company (X) prospered'
as the basic framework, with other rules to elaborate (X) into its possible varieties. This is a simple hierarchical procedure. It can even be used recursively, that is to say repetitively within itself, so that a procedure for producing subordinate clauses may include yet further subordinate clauses within those it produces, by invoking *itself* halfway through, giving for example

'The company the people the government taxed favoured prospered'. If on the other hand the sentence is viewed as a succession of words built up in order, each relating to its immediate predecessor then it would seem that tax was favoured and favour prospered. Using that approach other forms of structural and semantic anomaly would tend to arise as well.

　　In the planning of activity generally the same kind of thing is to be seen. No-one (in his right mind) plans a holiday for instance by thinking 'First I will go out of the house and lock the door, then I will get into the car, start the engine and engage reverse . . .' Planning occurs from the larger activity units down towards the smaller ones that make them up, so the first stage might be to decide on a package holiday in Spain; next to consider dates, reservations and cost; under reservations to consider which travel agent to go to and when to book, and so on. There is a complication, however, when we come to incidents involving several people. Unlike a sentence or some holiday plans, these are not entirely under the control of one person, and therefore a purely hierarchical process seems less likely. How could a sequence be generated by the elaboration of one overall descriptor, when no one actor is in a position to dictate how the contributions of others will be deployed in the final structure? Neither can they plan the unfolding of the hierarchy collectively, at least in those cases where any communication in the service of joint planning would itself count as an output pattern whose coordination needed to be explained. In this respect conversation is particularly problematic. Its structure is neither entirely hierarchical nor entirely left-to-right, and any hierarchical organization it does display must be engineered from the bottom upwards, since by definition it is only the exchange of messages that could be a medium of coordination, and yet it is precisely that exchange of messages whose hierarchical arrangement is to be explained. To put that another way, the problem is that conversation involves several generative subprocesses (corresponding to the individual people), which collaborate to produce a single structured entity (the conversation), and this has only its own past history with which to organize and coordinate its future structure.

Hierarchical control structures in action sequences also mean that special techniques of analysis have to be used, but we shall come to that later.

4. *Temporal extent*. Incidents do not occur in a flash but occupy a period of time. Furthermore their structure exists in the time dimensions. It is diachronic. In contrast to the morphology of a crystal, which is a synchronic structure, the parts of an incident are separated by time rather than space, and the relations that exist between them have various temporal implications. For instance causation, means–ends relations, and strategies and outcomes relate past, present and future in different ways.

5. *Discrete events*. The duration of an incident is divided into a series of discrete events, happening (more or less) one at a time and in succession, like words on a page, or beads on a string. They lend themselves to description in narrative form as opposed to a map showing the arrangement of objects on a two-dimensional surface.

6. *Polygenesis*. Incidents typically involve several parties, none of whom can completely foresee or control what will happen.

7. *Discrete outcomes*. Incidents tend to result in one of a set of clearly differentiated outcomes, amongst which people hold strong prefer-

ences. An interview results in a job or not for each candidate, and one as opposed to another person being employed, as far as the interviewer is concerned. Note that the set of outcomes may not look the same from the viewpoint of different participants. Likewise a trial may result in conviction or acquittal, peace talks may lead to reconciliation or renewed hostilities, and so on.

8. *Strategies and outcomes.* Often the content of the incident exists in order to determine the outcome. It is *just* because there are different states of affairs that could be engineered to be outcomes, that people are engaged in the activities they are, employing actions as strategies, often competitively, to bring about the result they prefer. Therefore the form the incident takes will depend largely upon the outcomes available, the participants' preferences between them, and the means–ends relations allowable by social convention and natural law.

The analysis of structure

As with all interesting problems in science there are obstacles to understanding. The Duke of Wellington once said 'All the business of war, and indeed all the business of life, is to endeavour to find what you don't know from what you do; that's what I called "guessing what was on the other side of the hill".' In this case there are two hills obscuring our view of action structure. First is the difficulty of reading other minds to know what feelings, plans and motives lie behind a pattern of observable activity. The second problem, of greater concern here, arises from the need to describe *sets* of incidents or sequences, not just individual cases. The single instance presents no problem. Ultimately its description boils down to a list of things that happened, in their order of occurrence. General patterns and laws are much harder to represent. Returning yet again to the example of language, the description of a single sentence is unproblematic and uninteresting. The concoction of some formula or grammar, however, that can represent simultaneously all and only the sentences of the language is an enormous undertaking. So too a canonical description of the incidents in a given class, or typical of a certain situation or person, is very difficult to arrive at. It becomes particularly important when the diachronic structure of incidents is to be used in the construction of forecasting models.

Any given circumstances could give rise to a number of alternative future scenarios, just as any chess position can be played out in a large

number of ways. If all the possibilities could be represented economi-
cally, the same procedure of optimal choice could be employed, but a
combinatorial explosion sets in, and the set of possible future sequences
becomes unstateable. If it were possible to write some kind of behaviour
'grammar' which could express the combinatorial constraints on future
events for a given set of circumstances, there would be considerable
scope for policy analysis, planning, modelling and forecasting of kinds
that do not exist today.

How then should a structural analysis of incidents be carried out?
Clearly experimental methods are unlikely to help, since the criteria of
an experimental topic are not met. The study, however, need be no less
scientific for that, as witness the non-experimental but highly respected
sciences like cosmology and anatomy. The experimental method is most
suited to phenomena having a small scale, short duration, manipulable
causes, observable effects, and traceable connections between cause and
effect (rather than long and variable delays, and the convoluted interactive many-to-many mappings between influences and outcomes). As
general characteristics of human activity patterns, no list could be less
promising. It is not even clear that the criteria apply to all that many
physical systems either. Since quantum/field theories, complex mani-
folds, systems theory, cybernetics and computer modelling have become the stuff of the advanced sciences, the experimental method, as
advocated by some psychologists, has joined the brass astrolabe and the
Leyden jar in the museum of scientific history.

Exploration by virtue of cause, or sufficient prior conditions, is not
the only goal of science. Many sciences are structural rather than causal
and they work by analysis and resynthesis, dissection, decomposition
and parsing. Their aim is to tease apart the fabric of nature, following
connections, noting boundaries and configurations, charting, mapping
and finally modelling. It is perhaps true that on the whole
those phenomena that consist of non-random distributions of events
in time have been treated causally, while those involving configurations of matter in space have been looked at structurally, but there is no
absolute reason why this must be so. Patterns of events in time
are just as amenable to a structural analysis as objects in space, and
this alternative view has distinct advantages in the interpretation of
incidents.

A third category of explanation, by virtue of sense, reason or meaning
has been proposed by Harré and Secord (1972) as particularly appropriate for human social action. Briefly their argument is that we tend very

reasonably in everyday life to explain mechanical events by cause and human actions by reason. The belief that causal explanation is more scientific is only a misconception brought about because most of the sciences we might look to for examples have quite appropriately used causal explanations as they have been studying material–mechanical processes. When we come to consider a science of action, what should be retained as the guiding principle of scientific thought is not the preoccupation with causation, but the *appropriateness* of the style of explanation we use to the nature of the thing to be explained. If our common sense is any guide, we should be explaining action according to reasons, rules and goals, and if the precedents of science are to be followed in a more general way, then it should be just that kind of insight that we attempt to formulate in precise theories, and test according to its implications for future observations, and the quality and coherence of our intellectual scheme.

Aristotle went one step further still, to suggest four classes of 'cause' or explanation, called material causes (the enabling conditions or powers that make something a possibility), final causes (the purposes or reasons for which something is done, as in the Harré and Secord scheme), efficient causes (which are like causal explanation as we know it today), and formal causes (which are the shaping factors governing the form of something which *other* factors have caused to happen in some form or another). This last category of formal causation or explanation has a great deal in common with the notion put forward here of a structural analysis of action, based on precedents from the structural sciences (see also Harré, this volume).

Linguistics and systems theory are already well on the way to producing a structural account of some aspects of human action, and in consequence the vocabulary of action analysis is starting to change from cause and effect, to embrace richer and more varied notions of equilibrium, stability, perturbation, feedback, field effects, attractor surfaces, resilience and trajectories, in the case of the systems sciences, while linguistic ideas are making people look at other activities besides language in terms of their terminal and non-terminal vocabularies, immediate constituents, commutable sets and deep structures. Yet another vocabulary for the description of action is growing up around the analogy with games, drawing attention to the importance of social rules and the analogues in social life of teams, points, referees, penalties and so on.

Social rules can be likened to game rules or linguistic rules. If the former comparison is made then those rules which are known to the actor, followed explicitly, and capable of being reported, will come to the fore. If the latter metaphor is used (which I find far more appealing) then rules will become technical devices, analysts' representations like equations or graphs, neither referred to nor necessarily followed by the actors, but in a way descriptive of what they do with far more precision and rigour than their own limited commentary. That is not to say that the collection of actors' accounts is unnecessary for this kind of study, only that they are insufficient. In fact they may be the prime data, even the only data which are available and suitable.

The linguistic analogy suggests a mode of operation for structural analysis, as well as a number of similarities between sentence structure and action structure (Clarke 1979). In the analysis of action as in the analysis of language the tacit knowledge of the folk is good on particulars but poor on generalizations. Anyone can recognize and produce particular sentences, and say what they mean. Anyone can complete a plot or story, replace deleted passages and describe the implications of each event, when they have something concrete to work on, but who can describe the regularities they trade on in doing this in a comprehensive and coherent form? One of the main tasks for a science of action will be to account *in general* for the regularities that we can all see in particular cases. In doing this, as in writing a grammar, the method of choice will not be to induce patterns from collections of data, but to undertake careful conceptual analysis of small numbers of examples looking for recurring events, processes and relations, so that precise models can be formulated like grammars or system models, capable of anticipating or reproducing the combinations of events and circumstances that observation and intuition tell us to be realistic, but which are, in the nature of the case, complex. Observation and intuition are both needed, since observation indicates probability, frequency and actuality; intuition indicates propriety, meaning and significance. There is also another reason for applying both criteria of 'adequacy' (see Chomsky 1965) to the characteristics of a model. Ideally an adequate model would reproduce all and only the action configurations consistent with a given set of constraints, or to put it another way, any structure produced by the model should be found in nature, and any structure found in nature should be reproducible by the model. These are quite separate criteria and they involve different practical problems when applied. To see if structures in nature conform with the model, natural structures would be observed and the model 'steered' towards their reproduction insofar as that is within its capability. The steerage of generative models for the purposes of analysis-by-synthesis (Neisser 1966) is a technical matter that cannot be gone into here. Note only that observation rather than intuition is required. For the opposite test, to see if all model productions are realistic, observation may also be possible, but since we discounted experimental procedures *per se*, there is the problem of finding the right observation when you want it, if you cannot engineer it, and worse still of ever being able to say that a particular structure is *not* naturally occurring on the basis of a limited sample of observations which might simply have missed it. Here intuition can come to the rescue. It is much more practical to detect erroneous outputs of a generative device by their implausibility to the intuitions than ever it would be to search the world for examples until they could finally be said to be non-existent.

Note that the models referred to here are not models of the action structure; they are generators, models of an underlying system whose output describes and corresponds to the action structure, but whose constitution does not. The parts of the model may be factors, forces and constraints which shape the behaviour, but they will not map to the behaviours directly, any more than the major parts of a particular grammar such as base rules, transformational rules and a semantic component correspond directly with the noun-phrases and verb-phrases which are major parts of the sentences the grammar produces. In the case of a grammar there is a third structure, which might be called the trace or generative history of a string, often represented in part by a tree diagram, in which a record is displayed of particular operations which can be identified with parts of the grammar, producing particular concatenations of the non-terminal vocabulary, which may be associated with parts of the sentence. In this terminology I would regard the deep structure as an intermediate phase through which the trace passes.

Gradually as this argument unwinds the analysis of action structure is coming to resemble a formal discipline such as algebra or logic which serves to explicate the nature of our reasoning about something. The ultimate aim of this line of enquiry would be to represent the regularities of action structure axiomatically in a scheme like geometry.

Unlike a simple form of causal account, this type of analysis avoids the embarrassment of having to explain where cause-and-effect relations or tendencies go when the cause is not present, the effect is not apparent and the relation not manifest. If a system is so constituted that an effect would materialize if a particular cause *were to be* present, then that tendency must inhere in the system in some material form. In our case these tendencies present no problem: their representation in the real mechanics of the brain is of no concern, and they can be engineered in the artificial system (the model) by the use of the appropriate kinds of rules with known call-conditions.

Let us turn briefly to the relation between hierarchical structure and reductive explanation. Both seem to suggest that an object to explain such as an *act* can be taken apart into its finer constituents to discover what it is made of, but the notion of hierarchy extends in principle to the grosser levels of structure than we are normally aware of, as well as the finer ones. This suggests we might also try putting the original entities together to discover what they are part of. Another virtue of structural methodology is that it encourages us to look for patterns that were previously unnoticed because they were too large to be seen, as well as assuming, as is the more common practice, that behind every phenomenon there must be an order of regularity too small to be seen. It might even be argued that this 'upward explanation' (in the sense that we are now working towards the top of a hierarchical structure from a given starting point) has a special appropriateness in the case of human action, where events do generally become more intelligible as we discover what they are part of but not so when we take them apart to see what they are made of. This is an interesting property of action since it is at variance with the nature of natural systems. It is tempting to speculate that there is a fundamental and important dichotomy between those phenomena in nature whose macroscopic properties derive from microscopic ones, and which are therefore explained by reduction, and the patterns of human affairs where subprocesses and subgoals are controlled from above, and satisfactory explanation is only achieved by synthesis.

Another consequence of structural analysis is that incidents rather than persons become the fundamental units or objects of study. This may impose a quite different partition on what in total is the same subject matter, rather like a road map of Britain as compared with a geological map sharing the same outline and covering the same ground, but distinguishing a different set of regions on a different basis. A science of persons tends to become a science of faculties, in which a number of more or less independent capacities like reading, memory and cognition are seen to reside in the head of each individual. This jeopardizes our understanding of the interplay between faculties and processes, and gives rise to a methodology where a human volunteer subject is taken to be a complete and representative system, whose constitution can be probed satisfactorily in the confines of a laboratory, using input–output contingencies to establish its transfer function. If on the other hand human *enterprises* are taken to be primary, such as policies, disputes and careers, it becomes unthinkable to look for their regularities in any example which does not share their spatial and temporal extent, or to look at the functioning of one component across instances, before examining the structure of one instance with all its components. Explaining human behaviour one faculty at a time, is like analysing *Hamlet* by looking first at the distribution of *a*s in the text; and then as a quite separate study the *b*s, and so on. Ultimately the same ground would be covered, but at what cost to the integrity of the phenomenon, and the *real* issues structure and function?

To say that incidents or episodes should be given priority, with persons and faculties being treated as contributors to, or derivatives from their structure, is, in an intriguing way, like the view that has been advanced in physics that our conception of particles and forces should be reversed. Although it seems natural at first to think of particles as fundamental, with their inherent attributes like mass and charge determining the forces that will act between them, it is in some respects more realistic to see fields as fundamental and all-pervasive, so that any one field is distributed throughout the body of the universe in such a way that certain discontinuities arise like interference patterns between waves, creating the illusion of solid particles of matter. In the psycho-social counterpart of this view we might take a second look at the assumption that people (at least in the sense of social personas or personalities) are fundamental, and that their attributes determine a pattern of interactions, and ultimately the nature of society. On the contrary it may be that 'forces' of knowledge, power, interest and value are distributed diffusely throughout society, and that the illusion of an identity is created when they intersect consistently in the vicinity of an organic individual.

Returning to the style of analysis that will make most sense of incident structures, there is a choice to be made between intensive and extensive methodology. As the name suggests, intensive methods aim to show the interplay of a large number of factors in a small number of instances, whereas extensive methods (which are much the more common in the behavioural sciences) are supposed to show the interplay between small numbers of factors in a large number of instances. Ultimately the purpose of either approach would be to produce laws relating all factors in all cases, so the question is really one of the order in which to do things.

Is it better to understand specific cases in detail and then check how general the findings are by consideration of further examples, or better to know that a pattern holds generally between some of the relevant variables, and then try to enrich the picture by adding more factors while maintaining the level of generality? Advocates of intensive methodology (including myself) would argue that the former is preferable because it results in a stronger form of generalization. The proposition we arrive at in either case will apply to a set of individuals or examples. However, paradoxical though it may seem, if the propositions involve non-distributive attributes of the objects of study, such as group averages, these propositions will not necessarily apply to the individual members of the set as well as to the set itself. This is one of the main drawbacks of the over-use of statistics in psychology: findings are produced about groups of people making up particular studies or experimental conditions which bear no necessary relation to the individuals making up the groups. Propositions formulated so as to be true of a set *and* of the members of the set are called general propositions; propositions which refer to properties of a set which are not necessarily shown by its members are called aggregate propositions. The real point of all this is that extensive designs tend only to yield aggregate propositions, since measures are aggregated over the extent of the study, and relations sought between the aggregates; whereas intensive designs, properly used, will yield general propositions by finding regularities in unaggregated data which may well stand up to eliminative induction, showing them to be generally true of an ever-growing set of instances. Put another way, that is to say that regularities that hold between all factors in a few cases may recur in further instances or not, but they will not *interact* between instances, thereby invalidating their own description. Extensive design is much more dubious. Here it seems that regularities that hold between some variables not only recur but interact when further variables are considered, so nullifying the original finding, at least as part of a general law. Interestingly enough intensive study has often been the preferred approach in structural subjects like anatomy, crystallography and linguistics. Needless to say the aim of structural or sequential analysis as proposed here would be to produce general rather than merely aggregate propositions about a set of incident structures produced under common constraints.

The syntax of action

As we have seen, the cause of events over time is usually described and analysed in one of two ways, corresponding roughly to continuous mathematics on the one hand, and discrete (meristic) mathematics on the other. Some systems lend themselves to descriptions in terms of continuously present, continuously varying (that is stepless) measures. An economic forecasting model or an engineer's model of stress and strain in a bridge make use of this kind of description. At the heart of each model is a number of (usually differential) equations sharing a set of relations between variables which the system preserves, and thereby predicting which configurations of values would be viable states or potential behaviours of the system. Other systems are not like that. Imagine writing the equations of chess, or of English grammar. These things are more like jigsaw puzzles than the interplay of sliding scales and flexible forces that go into a continuous system. The variables that make them up change in discrete steps from one time or place to another. Quite separate categories of component parts exist, within which there is a relative homogeneity, and between which differences are of kind, not merely of degree. Furthermore the considerations which go to make up a description of components of the structure at one time or place, may not apply *at all* elsewhere, unlike continuous variables fluctuating in strength, magnitude or relevance, but always having a value. A pawn does not have the same qualities as a bishop; but in different propositions a verb is not a less nominal kind of noun: they are members of different sets. So too with action, there seem to be categorical differences between the things done at different times or by different people, and these categories of event and circumstances come together in a combinatorial system, tolerant of some configurations but not others. What is being proposed here is a *combinatorial* theory of action, and its purpose is to express the range of possible combinations in a given instance, and the reason for that set of possibilities being appropriate rather than some other set. It is in this respect that the theory of action is 'syntactic', although other similarities also exist between action theory and linguistics, such as the similar use that can be made of lay knowledge of specific structures in building up a general theory of structure that goes beyond commonsense insight.

Basic building blocks, the 'morphemes' in the 'syntax of action' are likely to be social acts, rather like Austin's (1962) speech acts, but with a more general definition embracing speech acts as a special case. The categories to which these fundamental particles of action structure belong are unlikely to be 'categories' in the strict sense that each event will be described fully by its membership of one and only one of an array of types. Instead they are more likely to be features which themselves combine in the description of any one event, representing its illocutionary force, actor, recipient, mode, instrument, modifier and so on. In this respect the system (like language) could be said to have two distinct levels of articulation or combinatorial regularity: one making up individual acts or events from more basic feature descriptions, and the other showing how act sequences come to make up well-formed projects, lives, strategies and other incidents.

To describe this second, higher level of articulation, which is of prime concern here, it is necessary to identify structures on three levels of description: roughly parts, wholes, and the set of wholes to be distinguished from its counterset. In the case of linguistics these would be morphemes, sentences and a given language L, and the theory of that language would contain (or generate) all and only those strings of morphemes that were well-formed sentences of the language L. In a similar way an incident analysis must deal with basic acts (or their types or descriptions), the incidents they make up, and the class of incidents whose well-formed examples are to be examined collectively. In this way it may be possible one day to present a set of acts and a set of rules by way of an analysis of some specific situation, let us say, and to claim that all and only the combinations of the acts which may be found by following the rules are representative of the conduct associated with the situation. This sounds easy in principle but there are problems in practice arising from the odd combinations that human action structures happen to display. Note that some phraseological sleight of hand went into the notion of 'conduct associated with that situation', the reason being that unlike linguistics where there are probably only as many sets of strings worth delineating as there are languages, action analysis can usefully examine sets of sequences of many different kinds including the sequences that are *probable* given certain constraints, *permissible* and *proper* given the circumstances, *effective* in achieving one rather than another outcome, and so on. In the special case of forecasting and optimization the way to proceed would probably be to start with a 'grammar' defining the set of relevant and sensible future scenarios arising from a given point, and then if the system were interactively influencible a probability mapping showing the likelihood of achieving certain end states by certain means and hence the optimum strategy. If the incident were only to be anticipated but not controlled, the second step would be to construct a switching component, showing what combinations of additional factors would be necessary to nudge the pattern of events into one version as opposed to another, and thereby to make the actual outcome predictable, at least insofar as the probability of occurrence of these impact factors could be determined.

So far, the idea of expressing common patterns and constraints in sets of combinations or sequences has been used light-heartedly, as though once the point of doing such a thing became apparent, anybody could get on and do it without difficulty. In practice quite the reverse is true. It is simple enough to see why a combinatorial theory of circumstance and action might be a magic key with which to unlock many doors, but it is *very* hard to arrive at it satisfactorily. One of the problems, as we have seen, is that the regularities we are dealing with do not consist of mathematical functions relating continuously present, continuously changing variables, and therefore the language of equations is inappropriate. Instead particular combinations of categorically described events give rise to or give way to other combinations of categories. The usual representation for this state of affairs is the language of transformational or rewriting rules, showing which combinations of categories can arise from which simpler antecedent combinations. These rules share many of the properties of equations as they are used in generative models, and they are much better likened to equations than to the rules of a game in the everyday sense, as we have seen, provided three dissimilarities are borne in mind. Combinatorial rules unlike equations have discrete arguments, only concatenation operates, and their two parts or expressions are related by commutability but not equality.

Rule systems for combining symbols or categories into sequences, come in various basic types with different capabilities corresponding to four fundamental design principles. This fourfold distinction arises in automata theory where the four possibilities, in increasing order of power, are called finite-state automata, push-down stack automata, linear banded automata and Turing machines; and in linguistics where they are called language types 3, 2, 1 and 0, or finite-state, context-free, context-dependent and transformational grammars. Briefly the principles of the four types are as follows. A finite-state device has a finite number of discrete states and is entirely governed and described by two types of function; a next-response function determines the next output given the last input and last state; and a next state function determines the next state given the last input and the last state. The main limitation of this class is its inability to produce indefinitely many levels of embedding. This is remedied in the next most complex device, the simplest of the infinite-state machines. This uses a push-down stack (a memory having the property of the spring-loaded stacks of trays in cafeterias from which it takes its name, that items are added and removed in the opposite order). By storing 'where it had got to' in one sequence every time it starts on another embedded one, by adding a reminder to the stack, and later discharging these commitments to continue in the order in which they come off the stack, such a device can employ any number of nested brackets correctly, according to the laws of algebra, arithmetic or sentence construction. A linear banded automaton does all this too, and also makes other transpositions and substitutions within a restricted range. Finally a Turing machine or transformational grammar makes unconfined transpositions, and is co-extensive in its operations with the set of effectively computable procedures (Minsky 1972). That is to say any conceivable form of calculation that consists of clear unequivocal steps with one outcome for each operation can be expressed in this form.

Now the problem arises that a behaviour grammar should have some overall design principle: it should be a recognizable class of automaton, but all of the four above seem unsuitable. The finite-state types do not cope well with nesting, and the infinite type automata are deterministic and non-interactive. Human action seems to require an interactive, probabilistic model with fuzzily-defined vocabularies (Westman 1978), and while such things can be imagined, as tools for casting light on a problematic phenomenon they introduce more complications than they resolve.

Alternative methods

If, as it seems, formal models are doomed to run out of mathematics before they run into the substance of the problem, what are the alternatives? Experimentation *per se* is unsuitable as we have seen, but a kind of 'secondary experimentation' may be employed in which naturally occurring incidents are used as material in subsequent experimental tasks sorting, completion, reordering and so on. Here of course the subjects are being used to cast light on the experimental material rather than their more familiar role where the reverse is true. Alternatively incidents can be 'coded' for computer analysis, usually having a number to stand for each category of event, and then subjected to a kind of statistical 'code-breaking' procedure. Here as in secondary experimentation the methodology tends to become recipe-like and sterile, and the results are all too often piecemeal and superficial. However, to react against this and adopt 'inspirational methods' where no analytical procedure exists, and each case yields its own unique weight (or not), is probably unprofitable too. In principle it seems sufficient merely to take each incident on its merits and employ whatever concepts it suggests in formulating an analysis. After all those which are inappropriate will give rise to unrealistic properties in subsequent generative models, and can be weeded out that way. In practice, however, the concepts are all too often peculiar to the specific incident; the need to assemble a complete model before any ideas can be assessed makes for an impossibly large 'working unit' of analysis; and interesting case studies involve too many problems of access to privileged information for the beginner ever to get started.

A satisfactory compromise appears to be the use of heuristically specified stages of analysis to avoid the opposite perils of rigidity and aimlessness, and a basic unit of study consisting of specific questions about incidents rather than complete models, although these represent a goal of analysis in each case, just as linguistic papers dealing with matters of detail would still be written with a notion of the overall grammar in mind. Some compromise is also required on the matter of 'top–down' or 'bottom–up' analytical methods. Top–down methods require an overall design principle to be apparent where often it is not, and bottom–up methods though workable are disappointingly piecemeal in what they produce. Some kind of middle–out and alternating upward and downward analysis offers the best result, particularly when guided by the substance of the material itself, rather than some rigidly preordained schedule.

'Analysis' reviewed

The term *analysis* smacks of induction, suggesting that some procedure will be applied to collections of data to yield basic patterns and structures, and the validity of the result will be apparent from the soundness of the procedure. By now, though, it must be clear that analysis as applied to incidents is a very tentative and speculative business, and the conclusions require far more support if they are to be credible than an appeal to the soundness of the reasoning behind them. The role of analysis as envisaged here is only to suggest properties that might be built into some predictive or generative model (whether specified formally and algorithmically or heuristically), with a view to testing their validity according to the properties they confer on the model. This raises the question of the adequacy criteria the model must satisfy if it is to be acceptable, at least provisionally. So far it has been assumed that the adequacy criterion for a model is to produce all and only the set of sequences characteristic of the system being modelled. That may be unrealistic, though. Even physical models fail to pass that test, since they very often suggest more solutions or structures than actually exist in nature. They tend to be over-generative. One solution to this is to leave the model in an elegant if over-generative form, and then add additional boundary conditions so as to 'edit out' the unwanted predictions. Some of the most remarkable findings in science of course, such as the discovery of the positron, or the expanding universe, have themselves been predicted by theory and edited out as implausible, until it was discovered that it was the boundary conditions not the theory that were misconceived, and the 'unacceptable' consequences of the theory were true. This is still a long way from happening with incident structures. In the present state of the art it would be a feat enough to have a combinatorial formula that reproduced intuition, let alone transcended it. But the day may come when an analysis of dilemmas and conflicts serves not only to summarize the possible scenarios which are apparent, but to generate those alternatives which the untutored eye may not have noticed.

If we take the 'instrumentalist' view of science it will be enough for an analysis to behave as an accurate canonical representation of a set of incident structures. If we wish to be 'realists', however, then theories and models must do more than that. They must describe the real operations of genesis and control lying behind the observable stream of events. In the case of action theory, this may be unattractive and unnecessary. A realist account of action may quickly turn into an exercise in neurophysiology, and even if couched mentalistically, will be hampered by the fact that real social action is confined by the periodicity of turn-taking. The *real* process consists of each person reacting to the others in turn-by-turn basis, and that yields only one 'micro' level of analysis. If we wish to exploit the transfer of technique across scale which the hierarchy of action seems to invite, then a blow-by-blow account of the thoughts and reasons behind action may have to be abandoned in favour of a more abstract language of cycles, symmetries and equilibria in the fabric of action itself.

In conceiving of a science of action there is a temptation to assume that other sciences must provide the point of departure. In that case the reconciliation between science and action would be effected by drawing together the lessons of scientific methodology and applying them to the new domain of human affairs. However, it could be argued that science springs as readily from the body of folk wisdom about each new phenomenon to be considered as from the collective doctrine of the other sciences, and that a more sensible procedure would be to draw together the lessons of everyday conceptualization and vocabulary as it applies to action, and to look for gaps, inconsistencies and anomalies with a view to 'crystallizing out' of the mixture of lay beliefs a precise scientific formulation, much as linguistics has attempted to do given the intuitions of the native speaker as data.

Incident dynamics and forecasting

It has been suggested that a sequential or combinatorial theory of the unfolding pattern of events with time would lend itself to uses in forecasting and optimization of policies and strategies. Often there is a one-to-one correspondence between 'incidents' as defined here and problems to be solved, which is not the case if the unit of study is taken to be a person, a faculty or a behaviour. One of the few properties that problems seem to share, as a basis for general theory of problems and their solution, is that they arise as a progression of events or states of affairs which reaches a point where it gets out of hand, threatens to manifest one of its less desirable outcomes (such as the escalation of a conflict), or comes to require more systematic guidance than can easily be given. In this respect a problem is a matter of turning one state of affairs into another desirable one, avoiding undesirable outcomes on the way. It is a kind of navigation problem where the different courses that events could take are like the routes on a map, and the problem-solving strategy is simply a matter of taking the right turnings on the way to arrive at the chosen destination by an effective path. One difficulty in an interactive problem like chess, for instance, is that routing decisions in the point-to-point development of the game state are taken by different parties with mutually exclusive goals. The other problem is that the map itself is unknown, or at any rate too complex to draw out in full, like the 'game tree' for chess. A combinatorial theory of action would be a generative formula for such a map, and as such may be subject to procedures of optimization without the map itself ever being created in full.

Let us pursue the metaphor a stage further. If problems are problematic because we do not have the right kind of map of options and outcomes to allow us to steer systematically towards a chosen goal, albeit probabilistically, what is wrong with the maps we do have, and what can be done to improve them? With any map, concrete or abstract, certain properties are required if it is to be useful for systematic navigation. It must be accurate and the right features must appear in the right place, distances must be shown to scale and so on. It must be general: separate 'strip' maps for each journey would be tiresome. It must be consistent, and not allow contradictory inferences to be drawn. It must be complete, without blank uncharted areas. Lastly, and in a way most importantly, it must be *coherent*. Otherwise all the other criteria could be satisfied by a list of propositions like 'outside Banbury is a windmill on a hill', 'Southampton is on the coast', and so on. Such a list would be useless for getting about even though it could well be as accurate, general, consistent and complete as the Ordnance Survey. This is just the problem with our everyday knowledge of the world of actions and consequences and its drawback as a problem-solving tool: it is *incoherent*. Often the shortcoming is *mistaken* for inaccuracy or incompleteness, and so studies are directed to correcting or supplementing lay beliefs where it is not necessary, with the result that findings seem obvious or trivial in retrospect. What a science of action can really offer the problem-solver is not a way of putting new points on his map, or realigning more accurately those that are already there, it is a way of building the map in the first place in an integrated overall form, from the vast library of observations and measures that are already to hand. System dynamics, generative linguistics and incident dynamics all share this crucial feature: they are not ways of discovering new facts as such, since they all deal in matters where the primary facts are already well known. They are ways of assembling disordered collections of facts into consolidated schemata, and *that* is the crucial weakness of lay and scientific accounts of action, and the greatest hindrance to a well-grounded science of policy.

The combinatorial view of action, unlike more orthodox 'empirical' analyses, can research things before they happen, and determine the properties of states of affairs yet to be brought about. This is the crucial test of any science, be it empirical or rational, that it can extrapolate beyond its retrospective commentaries and reach into the future.

Action theory as a problem-solving method would produce a profession as well as a science, which like any other profession would learn as much by case-history-taking and by eclectic problem-centred forms of enquiry as by systematic research in search of general laws. In framing the concepts and practices of incident dynamics as much is to be learned by comparison with medicine, law and architecture as by the extension of physics, chemistry and biology. The new science-professions too are particularly strong in setting precedents for this field: systems engineering, management cybernetics and operations research combine much of the *modus operandi* of the helping professions, with a scientific information base that goes beyond professional acumen and experience.

The content of a problem should determine the form of analysis, not the reverse. Methods and techniques should be used as tools, employed as and when the subject matter itself dictates, not according to some preordained recipe. There may not be, and there need not be discovery procedures for incident structure. It is a fallacy to believe that scientific method requires discovery to be made by previously statable methods. No problem or puzzle worth its name is solved by methods chosen in advance of examining the problem in detail. The canons of science only require that the discovery *once made* can be justified by repeatable public procedure. *Evaluation* procedures do have to conform to a discipline, but the original mode of analysis and discovery can be completely unfettered, or guided as much by intuition, insight, and the peculiar association of each particular case as by any previously articulated conception of research procedure.

It may be noted in passing that in this as in many other respects, the requirements of good research and the requirements of research findings are diametrically opposed, and that the idea of writing proposals in advance of doing research is as conducive to real discovery as requiring explorers to set out only in search of known places they could guarantee to find.

In summary, then, there is no recipe for incident dynamics, only guiding principles. Analysis should proceed as particular instances, using intensive methods and a pretheoretical conceptual scheme as the point of departure. Synthesis or 'upward exploration' should seek for wholes given the parts, as well as the reverse. Abstract and idealized descriptions at the level of acts should be used in place of concrete behaviours, and explicit evaluation procedures may be employed to test models, although discovery procedures should not be sought for producing them. Specific questions about action models should form the working unit of study, and these questions should determine the subsequent styles of information collection and inference that are employed. A complete cycle of analysis would begin with a set of sequences or structures, decompose them into parts and relations and then impose some combinatorial formula or rule system according to which the original structures could be reassembled, together with all others of their kind but no anomalous examples. Boundary conditions might be imposed to meet the latter condition, and coherence of description should be a major object of analysis, and the particular respect in which it seeks to go beyond everyday intuition.

If these guidelines can be put to good use in the analysis of small-scale sequences, conversations, arguments and decisions, then the scene will be set to build up a facility for microfutures research, news forecasting and policy optimization based for the first time on the fundamental regularities of action structure and whatever natural calculus or 'psycho-logic' most elegantly expresses the syntax of events.

I would like to thank Rom Harré for inspiring the ideas which make up this article in more cases and in more ways than it was possible to acknowledge adequately in the text.

References

Austin, J. L. (1962) *How to do things with words*. Clarendon Press, Oxford.

Chomsky, N. (1965) *Aspects of the theory of syntax*. Mouton, The Hague.

Clarke, D. D. (1975) 'The use and recognition of sequential structure in dialogue.' *British Journal of Social and Clinical Psychology* **14**, 333–9.

— (1979) 'The linguistic analogy: when is a speech act like a morpheme?' In G. Ginsburg (ed.), *Emerging strategies in social psychology*. Wiley, London.

Forrester, J. W. (1972) 'Understanding the counter-intuitive behaviour of social systems.' In J. Beishon and G. Peters (eds.), *Systems behaviour*. Harper & Row, London.

Harré, R. and P. F. Secord (1972) *The explanation of social behaviour*. Blackwell, Oxford.

Minsky, M. (1972) *Computation: finite and infinite machines*. Prentice-Hall, London.

Neisser, U. (1966) *Cognitive psychology*. Appleton-Century-Crofts, New York.

Westman, R. S. (1978) 'Environmental languages and the functional bases of animal behaviour.' In B. Hazlett (ed.), *Quantitative methods in animal behaviour*. Academic Press, London.

Actors' powers

MICHAEL BRENNER

1. Introduction

It is, in a sense, trivial to note that we spend much of our time interacting with other people; it is puzzling, however, and at the heart of social psychology, to ask why we act in the ways that we do. An established line of reasoning, as regards the causes of our actions, is to locate these predominantly *within* ourselves, for example, in terms of various kinds of social motivation guiding our actions. Argyle (1978a, p. 18), for example, notes seven distinct social motivational sources: biological needs, dependency, affiliation, dominance, sex, aggression and self-esteem, and ego-identity, these affecting the genesis of action.

In contrast to a kind of social psychology which sees the causes of action predominantly as internal to the individual, there is another view, opposite to the former, which maintains that actions are explained better when viewed as the products of certain properties of *social situations*. It is through the individual's knowledge of various situational constraints on action that sensible interaction between people becomes possible. How may such situational constraints be expressed?

Argyle (1978b), for example, suggests for their explication that we should liken social situations to *games*, that is, imagine all social situations as rule-governed. The idea that action is constrained by rules, and that the individual needs to have knowledge of these before effective action can take place, has inspired another analogy, that between *language and action*. As language use, if well formed, involves syntax, so may social action be characterized as 'grammatical'. As Harré and Secord (1972, p. 123) point out:

> In our view human social life is through and through linguistic, and the best understanding of it can be obtained, we believe, by the use of linguistic and quasi-linguistic concepts. It may not prove too fanciful

to take this idea so seriously as to seek for the grammars of the social order, and perhaps even for the deep structure of social universals that may lie behind all human communities.

In order to comprehend action as 'grammatical', Harré and Secord (1972) emphasize that we should study two dimensions: the role–rule dimension and the act–action dimension. The concept of rule is of primary importance as rules 'guide action through the actor being aware of the rule and of what it prescribes, so that he can be said to know what to do in the appropriate circumstances by virtue of his knowledge of the rule' (Harré and Secord 1972, p. 181). Rules generate roles as particular positions for action, as roles are 'derived from a particular way of partitioning the rules' (p. 183) among participants. As the role–rule dimension is most explicit in formal situations, such as rituals or ceremonies, these are suggested as paradigms for the analysis of all other situations, including those which appear to be 'enigmatic'. Whilst a consideration of the role–rule dimension leads to an explication of why actions appear in certain ways, reference to the act–action dimension of social situations provides an understanding of what is done by social action. For example, the exchange of greeting actions, if well formed, that is, if participants act according to the appropriate role–rule dimension, accomplishes the act of greeting.

Clarke (1978a, b) employs the analogy between action and language in, perhaps, its most extreme form. As he (1978a, p. 240) points out:

Social interaction is like discourse and discourse is like language. More precisely, the rules which will generate all and only the speech act sequences which are sensible conversations are so like the rules which will generate all and only the morpheme strings which are well-formed sentences, that the study of the former may be assisted by the techniques for investigating the latter.

As Clarke's approach is entirely rule-based, in the fashion of Chomskyan generative syntax, an explanation of social interaction involves the discovery of the appropriate 'syntax of action' by which the observed actions are called into being. How may we produce a syntax of action? Clarke (1978b, p. 10) suggests thus:

Working at first from native actors' intuitions of a familiar behavioural structure we should propose a set of formal generative rules. A grammar is said to have no discovery procedure only an evaluation procedure. The rules would then be tested for their adequacy, that is their capacity to produce all well-formed *wholes* in the *domain*, and possibly provide other information correctly about each one as well.

The rule-based approaches summarized above have introduced a new sense of realism to social psychological work, as social action is here taken seriously in its naturally occurring forms, as being specific for particular social situations (see, for example, Marsh, Rosser and Harré 1978) rather than being decontextualized as frequently happened in experiments. I feel uneasy, however, about some assumptions on which the approaches seem to be based. First, the approaches seem to assume the quite straightforward researchability of social actions. Social actions seem to be regarded as quite unproblematic in that they are hypothesized to occur in well-formed or game-like situations; if they are apparently 'enigmatic', then it is thought possible to tease out the implicit structure of formality on which their occurrence relies. Secondly, the three approaches imply particular assumptions about the powers for action which people have. 'Powers' is here to be understood, in analogy to Harré and Secord (1972, pp. 264–90), in terms of people's competencies and capabilities for action. I believe that the rule-based approaches *underestimate* actors' powers, and it is therefore worthwhile to ask whether people *are* what they are expected to be when understood as rule-followers.

It is these two issues which I wish to investigate in this paper. I will first try to demonstrate some limits to the rule-based approaches by pointing at some practical research problems in the study of action. The exposition of research problems is then taken to suggest a more differentiated approach to the analysis of social situations than is presently being favoured by the rule-based approaches.

2. The issue of indexicality

Can we always unambiguously say which kind of social situation it is with which we are dealing? If not, this implies either that we are unable to determine exactly what the situation is *about*, this preventing us from ascribing precisely the relevant role–rule and act–action dimensions, the generative rules, and so on, or that we attribute the *wrong* meaning to the situation, which renders our subsequent analysis invalid. Let me illustrate these two points by looking at some examples of social action.

The majority of ordinary language expressions have been found to be incomplete in that they are not absolutely informative about their precise status as parts of a social situation. The fringe of incompleteness that they carry must be filled in by participants or observers before they can become more comprehensible. Such utterances which require attributions of meaning in the form of an understanding of the situation context implied by them are called 'indexical expressions' (Bar-Hillel 1954). Even apparently 'universal' and 'objective' statements, such as 'ice floats on water', rely on the use of contextual background knowledge to be understood properly, that is, by attributing correctly a domain of *ceteris paribus* conditions. 'For example, yes, ice floats on water, but not a single ice cube with a weight on top of it. Or, yes, it is "universally true" that ice floats on water, but only if there is "enough" water, the et cetera of our *ceteris paribus* adds. That an iceberg will not float on the water in my bathtub flatly contradicts this universal truth.' (Mehan and Wood 1975, p. 94.)

One can, rightly, argue that the issue of indexicality need not be considered all the time, in that the flow of action in a multitude of social situations will be sufficiently informative to allow accurate descriptions of the actions and the acts performed. This is particularly true for social situations which are rituals or ceremonies, or, in fact, are games. Yet, I would argue there are situations where we cannot so unequivocally understand what the exact definition of the situation is. It is here that the issue of indexicality needs to be involved, and it may happen that problems in understanding social actions correctly cannot be overcome.

Consider, for example, the following stretch of conversation (Mehan and Wood 1975, p. 123):

Actor₁: Hi, my name is Bud Wood, what's yours?

Actor₂: Chris Isaac. I'm an engineer.

Actor₁: Oh, that's interesting; I'm an alchemist.

If one abstracts, for a moment, from *what* is said and looks at the *form* of social exchange involved in the piece of conversation, one can quite easily conduct an act–action analysis. The situation involves three particular acts: a greeting, the disclosure of names and the disclosure of occupations. The actual actions are: Actor₁ greets Actor₂, Actor₁ discloses his name, Actor₁ asks for Actor₂'s name, Actor₂ discloses his name, Actor₂ discloses his occupation, Actor₁ gives Actor₂ some appreciative feedback, and, finally, Actor₁ discloses his occupation. We also notice a particular form within which the exchange takes place, namely, that the current speaker selects the next topic or act.

By analysing many situations of the above type, using an act–action approach, we may be able to discover the various ways in which actions typically combine to form particular acts. Yet it must be borne in mind that such an approach relies on a low level of ambiguity in understanding *what* the actors are doing. In the above stretch of conversation it may be the case that Actor$_2$ finds the utterance 'I'm an alchemist' problematic, as we as observers could. What was Bud Wood doing when he told Chris Isaac that he is an alchemist? Was he truthfully disclosing his occupation, or was he doing something else? For example, was he joking or involving Isaac in an experiment? Whatever it was that Wood did to Isaac actually, it is apparent that if Wood *were* joking or staging an experiment or doing something else with his utterance, this would render part of the act–action analysis offered above invalid as we cannot precisely define the contextual status of 'I'm an alchemist'. Notice that inviting Wood after the event to account for his action might not necessarily improve our analytic positions, for two reasons. First, Wood might not be able to offer an unambiguous reason for his action; he might say, for example, 'I don't know *why* I did it; it just occurred to me.' Secondly, Wood's account, even if providing an unambiguous reason for his action, would leave Isaac's position unconsidered, as Isaac, being *in* interaction with Wood, had to deal somehow with Wood's action whatever it meant to Wood. That is, for Isaac, a particular practical issue of indexicality may have been involved. The lesson to be learnt here is, I believe, that, in conducting act–action analyses of social situations, we cannot always assume that the issue of indexicality will be unproblematic, for actors do have the power to vary the contextual uses to which utterances and other forms of social action are conventionally put.

In the above conversational example we encountered a problem of indexicality related to just one action. Sometimes, however, it can be that an overall situation does not simply 'speak for itself', although it may be experienced as structured in some way. In this case, we have to fill in a working definition of the situation; otherwise, we could not comprehend what is 'going on'. It is here that we can go very wrong. Let me illustrate the problem with a story called 'Altruism on the Bowery' (Menzel 1973, p. 3):

On a recent afternoon I was walking along the Bowery, when I saw a man lying on the sidewalk some distance away. His clothes were dirty and torn, an empty whisky bottle lay near his hand, and he seemed to be unconscious. Another dishevelled man, not too steady himself, was squatting next to him, looked into his face, said some words, and pulled the lying man's jacket up around him. It was the first time I had seen one drunk help another in that neighbourhood, and I said to myself: 'There is still some solidarity left in the Lumpenproletariat. There is altruism in the streets! I saw it with my own eyes!'

Just then another man, dirty and dishevelled like the first two, but a little steadier on his feet, came up from the other side and started to yell at the good Samaritan. It was not until he yelled a second time that I understood his words: 'Get out of the man's pocket! Get out of the man's pocket!' One drunk robbing another who is unconscious is what he saw with *his* own eyes.

Notice that we do not know what it *actually* was that went on. Was it an act of altruism or a robbery or both or something else? Whatever it was, it is clear that we as observers, like the participants themselves, need to define the situation in *some* way before the actions start to make sense. In this instance, I believe, it would be fallacious to insist that the situation 'speaks for itself', that the meaning of the situation exists *independently* of us being in need to impute it for the purposes of analysis. The lesson to be learnt here is, I think, that act–action analyses of social situations may involve considerable interpretational work, which, where this work fails to solve problems of indexicality correctly, makes nonsense out of any subsequent attempts to explain a social situation in more specific terms.

3. Problems of description

In the rule-based approaches, dimensions such as 'rules', 'roles', 'actions', 'acts', besides others, have been proposed for the purpose of clearly differentiating the various salient features of social action. However, it is not at all clear how these ought to be employed in empirical research. For example, while 'actions' and 'acts' may, in principle, be taken as dimensions for categorizing observable behaviour, the following of rules, for example, may refer to unobservable characteristics of social action which are, however, regarded as crucial in that they are presumed to have some generative force or other. The problem here is, therefore, first, to suggest ways in which the surface flow of action may be categorized adequately, and, secondly, to suggest valid and reliable procedures for making inferences about the unobservable properties of action. There are a number of difficulties here, some of which have been mentioned by Clarke (1978b, p. 10) in his discussion of how to make a syntax of action empirically testable:

Unlike a grammar for a natural language, a syntax of action has to deal with the ordering of a set of *parts* which is indefinitely large and possibly infinite. There are no direct counterparts of the morpheme set which can be used as the vocabulary in which *wholes* are to be

created and described. Speech act or action taxonomies . . . are a help
but in themselves are insufficient as a set of descriptions for activity
parts. Consequently the rules which specify how *parts* may combine
into *wholes* cannot be written until there is a descriptive language for
parts which is concrete enough to be governed by a formal generative
system . . . while at the same time being rich and human enough that
a string of such descriptions will provide a satisfactory representation
of the activity sequence under study.

In other words, Clarke points out that, at present, we do not know how
to categorize the 'parts' of behaviour *exhaustively* so that we may become
able to write *specific* generative rules which help to combine the 'parts'
into 'wholes'.

Let me now look at more general problems of description in the
analysis of social action. Collett (1978, p. 2) has suggested considering
the following example for a discussion of some elementary problems of
unitization and categorization of social action:

Suppose I move my arm through the air. There is a sense in which it
would be impossible to offer an objective description of the separate
actions that I have performed. Any attempt to identify the constituents, let alone the boundaries of the actual movement itself, would
necessarily arise out of a set of assumptions that I entertain about the
nature of such action. In other words, the stream of behaviour is, for
all practical purposes, homogeneous in time. It is seamless, and it is
only by virtue of the segmentations that I impose on it, and the way
in which these segments are seen as relating to each other, that it can
have any meaning or significance for me.

Collett's observations are important in a number of ways. First, even if
we would wish to give an analysis of the 'arm moving through the air' in
behavioural terms, without ascribing a particular social meaning to it,
the analysis would not be observer-independent. It is we who have to
superimpose a structure on the 'arm moving', in the form of particular
units of movement, before we can come to see it as having this or that
form of movement. This implies that a number of structures may be
imputed to the same 'arm moving' when observers find reason to do so.
Similarly, if we were to study the 'arm moving' in terms of social action,
it is we who have to understand its meaning before the 'arm moving'
can be seen as fulfilling some social function or other and can be
categorized accordingly. Surely, our attributions of meaning can usually
be informed quite safely by referring to knowledge of the particular
situation in which the 'arm moving' occurs. Sometimes, obviously, this

means quite unambiguously a 'waving good-bye' or a 'warning' or 'asking for a turn in a discussion'. But who can say whether in ascribing a particular meaning to the 'arm moving' we have *exhausted* the realm of meaning it has for the performer and the receiver of the message as well as for other observers?

In essence, then, there are two major issues in the description of action. First, we need to structure the behaviour stream under study in such a way that we become able to speak of particular 'behaviours'. Secondly, these behaviours must then be viewed as carriers of meaning, as social actions. The crucial point here is that our analyses of behavioural and action structure are not independent of us, as we must *interpret* the behaviour stream before we can describe it. This implies that we have particular interests in, and purpose of, description which, in turn, determine the character and the quality of our investigations. This issue was particularly well noted by Crowle (1976) who pointed at problems in social psychological experimenters' attempts to interpret unambiguously subjects' responses to certain experimental manipulations, that is, without making subjectively biased inferences about the 'real' meaning of experimental responses. As Crowle (1976, pp. 167–8) puts it:

> Though more could be said, I think that it is now plain why even the most carefully designed experiment will be ambiguous: the subjects are individually complex, and they differ greatly from one another. The result of these difficulties is that far from there being just one possible inference concerning the direct effect of a single variable, there are many possible inferences, each of which specifies a path from a possible independent variable *via* a possible mediating mechanism to the observed effect. The selection of one path as the interpretation of the experiment is not entirely arbitrary but reflects the interpreter's beliefs about what variable was operating, and about what psychological states the subjects were in. These beliefs will be derived from the interpreter's experience and knowledge. Since different experimenters experience and know different things, they arrive at different interpretations.

I believe that, *mutatis mutandis*, Crowle's (1976) observations for experimentation are equally valid in other areas of social psychological enquiry, for the simple reason that the community of social psychologists is collectively uncertain about which concepts and descriptions of social action are acceptable (see, for example, Shaw and Costanzo 1970). Given that the social psychological community as a whole is uncertain about the true nature of social action, why is it, we may ask, that individual

social psychologists are frequently so convinced of the absolute propriety of their understandings of action? It seems to me that this has
partly to do with the fact that certain descriptive assertions about action,
such as, for example, Argyle's (1978b, p. 15) that 'all social situations are
rule-governed', are taken as *a priori true*, as *ontologically correct*, but not
just as particular interpretational devices, which they actually *are*, useful
in enabling the meaningful analysis of features of action. Given that
there may be an indeterminate number of fruitful ways of making sense
of action, it is most likely, I think, that employing just one mode of
description, based on just one particular theoretical perspective, will
lead to an incomplete, if not partly invalid, understanding of action. If
this is true, then the lesson to be learnt at this point is that, contrary to
the current fashion, we must try to underplay in social psychology the
relevance of *particular* theories of action, as their single use may only
facilitate a selective, if not distorted, analysis of social action.

4. The analysis of social situations

One of the most obvious prerequisites for a rule-based social psychology is that social situations involve some definite structure or other. If
there were no structure to detect, a rule-based approach would fail
altogether. But is the assumption of definite structuredness always
appropriate? If not, this implies that we need some other social
psychology for the study of those situations which apparently lack
structure; otherwise, no explanations of these forms of social life could
be given.

I would like to argue, in contrast to the rule-based position, that most
social situations involve ambiguity and lack of structure, this meaning
that there is no simple one-to-one relationship between rules and action.
This is so because only very few social situations are 'closed' to the
extent that a fully rule-guided character of action can be demonstrated,
as is the case with rituals and ceremonies where there are no problems
of identifying 'who has done what why'. The majority of social situations in everyday life may, however, be better characterized as 'defined'
or 'open'. By 'defined' I mean that action in a social situation, rather
than being primarily rule-following originates from certain objectives for
action which, in addition, do not necessarily involve a definite routine
for their realization. 'Objectives for action' implies that the actor, when
entering the social situation, has goals related to the achievement of
certain outcomes of action as well as the skills necessary for the goals to

be obtained effectively. By 'open' I mean that action in a given situation involves neither *a priori* objectives of a specific kind nor any definite routines for action.

It is quite obvious that all social situations involve rules, if only sometimes minimally those which are required in the effective management of co-presence, such as the rules which are employed most of the time in turn-taking in conversations (see Sacks, Schegloff and Jefferson 1974). I wish to emphasize, however, that rules have a variable impact on action depending on which kind of social situation it is with which we are dealing. Consider, for example, buying and selling. This may be done within a wide range of different social situations. Buying and selling by means of auction sales require from the seller, the auctioneer and the bidders the adherence in their actions to rigid rules of sequence (see Argyle 1979, p. 33). For example, it is not possible to bid meaningfully after the auctioneer has closed the bidding. Given that auction sales are social rituals, or 'closed' situations, the pursuing of personal goals in an auction sale must be seen as a straightforward function of the rules appropriate for such a situation.

This is surely not so if we imagine a car showroom as a context for buying and selling. In this case, the first problem for a salesperson and a customer is to define the conditions under which they will then act. In contrast to an auction sale, where there is a clear-cut definition of the situation, the actors need to achieve some 'working consensus' (McCall and Simmons 1966, p. 129) in order to obtain a reasonably stable ground on which to base the interaction. Instead of viewing the beginning of the transaction between salesperson and customer in terms of selecting a ritual for the interaction, Ball (1972, p. 76) suggests a much more subtle psychological process:

> More usual is a process of mutual testing, cue-reading, elaboration and modification, leading to some kind of definitional consequences. Definitions are tried out by participants and their partners and accepted, rejected, or modified on the basis of the reaction of the other in a process of situational–definitional negotiation.

Once a working consensus has been worked out about which kind of social situation it is that will be involved (an enquiry, a test drive, ordering a car), the participants can act. As Weinstein and Deutschberger (1964, p. 453) point out, action in 'defined' situations, once the situation is initially defined, may have little in common with action constrained by fixed rules of sequence. They note that:

> the problem for each participant is to choose a line of action adequate

to his purposes (whatever they may be, and whether or not they accord with the purposes of others) while still keeping the others bound in the relationship – that is to say, not terminate the interaction unsatisfactorily. Ego and alter *must* cooperate if either is to achieve his own imperative, even if these imperatives are not in themselves entirely compatible. The problem for the actor is either to bring both imperatives into agreement by means of some sort of bargaining, or to persuade the other that they are 'really' in agreement by manipulating the symbolic content of the situation. In this process, Ego may be required to modify his original purposes or to settle for some unanticipated payoff. Thus *novel outcomes also exist as possibilities* in the initial conditions of the interaction. (My italics.)

In other words, Weinstein and Deutschberger (1964) suggest that social interaction in 'defined' situations is, in contrast to fully rule-governed action, underidentified for participants in a number of ways. Not only may the goals pursued by salesperson and customer be antagonistic rather than complementary (for example, when the customer does not want to buy model X which the salesperson, however, tries to sell), but it may also be that the goals in themselves may change during the encounter, thus affecting the definition of the situation. It can be, for example, that the customer, although initially only vaguely interested in model X, decides at a point to order model X. The fact that initially unlikely outcomes are also a possibility in the interaction makes it worthwhile for the salesperson to employ effective selling skills, that is, to try to manipulate in various ways the customer's goal state, if he is not in the desirable mood of buying outright. Finally, it is worth noting that the customer himself can try to influence the salesperson's goal state, for example, by bargaining for a higher trade-in price for his present car than the salesperson is willing to allow.

In all, rather than taking rules as the main causes for action, action in 'defined' situations is better characterized as, primarily, a form of structured bargaining. Bargaining involves, of course, rules, for example etiquette rules, but the pursuing of goals, as well as their negotiation, and the employment of effective skills are much more crucial determinants of the action flow. A major consequence of the lack of impact of rules on action is that stability in interaction may be a transient phenomenon. Whilst it is the most prominent characteristic of rule-governed situations that they are stable in their situational definition, this is not so in 'defined' situations, as Weinstein and Deutschberger (1964, p. 453) indicate: 'The bargain may not stand, for as others elaborate their lines of action, the actor may find it unrealistic and proceed to negotiate a new one with himself on the basis of a raised or lowered set of aspirations.'

The idea that 'defined' situations may be better understood in terms of bargaining than of rule-following action makes it possible to admit ambiguity in interaction as a fruitful concept. The notion of bargaining obviously implies that not all actions performed by a participant during an encounter are structurable in advance. Actions may be planned, yet the initial plan may fail as a working consensus may not stand. The fact that an actor may experience problems in effective goal-pursuing or goal change may result in a felt degree of unstructuredness in the situation. McCall and Simmons (1966, pp. 128–9) mention part of the psychological process involved here:

> The degree of unstructuredness results either from the uncertainty of the actors about which of the identities will be involved or from ambiguities in the meanings of the situation for the identities that have already become involved . . . Typically, the problem in such cases is not that there are no available interpretations but rather that there are two or more *alternative* interpretations that could be placed upon the situation, each of which implies a somewhat different and perhaps conflicting meaning for the persons involved.

McCall and Simmons (1966) stress an important point, namely, that it may be quite illegitimate to interpret the bargaining process involved in 'defined' situations as just a sequence of various rituals, as the psychological states of participants, in order to be correctly understood, may require the ambiguity of meaning and the felt unstructuredness of the interaction as the major working concepts. This implies that we need to reconstruct carefully the actual conditions under which people find themselves acting in 'defined' situations.

So far, I have tried to indicate some differences between social situations involving rigid rules of sequence for action and 'defined' situations where the pursuing of goals under, possibly, some ambiguity and unstructuredness of the interaction is prevalent. There is an interesting kind of social situation, games, which are, in a sense, both 'closed' and 'defined' situations. Games are entirely rule-governed, that is, there are specific sets of admissible actions, yet they allow a much higher degree of self-expression and self-fulfilment for participants than 'closed' situations. The reason for the latter characteristic is, I think, that, unlike 'closed' situations, games have not emerged for the purpose of making people follow rules. Quite the contrary: games are played because they provide a maximum opportunity for self-enjoyment by involving explicit criteria for the interaction which in ordinary life may be neither explicit nor shared.

Given this gross identification of games as being both rule-governed and enjoyable to play, how does one explain, for example, the moves of participants in a rugby match? In order to understand *what* is done, the *instrumental* dimension, it is useful to define the various actions performed as being functions of the rules of rugby, the various roles available and the skills necessary to enact the game properly. Much of such an analysis would be rather obvious as the game is, of course, an instrumentally predetermined situation, that is, there are definite *a priori* boundaries to what can be done in a rugby match, these being self-evident for anybody who knows the game well. It is correct, in this sense, to characterize the rules of rugby as 'enabling rules' which provide boundaries for things to be done, but do not prescribe *how*, in detail, the game should be performed. This is to say that the *expressive* dimension of the game, the dimension related to the realization of personal goals and projects, is undetermined by the rules. For example, there are no rules for how hard to kick the ball or for how courageously or co-operatively the players must play or for which strategies for playing the game must be employed. It is the expressive dimension, of course, which provides joy and entertainment for both players and watchers, while the rule-based character of the game is typically taken for granted as long as the action is 'within the rules'. Interestingly, although most of the action in games is just rule-following, an explanation of the action by rules only would miss the point of such action nearly entirely, namely, that game action is carried predominantly by the players' realization of goals, projects, strategies and styles of action.

What would happen if we were to transform rugby into a 'closed' situation? This would mean that both the instrumental and expressive dimensions of the game would become rule-governed, as is the case, for example, in theatre where actors rehearse not only the performance of the content of a drama, but a particular expressive style of performance as well. If this were to happen in games, that is, if there were rules and directions as to how hard to kick the ball and how high given certain circumstances, surely, games would be experienced by us as having only very few degrees of freedom for action, as painful to play and as, perhaps, rather boring to watch. Luckily, however, games are, in a sense, just 'defined' situations which, however, in contrast to many everyday 'defined' situations, involve the element of certainty that most action will remain within just one definition of the situation, yet also the elements of novelty, surprise, spontaneity, self-expression and enjoyment for participants. In order to arrive at a sufficient explanation of social action in a particular game, we need to consider, therefore, the various expressive elements of action variably employed by players within the shared rule structure of the game. This was first seen, I believe, by Wittgenstein (1968, §68) who suggests the following concept of game:

> It is not everywhere circumscribed by rules; but no more are there any rules for how high one throws the ball in tennis, or how hard; yet tennis is a game for all that and has rules too.

While action in 'closed' situations is entirely predictable, as there are rigid rules of sequence operating on the action flow, this is not so with other kinds of social situation as they involve the element of *choice* for participants. In order to 'bring off' games and 'defined' situations, one might even say that people *must* develop choices as they cannot simply rely on rule-following in their actions. This means that the analogy of ritual suggested by Harré and Secord (1972) as a template to be used in the analysis of *all* social situations is, in a sense, inadequate, as action in situations other than 'closed' ones relies on active goal-pursuing, bargaining and the negotiation of situational definitions, the expression of skills and self-fulfilment, among others, and not just following rules.

The point that action, to be explained adequately, must be conceptualized in richer terms than just rule-following becomes most apparent when looking at 'open' situations. Here people act without relying on some broad *a priori* definition of objectives to be achieved in an encounter. It is in 'open' situations where people have the most degrees of freedom for action as it is up to them to create, live and abandon various forms of social interactions as they please. 'Open' situations do, of course, involve rules, for example, etiquette rules, but the overall impact of rules is minimal. There are hardly any ways, therefore, in which the course of the interaction can be predicted from past actions, as frequent change of the topic and the style of the interaction may be prevalent, as is the case in casual conversation among friends, for example. Also, particular actions may appear to be strange in that they just occur without suggesting to participants or observers a definite function or purpose. I believe that an explanation of action in 'open' situations in terms of following of prescribed rules is fundamentally misleading as it is not the givenness of a rule structure which needs to be accounted for, but the ongoing creation and variation of social life forms by the actors themselves who, for example, may make up the rules, and alter them, as they go along in the situation (Wittgenstein 1968, §83). Wittgenstein provides an example of social interaction within an 'open' situation:

> We can easily imagine people amusing themselves in a field by playing with a ball so as to start various existing games, but playing many without finishing them and in between throwing the ball aimlessly into the air, chasing one another for a joke and so on.

The lesson to be learnt from this consideration of some of people's powers for action in a range of social situations is, I believe, that the assumption of actions generated by, basically, the rule structure of social situations can be at variance with the actual human characteristics of action. I have been at pains to point out some of these characteristics here, as without them there would not be the particular human world in which we are allowed to dwell. As Shotter (1978, p. 18) remarks in this context:

> Human behaviour would seem to be unique not because, from an external observer's point of view, no other behaviour is quite like it, but because it is only about human behaviour that we are able to make *and sustain* certain assumptions. Observing a projectile now (as beneficiaries of the Cartesian metaphysics and modern science) we ascribe the pattern of its trajectory to the operation of impersonal general laws, but in observing people's motions we still ascribe their trajectories *to them*; we still think of them as controlling their own movements in relation to their own thoughts and feelings.

5. Conclusion

It was not my aim in this paper to negate the propriety of a rule-based approach to the study of action. This would be silly, as rules do indeed play a crucial role in the regulation of social action. My intention was to make us aware of some problems that can arise in specific contexts of enquiry when we may wish to explain action. First, there may be real problems of understanding properly what is meant by action. When such problems cannot be solved adequately, this implies that the quest for elegance and rigour in the scientific description of action may be misguided, as only rather messy and imprecise findings can be gained. Secondly, it may be that our theoretical concepts of action are inadequate. This means that we should exercise considerable care in the use of claimed-to-be-universally-valid interpretations of the causes for action, as we may go very wrong when taking these uncritically as *the* cognitive guidelines for research. Instead, I suggest that we may use in our enquiries a sense of amazement and puzzlement rather than just one particular theoretical orientation. By this I mean that we could employ in our work a serious attempt to understand the relevant characteristics of human conduct in *their own right*, instead of just superimposing, without much further consideration, forms of explanation of people's actions which may prove to be inappropriate.

References

Argyle, M. (1978a) *The psychology of interpersonal behaviour*. Penguin, Harmondsworth.
— (1978b) 'The analysis of social situations.' In M. Brenner (ed.), *The structure of action*. Blackwell, Oxford.
— (1979) 'Sequences in social behaviour as a function of the situation.' In G. P. Ginsburg (ed.), *Emerging strategies in social psychological research*. Wiley, Chichester.
Ball, D. W. (1972) '"The definition of the situation": some theoretical and methodological consequences of taking W. I. Thomas seriously.' *Journal for the Theory of Social Behaviour* **2**, 61–82.
Bar-Hillel, Y. (1954) 'Indexical expressions.' *Mind* **63**, 359–79.
Brenner, M. (ed.) (1980) *The structure of action*. Blackwell, Oxford.
Clarke, D. D. (1978a) 'The syntax of action.' *Oxford Review of Education* **4**, 239–55.
— (1978b) 'Developments in the syntax of action.' In M. Brenner (ed.), *The structure of action*. Blackwell, Oxford.
Collett, P. (1978) 'Segmenting the behaviour stream.' In M. Brenner (ed.), *The structure of action*. Blackwell, Oxford.
Crowle, A. J. (1976) 'The deceptive language of the laboratory.' In R. Harré (ed.), *Life sentences*. Wiley, Chichester.
Harré, R. and P. F. Secord (1972) *The explanation of social behaviour*. Blackwell, Oxford.
McCall, G. I. and I. L. Simmons (1966) *Identities and interaction*. The Free Press, New York.
Marsh, P., E. Rosser and R. Harré (1978) *The rules of disorder*. Routledge & Kegan Paul, London.
Mehan, H. and H. Wood (1975) *The reality of ethnomethodology*. Wiley, New York.
Menzel, H. (1973) 'Actor's meaning – who needs it' (revised version). In M. Brenner, P. Marsh and M. Brenner (eds.), *The social contexts of method*. Croom Helm, London.
Sacks, H., E. Schegloff and G. Jefferson (1974) 'A simplest systematics for the analysis of turn taking in conversation.' *Language* **50**, 696–735.
Shaw, M. E. and P. R. Costanzo (1970) *Theories in social psychology*. McGraw-Hill, New York.

Shotter, J. (1978) 'Action, joint action and intentionality.' In M. Brenner (ed.), *The structure of action*. Blackwell, Oxford.

Weinstein, E. A. and P. Deutschberger (1964) 'Tasks, bargains and identities in social interaction.' *Social Forces* **42**, 451–6.

Wittgenstein, L. (1968) *Philosophical investigations*. Blackwell, Oxford.

Rules in the organization of action: empirical studies

P. MARSH

It has become commonplace in psychological research to employ the notion of rule in the explanation of social action. Often, however, rule is used as a metaphorical device, one which usefully summarizes the regularities of day-to-day behaviour but says little concerning the forces which shape such behaviour. In some types of research that approach might be considered legitimate and fruitful. In many other cases, however, the moral imperatives which are embodied in rule frameworks far greater significance than the surface regularities of interaction which might be the products of the framework and which can be described in terms of transitional probabilities. The fundamental point here is that rules in the form of moral imperatives may not *necessarily* give rise to regularity. In addition, observed regularities in behaviour cannot, *automatically*, be attributed to the presence of moral codes of conduct.

The empirical work I wish briefly to describe here has been oriented towards the development of discovery procedures whereby social rules (as moral directives and interpretative devices) may be elicited. The main focus of this work has been on the expression and social management of aggression in a number of contexts and two particular examples will be considered. The first concerns the highly complex and ritualistic pattern of social action to be found on the British soccer terraces. The second is to do with interactions between licensee and client in that most timeless of British institutions, the public house.

For some time the behaviour of British football fans was considered, by those acting in the role of moral commentators, as violent and anarchic. Aggressive activity was random and gratuitous and, because of its 'senseless' nature, defied rational explanation. This is not the place to enter into sociological analysis of the origins and functions of such hysterical 'moral panics'.[1] Nor is there the opportunity to discuss why

[1] See, for example, S. Cohen (1973).

231

working-class youth (and their counterparts in other European countries) see such arenas for displays of aggression and masculine virtue. The point at issue is the extent to which an alternative perspective regarding the structure and nature of such activity can convincingly be developed. To what extent might this apparently random behaviour be governed and even constrained by coherent sets of moral codes or tacit rule frameworks?

The most tempting analysis to perform would have been one which dealt with the sequences of observable behaviour. Regularities apparent at this level might have been taken as a demonstration of an underlying rule framework. Immediately, however, considerable problems would have arisen concerning the coding of such behaviour and with the segmentation of the behaviour stream. Action on the terraces, or indeed within any other microsocial or subcultural context, cannot be rendered intelligible using frames of reference current outside of such contexts. The problem, in essence, is the inadequacy of imposed etic categorical and conceptual schemas in social research of this nature. Without some guidelines concerning functional or conceptual equivalence the outsider's schemas for making sense of enigmatic and foreign social worlds are likely to be very misleading and unproductive (see for example Berry, Frijda and Jahoda, Whiting). At best such an approach is likely to yield only a description of consistencies and regularities in motoric behaviour – the social meaning and import of such behaviour remaining opaque and mysterious.

The problem of meaning is one that has to be tackled if rules are to be discovered. Indeed, the ascription of meaning to objects and events within a given social world is itself clearly rule-governed. And the rules which apply at this level can be labelled *interpretative*. What constitutes 'provocation', 'riot', 'fight', 'cowardice', 'victory'? How shall a thing be called? What rhetorical devices should be used to refer to specific acts and situations?

The discovery of such rules is an essential prerequisite for conducting any serious research concerned with the internal life of subcultural groups. To assume that one's own lexicon and tacit set of conceptual reference points can be transported across subcultural frontiers without a care is both unnecessarily chauvinistic and scientifically quite untenable. In practice, the discovery of interpretative rules is straightforward and often very illuminating. One need only elicit accounts from members and juxtapose the material contained within such accounts with observations of the objects, acts and situations to which such accounts refer. Thus, one finds that a 'fight' may refer to a sequence of behaviour in which protagonists did not make physical contact with each other. In the world of soccer fans, 'fights' may be spoken of in which only insults, threats and imprecations were exchanged – the key feature being the belief, on the part of onlookers, that there was a *readiness* to engage in physical acts of violence if the occasion called for it (cf. Fox 1977).

Similarly, from such an elementary analysis it can be seen that certain items of clothing have sufficient symbolic significance as drastically to alter the perceived status of the wearer. Subtle variations in the way scarves are knotted, the precise style of footwear and the length of trousers all contribute significantly to attributions made on dimensions of hard–soft and loyal–disloyal.

The isolation of such interpretative rules, which constitute a reference framework for collective negotiation of meaning, open up the possibility of discovering a second type of rule which directs and shapes action. These *prescriptive* rules most cogently embody the moral concerns and values of a social group. Given that, through reference to interpretative rules, one understands what is happening, what should one do? The word 'should' is important here for the major characteristic of these rules is their potential for sanction being inflicted on those who breach them. The form of such sanction will depend, to a large extent, on the significance of a particular rule within the existing heirarchical rule framework. Such frameworks can be extremely complex, but in the case of soccer fans a three-tier structure appears to be present.

The highest order of rules within this structure are almost isomorphic with values. Accounts offered by soccer fans contain statements such as:

You should always stand up for yourself, no matter what the cost.

To be a *man* you should not run away.

Never let rival fans think you are scared.

These are statements which can clearly be embraced by the concept of rule and are, of course, very familiar. Reflected in this high-order rule set is a selection of values from the mainstream, male-dominated society in which the subculture is nested. The selection of ideals of masculine virtue, honour and reputation as dominant themes serves to shape, but not dictate, the more immediately significant rules existing at a second level. Given that one should stand up for oneself, how should that act be performed in the particular contexts in which fans find themselves? In other words, what social actions should be carried out in order to achieve that act?

It is at this point that research in this field becomes much more problematic. The discovery of basic frames of reference and values poses little difficulty to those who conduct what used to be called participant-observation work. But obtaining a meaningful picture of the rules which apply in an immediate sense at the level of social action is, to use an appropriate metaphor, a different ball-game. It is also here that the accounts methodology, on its own, begins to become a little ineffective. The real problems may be summarized as follows.

Folk do not ordinarily go about their lives with a conscious appreciation of the rules which govern day-to-day activity. One cannot, therefore, simply ask what the rules are. The question is inappropriate. Instead one must find some alternative way of teasing them out. To some extent this can be done by inferring them logically, from statements contained within accounts. For example:

There's an organized pattern of events, I mean, you know what is going to happen, bringing a knife, I mean, probably by your own supporters, is looked down on as being a sort of form of cowardice. There is not many people will carry knives about – there is not many who will set out to harm someone. Not many people have got that killer instinct, once you have kicked them to the floor and made them bleed, I mean, that's it, it is left at that and they will say 'Leave him'. Someone in group who has been fighting them will just say, leave him, he has had enough. It is not very often it goes on to the point where he is kicked senseless.

Such a procedure, whilst illuminating, is rather haphazard and hardly likely to be comprehensive or exhaustive. A more precise, but less direct approach, is to elicit examples of rule breach. When tacit rules are broken, the existence of the rule becomes visible through the remedial strategies members bring into the situation. Whilst rules may remain for most of the time unarticulated, a breach is a 'remarkable' event which calls for explanation. From a research point of view, one might test hypotheses concerning the existence of a rule by posing, for comment by members, an example in which such a rule was breached. For example: 'What would you think about the fan who throws a stone at a player in the team he supports?'

To be in a position to develop such hypotheses in the first place, one usually needs a degree of knowledge in order not to pose questions or examples of such banality that one's credit in the eyes of informants is completely destroyed. A particularly useful feature of fans' accounts in this context is reference to actions which are deemed 'out of order'. In fact, this term is one of the keys. Not only does it affirm that there is, indeed, an order out of which it is possible to be, but it leads to a quite precise definition of boundaries of acceptable, legitimate or 'moral' behaviour. In parallel with this, an examination of the activity of deviants within the subculture can also provide similar illumination. On the soccer terraces certain individuals are referred to as 'nutters'. They engage in activities which are not only 'out of order' but seen, by other members, as mad. Thus by observing what nutters actually do, and by listening to how other fans describe their behaviour, one gains a fair appreciation of what is not allowed. This knowledge of existing *pro*scriptions complements documentation of *pre*scriptions and allows for a full mapping of second-order rules.

In addition to methodological problems encountered at this stage, a much more serious problem exists which concerns the relationship between rhetoric and action. Before pursuing this, however, mention must briefly be made of the third level of rules.

The first two levels of rule apply to established situations and routinized contexts. In the world of British football fans Saturdays bring with them predictable scenarios and rules exist to structure and deal with them. From time to time, however, routines are interrupted in an unexpected fashion. At such points not only are appropriate interpretations negotiated but ways of dealing with the new situation are created on the spot. Thus the third level of rules are 'one-off', non-generalizable ones which, whilst they may strongly reflect the dominant imperatives of the value framework, have a radically different status. To some extent they can be ignored in the development of general explanations of recurring social action. Attention to this area, however, is of importance since the 'mechanics' of negotiation of rules become visible. When mapping first and second order rules their genesis is not available for examination. The actual processes of negotiation and renegotiation are lost in an irretrievable history. Whilst the often frenzied running up of temporary rules might not reflect with total accuracy the development of their more stable and enduring counterparts, the involvement of certain members with definable roles within the subculture might be taken as a guide.

The remaining problem alluded to a moment ago concerns the manner in which social action is reflected in social talk. In research which relies heavily on accounts (or self-reports) it is essential to tackle this question despite the temptation to retreat to a purely phenomenological stance. A given pattern of behaviour is capable of being viewed from a number of standpoints yielding a set of different perspectives. These perspectives are encapsulated in the various rhetorics which people use in the description and explanation of the behaviour. Following a phenomenological line there is no way of choosing between such perspectives since the notion of there being an *objective* reality against which the perspectives can be juxtaposed is abandoned. I do not wish to quarrel with this at all. Apparent mismatches between account and observed (from the outside) behaviour can be accommodated by reference to interpretative rules. However, I would argue that to assume the rhetoric and the action are isomorphic (i.e. action becomes a meaningful entity in the gloss which members place upon it) is unnecessarily optimistic. The study of football fans highlights this most significantly since here the rhetoric embraces not one but two distinct perspectives. A failure to detect this duality in the rhetoric would render analysis of action on the terraces quite meaningless.

This seemingly peculiar state of affairs results from the fact that whilst rules clearly direct action on the terraces a further set of rules exists to govern how such action should be spoken of and, most significantly, what exaggerations and distortions may legitimately be introduced into the rhetoric. Thus an account will contain not only a reflection of the rules employed to define events and situations and those which are instrumental in the organization of actions, but also a level of exaggeration (for the purpose of self-enhancement) which members will tacitly conspire to accept. These two aspects of the account must be disentangled before even a purely phenomenologically oriented enquiry can be pursued (see Marsh 1978).

The existence of rules of distortion is clearly illustrated in the cross-negotiation of accounts among members but can also be evidenced through observation of the creation of a rhetoric relating to a particular event. Football fans talk endlessly among themselves about what has happened during a particular Saturday. Routine events gradually become a little larger than life. There is a careful testing-out procedure during which various distortions and exaggerations are introduced and their acceptance or rejection monitored. Thus, at the end of a regular day, prestige and a sense of worth can be created even though the opportunities might not have existed in the action itself.

I do not wish to labour this point here (it is covered more fully in Marsh and Campbell 1981). An example of a transcript taken from a tape-recorded discussion with fans on a train to an away match should serve to establish the point quite fully. Here one sees how certain distortions may be tacitly accepted whilst others, which lie outside the rules of rhetoric, are discarded as 'bullshit'.

Fan A: You go somewhere like today, we will go down Southampton, Millwall will turn out in force, if they go up Millwall, we know they are going to bring some supporters, if the other team, the home team, knows that the away team is going to bring supporters, they will come out for a fight, half of them.

Fan B: It's a shouting match to start off with but it kind of gets emotional, don't it. If you can imagine it, really good Millwall supporters, they can't stand their club being slagged down, you know and it all brings up, it builds up . . .

Fan A: It builds and it gets, you got to hit someone . . .

PM: How many people actually get hurt in those kind of things, though?

Fan A: When we played Everton in the FA Cup, I spent two weeks in hospital, I got seven busted ribs and a broken nose.

Fan B: Ah, na, that's exaggerated . . . The young fellas, they are giving each other verbal and they are running each other down, that's all harmless fun, you know, even if they chase each other round the ground or something. When it comes to people bringing out knives, that's out of order.

Fan A: Yeah, but it's changed, it's changed, everything comes out now. When we go away, I admit, I do people in the eyes with ammonia, so what? I got done at Everton; since I have been there, I have carried that ammonia with me all the time. There is no way that I go away without that ammonia . . .

Fan B: Where is it now then?

Fan A: Today, I haven't got it, right . . .

Fan B: Ah, I don't believe you. If you take it everywhere, why haven't you got it today?

Fan A: Because I haven't been home to get it.

Fan C: If you went down this train and asked everybody honestly, if they have had a fight, a battle with anybody at a football match, they might say 'We have done this, and we have done that' but they never actually done it. It's always 'We' you know – 'We' – it's the group. We done this, we done the college, but it's never actually them that have done it. The majority done it, you know. 'We' – it's never 'I'.

The research approach briefly described here has been applied in the investigation of other arenas for aggressive behaviour. One such study centred around fights and disturbances in public houses, and here special attention was paid to the patterns of social interaction between landlords and customers. Accounts from both publicans and 'punters' were elicited and juxtaposed with data derived from observation work. More formal questionnaire methods were also used to provide both quantitative and qualitative material. Clear evidence of rules in the organization of action on the part of landlords was revealed, and a set of 'ground rules' for pub-goers was also articulated. In the interests of brevity only a few examples are given here (see Marsh and Campbell 1979).

Fights in pubs and bars are rarely random or unpredictable events. Assaults on landlords and bar staff, in particular, were found to result in a statistically predictable fashion as a consequence of particular social acts which they themselves performed. It was quite clear that coherent interpretative rules existed within most pubs to define certain actions by staff as warranting reaction and moves to remedy perceived denial of status and worth. Such actions included inappropriate measures to conform with the drinking-up rule, pre-emptive refusal to serve particular customers (defined in advance as 'troublemakers') and, more generally, exceeding the authority thought to be fitting in the case of a particular publican. Evidence of such rules was implicit in many of the justificatory accounts offered by customers. For example:

I was sitting there with three of my mates. It was just after eleven and we'd got last orders in . . . He says, 'Come on, we've had your money, now let's have you out' – real flash bastard . . . We've nearly finished, and he comes over again and says 'Look, I've already told you: come on, out,' and he picks up my mate's glass and then reaches over for mine. So I put my hand on it and said, 'What about all those over there, then (pointing to a corner table)? They're still drinking and you haven't said anything to them.' He says, 'Never mind about them,' and grabs my arm and pulls me up. He was trying to push me out of the door. So I hit him. My mates had a go at him as well . . . Then we made a run for it.

To regular pub-goers, especially those who frequent those houses where fights and acts of aggression are not uncommon occurrences,[2] the

---

[2] It must be pointed out that acts of violence in British pubs are statistically rare. From a sample of 2000 pubs it was found that events warranting description as 'violent' occur with an average frequency of less than three per year. In some particular pubs, however, fights occur weekly or even daily.

notion of rule-directed behaviour is present in everyday talk. Indeed, many will offer the existence of a tacit rule as a justification for aggressive action. For example:

> One thing you *don't* do is spill somebody's beer. If you knock into him and his beer's spilt you've got to do something – you've got to get him another, and quickly. It's like smoking somebody else's fags on the counter. You can pinch his girl friend – you can do anything, but you don't spill his beer, you don't drink his beer and you don't steal his fags.

Failure to engage in remedial actions to redress some offence is a common precursor of assaults. Customers perceive that many offences are accidental in nature and accept appropriate measures to reinstate the *status quo*. However, lack of social knowledge on the part of the offender would not be seen as mitigation. As one drinker pointed out after two students had accidentally walked off with a regular customer's pint of lager, and failed to take appropriate remedial steps, 'If they don't know the rules, they shouldn't be in here. They both need a smack in the mouth to make them learn.'

Whilst customers have their own ground rules for orderly pub life, landlords appear to follow strict (and often rigid) codes for both identifying and dealing with 'troublemakers'. For example:

> The people we get most trouble with are the 18–21 year olds – these are the people that cause the trouble. And quite literally you can smell them as they walk in the door.

> If you have been in the trade a while you can tell more or less, when they (troublemakers) are coming through the door. Instantly, you tell the barman or whoever is on duty 'keep your eyes open' . . . It's just a feeling. You just know.

> I don't know whether it's me or what, but I can usually spot them as they walk through the door. In a pub you never know what's going to walk through the door.

At times these rigid approaches conflict with what customers take to be appropriate publican behaviour. Assaults on publicans can, therefore, be seen as resulting from a clash of distinct perspectives existing within one social arena. Although the publican's and the customers' rules overlap to a great extent, ensuring a usually harmonious pattern of interaction, small areas of incompatibility can exist which lead to aggressive action – this being seen as the only way of resolving the dilemma.

In some pubs, with a long-standing and regular clientele, the rule framework is often highly complex and, to the outsider, largely hidden. Certain seats or stools, for example, may be acknowledged as 'belonging' to a particular person because he has sat there for twenty years or so. Naive outsiders sitting in such a seat and refusing to move will be seen as in serious violation of an absolute rule and strong sanction will be inevitable. In contrast, those pubs catering for a more transient and casual clientele may have few coherent ground rules apart from those which customers see as applying to pubs in general. Where a strong internal framework is absent, acts of violence may be seen, on occasions, as resulting from this partial anomie and the ability of individuals to act without anticipation of group sanction. For example: 'If you want a bit of aggro you go down to — (a late-night bar with a disco). It's OK there. But you don't do it in your local. That's different.'

Attention to the rules which are salient features of the organization of action within definable social contexts appears to be a profitable research strategy. Its particular value is that explanations of behaviour, because they are initially couched within the framework of member's own terms of reference, are immediately relevant and 'intensive'. In addition, the derivation, through 'glossing' of the emic material, of etic perspectives opens the way for comparative research. The structure and content of extant rule frameworks might be seen as having sufficient functional equivalence to enable cross-cultural and cross-subcultural work to take on a new dimension. This possibility is currently being explored empirically in a project centring on the expression and social management of aggression among teenagers in Europe and America. Cross-sex differences are also being explored.

References

Berry, J. W. (1969) 'On cross-cultural comparability.' *International Journal of Psychology* **4**, 119–28.

Cohen, S. (1973) *Folk devils and moral panics.* Paladin, London.

Fox, R. (1977) 'The inherent rules of violence.' In P. Collett (ed.), *Social rules and social behaviour.* Blackwell, Oxford.

Frijda, N. and G. Jahoda (1969) 'On the scope and methods of cross-cultural research.' In D. R. Price-Williams (ed.), *Cross-cultural studies.* Penguin, Harmondsworth.

Marsh, P. and A. Campbell (1979) *Report to the Whitbread Foundation*. Whitbread Ltd, London.
— — (eds.) (1981) *Aggression and violence*. Blackwell, Oxford.
Marsh, P., E. Rosser and R. Harré (1978) *The rules of disorder*. Routledge & Kegan Paul, London.
Whiting, J. M. (1969) 'Methods and problems in cross-cultural psychology.' In S. Lindzey and E. Aronson (eds.), *Handbook of social psychology*, vol. 4. Addison-Wesley, Reading, Mass.

4. Knowledge

Introduction

In this chapter Luckmann and Kreckel examine the idea that social action is the realization of a store or stock of knowledge. The sharpest distinction between behaviourist and ethogenic psychologies appears in the relevance each accords to the attribution of knowledge to actors. In action psychologies people are thought of as drawing on a stock of knowledge in acting. A general theoretical framework for dealing with stocks of knowledge is developed, and detailed empirical support for the distinctions proposed in the theoretical part is provided.

The theoretical derivation of the idea of a 'stock of knowledge' starts with the observation that actions are related to projects. But projects may themselves be related to human requirements as a species of animal, to social requirements relative to a culture with a particular history and to personal requirements of an individual with a certain autobiography. Action to realize projects at each 'level' has its own proper mode of explanation. The requirement that action must be seen as embedded in history, both social and individual, can be expressed in another way. Actions so conceived have meaning, relative to the 'themes' they realize. To project and to understand an action as realizing a theme requires that actor and interactor draw on a stock of knowledge.

Individual stocks of knowledge are partly idiosyncratic reflecting distinctive autobiographies, but they are partly common, reflecting the social processes by which humans become persons. The necessities of transmission alone, for example a communication code, and the time taken to transmit such a stock, lead to the stock becoming differentiated among different categories and classes of persons, such as the old and the young, the male and the female. Each identifiable group has both a proper stock of knowledge peculiar to itself and shares in a common stock. The more complex the society the more elaborately differentiated becomes the stock of knowledge.

Empirical studies of the way family members are able to carry on a social interaction reveals that, just as theory predicts, there is a stock of knowledge (homodynamic code) concerning the meaning of speech actions that is peculiar to a family; and there is another stock (heterodynamic code) that is common to family members and outsiders.

In the empirical study reported in Part 2 of this chapter, social interactions mediated by speech between family members were recorded. The social meanings of the speech (tone) units as performative utterances were investigated by asking family members to interpret the events. This reveals the homodynamic code used within the family, the family's stock of knowledge. Then outsiders were asked to do the same thus revealing the heterodynamic code, the common stock of knowledge shared by all members of the local English-speaking community. It became clear that the family members had a stock of very detailed knowledge as to how to produce and interpret social acts by speaking. This knowledge included even the proper location of stress to use the same sentence for the performance of different speech acts. Outsiders, dependent on a common stock of knowledge, shared some *but not all* the family's interpretative conventions.

This very detailed and thorough empirical study shows that stocks of knowledge are indeed differentiated in just the ways theoretical analysis predicts.

However, an important dimension of research has been omitted from this chapter. The next step in the evolution of the study of the role of knowledge in action production ought to be the investigation of how individuals actually use their action-related knowledge. This would involve research into the way people bring about their own actions as the correct ways of realizing the acts that the social demands momentarily put upon them require. To complete an action study we need to know how individuals process knowledge. There is a pretty exact parallel in linguistics. Modern studies of syntax are aimed at revealing a native speaker's 'competence', so called. In this sense 'competence' is the totality of knowledge and skill that an individual requires to perform linguistically. But though a fully adequate competence theory could be used to specify all and only the correctly formed strings of lexemes admitted as proper in a certain language, it is far from answering the question as to how an individual speaker uses his knowledge and skill in the moment-by-moment production of action. As they say in linguistics, it is not a performance theory. In terms of the analogy, Luckmann and

Kreckel have demonstrated the importance of the discovery of the corpus of knowledge required for social action. The next step would be a performance theory, an explanation of how this knowledge is actually used in 'real' time to control action.

Individual action and social knowledge

THOMAS LUCKMANN

1. Introduction

It is natural that a topic so close to men's hearts as ours should provoke considerable disagreement. The briefest look at the way the concept of praxis traversed from Aristotle to Marx, and an inspection of the range of positions in our own day from the development of Max Weber's interpretative sociology to behaviourism's last stand in Skinner's writings shows that action is closely linked to basic prejudices. Where elementary metaphysical positions and general ways of looking at the world are involved, communication becomes difficult. This may be inevitable. But some of the difficulty is caused by outright misunderstandings which one may try to avoid. Many misunderstandings on topics of such wide implications as action follow from the fact that the arguments proceed from assumptions which are not stated. I should therefore like to begin by saying as clearly as I can what I mean by action.

Action is a privileged form of behaviour and it is also a privileged form of non-behaviour. It is privileged in that it is meaningful to the actor above and beyond the way in which ordinary experiences are meaningful to the human person. This is not attributable to some substantive trait of such behaviour (non-behaviour presumably cannot have any substantive traits in any case) but to the fact that it was originally projected by the person. It is behaviour or non-behaviour with a subjective purpose. That purpose is subjectively articulated in a project; the behaviour, or non-behaviour, occurs in accordance with, or, naturally, also in deviation from, the original project. This, as it seems to me extremely useful, precise and compelling way of looking at action, was developed by Alfred Schutz (see especially Schutz 1962). Evidently, not all behaviour is action; some behaviour may be a simple reflex without awareness on the part of the organism; some behaviour may be meaningful, i.e. a genuine experience for the person without having been projected by the person. Conversely, not all projected behaviour is action; some of it may remain mere phantasy. It hardly needs to be added, finally, that not all non-behaviour is action: only abstaining from behaviour is – provided that such abstention was projected by the actor. I shall return to a detailed analysis of this problem in the next section.

Turning now from preliminary definitions to analytic proposals, I suggest that the following main levels should be distinguished in the analysis of the 'causation' of human action: the level of the species (genetic populations); the level of social structures (institutions, social groups, social classes) and, more generally, social strata; and the level of individual life. Correspondingly, the following elementary dimensions of time should be kept separate in the analysis of the processes of human action: the evolutionary time of the species; the historical time of social institutions, groups and strata; and the biographical time of individual life.

It is obvious that the level of individual life is logically implied in the social-structural level, and that the social-structural level is implied in the level of the species. Biographies are thus inserted into historical time, and human history emerged in evolutionary processes. It may be said in the abstract that structures and functions on levels of higher generality define the range of possibilities on the next more specific level. Each level and each time dimension must be nonetheless considered in its own right. Different paradigms of explanatory interest and analytic procedure correspond to the various levels. Metaphysical prejudice, materialist as well as idealist, traditionally dictated reductionism from one level to another. Neither form of reductionism, one prevalent in modern physical science, the other in the study of history and other humanities, could account for the systematic organization of the 'elements' on the several interconnected levels and for the systematic enchainment of events in each dimension of time. Doubtless, evolution primarily refers to processes affecting the species, history to changes affecting social structures and biography to events that form individual life. But this is not the whole story. There is clearly a sense in which one may also speak of the genetic determination of individual actions. At the very least, individual actions are confined within the range of the possibilities of the species. It is so evident as to appear trivial that human beings neither lay eggs nor navigate by echo – but the implications are wide and the consequences enormous. There is also a sense in which one may speak of the historical determination of individual actions. Again it seems trivially obvious that a first-century Bedouin tribesman was not and could not have been motivated by the Puritan ethic or the Sioux warrior deterred by the Code Napoléon – but again the corollaries of these obvious truths are highly significant and, at least implicitly, under attack by reductionist preconceptions.

In trying to understand certain interesting and important things about human action one may place in brackets the genetic determination of human behaviour – provisionally. Certainly, the 'biogram' of the species accounts for a wide range of 'universals'. That range is not limited to the more obvious morphological facts. Nonetheless, genetic determinants explain little of the concrete patterns of individual actions. Turning, then, to the historical formation of social structures, institutions and social classes, we find much that helps to explain the differences between Bedouins and the Sioux. In some way 'history' is the necessary background for any human action. But even historical institutions rarely account directly for individual actions; and individual actions as such do not 'history make'. If one speaks of the historical determination of individual actions by social structures, institutions and classes one is forced to allow for something that mediates systematically between historical structures and individual actions. What can that be? Evidently something that is a principle of behavioural integration which takes into account the 'location' of individual life-courses in the temporal dimension of history.

Assumptions about some such principle are made in all but the 'black box' approaches to human behaviour. They are certainly also implied in common sense, in ordinary talk about human life and behaviour. But the assumptions and implications are rarely spelled out, as urgently needed as an explication of such assumptions seems to be in the present state of the biological and social sciences and the humanities. I shall return to this matter in the section that follows the analysis of the constitution of meaning in individual action.

2. The constitution of meaning in individual action[1]

The source of all meaning in individual actions is elementary conscious processes. Consciousness is, of course, nothing in itself, it is necessarily

---

[1] This section is based on the phenomenological investigations of Edmund Husserl, Alfred Schutz and Aron Gurwitsch. I have tried to use the results of their investigations as I think they apply to a theory of action and language some years ago (Luckmann 1973) and, more recently, in relation to certain methodological issues in social science (Luckmann, in press). The following account is taken from the latter with slight changes.

of something. But that which it is of, the object of intentional processes – which may or may not be an object in the ordinary sense of the word – has a universal structure. This consists of a thematic kernel of awareness which is surrounded by a thematic field which, again, is surrounded by an open horizon. 'What' it is that stands out as a theme in the stream of consciousness is a question difficult to answer. Very generally, it can be said that thematic kernels emerge in the stream of consciousness in consequence of an interrelated system of thematic, interpretational and motivational relevances. Thematic kernels may be perceptual, recollective, fictive, judgemental, etc. But experiences contain more than merely the actual presentation of a kernel. They involve continuing syntheses of the theme with the presentations of the kernel in the phase that has just passed and the automatic anticipation of a theme in the phase that follows immediately. It also contains appresentations, i.e. indirect presentations. In the case of perceptual experiences, for example the 'tail' side of a coin is appresented to the directly presented 'head'. All experiences, in particular those in everyday reality, contain automatic appresentations of a relevant type, a typification. This is a 'scheme' of subjectively sedimented, interrelated thematic elements. *Before* experiencing a policeman as a policeman, we experience a human body as a typical shape with typical visual, tactile, olfactory components which 'belong' together and form an elementary experience of the human body – although what is directly presented at a given time may be only a distant visual form. 'Before' is to be understood, of course, in a logical, not necessarily in a temporal sense. The most primitive source of any kind of meaning is located right there: in the automatic constitution of themes as typical 'objects', whether these are perceptual, recollective, fictive, logical–judgemental, etc.

Themes may simply follow one another in the stream of consciousness without any active involvement of the self, as in some forms of day-dreaming. But we may want to reserve the term *experience* for such sequences of themes which do not merely 'run off by themselves' but in which the self is actively engaged, to which the self is paying attention. Experiences are characterized, in addition, and as a consequence of this kind of involvement, by a higher degree of clarity and distinctness of the themes and by a higher degree of consistency among the themes that follow one another. Nonetheless, a specific *meaning* of experience emerges only in a further and more complex conscious activity. It is constituted in the retrospective or, one may also say, reflective grasp of an experience that has just come to an end or of a phase of experience that has just passed. The experience is thereby placed in a context that goes beyond the simple actuality of ongoing awareness. Meaning is thus constituted in the consciousness of the relation – and of the kind of relation – that obtains between a concrete experience and something else. That 'something else' may be a past experience; the kind of relation that obtains, may be one of similarity ('another man in that kind of uniform'). It may be a typificatory scheme ('this is a policeman') or a social norm ('don't jay-walk if policemen are around'), etc. The *why* and the *how* of the active performance of the mind in which the meaning of experiences is constituted depends again upon subjective relevance systems and, of course, on the structure of the situation. The subjective relevance systems determine in considerable measure not only the original experience, i.e. the experience just accomplished or recollected, but also the experience in which the meaning of that past experience is constituted. They also determine the action context in which both the original and the subsequent interpretative experience are located.

What, then, is an action context? As we have already seen in a preliminary consideration of the matter, actions are experiences which had been projected by the self and which are lived through in relation to that project. Actions are constituted in the relation of project and performance. A project is formed in the (fictive) anticipation of a state of affairs to be achieved by the self in a sequence of experiences. Projects evidently vary considerably as to their clarity and distinctness. This is partly a function of the type of action involved, e.g. a mathematical operation, the building of a house, going to the cinema, expanding one's consciousness, renegotiating the rate of interest on loans, etc. Most importantly, it depends on the degree of familiarity with this kind of action and the degree of routinization that characterizes the steps involved in reaching the end-result. Actions have thus two dimensions of meaning. They are defined as actions by the connection of ongoing experiences to the projected aim. That is one dimension of meaning. But once an action is accomplished – or a phase of an action is achieved – one may return to it reflectively just as one can turn to other experiences with a less complicated temporal structure, and link it to a superordinated context. This may be, in the simplest case, another action of the same type, it may be a social norm, a moral maxim, an entire rhetoric of justification, etc. One difference must be noted, however. Actions are self-determinations of conduct – at least partial self-determinations. They are, therefore, intrinsically meaningful to the actor at the time of action. That particular meaning is, in a manner of speaking, closed once the action has been performed. It does not change after the action is accomplished or the project has failed. But it can be reinterpreted, placed in different contexts, e.g. of self-justification, biographical recollection or mythologization, legal reconstruction in court proceedings, coding in interactional schemes by social scientists, etc. This dimension of meaning is 'open', both subjectively and inter-subjectively.

Social actions are actions whose project is oriented to others. These others may be concrete fellow beings. Here one may distinguish between actions in which the fellow beings are experienced directly in face-to-face situations and actions that are oriented to people who are merely recollected. This action is here geared to an anticipated effect, a reaction, etc of a person whose existence is, strictly speaking, merely assumed rather than an absolute certainty. It is structurally not quite the same thing whether I do not cross the street against red signals when I see a policeman or I merely assume that the policeman I saw on that street some time ago may return in another few moments. Furthermore, social action may be oriented to people whom I grasp exclusively in their typicality, social function and the like, e.g. policemen in general. Finally, it may be oriented to a fully anonymized social 'structure', e.g. the traffic regulations.

From many – although not all – points of view, face-to-face interactions are the most important kind of social interaction. They are its prototype. Evidently, at least, all social action that is behaviour and comes to the notice of others can be interpreted by them and, potentially, reacted to. But in face-to-face situations, all social actions that are behaviour come to the notice of others. More importantly, social action is in this case not only oriented to others in the original project but is determined by others in its concrete performance. All forms of social action are characterized, in addition to the two-dimensionality of meaning that is constitutive of action in general, by the specific and rather complex structure of experiences that involve others as concrete persons face-to-face, or in recollection and anticipation; or that involve them as social types, again face-to-face or indirectly; or that involves them as fully anonymized social 'structures'. Social action is thus always 'co-determined' by others. More precisely, the meaning of social action is co-constituted by the meaning which others have for the actor. And in addition to this 'determination by anticipation' others 'co-determine' social action in a variety of ways: directly by action and communication in face-to-face situations; and indirectly by various kinds of objectivated results of action. These range from buildings and paths and roads and traps and mines to the preservation of communicative acts in texts of various kinds.

One should consider carefully what the 'meaningfulness' of social action requires by way of 'interpretation'. We all 'interpret' social actions of our fellow-man. But most of the time we do so as routinely as the actions themselves seem routinized. In other words, the 'meaning' of such actions presents itself 'automatically' to us when we observe the actions of other people. We do not normally stop to think about them. If the course of an action does *not* fit the automatically appresented 'meaning', however, that is, if it constitutes a problem of some sort, the typical appresented 'meaning' must be modified or even abandoned completely and replaced by another typification. All this requires interpretative acts in the narrower sense. The acts will be continued until the pragmatic or theoretical 'problem' is adequately resolved. It hardly needs to be added that interpretative acts of this kind draw upon a subjective stock of knowledge. Now it is the case that only part of a subjective stock of knowledge is built up in interpretative acts of the self. For the most part it contains socially derived and transmitted elements, i.e. elements derived from a social stock of knowledge: the systematic repository of objectivated past interpretative acts by innumerable other people.

3. The actor: personal identity[2]

Human actions are determined by evolutionary processes in a manner which is only partly analogous to the genetic transmission of highly specific behaviour traits in most other species. Genetic codes which embody the results of selection and adaptation in the evolution of our species indubitably also define the range of possible behaviour for living human organisms. Evidently, the possession of certain traits will have cut down the chance for some individuals to transmit their genes. But to assume that individual organisms' reproductive success should have been 'favoured' by the possession of a definable set of specific behavioural traits within human history or, for that matter, prehistory, rather stretches the imagination. Individual traits, embedded in rigid patterns of social organization (themselves the indirect product of evolutionary processes), are much more likely to have played a strictly subordinate

[2] I have considered and documented the problems with which this section is concerned in more detail elsewhere (Luckmann 1980).

role in human evolution, a role certainly less prominent than that of total organismic responses within complex, highly individualized and variable patterns of social organization.

Total organismic response? It may be preferable, although cumbersome, to speak of systems of behavioural organization developing in the lifetime of organisms, systems in which specific behavioural items and repertoires are integrated into functional sets (i.e. complex actions) by individual organisms in conscious 'adaptation' to varied requirements. Perhaps the most important of these requirements consists of behaviour in relation to other organisms. Both the organisms and their interrelationship are thus highly individualized. In the human case social organization was decreasingly determined by the aggregates of genetically transmitted behavioural traits of individual organisms and became increasingly man-made, that is to say, historical. At some early stage of human evolution a kind of historical dialectic must have set in. Human behaviour, determined genetically in a less and less direct manner produced specifically human, historical forms of social organization. Historical forms of social organization determined, in their turn, often in a highly specific way, the behaviour (and non-behaviour) of individual human beings. This was possible by the historical 'coding' of the results of past human actions: their communicative transmission by social institutions. Yet again, it is not so much specific institutions which directly determine specific actions, although that of course is part of the story. More important is the general formation of specific types of behavioural organization in an individual course of life by specific historical societies. The common terms which I consider most appropriate to refer to these types are person, or personal identity. Without recourse to philosophical idealism or materialism we may say that human beings determine their own actions as persons.

Human beings determining their actions? Are then actions not autonomous on any account? Evidently not: they are 'determined' on many different levels in many different ways. But are actors autonomous? They are and they are not. Personal identity may be persuasively considered as the principle of autonomy in behaviour – yet personal identity as a form of life is itself a 'product' of evolution and history. Personal identities are constructed socially, i.e. historically, in processes in which the individual organisms participate actively – but under natural and social constraints. Furthermore, the enchainment of actions in the time dimension of individual life produces a 'history' of its own: a biography. Here we meet with another set of determinants of action which, in this case, is neither derived from nature (in the sense of evolutionary determination) nor man-made (in the sense of human production of 'history'). That set of action-determining factors is *self-made*. In choosing future courses of action human beings are autonomous, in general principle. But the choices are based on accumulated past experience, an individual stock of knowledge. And the choices are made under the weight of past commitments – whether they were freely chosen or socially imposed and whether they are devised with an eye to the future or with both feet in past routine.

Phylogenetically as well as ontogenetically, personal identities presuppose the specific morphology and physiology of the human body and the elementary structures and functions of human consciousness; and they develop within a wide but nonetheless limited range of social organization that evolved in the human species. These presuppositions are 'universal', at the same time they are specific and concrete. But a human person does not emerge automatically. A personal identity is actively 'constructed' in social processes. These processes are essentially processes of direct inter-subjective communication. Their key characteristic may be described in the abstract as a reciprocal 'mirroring' of behaviour. The concrete content of these processes is, however, predetermined by a historical social structure, i.e. a social organization of behaviour, and a culture, i.e. the socially objectivated categories of the subjective orientation of behaviour. The former consist of systems of production and distribution of power, etc, the latter of a language, rules of conduct, legitimations etc.

Personal identity is a form of life characterized by central, long-range control of behaviour by an organism. Even if occasionally short sequences of overt behaviour might be or might seem to be adequately explicable functionally (to use the term in its ethological connotation) without reference to personal identity, this becomes increasingly difficult with higher-level action, as e.g. with action that spans long-term sequences of continuous behaviour. It becomes impossible with action that spans sequences of discontinuous behaviour. Finally, to try to explain action that consists of *non*-behaviour without allowing for an actor who is a person or is characterized by some such principles of identity is downright absurd.

The level of determination of individual action which is of main interest to the sociologist is obviously that of social structure. The distinction between social-structural determination and genetic determination of behaviour is normally taken for granted by social scientists, although the line that separates highly routinized action from behaviour that is 'directly' determined by genetic mechanisms is empirically blurred. When it comes to the peculiar and complex relation between social structure and personal identity, however, social scientists are likely to forget the metaphorical character of statements about the social 'causation' of individual behaviour. A sociological theory of personal identity is therefore urgently needed. Unfortunately, it is still in its infancy.

The modern sociology of knowledge attempts to overcome one theoretically fatal consequence of this deficiency. It shows how individual stocks of knowledge, which are the foundation of individual action projects, are derived from social stocks of knowledge, and it analyses the structure of social stocks of knowledge. Individual stocks of knowledge are formed in biographically unique sedimentations of experience of an individual. The necessary condition for their being built up is a substructure of cognitive operations, an elementary structure of consciousness which, as it may be said here without further elaboration, is the product of evolutionary processes. But it is evidently not a sufficient condition, and, in fact, it explains very little of the concrete systems of orientation in the world. Generally, no more than a small portion of knowledge in any individual stock is constructed in autonomous problem-solving activities. The larger portion is derived from a social stock of knowledge, i.e. a *socially* objectivated and *socially* distributed reservoir of meanings which is capable of functioning as an *individual* system of orientation in 'the world'. The processes by which elements of a social stock of knowledge are transmitted to individual stocks of knowledge are determined by a historical social structure. The social structure is a network of institutions and a set of inequalities; as such it restricts the distribution of elements of the social stock of knowledge of typical individual members of the society. The social structure thus always also contains typical transmission processes, regulations of access to knowledge, and strategies and rhetorics of legitimation for the inclusions and exclusions of potential recipients of knowledge, as different as all these elements may be in different societies.

4. Acquisition and transmission of knowledge

It could be asserted that individuals acquire knowledge whenever an experience is stored away. Is not knowledge acquired continuously, at least during the waking hours of human life? Indeed, all experiences – in the sense in which the term was introduced in the discussion of the ways in which meaning is constituted in action – impress themselves on memory. All experiences *are* sedimented in subjective structures of meaning according to their typicality and relevance. All sedimentations do contribute something highly or minimally significant to an individual stock of knowledge, no matter how large or small that stock is at any given time.

On the other hand, mature human beings learn little from most experiences. This is not surprising: in a manner of speaking, there is not much to learn. In the routine of everyday life most experiences are unproblematic. After all, many situations occur again and again, and the problems that they may have originally presented were solved long ago. The solutions were stored in the stock of knowledge, and, upon the individual's being faced with a similar situation, are used to master it. The oftener the solutions were applied successfully, the more routinized the application. Further sedimentations of such experiences merely supported the established routine by reinforcing the credibility of the appropriate elements of knowledge.

It is a different story whenever a situation 'resists' the application of old routine. If appropriate elements of knowledge cannot be applied without difficulty to cope with the problem at hand, one must begin to think. What this means is fairly obvious: one starts to review deliberately all available and potentially relevant elements of one's stock of knowledge and applies them to the situation to see whether they fit at all and how well they fit. Appropriate knowledge may consist of typifications of objects, events, qualities, persons, in one word, of taxonomies. Such taxonomies are pragmatic, action-oriented. They contain evaluations, typical motives of behaviour and means–ends relationships. They are inserted into superordinated paradigms of looking at reality and general strategies of action – as well as, prophylactically, justifications of such strategies. Thinking in problematic situations thus consists of interpretive procedures. On the individual commonsense level, such cognitive operations are comparable to the hermeneutics of more ambitious systems of thought on the level of mythology, religion and science. They evidently contribute something of significance to the individual stock of knowledge; they change existing typifications, revise taxonomies and even formulate new strategies. Thinking in problematic situations normally proceeds until the problem is adequately resolved. What is 'adequate' coping with a situation, what represents an 'adequate' solution of a problem to an individual, is a joint function of several factors. One is the individual's subjective system of relevance and, more generally, his stock of knowledge at the time, another is his pragmatic interest in the situation, still another the external, imposed requirements of the situation; finally – especially if the situation in question should be a social one –, the 'adequacy' of solutions will also depend upon the social definition of the situation.

It is impossible now to discuss the way in which knowledge is acquired in much further detail; an analysis is to be found in Schutz and Luckmann (1973, esp. Ch. 3). Furthermore, it is hardly necessary to elaborate here on the point that the human ability to acquire knowledge rests on general and elementary structures of consciousness. It may be useful to stress, however, that, *logically*, subjective processes of the acquisition of knowledge suffice to explain the formation of individual stocks of knowledge. In addition, they suffice to explain the structure of such stocks; the interrelated hierarchies of specificity and distinctness, familiarity, credibility and compatibility which constitute them can be traced back to the original sedimentation processes. By the same token, social stocks of knowledge, no matter how anonymously impressive, can accumulate only if fed by subjective processes in which knowledge is acquired – whatever other conditions may be required for knowledge to accumulate socially. *Empirically*, however, social stocks of knowledge play a decisive role in the individual development and accumulation of knowledge. Human beings do not acquire knowledge by starting from scratch. They are born into a world in which other people already know *something*. They must indeed sometimes themselves solve problems; more often they only need to learn the solution found long ago by others. There is not only a division of labour in the functioning of society, there is also something akin to a division of labour over the generations in the history of culture.

If individually acquired elements of knowledge are to become available to others, they must be communicated. Some elements of knowledge – especially those pertaining to physical skills, work, war, sex, etc – may be communicated in the directness of face-to-face situations. Anything but transmission of the most rudimentary knowledge, however, requires a system of communication which is capable of referring to past and absent objects, qualities, events and persons, a sign system that transcends the expressivity and deixis found in face-to-face situations. Human language is such a system. By means of language, individuals may communicate to others such elements of knowledge as are likely to be relevant to them, not only here and now but also in the foreseeable future.

Nonetheless, communication is not yet social 'storage' of knowledge. Something like a *social* stock of knowledge accumulates only when the transmission of typical and specified elements of knowledge to typical and specified individuals is institutionalized, i.e. made mandatory and enforced by various kinds of sanctions. Institutional regulation of direct transmission – mainly by oral tradition in socially defined 'chains' – is certainly a necessary component of storage. Presumably it was the only one available in early prehistory and it is the normal one in early socialization. But artifacts of various kinds and language-independent notational systems – which probably also go farther back in human prehistory than was commonly thought – are also constitutive elements of social 'storage'. Finally, the importance of writing in early civilization is almost as well known as that of printing in modern history and that of other mass media in still more recent times. It requires no additional comment here. The history of religion, science and technology, and now also the sociology of knowledge attempt to relate these factors in the social accumulation of knowledge both to the intrinsic developments of various branches of knowledge and its external 'environment': human ecology and social structure, in particular the modes of production and distribution, and the organization of power (for further discussion see Berger and Luckmann 1966).

Our historical and systematic understanding of these matters was prepared by the political economies and sociologies of the early nineteenth century and it was significantly advanced first by Marx, later by Max Weber and more recently by the exponents of various forms of structuralism, especially Lévi-Strauss, and new developments in the sociology of knowledge. Nonetheless, our grasp of a key problem in the relation of individual and social knowledge, the social distribution of knowledge, is not as strong as could be wished. Durkheim, Mauss, Halbwachs, Scheler, Mannheim and Schutz, to mention only the most important names, approached the problem from quite different starting points. As a result of their work at least the contours of the problem are becoming fairly clear. Without doubt, the social distribution of knowledge is systematically related to the overall forms of social organization. I shall sketch an elementary model of this relationship in a moment. What is not yet sufficiently understood – and must be left open here – is the degree of autonomy of the system of knowledge from the basic structure of society. We do not know with any degree of certainty to what extent historical transformations of knowledge and the social distribution of knowledge are consequences and to what extent causes of general social change.

5. The social distribution of knowledge[3]

A completely equal distribution of knowledge is impossible except under highly unrealistic conditions. One is that the biological differentiation of human beings should be without any social consequences. Although the differences between man and woman, young and old, strong and weak, etc, are socially expressed, diminished or exaggerated, we cannot assume that without such social definitions all problems of life would be imposed on everybody in the same way, nor that the 'same' would appear to them in an identical fashion. Another condition is that the biographically unique sequence in which knowledge is acquired should play no role. Furthermore, the concrete intersubjective, face-to-face conditions for the communication of knowledge, one of the essential presuppositions for the development of any social stock of knowledge whatever, would have to be eliminated and the accumulation of knowledge would have to be stopped at a given level. But once granted that this is impossible, how would an *almost* equal social distribution of knowledge look?

First, some biological differentiation, no matter how minimal, must be assumed to be the evolutionary starting point for the expression of relatively simple differences in social relevance. It hardly needs to be stressed that 'biographically' established social relevances are not simply reducible to biological differences. In the present context all that is significant for us is that the most elementary differences in social relevances are founded on biological differentiations of some sort, and that these are elaborated historically in various directions – at least some of which may be assumed to have been 'functional'.

Next, the temporal and biographical differences in subjective streams of experience which determine an individual perspective cannot be entirely neglected. Such perspectives play a role in the processes by which elements of the social stock of knowledge are transmitted. They are socially relevant and are themselves in a certain sense 'socialized': learning sequences are embedded in social relevance contexts. The processes of transmission are differentiated in the dimension of social

---

[3] What follows is taken, in the main, from parts of the Ch. 4 of Schutz and Luckmann (1973).

time and with reference to socially defined, biographical categories. An obvious concrete example is the socially determined conjunction of institutionally defined age levels with learning sequences.

And finally, minimally unequal social distributions of knowledge presuppose that knowledge accumulates only very slowly. There is little specialization of knowledge. From this follows that all knowledge stored socially is, in principle, accessible to everyone. More exactly: there is nothing in the *structure* of knowledge that would stand in the way of its acquisition by anyone. If we disregard institutional barriers, which may stand in the way of the acquisition of certain kinds of knowledge by specified social types (as for example in the case of secret knowledge), the uneven distribution of knowledge is based on the social differentiation of routine processes of transmission of general knowledge.

The fact still remains that not all problems appear in the same way to all people, that they are not imposed on everyone at the same time, and that newly accumulated knowledge cannot be transmitted to everyone at once. The routine transmission of solutions to problems is therefore differentiated, first, according to the social definitions of the kinds of people for whom the solutions are considered relevant, second, according to the social definition of urgency of transmission and third, according to socially defined phases and sequences of acquisition. It is impossible to conceive of a social stock of knowledge which did not at least exhibit an unevenness of distribution of its elements in these respects.

A simple social distribution of knowledge, characterized as briefly as possible, thus looks as follows. Its core consists of elements relevant for everyone. Accordingly these elements are routinely transmitted to everyone, and the transmission is institutionally enforced. The processes of transmission are phased temporally and they are biographically graduated. At every given point of time all 'normal adults' therefore possess all those elements of the social stock of knowledge that are socially defined as relevant for 'everyone'. Young people, in contrast, possess only one – socially determined – part of the total supply of knowledge, but they expect that in due course other parts of generally relevant knowledge will be added.

Furthermore, there are elements relevant only for men and others relevant only for women – precisely as men, women and relevance are defined in a given society. Some knowledge will be routinely transferred only to men, some only to women. Thus 'normal men' should be in possession both of generally relevant knowledge and of that relevant only for men. Moreover, 'normal women' should likewise be in possession of generally relevant knowledge and of that relevant only for women. But because the institutionalized temporal–biographical differences of transmission also apply to the specifically 'masculine' and 'feminine' elements of knowledge, a further distributional factor is added. At any given point in time, only 'adult men' are in possession of the elements of knowledge relevant for everyone as well as those relevant only for men, while 'normal young men' possess only the socially defined components of common knowledge as well as the 'young' parts of knowledge relevant for men. And correspondingly for women.

Though we have used obvious and, empirically, the most important concrete examples of factors contributing to the social distribution of knowledge in 'simple' societies, it must be stressed that a generally valid *material* determination of the kinds of knowledge involved is not possible. The structural factors on which rest simple social distributions of knowledge generally determine the distinction between 'general knowledge' and 'special knowledge'. But what belongs to special knowledge in a society can be general knowledge in another and vice versa. General as well as special knowledge includes skills, usages, recipes, and explicit elements of knowledge. Without doubt there are definite skills and items of practical knowledge, 'recipes' of action, that belong almost universally to 'normal' general knowledge: walking, typical orientation in time and space, 'generally valid' norms of conduct, language. Together they form the inner core of everyone's relative–natural world view (to use a term coined by Scheler). But beyond this few generalizations can be offered. Only detailed historical and ethnological studies may yield additional conclusions.

General knowledge is routinely transmitted to everyone, special knowledge only to certain kinds of people, but fundamentally all knowledge is accessible to everyone. Evidently, there is no compelling motive for everyone to acquire special knowledge, and it happens that institutional barriers oppose such an acquisition. But everyone knows who is in possession of which forms of special knowledge. The social distribution of special knowledge is an element of general knowledge. In societies with simple social distributions of knowledge, everyday reality and above all, the social world, remain *relatively* manageable for everyone without permanent recourse to experts.

Complex social distributions of knowledge are characterized, first of all, by a certain 'inequality' in the distribution of general knowledge. No doubt, this at first seems paradoxical. General knowledge, it was said, consists of the socially objectivated solutions to such problems as are relevant for 'everyone'. But what does 'everyone' mean here? It hardly needs to be stressed again that problems confronting 'everyone' also appear individually in the perspective of a unique biography. The typical, socially objectivated solutions to problems that are taken over by the individual thus necessarily undergo certain idiosyncratic variations within his 'unique' subjective perspective. In addition the transmission of the elements in the social stock of knowledge takes place in concrete social interactions, which are also 'unique' for the individual. This is a source of the 'idiosyncratic' modifications of typical solutions to problems. But all this only means that absolute equality in the distribution of the elements in the social stock of knowledge is in principle impossible – a circumstance which was already mentioned. As long as it is a matter of nothing but 'idiosyncratic' modifications which occur 'after' the subjective acquisition of the socially objectivated elements of knowledge, the social stock of knowledge is not directly affected.

But where can it remain a matter of idiosyncratic variations only? In societies with an extremely simple division of labour and without established social strata the problems that are imposed on 'everyone' may be also assumed to be presented to everyone in essentially similar perspectives. As soon as the division of labour becomes more complicated, and as soon as clear-cut social strata – castes, feudal estates, classes – emerge, few problems, even those that are basically the same, are seen in the same way. Similar 'biographies' develop for obvious structural reasons, in the course of the progressive division of labour. These similarities in 'biographies' are responsible for the emergence of similar ways of looking at the world. The transmission of elements of general knowledge is modified accordingly, at least on the part of the recipients. Language offers an obvious, but by no means the only, example. As a component of the general knowledge of every society, language can – and must – be distributed in a relatively equal fashion. Subjective variations in the form of the idiosyncratic usages on the phonetic and lexical levels remain socially almost irrelevant. Given a certain complexity in the social structure, and the emergence of different types of biographies that are ultimately linked to the division of labour, a common language is converted into socially conditioned, socially established, and socially transmitted 'versions': as dialect, court language, 'social dialect', etc. In this restricted sense one can speak of an 'inequality' in the social distribution of general knowledge. It is this 'inequality' which is one characteristic of complex social distributions of knowledge.

The latter involves further subdivisions and developments of special knowledge. This can be regarded, first of all, as simply a quantitative difference. Through progressive subdivisions and internal developments (e.g. 'theoretization', 'professionalization') special knowledge gains a certain limited 'autonomy'. Special knowledge becomes institutionally divorced from general knowledge. The distance betwen 'laymen' and 'experts' becomes greater. Involved, often tedious, sometimes painful or even dangerous presuppositions (learning sequences, tests, initiations) precede the acquisition of special knowledge. Even the *transmission* of special knowledge becomes a job for specialists in the teaching of specialities. The subdivisions of knowledge are specialized as meaning-systems and the transmission of knowledge is itself institutionally specialized.

Given a complex social distribution of knowledge, special knowledge, in its totality, is no longer accessible to everyone – even in abstract principle. In addition, how specialized knowledge is distributed and where and when it is to be found, is no longer a part of the supply of 'equally' distributed general knowledge. What repercussion this has for society is a question of the greatest interest for the empirical sociology of knowledge. Knowledge can become more and more of a power factor in complex social distributions of knowledge. On the other hand, what consequences such a distribution of knowledge has for the social determination of individual action, is a question that only a historical, comparative social psychology will be able to answer.

References

Note: this list only gives references to such studies as contain more detailed analyses of the arguments presented in this essay. For references to evolutionary and ethological literature see Luckmann (1980); for phenomenology see Luckmann (1973) and for sociology, especially the sociology of knowledge, see Berger and Luckmann (1966).

Berger, P. and Th. Luckmann (1966) *The social construction of reality*. Doubleday, Garden City, N.Y.

Luckmann, Th. (1973) 'Aspekte einer Theorie der Sozialkommunikation.' In H. P. Althaus, H. Henne and H. E. Wiegand (eds.), *Lexikon der germanistischen Linguistik*. Niemayer, Tübingen. (Revised edn, 1979.)

— (1980) 'Personal identity as an evolutionary and historical problem.' In M. von Cranach, K. Foppa, W. Lepenies and D. Ploog (eds.), *Human ethology: claims and limits of a new discipline*, Cambridge University Press, Cambridge.

— (in press) 'Hermeneutics as a paradigm for social science?' In M. Brenner (ed.), *Social method and social life*. Academic Press, London.

Schutz, A. (1962) *Collected papers, vol. 1*. Nijhoff, The Hague.

Schutz, A. and Th. Luckmann (1973) *The structures of the life-world*. Northwestern University Press, Evanston, Ill.

Communicative acts and extralinguistic knowledge

MARGA KRECKEL

1. Delineating the research problem

That communication via language is possible and regularly occurs is considered by most social scientists as a truism. This view is shared by the overwhelming majority of lay members of a society who usually take it for granted that they are able to understand what they are listening to and get across what they want to. However, when we ask both social scientists and laymen how they actually transmit and understand messages like 'complaints', they must admit defeat. All they can say is that they do occasionally 'complain' and that they recognize 'complaints' in concrete interaction. Furthermore, they recognize them the more confidently the better they know the speaker, that is, the better they can tell what is *not* a 'complaint'. Hence, if we are able to produce 'complaints' and recognize them when issued by different persons, phrased in different words, spoken under different circumstances, then we have to assume that there are *physical indicators or cues* which assist us in the process of *encoding* and *decoding* these messages.

In this paper it will be argued, first, that the very attempt at discerning and empirically analysing cues in natural interaction has to start where speakers rely on a large body of *shared knowledge* acquired in *direct interaction within close-knit groups*, such as families or long-standing groups of friends; and, second, that cues can only be explored if the *participants* in the social interaction under investigation *actively co-operate* in *interpreting their own communicative behaviour* in a detailed and systematic way.

This paper will consist of three sections: in the theoretical section I am going to discuss the conditions under which the research questions can be approached; in the procedural section I shall develop a discovery procedure which has proved to be fruitful for the empirical investigation

267

of cues used in the process of encoding and decoding messages; and in the empirical section I shall give an illustration of the application of both theoretical framework and procedures by means of an extract from the recorded interaction of an English working-class family filmed continuously over a period of four months (part of the material was broadcast as the BBC television documentary, *The family*[1]).

2. Theoretical framework

2.1. A pragmatic approach

Numerous social scientists interested in exploring the necessary and sufficient conditions for communicative behaviour have chosen *discourse analysis* as their point of departure. By making use of Austin's (1962) and Searle's (1969) theoretical insights they could conceive of discourse as of one form of communicative behaviour more easily amenable to theoretical and empirical analysis than non-verbal aspects of communication. Their common concern was, and is, the bridging of the gap between observable language behaviour and the meaning attributed to it. The hope that generative grammarians might provide the missing link crumbled when it became obvious that even the most elaborate transformational rules could not sufficiently account for the frequently encountered fact that the same utterance can have different meanings in different circumstances and that different utterances can stand for the same semantic construct.[2] The realization of the limited explanatory value of the generative approach for actual performance promoted a shift of research interests to *pragmatics*.

Empirical pragmatics, the inquiry mainly undertaken by psycholinguists, sociolinguists, and linguistic anthropologists, is concerned with different realizations of comprehensible and appropriate speech under

---

[1] In order to film the everyday life of a British family many precautions were taken to minimize possible distortions:
(i) the family was chosen amongst other contenders since its members did not seem to be concerned with presenting themselves at their very best.
(ii) The series was shot by three persons only, film director, cameraman, and sound-recordist. No artificial lighting was used. During a habituation period of two months in which no filming took place, family members got accustomed to the constant presence of the film crew.
(iii) The family was filmed continuously for a period of four months. Everything but the most intimate activities was recorded.
I was fortunate enough to obtain the entire material.
[2] See in this respect Harris's (1978) excellent critique of the current state of linguistics.

different communicative conditions.[3] That is, empirical pragmatics attempts to investigate the *extra- and intralinguistic conditions* necessary and/or sufficient for actual performance. Research workers who adhere to such an approach can begin their inductive analysis either with communicative behaviour classified as successful by the participants themselves or with cases of patent miscommunication like in pathological interaction. In other words, they can start from the idealized assumption that, given the 'right' knowledge, speakers can communicate and try to determine the features on which successful communication depends or they can explore pathological exchanges with the aim of learning something about the missing ingredients. Choosing the first avenue, I am going to delineate the conditions under which optimal communication may be expected. For this it will be of central importance to explore the structure of knowledge in general and of shared knowledge in particular.[4]

2.2. Knowledge and reality

Knowledge about the world can be of three kinds: it can pertain to 'the' world, to the 'own' world of the individual, or to the 'shared' world of the communicants. Habermas (1976b) speaks of *three pragmatic functions of speech* which reflect three different relations of knowledge to reality:[5]

(i) The *representative function* of speech is concerned with the analysis of universal, context-free conditions for making statements about the world. This function falls usually in the domain of analytic philosophy.

(ii) Speech in its *expressive function* reflects the subjective experiences of the speaker. For a theory of communication this function presents a boundary condition since the 'own' world of the speaker becomes only a communicative event when the actor successfully converts

---

[3] The problem of different realizations of Grice's maxims of quantity, relation, and manner under different communicative conditions has been treated more extensively in Kreckel (1979).

[4] Within the framework of this paper I shall not be able to discuss authors who are concerned with related research questions. I feel justified in not doing so since I am going to present an approach which differs sufficiently from other attempts at theoretically and/or empirically analysing what has been termed 'representational communication' (Fraser 1978) or 'conversational inferences' (Gumperz 1977).

[5] The three pragmatic functions of speech have to be distinguished from Halliday's three semantic functions. He stresses: 'the terms "ideational", "interpersonal", and "textual" . . . are to be interpreted not as functions in the sense of "uses of language", but as functional components of the semantic system – "metafunctions" as we have called them.' (Halliday 1978, p. 12.)

'his' world into a 'shared' world. If not shared it remains idiosyncratic and, as such, non-communicative.[6]
(iii) Speech is factually communicative only in its *interactive function*, i.e.
when based on the 'shared' world or a reciprocity of knowledge.
Communication as defined by its two Latin roots *communio*, a two-way
process of sharing, and *communicare*, a one-way process of transmitting
information, is concerned with speech in its interactive and its expressive function. Reciprocity of knowledge or interactive use ensures the
communio-aspect of communication, whereas the expressive use provides the *communicare*-aspect, i.e. the conversion of new, idiosyncratic
experiences into shared knowledge. The interrelationship between
these two functions will occupy us in the next sections.

2.3. Acquisition of knowledge through direct interaction

One of the most fundamental tenets of Piaget's (1950) genetic epistem-
ology is that the individual acquires and accumulates knowledge in
active interaction with his physical and social environment. Since socially
mediated acquisition of knowledge is recognized as being of the utmost
significance (Brown 1965), I shall concentrate exclusively on this aspect.
A concrete example resulting in 'faulty' knowledge serves to illustrate
the mechanism of social mediation at work. This instance is taken from
Maccoby, reproduced in Clark and Clark (1977):
> *Mother*: We have to keep the screen door closed, honey, so the flies
> won't come in. Flies bring germs into the house with them.
> *Child (when asked later what germs were)*: Something the flies play with.
The child has obviously used his already existing knowledge, namely
that friends are brought home for playing, as context for the new item of
knowledge provided by his mother. Hence, knowledge about the world
is frequently mediated directly by parents, teachers, friends, etc. The
most basic of all institutions, the family, plays a key role in the kind of
knowledge acquired in the process of socialization.

It is one of my basic contentions that knowledge acquired in *mutual
interaction with one or more relatively stable reference persons* is *qualitatively
different* from knowledge obtained through books, television programmes, or ephemeral encounters such as interacting with a shop assistant.
This qualitative difference, which is of special importance for com-

---

[6] The question of communicative versus non-communicative has been discussed in more
detail in Kreckel (1978b).

municative behaviour between people and for the study of this communicative behaviour, will be the focus of the next sections.

2.4. Conceptual knowledge acquired in mutual interaction

Analysing the different uses of meaning Frege (1892) introduced the famous distinction between sense and reference. For example, the sense of a word, or its intension, is the concept associated with this word, whereas its reference, or its extension, is the set of things the word applies to in any real or imaginary world, i.e. its truth-value. In communicative interaction it is the sense or the *concept* of 'germ' (see the example introduced above) which is of relevance and not its reference or its true relationship to the world.

In accordance with Frege and numerous psychologists interested in 'concepts', 'cognitive categories', or 'cognitive constructs' (these terms are often used interchangeably) such as Bruner (1967), Harvey, Hunt and Schroder (1961), or Kelly (1955), concepts can be defined as products of classified knowledge an individual has accumulated of all facts and generalizations about objects, events, and states.[7] One of the essential characteristics of concepts is their *dynamic* quality: concepts are based on past knowledge and change in the light of new knowledge.[8] This implies that no two individuals will ever form exactly the same concepts since no pair of individuals will ever interact with the world in exactly the same way.

However, this logical conclusion does not exclude the possibility of communication. It only imposes certain constraints on communication which have to be taken into account. For instance, the likelihood of two people having a similar concept of 'car' is relatively high if they are twin brothers who always drive the same car, repair it together, and feel jointly responsible for its current and future maintenance. In contrast, a Bedouin, riding usually on a camel's back, and an English car fanatic, buying every year the newest model of his favourite make, will have very different concepts of 'car'. From these examples one may deduce that *mutual interaction in the past* provides the opportunity for acquiring similar concepts with regard to the respective subject matter. In other

---

[7] A more extensive discussion of the problem of categorization can be found in Jones and Gerard (1967) and Zajonc (1968).
[8] Tajfel (1978) defines 'dynamic' as the interplay between stability and change which provides a successful fit between the organism and the environment.

words, mutual interaction in the past facilitates the conversion of *individual knowledge* into *shared knowledge*.

However, the *status quo* of conceptual similarity between two or more people, i.e. the degree of conceptual convergence, is not only dependent on the *retrospective variable* of mutual interaction in the past, it must be complemented by an additional *prospective variable*, the one of *mutual perspective*. I shall define *mutual perspective* as the desire to participate or share in future encounters. The prospective variable represents the *active* part communicants have to play in converting individual experience into shared knowledge and, thus, affecting the convergence of concepts used. This active involvement becomes salient in the above-mentioned example of the twin brothers who 'feel *jointly responsible* for . . . (the) *current and future* maintenance' of their car(s). The contribution of both retrospective and prospective variables to the present *status quo* of conceptual convergence between two or more individuals can be represented as in Fig. 1, which indicates that 'conceptual *status quo* prior

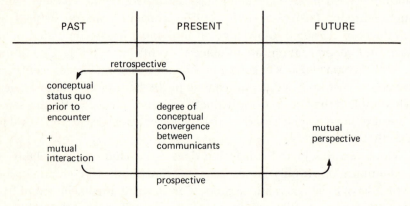

Fig. 1. Variables influencing the convergence of concepts between communicants

to encounter' and 'mutual interaction' contribute jointly to the 'degree of conceptual convergence between communicants'. For instance, two persons having been brought up under similar environmental conditions such as same culture, subculture, region, and education will need less direct interaction for achieving relatively high convergence of concepts as compared to persons with very different background knowledge. In the first case, we can assume that the two people have a great deal of *knowledge in common* (such as two English car fanatics who have never met) which, after a short process of negotiation, will become *shared knowledge*. Where a wider basis of *common knowledge* is lacking (as in the instance of the Bedouin and the English car fanatic), negotiation via mutual interaction will be more complicated and more time-consuming.

The importance of the retrospective variable *mutual interaction* for establishing shared knowledge can be attributed to two well-known mechanisms of behavioural (and by the same token, conceptual) adjustment: *overdetermination* and *feedback*. *Overdetermination* implies that what is communicated in interaction is not a 'once-and-for-all' phenomenon. As Pittenger, Hockett and Danehy (1960) stress, 'anyone will tell us, over and over again, in our dealings with him, what sort of person he is . . . what his likes and dislikes are, and so on'. That is, given relatively frequent encounters and, for example, the particular hypothesis from our example that 'germs' are 'friends', there will be ample opportunity for testing one's initial interpretation. If overdetermination provides the possibility for checking and rechecking, *feedback* supplies the individual with reliable knowledge as to what is actually shared. Thus, in observing their respective behaviour via feedback, mother and child will soon realize the discrepancy between their concepts of 'germ'. They will be able to make the necessary adjustment towards relative convergence and obtain thus a reliable basis for communication.

The prospective variable *mutual perspective* emphasizes the individual's *active* contribution in categorizing his environment in taking his social relationships into account. General support for this phenomenon can be drawn from a number of authors ranging from cognitive psychologists of the late fifties like Cherry (1957) to social psychologists writing about categorization in the late seventies such as Tajfel (1978). Tajfel discusses two cognitive activities, the one of 'selecting' and the other of 'modifying' aspects of the environment in order to achieve a better fit within a category. It seems convincing that these activities of selecting and modifying are also used to achieve a better fit between categories or concepts held by individuals interested in future interaction since 'the pressures to develop common modes of interpreting, perceiving, and labelling have dramatic effects on cognitive structures' (Jones and Gerard 1967, p. 133).

The importance of the variables discussed above can be underlined by the following quotation: 'If social psychology could throw light on the interweaving of social relations [Kreckel: mutual interaction in the past plus mutual perspective] and presuppositions [Kreckel: degree of conceptual convergence between communicants], it would be much nearer to the heart of communication than it has ever been before.' (Fraser 1978, p. 140.)

This brings us back to my general assumption that, for communicative purposes, there is a qualitative difference between knowledge acquired and modified in mutual interaction with stable reference persons or reference groups as opposed to knowledge acquired in interaction with a social environment of a more ephemeral nature (the latter will be referred to as 'separate' mode of acquisition). Since separately acquired knowledge lacks the essential ingredient of 'mutual perspective' defined above as the desire to participate and/or share in future encounters, one can assume that the individual's activity of selecting and modifying aspects of his environment is not geared towards bringing his concepts into convergence with the ones his interaction partner holds. This implies in addition that the adjustment mechanism of feedback will play a less prominent role as it requires the *active* taking up of information available in the situation. The distinction between the two modes of acquisition of knowledge, the 'mutual' and the 'separate' one, is of strategic importance for the arguments presented in this paper.

2.5. Relationships between concepts and codes

So far we have treated concepts, such as 'germ' or 'car', as if they were isolated entities. However, since Saussure's (1974) now classical insights, it has become common knowledge that concepts are created in relation to each other. For instance, the person's concept of 'germ' will depend on his concept of 'health', 'illness', 'hygiene', which are in turn elements of a larger whole or a *code*. Different codes organize knowledge, i.e. the components of concepts, according to different principles. In other words, the concept of 'health' may have different ingredients when used by the same person within the frame of reference of his family (his pretheoretical knowledge of health), the university of which he is a member (his scientific knowledge about health), or the nation at large (e.g. his views on the National Health Service). Thus, elements of the general body of knowledge a particular person holds can be taken up or ignored according to the code used under specific circumstances.[9] This implies, first, that individuals have a repertoire of different codes at their disposition and, second, that these codes are acquired through

---

[9] 'Codes' and related terms such as 'registers' and 'speech variants' are discussed in Halliday (1978).

practical use, i.e. through direct and indirect interaction with the environment.

In order to emphasize these two implications, I have introduced in earlier papers (Kreckel 1978b, 1979) the term *practical code(s).* *Code* is used in Bernstein's sense, namely as 'social structuring of meaning *and* . . . (its) related contextual linguistic realization' (1970, p. 158). Practical codes represent the underlying patterns of the culture and/or subculture(s) to which the individual has been exposed. Halliday (1978, p. 111) writes in this respect: 'As the child comes to attend to and interpret meanings, in the context of situation and in the context of culture, at the same time he takes over a code.'

The relationship between and the communicative function of practical codes needs further differentiation. In view of the problem discussed in section 2.1 of where to locate the potential for successful communication and of where to commence an analysis of principles used in encoding and decoding knowledge, I shall advance several claims:

(i) Practical codes are not clear-cut wholes without any overlap. Rather we have to conceive of practical codes as of systems with a relatively solid central core and fuzzy edges. The solid central core of a practical code developed within, for example, families would consist of the members' conventions for communication about their own relationships. The less familiar the subject matter of the interaction becomes, the more overlap with other practical codes.

(ii) Thus, the central core of practical codes, acquired in mutual interaction with stable reference persons, has a special communicative status due to the effect of the retro- and prospective variables discussed above.

(iii) Within a language community we must, therefore, distinguish between practical codes developed in mutual interaction in view of 'mutual perspective', and practical codes acquired by virtue of one's membership of a specific culture, class, or region i.e. separately. I shall introduce for these two extremes the terms *homodynamic* and *heterodynamic. Dynamic* emphasizes the interrelationship between stability and change referred to above when discussing the acquisition of concepts. Practical codes[10] and their elements, concepts, are of a dynamic nature as they are acquired through past interaction with the environment and change through present and future

---

[10] *Homodynamic code* is used as a heuristic device. Its existence has to be empirically demonstrated. See in this respect the concluding remarks of Kreckel (1978b) and section 4.3.6 of the conclusion of this paper.

interaction. *Homo-* underlines that both acquisition and change have occurred under the same or similar conditions for two or more individuals, and *hetero-* stresses the different conditions of acquisition.

(iv) The *potential for optimal communication is highest* under *homodynamic conditions*, where members of long-standing, close-knit groups, e.g. family members, speak about matters they are most familiar with.

The reader should not be under the impression that my claims imply either a 'harmonistic' conception of family interaction or the view that everything is shared within the family. As for the 'harmonistic' conception of family interaction I wish to distinguish between *shared knowledge* and *shared interests*. One can assume that family members do know a great deal of one another and use this knowledge in their daily communication. However, knowing is not equivalent (a) to acknowledging that one knows, or (b) to not having conflicts of interest. Furthermore, the frequently reported experience that the deepest misunderstandings occur between people who are closest to each other may be due to two aspects related to the emotional assessment of interaction: (a) expectations with respect to mutual understanding and (b) tolerance of frustration. In other words, the better people know each other, the more they expect complete understanding, an ideal never to be achieved, and the greater the frustration if the interaction does not live up to it. Conversely, the less people know each other, the lower the level of expectation and the higher the tolerance of frustration. This may account for the occasional experience of 'perfect' understanding between complete strangers. Hence the emotional appraisal of what is going on in communication need not reflect the actual understanding achieved. One might conclude that whether communicants interpret their own interaction in the same way can be considered an empirical question, one that is at the very heart of this type of research.

The second problem of discrepancies in knowledge between family members is not underrated either. What is communicable, what is potentially communicable, and what remains idiosyncratic can be shown in diagrammatic form (Fig. 2).

2.6. Conceptual v. expressive plane

In the previous section, a code was defined as a system of knowledge, or a conceptual system, realized in communicative behaviour in general and in speech in particular. Furthermore, I pointed out that a specific

SPEAKER   ADDRESSEE

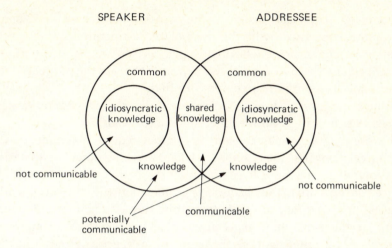

Fig. 2. The effect of different kinds of knowledge on communication

system of knowledge is the defining feature of a practical code. This organized knowledge can be *expressed* in a number of ways more or less characteristics for a particular practical code. Before trying to tackle the problem connected with the *expressive manifestations of systems of knowledge*, I am going to present a justification for separating the conceptual from the expressive plane.

As mentioned in section 2.1, the social scientist adopting an empirical pragmatic orientation can start his investigation either by analysing successful communicative performance or by studying pathological interaction. For the distinction between expressive and conceptual planes, evidence from the speech pathology of executive and receptive aphasia is of interest. Generally speaking, aphasia involves the loss or impairment of the ability to use language. In its executive version the patient has difficulties in expressing concepts. However his ability in forming concepts is not impaired as he can identify objects or persons by pointing. Receptive aphasia, on the other hand, is characterized by difficulties in understanding written or spoken language. In this case, the patient can produce the expressive unit, e.g. 'car', but he cannot relate it to the corresponding concept. Hence, in pathological cases concepts and their expressive realization can be divorced.

This failure of cognitive abilities can be seen as empirical support for the distinction first made by Saussure between two planes, the expressive and the semantic (or conceptual in the terminology of this paper). In mapping *units of the expressive plane* onto *units of the conceptual plane, signs* are created. This basic insight is the cornerstone of a whole scientific discipline concerned with the symbolically structured social world, semiotics. The main tenets of this perspective are more extensively described and discussed in Kreckel (1978b, 1979). For the purpose of this discussion it is sufficient to emphasize that:

(i) the same concepts can be expressed in different ways and the same expression can stand for different concepts, and

(ii) expressing a specific concept may often require a combination of lexical items like 'the red Mini that kept breaking down' or 'that rusty Volvo that saved our lives'.

Since concepts are mainly acquired in interaction with the social world, that is, in a specific expressive form, one can assume that individuals learn at the same time *conventions or accepted practices of expressing concepts*.[11] In other words, members of a specific group establish accepted ways of saying things with an accepted meaning and vice versa. This implies that *the likelihood of communicants holding convergent concepts and expressing them in a form accepted amongst themselves* is highest when they share the same homodynamic code.

For the research worker interested in bridging the gap between speech and its meaning this implication is of strategic importance. For only under conditions where he can assume that (almost) the same shared knowledge is used for encoding and for decoding meaning, and that this knowledge is expressed in (almost) the same way, can he even start thinking of how to analyse cues used in the process of communication. Therefore I would claim that the appropriate vantage-point for investigating communicative performance is where empirical data meet homodynamic conditions. It is for this reason that in my own empirical work I have opted for recorded family interaction and have selected from these recordings extracts where relationships between family members are the focus of verbal exchanges.

3. Development of an appropriate discovery procedure

3.1. Delineation of units of analysis

Concepts as elements of practical codes may be delimited in a number of ways. Within the framework of this paper I am concerned with two types

---

[11] In defining conventions as 'practices accepted between at least two people' I try to circumvent the long-standing controversies connected with the problem of convention versus arbitrariness.

of concepts, the ones corresponding to acts of communication and the others being part of these acts. This distinction will become clearer in the following sections.

Within the framework of speech-act theory (Austin 1962, Searle, 1969), saying things is seen as doing things. That is, in using language the speaker performs acts like 'complaining', 'advising', 'informing', etc. The constitutive rules accounting for speech acts have occupied numerous philosophers and linguists in the last decade. The analysis of these rules for direct speech acts like, 'I hereby promise that . . .', and/or indirect ones like, 'I'll do it', were usually carried out on *decontextualized* specimens of specific categories such as 'promising'. I am not going to discuss speech-act theory in detail, since I have done so in Kreckel (1978b). I shall take a working knowledge for granted.

This decontextualized approach has its obvious empirical limitations, as acts such as 'promising', 'complaining', and 'threatening' always occur within communicative situations and thus depend on a number of extra- and intra-linguistic factors which have to be taken into account. These factors not only influence the way a specific act of speech is physically realized in speech (and action) but also, and more importantly, the subset of constitutive rules chosen for a specific use. That is, the philosophers' claim that specific combinations of constitutive rules like the constitutive rules for 'promising' are universal might need further investigation.

My contention is that the concept underlying an act of speech and the rules constituting this concept can only be explored within a practical code. In order to distinguish this *contextualized* approach from the decontextualized one I have replaced the term speech act by *communicative* act. Communicative acts may be performed within the framework of either homo- or heterodynamic codes. In the present paper, I am primarily concerned with communicative acts as elements of homodynamic codes.

3.2. Tone-units as units of analysis[12]

In trying to explore the meaning conveyed by speech the research worker is faced with the problem of how to segment the continuous

---

[12] The term *tone-unit* is equivalent to what Trager and Smith (1951) named and described as 'phonemic clause'. Kreckel (1981c) discusses in detail experimental work done on tone-units.

stream of verbal behaviour. Linguists conceive of speech as of 'a sequentially organized communication system in which judicious ordering and placing of emphasis may be important for the proper understanding of the message and its implications' (Quirk and Greenbaum 1973, p. 406). They suggest that the most prominent ordering device the speaker has at his disposition is the placement of *tone-unit* boundaries. According to Laver (1971), tone-units are the fundamental units of neural encoding. He arrives at this conclusion from empirical findings which indicate that slips of the tongue rarely cross tone-unit boundaries. In discussing the defining properties of tone-units both Crystal (1975) and Halliday (1976) take a basically syntactic view. Halliday points out that tone-units represent 'the speaker's organization of discourse into message blocks . . . roughly equal to the number of clauses' (pp. 175–6). Crystal supplies more stringent criteria for tone-unit boundaries in writing: 'If a sentence consists of one clause, and if this clause consists maximally of the elements Subject + Verb + Complement and/or Object, with one optional Adverb, in this order, and if each of the elements S, C, O and A is expounded by a single nominal group, then the sentence will have a single tone-unit. This is considered to be the basic pattern.' (1975, p. 16.) Quirk and Greenbaum (1973) stress in their *University grammar of English*, the first grammar based on conversational English, that 'the clause is the unit of grammar that most closely corresponds to the tone unit' (p. 406). Crystal, Halliday, and Quirk and Greenbaum emphasize in addition the importance of prosodic features for the placement of tone-unit boundaries. A comprehensive model of 'operations for assigning tone-unit structures to sentences' has been developed in Crystal (1975). According to this model a tone-unit can consist minimally of one lexical item as in the case of vocatives and maximally of one sentence.

For the purpose of this analysis it will be sufficient to define a tone-unit as a continuously spoken clause, i.e a clause not interrupted by a pause. I shall illustrate this point by means of a short extract taken from the family recordings in which the eldest daughter has a discussion about marriage with her boyfriend:

Marian: //You never told me you'd never marry me//
            //that's what you told Mum//
Tom: //I see//that's it//we've had this out with your Mum
            already//love//I didn't say I wouldn't marry you//

(double slashes signify tone-unit boundaries: note the vocative//love//).
The general consensus amongst linguists, in conceiving of tone-units

as of the organizational device the speaker employs for dividing discourse into message blocks, provides me with a strong argument for parsing continuous stretches of speech into tone-units. In view of the search for procedures for making the implicit knowledge of communicants explicit one can thus argue that a message block is realized by a tone-unit and that their combination constitutes a communicative act (see Fig. 3 below). Under homodynamic conditions the question of *which communicative act is performed can only be decided by the communicants themselves*. This point will be illustrated later.

3.3. Internal structure of communicative acts (intra-unit structure)

Quirk and Greenbaum underline that 'each tone unit represents a unit of information, and the place where the nucleus falls is the focus of information' (1973, p. 406); 'Focus is related to the differences between GIVEN and NEW information; that is to say, between information already supplied by context and information which has not been prepared for in this way.' (p. 408.) Assignment of *nucleus*[13] falls in the domain of *tonicity*. Crystal argues that the placement of nucleus is 'primarily conditioned by the speaker's view of how to distribute the semantic weight of his sentence, for which it is necessary to take account of the entire context' (1975, p. 6). The view that tonicity reflects the distribution of 'new' information in a tone-unit directly mirroring the speaker's intent (not necessarily conscious) and essentially independent of the syntax is generally accepted amongst linguists. Controversies have arisen with respect to, first, terminology: giving–new, presupposed–focus, topic–comment, known–unknown; second, the nature of information; and third, the dichotomous versus the dynamic perspective (i.e. given–new versus communicative dynamism as expounded by the Prague school of linguistics (see Daneš 1974)). Dahl (1976) discusses most of these problems in his excellent paper on 'What is new information'. Being only interested in the generally accepted fact that the internal structure of a tone-unit is characterized by tonicity, I feel entitled to ignore the first and second controversies and concentrate on the problem of information in its relationship to GIVEN and NEW.

---

[13] The entity that I shall call the 'nucleus' has been variously described as: 'primary stress' (Katz and Postal 1964), 'tonic syllable' (Halliday 1967), 'intonation center' (Chomsky and Halle 1968), 'contour center' (Stockwell 1972), 'primary contour' (Pike 1948), and 'accent' (Bollinger 1958).

To avoid misunderstandings I would like to point out that GIVEN and NEW as well as the alternative labels mentioned above are used in linguistics as technical terms. The rather unfortunate choice of these labels seems to stem from the linguistic bias of trying to relate preceding elements to following ones. Hence, NEW becomes a residual category for everything that cannot be linked up with what has been said before, i.e. with what is intralinguistically GIVEN. Problems connected with the 'gradedness' of both GIVEN and NEW will be discussed below.

Dahl points out that 'a speaker chooses the form of message in such a way that his addressee can reconstruct the content of the message' (1976, p. 45). He adheres, according to Dahl, to the 'laziness principle' which reads: 'Omit everything that the adressee can figure out by himself.' (p. 46.) Following on from this one might distinguish between four kinds of information:

(i) information the speaker takes for granted and therefore *omits completely*, examples being the layout of the house in which the interactors live or personal characteristics of the speakers;

(ii) information the speaker considers as *previously mentioned*, i.e. as intralinguistically given;

(iii) information which the speaker assumes to be *partly or entirely new* to the hearer, and

(iv) information the speaker chooses to *emphasize*.

As already mentioned, stressed lexical items are seen by linguists as being equivalent to NEW information and the unstressed ones to GIVEN information. However, taking into account the four kinds of information dicussed above, it seems appropriate to introduce a further differentiation for both NEW and GIVEN: The speaker can stress or treat as NEW, first, what he considers as entirely new information; second, as partly new information; and, third, as known information that he wishes to emphasize. In addition, GIVEN can be perceived by him as either intra- or extra-linguistically retrievable. This state of affairs is presented graphically in Fig. 3.

But how does the gradedness of 'information' relate to the approach introduced in the theoretical section? When dicussing the problem of GIVEN versus NEW, Chafe (1970) refers to *concepts*. He postulates that 'expressing a concept' equals 'conveying information'. This view is in accordance with the argument presented in this paper, namely that the speaker conveys *aspects of knowledge* when expressing concepts.

In general, the speaker will use lexical items where he can expect complete or partial conceptual convergence. Lexical items, where per-

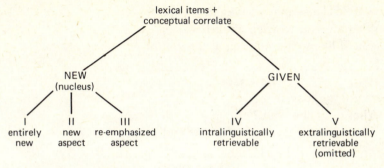

Fig. 3. Differentiation of NEW and GIVEN

fect conceptual convergence is taken for granted, can either be omitted (V) or uttered without focal stress (IV). The use of entirely new lexical items (I), that is, entirely new words and their conceptual correlates, is a relatively rare case in adult communication[14] and especially in communicative interaction within the family. With respect to items where complete conceptual convergence is seen as lacking the speaker can either introduce the relevant new aspect (II) or re-emphasize the aspect (III) he wishes to convey. Choices I, II, and III will be realized by assigning the nucleus to the particular item. Consider in this respect the following three versions of the same sentence taken from the family recordings:

(1) //She'd like to get married at the end of April//

(2) //She'd like to get married at the end of April//

(3) //She'd like to get married at the end of April//

One can safely assume that none of the lexical items and the corresponding concepts is entirely new to the hearer. Thus, in placing the nucleus on 'she' (1), the speaker introduces either a new aspect or re-emphasizes an already known one. The same holds for example 2 where the speaker shifts the nucleus to 'married'. In both 1 and 2 the lexical items that are not part of the nucleus can be considered as given (IV). Example 3 is of a more complicated structure. Quirk and Greenbaum point out that 'if the nucleus falls on the last stressed syllable of the clause (according to the end-focus principle), the new information could, for example, be the entire clause, or the predication of the clause, or the last element of the clause' (1973, p. 408). Which one of the three possibilities applies depends on how much the speaker expects the hearer to know. To delineate the three possibilities I have invented three questions.

[14] Only words which are completely new for the hearer qualify as 'entirely new'.

The whole clause may convey new aspects:

(4) What are you worried about?

//She'd like to get married at the end of April//

[_____]

new aspects

The predicate may be new:

(5) What does she want?

//She'd like to get married at the end of April//

[_____]

new aspects

Final adverbial phrase may be new:

(6) When does she want to get married?

//She'd like to get married at the end of April//

[_____]

new aspect

Hence, tonicity or the assignment of nucleus to an element in a tone-unit can display different patterns: *pre-final* tonic placement as in examples 1 and 2, *final* tonic placement as in examples 3–6, and finally, according to Crystal, *compound* tonicity in which a tone-unit has double focus, as in:

//She's the most <u>miserable</u> person I've ever <u>seen</u>//.

As mentioned under 3.1, concepts may be delimited in a number of ways. They can either correspond to physical entities on the expressive plane delineated by tone-units or they can correspond to smaller expressive units, such as lexical items, which are part of tone-units. I shall introduce for concepts mapping onto tone-units (and thereby forming communicative acts) the term *communicative concept* and for concepts relating to lexical items the term *lexical concepts*. The distinctions introduced so far are summarized diagrammatically in Fig. 4.

In the example used for illustrative purposes in Fig. 4 the tone-unit //I didn't say I <u>wouldn't</u> marry you// stands for the communicative concepts of 'denying' and 'protesting'. The combination of tone-unit and communicative concepts constitutes the homo- or heterodynamic communicative act of 'denying–protesting' depending on whether it is issued under homodynamic or under heterodynamic conditions. This homo- or heterodynamic communicative act consists in turn of a number of lexical items and their related lexical concepts which again reflect the shared knowledge between family members.[15] Thus, in producing a

---

[15] I would like to point out that 'denying' can be a homo- or heterodynamic communicative act (tone-unit + communicative concept) as well as a single word (lexical item + lexical concept).

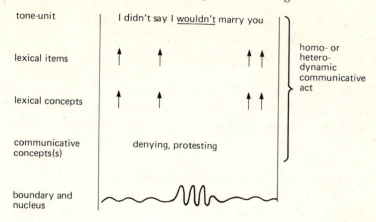

Fig. 4. Tone-unit: the unit of analysis

specific homo- or heterodynamic communicative act, the speaker not only decides (not necessarily consciously) on which lexical item to use or not to use, but also on how to place the focal stress (see underlined item wouldn't). The placement of the nucleus does not so much reflect the distribution between NEW and GIVEN as the speaker's view of how to *allocate the pragmatic weight within a communicative act.*

3.4. Structural and functional properties of communicative acts

Assignment of nucleus (or nuclei) can fulfil a double function. First, it can stand for the speaker's 'own' world and thus convey either lexical items and corresponding concepts which are entirely new (I) for the hearer or where new aspects (II) are presented (see Fig. 3). In this usage, speech is employed in its *expressive function* (see the three pragmatic functions discussed under 2.2). Seen from a homodynamic perspective, expressive use constitutes the innovative element in communication, i.e. it provides the grounds for converting 'own' knowledge into 'shared' knowledge.

Second, it can reflect the 'shared' world and thus be used in its interactive function. The *interactive* or *relationship-regulating function* combines re-emphasized aspects of concepts (III) with given ones (IV and V) in order to achieve specific goals within the relationship (this point will become clearer when discussing the empirical application of the theoretical framework in the last part of the paper).

At this stage in the exposé the ground is prepared for advancing the following three contentions:

(i) the nucleus (nuclei) is the defining feature for the interpretation of a tone-unit as a communicative act;

(ii) homodynamic communicative acts are characterized by nuclei in which aspects of concepts are re-emphasized; nuclei of heterodynamic communicative acts introduce predominently new aspects of lexical items or entirely new lexical items and their corresponding concepts;

(iii) this implies that homodynamic codes typically are 'tuned' to their interactive function and heterodynamic codes to their expressive function (which respectively are their most frequent, though by no means exclusive, ways of application).

To illustrate the first two contentions I am going to present two short extracts from the working-class family's interaction: one in which the mother is addressing her son (homodynamic example), and another in which the mother is talking to a local MP about housing problems (heterodynamic example).

Homodynamic example:

(7) //<u>You're</u> not working as well as you could//
    //if <u>you'd</u> only stop day-dreaming//

(8) //You're not <u>working</u> as well as you could//
    //if you'd only <u>stop</u> day-dreaming//

(9) //You're not working as <u>well</u> as you could//
    //if you'd only stop <u>day-dreaming</u>//

A comparison of the three versions of the same sentence suggests that the shift of nuclei influences the interpretation in terms of underlying communicative concepts and, thus, the constitution of communicative acts. Example (7) may be seen as 'lamenting', or 'complaining'. Example (8) highlights a 'criticizing', 'telling off' interpretation, and example (9) could be regarded as 'advising' and 'encouraging'. With regard to my second contention, the three versions of the same instance illustrate the point that nuclei in homodynamic communicative acts tend to *re-emphasize* already shared aspects of concepts.

Heterodynamic example:

(10) *MP:* //How <u>many</u> people are there in the house altogether then?//
     M: //Well// there's <u>nine</u> at the moment//
     MP: //<u>Yes/Well</u>// I'll get one of the councillors to come <u>round</u> and <u>see</u> you about this//

(11) *MP:* //How many people are there in the house <u>altogether</u> then?//

M: //Well// there's nine at the moment//

MP: //Yes//Well// I'll get one of the councillors to come round and see you about this//

In example 10 one could interpret the sentence as follows: MP 'asks for information', Mother 'gives information', and MP 'promises' that something will be done. Example 11 seems to have a different communicative structure: MP shows his 'disapproval', Mother 'hints' that there might be more to come, and MP 'reassures' her that he personally is going to look into it. In both examples *new aspects* of lexical items are revealed, since the knowledge is not shared between the interactors. Hence, examples 7–9 and 10–11 seem to give support to my third contention that homodynamic codes display a tendency of being used interactively and heterodynamic codes of being used expressively.

3.5. Relationship between communicative acts (inter-unit structure)

I have indicated that shifts of nucleus within a tone-unit may produce changes in conceptual interpretation and therefore may result in different communicative acts. The interpretation of a tone-unit as a specific communicative act is, however, not only dependent on its nucleus, but also on its *intralinguistic context* or its position within preceding and following tone-units. Consider the following example taken again from the family recordings. The first version is the original one, the second one has been rearranged:

(12.1) *Tom:* //I didn't say I wouldn't marry you//

(12.2) *Marian:* //Nobody bloody includes me//

(12.3) *Tom:* //I said//I didn't fancy getting married just at the moment//

(13.1) *Tom:* //I said//I didn't fancy getting married just at the moment//

(13.2) *Marian:* //That's a poor excuse I'm afraid// and if you can't come up with something better than that// then you know what to do//

(13.3) *Tom:* //I didn't say I wouldn't marry you//

Comparing the two lexically identical sentences (12.1) and (13.3), it becomes apparent that their communicative concept has changed due to the differences in focal stress *and* sequential position. Whereas (12.1) can be read as 'defence', (13.3) may be interpreted as 'denial'. A comparison between (12.3) and (13.1) again lexically identical, reveals changes in communicative concepts, too. (12.3) might be perceived by the hearer as 'refusal' and (13.1) as an 'excuse'. Thus, lexically identical sentences occurring in different sequences and displaying a different distribution of 're-emphasized' and 'given' are assumed to constitute different communicative acts. This corresponds to our everyday experience that utterances taken out of context can give a very distorted picture of what was actually going on. One of the main reasons for this is that what has been uttered before is treated by speaker and hearer as intralinguistically 'given', and thus as contributing to the interpretation of what follows afterwards.[16]

3.6. Summary of the theoretical and procedural inquiry

In the theoretical section of this paper I have discussed the conditions under which an empirical investigation of cues used for encoding and decoding messages in natural interaction can be attempted. In the procedural section, I have outlined an analytical procedure and advanced the hypothesis that the nucleus of a tone-unit issued within a specific intra- and extralinguistic context carries the semantic weight and, thus, contributes to the constitution of a communicative act. The arguments presented in both sections can be summarized in more detail as follows:

3.6.1. In order to empirically investigate the research question the data must meet homodynamic conditions, since only homodynamic conditions have the potential of (a) approximating a convergence of concepts between interactors which favours effective communication, and (b) ensuring that these concepts are expressed in a conventionalized way.

3.6.2. To investigate communicative concepts realized by speech, tone-units provide a theoretically and empirically warrantable point of departure.

3.6.3. Tone-units must be interpreted and analysed as parts of a code, or more specifically, where a homodynamic code can be expected (the empirical demonstration of the existence of homodynamic codes is part of the wider research project).

---

[16] Linguistically there are a number of devices of how to achieve the link between sentences. These devices fall under the general heading of 'cohesion'. Linguists interested in what constitutes a text, i.e. a coherent stretch of speech in the case of natural discourse, are concerned with endophoric, exophoric, cataphoric, and anaphoric references, with problems of substitution, ellipsis, conjunction, and, finally, with lexical cohesion. Within the framework of this paper, I cannot discuss these text-constituting devices. The interested reader will find an excellent presentation of them in Halliday and Hasan (1976).

3.6.4. Tone-units interpreted in terms of communicative concepts by the interactors themselves constitute homodynamic communicative acts.

3.6.5. Tone-units interpreted in terms of communicative concepts by outside observers constitute heterodynamic communicative acts.

3.6.6. The internal structure of communicative acts (or their intra-unit structure) is expounded by the speaker's distribution of NEW (entirely new, new aspect, re-emphasized) and GIVEN (extra- and intralinguistic).

3.6.7 The distribution of NEW versus GIVEN is different for interactors and outside observers; outside observers can neither take recourse to extralinguistic knowledge presupposed in natural family interaction nor can they discriminate between 'new aspects' or 're-emphasized' aspects of concepts used in family interaction (see 4.1.).

3.6.8 For homodynamic conditions the interactive use of speech is the prevalent one; heterodynamic conditions are predominantly characterized by speech in its expressive function.

4. Application of theoretical framework and discovery procedure

4.1. Homodynamic versus heterodynamic knowledge

I shall commence the empirical section with a quotation which introduces both a touch of caution and optimism. Gumperz writes:

> There is no such thing as impartial observation or measurement of verbal behaviour: measurement is always affected by distortions. To some extent these distortions can be overcome by analytical techniques, however; and the study of linguistic forms provides tools to deal with a level of subconscious behaviour which, when compared with an individual's actual behaviour on the one hand, and his expressed opinions about his behaviour on the other, can offer entirely novel insights into social processes. (Gumperz 1972, p. 204.)

In the next sections I shall give an illustration of the analytical technique used. Before doing this I shall expand on Fig. 3 with the aim of delineating the differences in distribution of conceptual knowledge between family members and outside observers. As Fig. 5 indicates, family members can use verbal interaction either expressively when

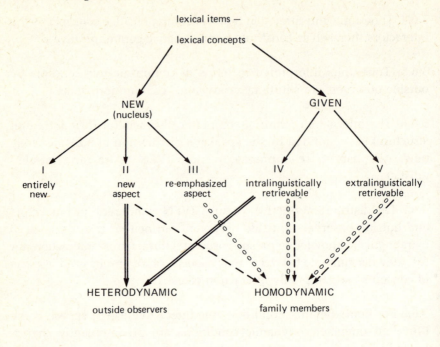

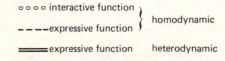

Fig. 5. Origins of homodynamic and heterodynamic codes

introducing a 'new aspect' or interactively when solely 're-emphasizing' what is known to speaker and hearer(s) alike. This point and the fact that 'entirely new' lexical items/lexical concepts are such rare cases in adult communication within families that they can be neglected has been discussed in sections 3.3. and 3.4. I have stressed, in addition that the interactive use is the predominant one when family members discuss their own relationships. Outside observers are in a very different position. They cannot differentiate between 'new aspects' and 're-emphasized' ones since they lack the extralinguistic background knowledge. Hence, they are restricted to what is intralinguistically given, stressed or unstressed.

On the basis of these differences in distribution of knowledge one can expect four tendencies of interpreting verbal interaction within the family.

(i) Family members as opposed to outside observers may well interpret tone-units differently, i.e. they should arrive at different communicative acts.

(ii) Family members who share a large body of conceptual knowledge should share the same or a similar view of family interaction.

(iii) Each family member should display, in addition, an idiosyncratic bias, that is, an interpretation which is characteristic only for him- or herself.

(iv) Each outside observer should come to a markedly different interpretation; this difference should be more pronounced the more dissimilar the respective cultural and subcultural background is (an illustration of this tendency cannot be attempted within the framework of this paper).

If these four trends hypothesized on theoretical grounds can be demonstrated empirically then one would be justified in arguing that family members use their shared knowledge in the same or similar way in order to encode and decode conceptual knowledge. Having suggested that the nuclei of tone-units are the elements or the physical cues which contribute essentially to the constitution of communicative acts one could then look, *inter alia*, for characteristics of nuclei with the aim of discovering certain principles of encoding and decoding.

Within the framework of this paper, I shall not be able to present the entire study and the investigations which led up to it. All I can do here is to give an illustration of the analytical technique used and the general findings obtained. This will be done with the aid of two extracts from the family interaction.

4.2. Illustration of the analytical technique

The first extract is an argument between the mother of the family and the fiancé of her eldest daughter, Marian, in which she is strongly putting across Marian's desire to get married. The extract is subdivided into tone-units. Nuclei are underlined.

		Pre-final nucleus
Mother:	1. <u>She</u> expects to be married	she
	2. before <u>she</u> moves into that <u>flat</u>	she
Fiancé:	3. Oh <u>no</u>	
	4. I don't <u>think</u> she does	think

Extract 1

Mother:	5. Well I tell you she <u>does</u>	I
Fiancé:	6. Well not by <u>me</u> talking about it anyway	me
Mother:	7. Well if she doesn't . . .	
	8. <u>She's</u> said she's not moving into it unless	she
	she <u>is</u> married	is

In section 3.3, I discussed three patterns of tonicity, i.e. three patterns of assignment of nucleus within a tone-unit: (i) pre-final tonic placement, (ii) final tonic placement, and (iii) compound tonicity. Furthermore, I argued, in accordance with Quirk and Greenbaum (1973), that only pre-final tonic placement can be considered as the speaker's assignment of NEW since stress on the final lexical item constitutes an unmarked case in which, maximally, the entire tone-unit can be treated as NEW.

Let us therefore consider the pattern of pre-final tonic placement:[17]

1. she
2. she
4. think
5. I
6. me
8. she is

Note that in five out of eight tone-units a *personal pronoun* is in pre-final position. Only in two instances does the speaker stress a *verb*.

Before analysing this pattern in greater detail, we will compare extract 1 with extract 2. This extract is part of a longer stretch of interaction, the beginning of which will be presented later (that this extract is part of a longer dialogue explains the numbers of the tone-units 27–32).

The interaction consists of an argument between mother and daughter, Heather. Heather is displeased about the fact that her sister-in-law, Karen, who has just moved out of her parents' flat, is constantly coming back to see them.

---

17 I shall not be able to discuss the special significance of compound tonicity within the framework of this paper. However, I would like to direct the reader's attention to the fact that the succession of nuclei within natural discourse displays to a high degree the message structure of this interaction:

Mother:	she
	she flat
Fiancé:	no
	think does
Mother:	I does
Fiancé:	me
Mother:	she is

Extract 2   Pre-final
                                                             nucleus

Daughter: 27. Well <u>you</u> have her <u>back</u> here then   you/back
            28. and I'll go in the <u>flat</u>   I
Mother: 29. I don't <u>want</u> her back   want
Daughter: 30. Well <u>exactly</u>
            31. you don't want her <u>back</u>   won't
Mother: 32. You <u>won't</u> try to <u>understand</u> people   understand

The pre-final nuclei of extract 2 are predominantly of a *verbal/adverbial* nature:

    27. back
    29. want
    32. won't   understand

Before showing how both extracts have been interpreted by members of the family, on the one hand, and by outside observers, on the other, I will have to describe briefly the coding procedure employed.

4.2.1. Coding procedure

The coding procedure adopted was as follows:

(i) Six extracts from the family interaction in which family members discussed their own relationships were chosen at random from the recorded material. These six extracts amounted to a total of 147 tone-units.

(ii) The coding was done by three family members[18] (extract 1 was coded by four family members) and by five outside observers. The outside observers were subjects from the subject panel of the Department of Experimental Psychology, University of Oxford. Four of them (subjects I, II, III and V) were matched for social and regional background, education, and age.

---

[18] Since the recording of the family interaction was done in 1974, family members interpreted their own behaviour four years after the event. This has both advantages and disadvantages. One of the major advantages is the fact that the experiences which – as the extracts indicate – were partly of a highly emotional nature could now be seen with sufficient detachment. All family members emphasized that only because of this lapse of time were they able to give as honest an interpretation as possible. A major disadvantage would be if part of the communicative significance of the concrete interaction were forgotten or had drastically altered. If this were the case we would expect a low degree of agreement between family members. However, since I am only interested in how messages are encoded and decoded on a level on which interactors lack conscious awareness, one can argue that high agreement between family members would theoretically justify a detailed investigation of the potential cues used to arrive at this shared view of the interaction.

(iii) Each individual coder was presented with the written transcript of the pieces of interaction, already subdivided into tone-units,[19] and the audio-tape of the same passages.

(iv) In addition, each coder was provided with an open-ended list of 100 labels[20] comprising items like 'complaining', 'ordering', 'disapproving', which were derived from previous experiments. She/he was asked to familiarize her- or himself thoroughly with these labels.

(v) The task consisted in interpreting the interaction by assigning as many labels to each single tone-unit as seemed appropriate to the individual coder. She/he was instructed to pay especial attention to the way the tone-unit was actually *spoken* and to what the speaker was *doing* in interaction with the hearer.

(vi) Family members coded the interaction verbally, that is, they interpreted each tone-unit in giving an account of what the speaker had done. They used the provided labels as an aid for condensing their inside knowledge.[21] The interpretation was tape-recorded and notes were taken simultaneously.[22]

(vii) Outside observers underwent two experimental conditions: in the first condition the five subjects were solely informed about the kinship relations, the sex, and the age of the family members involved in the interaction. In the second condition three of the five subjects repeated the task after a lapse of two months. Through the previous experiment they had become familiar with the recordings.

[19] The decision to present each subject with a transcript already segmented into tone-units seemed justified on the basis of an earlier experiment in which subjects had to parse written transcripts, transcripts plus audio-presentation, and transcripts plus video-presentation into the smallest meaningful units. For the audio-presentation subjects segmented the continuous stretch of speech with more than 95 % accuracy into the same tone-units. Thus, the boundaries of tone-units seem to correspond to the tacit knowledge of naive, native language-users. This corresponds to the findings reported by Boomer (1978). See in this respect Kreckel (1981b, c).

[20] I have argued in the theoretical section that an 'order' or a 'complaint' depend for their specific features on the code within which they are issued. For this reason, I asked three members of the family and three outside observers to define each label by using a concrete example taken from the everyday interaction within their respective families. This refinement of the analytical technique cannot be discussed within the framework of this paper.

[21] A *general* interpretation of each extract which was done by each family member before tackling the *detailed* analysis of each single tone-unit did only generate rather superficial accounts. All family members emphasized the fact that only the task of interpreting each single tone-unit enabled them to retrieve knowledge about the interaction which they would not have been able to retrieve without this method.

[22] All experiments were conducted by myself. I tried to be as neutral and as unobtrusive as possible. Any experimenter-effect, which can never be completely eliminated, should therefore lead to the same or similar consequences for all subjects.

In addition, they were given further information about the family. Their interpretation was tape-recorded and notes were taken at the same time.

4.2.2. Analysis

Table 1 shows the results obtained from the family members' coding of extract 1.

Despite the fact that family members could choose from an open-ended list of 100 labels there was a surprisingly high agreement between them.[23] This seems to support the second hypothesis, that, for communicative purposes at least, family members encode and decode their shared knowledge in a similar way. One may infer, thus, that they use the same or similar physical indicators or cues for transmitting communicative concepts. In correspondence with the third hypothesis, each family member introduced an idiosyncratic bias in assigning labels to tone-units that were not shared by other members of the family.

The relatively high agreement between family members seems to justify a closer inspection as to the relationship between interpretations given for specific tone-units and the physical properties of these tone-units. The most prominent regularity to be noticed was that tone-units with *personal pronouns* as pre-final nuclei are coded in terms of 'instigating action' (1, 2 and 5) or 'declining to act' (6); this assertion is based on the findings of the whole study where both pronominal and prepositional nuclei regularly coincide with 'action-oriented' interpretations. In other words, in this particular extract we have a rather clear-cut case in which the stress on personal pronouns concurs with 'action-oriented' communication. (See Kreckel 1981b.)

Tone-unit 4, which has a *verbal* nucleus, is of a very different nature. Here the 'defending' in simultaneously 'disagreeing', 'protesting', and 'doubting' seems to be in the centre of the interpretation. This more 'person-oriented' view of the interaction will be discussed in conjunction with extract 2. Tone-unit 8 displays both a pronominal and a verbal pre-final nucleus. This combination is equally reflected in the family members' coding. Three out of four insiders chose labels of both 'action-oriented' ('warning', 'challenging', 'threatening', 'provoking') and 'person-oriented' quality ('criticizing', 'reproaching', 'appealing', 'defending', 'disapproving').

[23] Since I am only going to give an illustration of analytical technique and general findings, I will not present any statistical data.

Table 1. *Family members' interpretation of extract 1*

Tone-unit no	Pre-final nucleus	Mother	Daughter	Son	Fiancé
1	she	ordering warning challenging giving information reproaching	urging insisting stating	ordering complaining	urging insisting giving information
2	she	ordering warning challenging giving information reproaching disapproving	urging insisting justifying stating	ordering complaining	urging insisting giving information
3		questioning disbelieving disapproving doubting	questioning disagreeing playing	disbelieving disagreeing hestitating	questioning disbelieving disagreeing rejecting stating
4	think	defending denying doubting	defending disagreeing playing	defending disagreeing protesting	disbelieving disagreeing stating
5	I	urging challenging	urging insisting telling off clarifying	urging ordering	insisting attacking
6	me	rejecting defending	rejecting avoiding evading brushing off	rejecting challenging defying	protesting denying
7		doubting warning threatening	doubting challenging provoking	warning threatening defending	doubting telling off disapproving
8	she is	warning threatening challenging provoking criticizing reproaching appealing	insisting challenging concluding	warning threatening declaring defending	warning challenging protesting disapproving appealing defending

Let us now peruse the outsiders' interpretation of the same piece of discourse. If one inspects Table 2 more closely, i.e. the outside observers' interpretation of the same extract coded without background knowledge, one is struck by the abundance of so-called 'neutral' labels such as 'stating' and 'giving information'. On this level, there is a relatively high agreement between coders. This is not too surprising

Table 2. *Outside observers' interpretation of extract 1 (no background knowledge provided)*

Tone-unit no	Subject I	Subject II	Subject III	Subject IV	Subject V
1	stating challenging advising	giving information warning attacking declaring	stating threatening	stating postulating giving information	stating making observation giving information
2	stating challenging advising	giving information warning urging	warning	stating postulating giving information	giving information making observation
3	disagreeing	disagreeing protesting	disagreeing questioning hesitating	disagreeing questioning	disagreeing giving information
4	disagreeing challenging making observation	defending avoiding stating	disagreeing giving opinion	disagreeing questioning	disagreeing amplifying information
5	disagreeing objecting warning stating	insisting emphasizing information	contradicting giving opinion	insisting contradicting protesting	insisting stating making observation
6	defending disagreeing giving information	defending evading	disagreeing giving opinion	defending explaining	defending giving information
7	reproaching	insisting warning	hesitating	conceding	doubting postulating
8	stating appealing approving challenging	giving information insisting warning	giving information stating	giving information giving reason contradicting	giving information asserting

since no special background knowledge is needed for 'neutral' interpretations. In Table 3 I have tried to condense the information of Tables 1 and 2 to give the reader a better impression of the general trend.

This comparison between family members' and outside observers' coding reveals that the 'action-oriented' interpretation for tone-units with pre-final nuclei only holds for family members. An 'action-oriented' tendency is equally prevalent in the coding of subjects I and II and, to a lesser extent, in the one of subject III. However, there is no exact correspondence with respect to concrete labels employed by insiders and outsiders.

In the second set of interpretations by outside observers, the trend

Table 3. *Comparison between Table 1 and Table 2*

Pre-final	Tone-unit no	Family members (Table 1)	Outside observers (Table 2)
she	1	ordering/urging/insisting	stating/giving information
she	2	ordering/urging/insisting	giving information/warning
	3	questioning/disbelieving/ disagreeing	disagreeing/questioning
think	4	defending/disagreeing	disagreeing
I	5	urging/insisting	insisting
me	6	rejecting	defending
	7	doubting	—
she is	8	warning/challenging/ threatening/appealing defending	giving information

towards 'action-oriented' interpretation becomes more apparent. As mentioned above, three subjects were asked to recode the same extracts after having obtained additional background knowledge.

The most apparent difference between the codings produced with and without background knowledge is the increase in labels used and especially the increase in labels with emotional connotations. Obviously, the additional information made subjects more eager to explore the subtleties of communication. Pittenger, Hockett and Danehy (1960) write in this respect: 'One observer may hear anger . . . while others detect remorse or depression or self-pity. They may all be right in that the actual signals may reflect all these contributing factors in a particular varying balance . . . The wise working assumption then is that always no matter how many possible contributing factors we have itemized, there may still be others that we have overlooked.' This quotation taken from *The first five minutes*, a study concerned with therapeutic interviews, is of extreme relevance for the interpretation of communicative interaction from an outside observers' perspective. However, as shown in Table 1, there seems to be much less scope for the detection of an infinite number of contributing aspects when the participants themselves interpret their own interaction. A finite number of possible interpretations does not only correspond to the theoretical framework suggested above, it also underlines the functional value of communication. Were there an infinite number of contributing factors, communication would become a counterproductive instrument for interactors who have to rely on it for the smooth running of their everyday activities. This point will be taken up again.

Returning to Table 4, one can point to two findings of more general interest: first, there is a relatively high amount of internal consistency within coders (compare Table 4 and 2), second, as Table 4 indicates, outside observers arrived at a more 'action-oriented' interpretation for tone-units 1, 2 and 5, than they did in Table 2. Corresponding to the family members' coding, tone-unit (8) displays both an 'action-' and a 'person-oriented' tendency. However, there is still little literal agreement between family members and outside observers. This lack of literal agreement seems to lend support to the assumption put forward in the theoretical section of the paper, namely that accepted ways of expressing concepts can only be expected where knowledge is acquired and categorized in direct interaction between communicants who share a common perspective. Hence, under heterodynamic conditions even the same assessment of a particular tone-unit may lead to the choice of different labels. However, the likelihood of arriving at exactly the same view of the interaction is not too high; for even if outsiders did obtain all the background knowledge relevant for the interaction they would still use this information 'expressively' whereas family members would employ it predominantly in an 'interactive' way.

In order to explore more closely tone-units with verbal pre-final nuclei I am going to introduce now the interpretation of family members of extract 2.

Tone-units 27 and 28 displaying *prepositional* nuclei are again interpreted in an 'action-oriented' way. This corresponds to what has been pointed out above, namely that pronominal and propositional nuclei are used for directing action.[24]

The interpretation given to tone-units 29 and 32 is of a very different kind. Here, family members have emphasized aspects of interaction that I have termed above 'person-oriented'. 'Person-oriented' can refer either to the speaker or to the listener. In both 29 and 32 we have listener-oriented interpretations such as 'assuring', 'mocking', 'criticizing', 'disapproving'. Tone-unit 4 in Table 1, displays on the one hand a speaker-oriented interpretation such as 'defending' and, on the other, a listener-oriented interpretation such as 'disagreeing'.[25]

---

[24] This preliminary result seems to correspond to insights obtained, from a very different perspective, in developmental linguistics. Bruner (this volume) stresses, *inter alia*, that children use locatives for directing the mother's behaviour.

[25] One of the problems of a condensed presentation is that certain subtleties have to be ignored. For instance, 'disapproving' can be used in the sense of 'disapproving of a person' (= person-oriented) or 'disapproving of an action' (= action-oriented). The same holds for a number of other labels. Since the interpretations given by the coders are, however, tape-recorded, this is mainly a problem when the assessment of the interaction has to be reduced to a single label.

Table 4. *Repeated interpretation of extract 1 by outside observers (background knowledge provided)*

Tone-unit no	Subject I	Subject II	Subject IV
1	stating appealing requesting agreement having a go at	giving opinion explaining warning attacking	challenging warning advising having a go at threatening provoking declaring giving information predicting
2	stating appealing requesting agreement having a go at	giving information warning urging	challenging warning advising having a go at threatening provoking declaring giving information predicting
3	disagreeing rejecting defending	disagreeing protesting	questioning disbelieving disagreeing denying wavering evading
4	defending disagreeing	doubting denying	doubting questioning brushing off evading dismissing refusing resisting avoiding postulating hesitating
5	disagreeing blaming reproving rejecting protesting warning requesting agreement	insisting confirming declaring	insisting challenging protesting objecting warning threatening appealing confirming declaring
6	defending scoring a point disagreeing arguing	defending protesting justifying	protesting compromising evading brushing off dismissing lamenting

			riduling doubting

7	hesitating	insisting warning giving information giving opinion clarifying	insisting challenging provoking warning disagreeing objecting predicting declaring
8	challenging provoking brushing off dismissing contradicting defending disbelieving	insisting warning explaining	insisting warning challenging having a go at proving a point reasoning persuading provoking reporting predicting

Table 5. *Family members' interpretation of extract 2*

Tone-unit no	Pre-final nucleus	Mother	Daughter	Son
27	you back	challenging requesting attention warning teasing defying	challenging provoking insisting arguing	challenging requesting agreement complaining arguing
28	I flat	challenging requesting attention warning teasing defying	challenging provoking insisting arguing	challenging requesting agreement arguing
29	want	assuring appeasing pacifying	assuring mocking	assuring mocking ridiculing
30		scoring a point teasing triumphing	scoring a point mocking triumphing	scoring a point agreeing
31		winning a point triumphing	scoring a point mocking requesting agreement	scoring a point agreeing provoking
32	won't understand	criticizing disapproving reproaching accusing	criticizing complaining pacifying appealing	criticizing disapproving rejecting

Table 6. *Outside observers' interpretation of extract 2 (no background knowledge provided)*

Tone-unit no	Subject I	Subject II	Subject III	Subject IV	Subject V
27	postulating	challenging mocking attacking	challenging concluding declaring	provoking reproaching	challenging declaring suggesting
28	challenging appealing stating requesting information	provoking mocking suggesting	challenging concluding declaring	provoking warning	challenging warning asserting
29	conceding giving opinion	admitting disagreeing stating	objecting explaining	declaring giving opinion	declaring giving information
30	emphasizing	attacking challenging	agreeing provoking	confirming accepting	confirming agreeing
31	concluding	justifying attacking ridiculing	declaring	confirming making observation insisting	agreeing
32	changing subject starting lamenting	stating reproaching	dismissing ignoring explaining giving opinion	reproaching protesting	criticizing

Turning our attention now to the interpretation given to the same piece of discourse by outside observers without any background knowledge (Table 6) we can observe, first, a marked trend to 'neutral' labelling even if the ratio of 'neutral' to 'emotional' is a more balanced one for extract 2 than for extract 1. Second, tone-unit 27 is, corresponding to the family members' assessment, predominantly 'action-oriented'. Third, tone-units 29 and 32 display, again in concordance with the insiders' view, a 'person-oriented' tendency.

The 'action-' versus 'person-oriented' tendency is even more pertinent in the recoding done by subjects I, II and IV. This can be shown in Table 7. Like in the corresponding condition for extract 1, subjects I, II and IV have again used predominantly 'emotional' labels. The 'action-oriented' tendency is strongly pronounced in tone-units 27 and 28, and the 'person-oriented' one almost exclusively represented in tone-units 29 and 32. Hence, both 'action-oriented' interpretation for pronouns/ prepositions and 'person-oriented' interpretation for verbs seems to hold for family members as well as for outside observers. Furthermore, there is a surprising degree of agreement with respect to the concrete labels used if one compares those items which were chosen by at least two out of three family members or outside observers. Before presenting this comparison in form of Table 8, I would like to reiterate the note of caution put forward above: even if the interpretation of outside observers coincides for several items with the one given by family members, the very fact that some outside observers produce such a large number of alternative labels may indicate their lack of agreement with the family members. For to know what something means implies to know what it does *not* mean.

4.3. Conclusion

The aim of this paper was theoretically to establish and empirically to illustrate the possibility of investigating physical indicators or cues used by communicants in the process of encoding and decoding messages. For this purpose, I have, first, advanced a theoretical framework within which criteria for adequate empirical data could be formulated (sections 2.1 to 2.6), and, second, developed an analytical technique with the aid of which the empirical investigation of the research question could be carried out (sections 3.1 to 3.6). The heuristic value of theoretical framework and discovery procedure was illustrated in sections 4.1 and 4.2. From the preliminary findings discussed under 4.2.2 certain pro-

Table 7. *Repeated interpretation of extract 2 (Background knowledge provided)*

Tone-unit no	Subject I	Subject II	Subject IV
27	challenging attacking pressuring disbelieving appealing seeking attention	challenging protesting threatening suggesting defending	threatening provoking warning defying
28	challenging pressuring attacking disbelieving appealing seeking attention	threatening pressuring requesting agreement	challenging threatening provoking having a go at warning protesting scoring a point prescribing
29	defending disagreeing resisting conceding a point reasoning	assuring ridiculing clarifying stating	assuring ridiculing defending losing a point consenting hesitating complying
30	scoring a point triumphing arguing	scoring a point triumphing mocking	scoring a point proving a point triumphing mocking teasing joking playing ridiculing demanding agreement
31	scoring a point triumphing arguing	triumphing justifying scoring	scoring a point mocking teasing accusing provoking challenging having a go at scoring
32	appealing reproaching reasoning rejecting	appealing criticizing reasoning defending	reproaching reasoning accusing complaining lamenting appealing advising

Table 8. *Comparison between Table 5 and Table 7*

Tone-unit no	Pre-final nucleus	Family members	Outside observers
27	you back	challenging/requesting agreement/arguing	challenging/threatening
28	I flat	challenging/requesting agreement/arguing	challenging/threatening pressuring
29	want	assuring/mocking	assuring/ridiculing/ defending
30		scoring a point/triumphing	scoring a point/triumphing mocking
31		winning/scoring a point	scoring a point/triumphing scorning
32	won't understand	criticizing/disapproving	appealing/reproaching

visional conclusions may be drawn and open problems formulated which will require further empirical investigation.

4.3.1

The homodynamic criteria outlined in the theoretical sections seem to have been corroborated. The communicative concepts used by family members for decoding their own interaction indicated a similarity of interpretation which was not displayed to the same extent by outside observers. However, the problem of how shared knowledge is used in the process of encoding and decoding messages within conditions where homodynamic codes can be expected needs further investigation. Research employing the same analytical technique is currently carried out on recordings of a middle-class family.

4.3.2

The segmentation of the continuous stretch of speech into tone-units has proved acceptable and useful. Family members as well as outside observers agreed, with very few exceptions, with the parsed sequences in spite of having undergone no linguistic training. They saw the task of assigning communicative concepts to tone-units as corresponding to their communicative intuitions, namely that both speaker and listener (within close-knit groups) know what is really meant over and above the words used. However, since interactors do not consciously perceive their everyday interaction as a sequence of communicative acts, coders required time and concentration in order to make their implicit knowledge explicit.

4.3.3

Due to the surprisingly high agreement between family members as to the message character of tone-units, an analysis of the physical features of these units could be carried out. This empirical analysis of the internal structure of communicative acts has produced promising results. On the basis of the investigation conducted so far, there seems to be a strong tendency to interpret tone-units with pre-final nuclei of a *verbal* kind as *person-oriented* interaction and tone-units with pre-final nuclei of a *pronominal/prepositional* nature as *action-oriented* communication. Hence, in accordance with the theoretical expectations discussed above the system of tonicity appears to be of crucial importance for the interpretation of tone-units in terms of specific communicative acts. This finding is currently being tested experimentally.

4.3.4

The analysis of additional physical indicators for communicative acts has not yet progressed very far. Subsequent research will centre around the type–token question. That is, in having tone-units coded by family members we obtain 'tokens' of a specific 'type' like 'ordering'. Only in comparing a number of tokens of the same type will we be able to detect the physical properties of the type under investigation. That is, 'family resemblances' of tokens have to be analysed in order to detect the 'defining' and/or the 'characteristic' features of specific types of communicative acts.[26]

4.3.5

The final aim of this genre of research is to establish empirically the existence of homodynamic codes. At the present stage of investigation, this goal is still rather remote. But only when we can empirically demonstrate specific paradigmatic and syntagmatic relations defining and/or characteristic for a specific homodynamic code can we really evaluate the significance of more detailed findings.

I would like to thank Jens Allwood, Michael Argyle, Rom Harré, Roy Harris, Jos Jaspers, Reinhard Kreckel, and David Pendleton for helpful criticism.

[26] This research question bears a certain resemblance to Rosch's (1977) featural approach to category names like 'birds'.

References

Allwood, J. (1976) *Linguistic communication as action and co-operation: a study of pragmatics. Gothenburg Monographs in Linguistics, no. 2.*

Austin, J. L. (1962) *How to do things with words.* Harvard University Press, Cambridge, Mass.

Bernstein, B. (1970) *Class, codes and control, vol. 1: Theoretical studies towards a sociology of language.* Routledge & Kegan Paul, London.

Bollinger, D. L. (1958) 'A theory of pitch accent in English.' *Word* **14**, 109–49.

Boomer, D. S. (1978) 'The phonemic clause: speech unit in human communication.' In A. W. Siegman and S. Feldstein (eds.), *Nonverbal behavior and communication.* Lawrence Erlbaum, Hillsdale, N.J.

Brown, R. (1965) *Social psychology.* Free Press, Glencoe, Ill.

Bruner, J. S. (1967) 'On perceptual readiness.' *Psychological Review* **64**, 123–52.

Chafe, W. L. (1970) *Meaning and the structure of language.* University of Chicago Press, Chicago.

Cherry, C. (1957) *On human communication.* Massachusetts Institute of Technology, and Wiley, New York.

Chomsky, N. and M. Halle (1968) *The sound pattern of English.* Harper & Row, New York.

Clark, H. H. and E. V. Clark (1977) *Psychology and language.* H. B. Jovanovich, New York.

Crystal, D. (1975) *The Engish tone of voice.* Edward Arnold, London.

Dahl, Ö. (1976) 'What is new information?' In N. E. Enkvist and V. Kohonen (eds.), *Reports on text linguistics: approaches to word order.*

Daneš, F. (ed.) (1974) *Papers on functional sentence perspective.* Mouton, The Hague.

Fraser, C. (1978) 'Communication in interaction.' In H. Tajfel and C. Fraser (eds), *Introducing social psychology.* Penguin Books, Harmondsworth.

Frege, G. (1892) 'Ueber Begriff und Gegenstand.' *Vierteljahrsschrift fuer wissenschaftliche Philosophie* **16**, 192–205.

Grice, H. P. (1975) 'Logic and conversation.' In P. Cole and J. L. Morgan (eds.), *Syntax and semantics, vol. 3: Speech acts.* Academic Press, New York.

Gumperz, J. (1972) 'The speech community.' In P. P. Giglioli (ed.), *Language and social context.* Penguin Books, Harmondsworth.

— (1977) 'Sociocultural knowledge in conversational inference.' In M. Saville-Froike (ed.), *28th Annual Round Table Monographs on Language and Linguistics.* Georgetown University Press, Washington, D.C.

Habermas, J. (1976a) 'Was heisst Universalpragmatik.' In K. O. Apel (ed.), *Sprachpragmatik und Philosophie.* Suhrkamp, Frankfurt.

— (1976b) 'Some distinctions in universal pragmatics.' *Theory and Society* **3**, 155–67.

Halliday, M. A. K. (1967) *Intonation and grammar in British English.* Mouton, The Hague.

— (1976) *System and function in language: selected papers* (ed. G. Kress). Oxford University Press, London.

— (1978) *Language as social semiotic.* Edward Arnold, London.

Halliday, M. A. K. and R. Hasan (1976) *Cohesion in English.* Longmans, London.

Harré, R. (1979) *Social being.* Blackwell, Oxford.

308   Marga Kreckel

Harris, R. (1978) 'Discovering languages.' Paper presented at the symposium 'Discovery strategies in social psychology', Oxford, 11 December 1978.

Harvey, O. J., D. E. Hunt and H. M. Schroder (1961) *Conceptual systems and personality organization.* Wiley, New York.

Jones, E. E. and H. B. Gerard (1967) *Foundations of social psychology.* Wiley, New York.

Katz, J. and P. Postal (1964) *An integrated theory of linguistic description.* Massachusetts Institute of Technology Press, Cambridge, Mass.

Kelly, G. A. (1955) *The psychology of personal constructs.* Norton, New York.

Kreckel, M. (1978a) 'Private versus public code: a conceptual analysis of the phenomenon of code-switching.' *Research Film – Le Film de Recherche – Forschungsfilm* **9/5**, 445–63.

— (1978b) 'Communicative acts: a semiological approach to the empirical analysis of filmed interaction.' *Semiotica* **24**, 87–111.

— (1979) 'A framework for the analysis of natural discourse.' In M. Brenner (ed.), *The structure of action.* Blackwell, Oxford.

— (1981a) 'Where do constitutive acts for speech acts come from?' *Language and Communication* **1**, 73–88.

— (1981b) *Communicative acts and shared knowledge in natural discourse.* Academic Press, London.

— (1981c) 'Tone-units as message blocks in natural discourse.' *Journal of Pragmatics* **5**.

Labov, W. and D. Fanshel (1977) *Therapeutic discourse,* Academic Press, New York.

Laver, J. (1971) 'The production of speech.' In J. Lyons (ed.), *New horizons in linguistics.* Penguin Books, Harmondsworth.

Piaget, J. (1950) *Introduction à l'épistémologie génétique.* Presses Universitaires de France, Paris.

Pike, K. I. (1948) *The intonation of American English.* University of Michigan Press, Ann Arbor.

Pittenger, R. E., D. F. Hockett and J. J. Danehy (1960) *The first five minutes.* Martineau, Ithaca, N.Y.

Quirk, R. and S. Greenbaum (1973) *A university grammar of English.* Longmans, London.

Rommetveit, R. (1974) *On message structure: a framework for the study of language and communication.* Wiley, London.

Rosch, E. (1977) 'Human categorization.' In N. Warren (ed.), *Advances in cross-cultural psychology.* Academic Press, London.

Saussure, F. de (1974) *Course in general linguistics.* Collins, Glasgow.

Searle, J. R. (1969) *Speech acts.* Cambridge University Press, Cambridge.

Sinclair, J. M. and R. M. Coulthard (1975) *Towards an analysis of discourse.* Oxford University Press, London.

Stockwell, R. (1972) 'The role of intonation: reconsiderations and other considerations.' In D. Bollinger (ed.), *Intonation.* Penguin Books, Harmondsworth.

Tajfel, H. (1978) 'The structure of our views about society.' In H. Tajfel and C. Fraser (eds.), *Introducing social psychology.* Penguin Books, Harmondsworth.

Trager, G. L. and H. L. Smith (1951) *An outline of English structure.* Battenberg Press, Norman, Oklahoma.

Zajonc, R. B. (1968) 'Cognitive theories in social psychology.' In G. Lindzey and E. Aronson (eds.), *The handbook of social psychology, vol. 1.* Addison-Wesley, Reading, Mass.

5. The ontogenesis and phylogenesis of action

Introduction

Many of this book's contributions deal with action of a highly developed form: as the goal-directed, planned, intended and more or less consciously guided behaviour of *persons*, that is mature and socially responsible human individuals. As such, goal-directed action can be characterized as the most human form of behaviour; but obviously it only represents the last result and final form of ontogenetical and phylogenetical development. Infants and animals pursue projects too, although in an imperfect way. As documented in this chapter, the study of these simpler actions provides insight into the organization of GDA in general.

The first and perhaps the most important of these insights is that the organization of infant and animal action can be seen as fundamentally similar to fully developed GDA in many respects; we must however assume very important differences in the form and quality of the corresponding mental representations. There are convincing reasons which forbid us to treat these as conscious cognitions. In this respect, the authors of this chapter agree. The consequences of dealing with non-conscious cognitions, the transition from non-conscious to conscious, and the discontinuity of the syndromes 'non-conscious–organic–social' and 'conscious–symbolic–societal (or institutional)', in contrasting infant and animal actors to persons, is one of the pervading themes of the discussion.

Thus, Bruner begins his presentation of the socialization for action with the presupposition that human action is steered by intentions. Intention is objectively defined as being present when an individual operates persistently towards achieving an end state, chooses among alternative means or routes and tests the results. The complete circle therefore comprises aim, option of means, persistence and correction. Bruner emphasizes that it is not necessary that intention be conscious or accountable (which would exclude its study in small infants): conscious intention however has a special status, and when and how a child achieves reportable awareness of what it is trying to do is important. In fact Bruner's paper documents in many details how the mother aids her infant to develop his practical and communicative action until the final state of reportable awareness is reached. In doing so, the mother relies on her social knowledge ('folk wisdom') about the child's intentions and the appropriate means to transform them into actions. Thus the process is imbedded into culture and society.

Vernon Reynolds considers general possibilities and implications of GDA in animals in comparison to man; he illustrates discussions with examples from his studies on the behaviour of rhesus monkeys. In the definition of his four basic terms, he follows Max Weber and Rom Harré: *behaviour* is what people and animals do. *Meaning* refers to reasons and ideas. *Action* is behaviour based on meaning, and the *act* is action in a social context. By the latter category, the social side of the action is included from the beginning.

The distinguishing feature of human action is seen in language, as the basis of communication, which serves as a 'transforming device' in socialization: it aids the child to acquire *meaning* in form of *social representations* (although many cultural meanings remain always implicit). It is the unique feature of the human social order that it is based on social representations; although the existence of analogous structures in monkeys cannot be excluded, these cannot form a useful basis for the scientific analysis of their actions.

As to the transmission of social life from generation to generation, *organic evolution* in animals is contrasted to *superorganic evolution* in man; the latter is characterized by verbal transmission of social representations. In the human individual, the integration of cultural and private experience culminates in the development of *the self*. The self is free in the sense that man, in his action, is constantly choosing between alternatives. Is there any correspondence in the mind of animals? Vernon Reynolds sees few possibilities to study the related mental activities, especially consciousness, in sufficient detail; instead he proposes a general theory of decision-making, which could serve as an integration of cognitive and behavioural analysis.

The paper by Peter Reynolds (the two Reynolds are not related) exposes a different approach; the author presents a comprehensive and detailed report of a method for the description of a specific GDA, the construction and use of tools in non-human primates and man, and reports some of the obtained results. This method is called the DAEDA-LUS program. Like many authors of this book, he postulates a two-dimensional organization of action, which he characterizes by the terms 'chain of command' and 'subsystems' autonomy'. Primate constructional activity, as GDA in general, cannot readily be described in terms of behaviour catalogues (e.g. an ethogram), but in functional terms. In consequence, Reynolds's method (which is in some respects analogous to the computer programming language LISP) performs a functional description. This method combines rigour with flexibility; the latter quality is achieved in analogy to the flexibility of skills, which is seen to be 'based on the ability to run the same program with different arguments' (after Bruner). Thus, the 'DAEDALUS function' for 'climbing up', 'climbing down' and 'pulling in' are rather similar. It is of little use to go into details here; instead let us turn to two problems also discussed by the other two authors. Peter Reynolds firmly claims that much animal behaviour is goal-directed. How can we, however, determine goals without access to verbal reports? The author argues that goals can be securely and correctly concluded from the observable behaviour and the circumstances of action. He enumerates and discusses some criteria for the inference of goal-directedness. Most important among these are behaviours which serve the function to get around a 'block', but also other behavioural indicators can be used. In his own words:

> Moreover, the inference of goal-directedness utilizes a wide range of behavioural indicators, including (1) reinstatement of entry conditions through repetition of a prior act in the sequence, (2) creation of a terminal consequence through repetition of the present act, (3) circumvention of a BLOCK through substitution of another act which produces a related consequence, (4) gaze direction toward anticipated consequences, (5) emotional reactions to consequences, and (6) the consequences which follow from altered performances of activities observed in other circumstances. To these should be added *anticipatory movements* which are acts appropriate to an external effect but which are given before that effect has taken place, as when a chimpanzee begins to climb the ladder before it is fully in position. Taking all of these lines of evidence together, the inference of goal-directedness in behaviour does not appear to be epistemologically weaker than many other kinds of scientific inference which have been generally accepted.

Obviously, these criteria can be applied to human actions as well.

The comparison of human and non-human action is also of general interest. By applying his methods to similar activities in chimpanzees, adults and children in different cultures, Peter Reynolds finds considerable differences in the organization of action, mainly consisting in a greater amount of differentiation and hierarchical nesting of operations in man. Another major difference is seen in the use of representations:

> The construction of many human artifacts requires the control of motor activity by an image of the final product that is being produced by the skill. That is, motor activity is controlled by simulated perceptual content that is only gradually created empirically.

Most important in their consequences, however, are Peter Reynolds's conclusions about the social differences in constructional activities of apes and humans. Besides individual interconnection, the latter are also functionally related to a social context. The author concludes:

> Since *technology*, in a human sense of that term, presupposes a social infrastructure for even individual performances, theories of the ape–hominid transition which attempt to derive 'co-operative tool use' from 'tool use' have placed the cart before the horse. Since intentional action is frequently co-operative and socially regulated in non-human primates, it makes more sense to derive co-operation from social interactions where it already exists than from object-using programs where it does not. Consequently, a theory of the evolution of human technology should place less emphasis on differences in the tool-using capacities between humans and apes (important as these are) but ask instead how emergent tool-using capacities become integrated into the domain of intentional social action.

So we have come back to the social nature of GDA.

The organization of action and the nature of adult–infant transaction

J. S. BRUNER

I wish to begin by baldly stating a presupposition about the organization of action, one which I shall take for granted; then I shall present evidence from the study of mother–infant interaction that would have forced me to come to a conclusion about the nature of human action very like that which I began with as taken for granted. I promise to perform this feat without mirrors. My argument will be simply: how could parent–infant interaction in the human species (and in some higher apes) be as it is unless the nature of human action is as I suppose it to be? This is not such an audacious enterprise as it may seem. It is what we researchers do all the time, though we suppress our presuppositions in communicating our findings and then feign surprise when we state our final conclusions. The evidence I shall use is material from studies in both the acquisition of language and the assisted acquisitions of action routines by infants.

What I shall take for granted for the moment (until forced later to conclude that I was right) is that most of what we speak of in commonsense terms as human action is steered by intentions of the following kind and in the following way. An intention is present when an individual operates persistently toward achieving an end state, chooses among alternative means and/or routes to achieve that end state, persists in deploying means and corrects the deployment of means to get closer to the end state, and finally ceases the line of activity when specifiable features of the end state are achieved. The elements of the cycle, then, comprise aim, option of means, persistence and correction, and a terminal stop order. There are several unspecified features present in this type of cycle. The principal one has to do with the nature of feedback and correction. In the nature of things, feedback in such an action cycle is always context-dependent: it is computed by reference to the feed-forward signal inherent in the action aim of the organism. A

313

correction procedure involves a redeployment of means whose objective is to minimize the discrepancy between one's present position and what had been anticipated as the position appropriate to achieving the sought-after end state – minimizing $\Delta_\omega = S_\omega - I_\omega$.

There is another matter hidden in my description that wants to be made explicit. It is not necessary that, in such human action, the actor be able to account for or be conscious of the nature of his intentions. Much of intentional action takes place below the threshold of reportable awareness. Driving a car whilst conversing with a friend provides a familiar case. But I would want to emphasize that a special status inheres in those intentional acts that *are* reportable and conscious. The distinction is important not only in the ethical sense intended by my colleague Tony Kenny (see Kenny 1975), but also from the point of view of how conscious reportability extends the range of corrections accessible to the actor. Perhaps it is by making conscious intentions more combinable through the use of language. I need to mention this rather banal point for reasons that will have already occurred to you. I shall be speaking of the support of intentional action in the relation that develops between infant and mother and it matters mightily when and how the child achieves reportable awareness of what he is trying to do.

Another preliminary remark. It has to do with the graininess of the theory of action I am presenting, its decomposability into elementary units. We know that intentional acts can become constituents of, serve as means subroutines in, other intentional acts. Intentions are obviously nesting and nestable or, in a technical sense, have the property of iterativeness and recursivity. In some systems of intentional behaviour, like talking a natural language, there are discernible, analysable levels that go to make up a communicative act – say an utterance. These have the property that they cannot be understood from bottom up, but are amenable of interpretation only from the top down. When we say that distinctive features are the constituents *en pacquet* of a phoneme, and that phonemes and their allophonic slippages are constituents of morphemes (whether derivational or inflectional), that morphemes somehow fill the grammatical slots of a sentence, etc, we imply top–down determination. Each level below is constrained by the level above in a fashion that makes it extraordinarily difficult to describe how language is produced or even comprehended. Language is a very special case in the sense that the design features of the system are in many ways quite unlike any other system of intentional action known in the biological world (and I do not mean to exclude the social world by using the term 'biological'). Yet, for any system of action – from skilled motor activity to such highly symbolic, rule-governed activities as flirtation or stock-broking – there is a possible description of the manner in which constituents are composed into higher-level action of structures. And the crucial point is that it is the task of anybody learning to carry out skilled, intentional action to figure out the rules of composition (and decomposition) of the system.

This brings me to the final preliminary remark I must make. It is quite the most typical thing of the actions of our species that in the course of growth our intentions outstrip our capacities for fulfilling them or, indeed, even for recognizing fully what they are about. The young infant will typically reveal a situation-related restlessness, a general activation before he is able fully to recognize means to an end, and indeed there is a body of data in the field of motivation that suggests that, under such conditions of activation, it may be necessary for the immature organism to learn what the end state is that terminates the diffuse intentionality (if I may use such a bizarre phrase as a synonym for activation). It certainly becomes necessary for him to learn how to deploy the means for achieving the desired end state. It is characteristic of organisms like man, with a conspicuously helpless immaturity, that they cannot operate to achieve their goals (or to learn them, for that matter) by trial-and-error behaviour, and they do not have enough of a wired-in repertoire of try-out routines to guide them much in such trial and error. In consequence, they are dependent, like no species yet ever evolved, upon a tutoring relationship with adults who can help them learn to carry out their intended actions directed to goals. It is quite obvious that something of this order occurs in language acquisition and in other forms of social skill learning. It is equally obvious that such also occurs when one observes the child learning to cope with the world of objects during the first two years of life. Or if it it is not immediately obvious, I hope I will be able to make it so shortly.

Now, a little reflection upon this interesting problem makes it plain that for such a state of transaction between infant and adult to prevail, adults must have a representation in their heads about the nature of human development. That is to say, to take the case of language, the adult, in order to help the child to his goals of linguistic mastery, must not only know what constitutes human mastery, but also have a developmental theory of the performance of the child en route toward that final state. If there is anything to the doctrine of an inbuilt, if not innate, Language Acquisition Device, LAD (Chomsky 1965), for young children faced with the flow of the language about them, on my view there must be something comparable in the adult that deserves the title Language Assistance Service (LAS). On this view as well, the acquisition of language is a dialogue between the child's acquisition device and the adult's assistance service, between LAD and LAS. Certainly the findings of Shatz and Gelman (1973) on 4-year-olds being able to talk appropriately in 'baby talk' register to 2-year-olds suggest that the adult assistance service opens its doors to potential clients at a very tender age indeed. And the past several years of research on mother–infant linguistic interaction points to the fact that there is an enormous amount of fine tuning in the mother's responses to the child's talk (or his very effort to talk) that could not have got there simply by virtue of the mother's having been exposed to other babies or having read John Lyons (1970) on Noam Chomsky.

With respect to helping the child to handle manipulation of the world of objects, there is a comparable problem. David Wood and his co-workers (Wood, Bruner and Ross 1976), including me, have explored what mothers do when helping their child to do things like drinking from a cup or putting together an interlocking set of blocks. The mother's performance is an interesting and uncanny set of manoeuvres on the theme we have been exploring. She is obviously operating on a very intricate and subtle and updatable theory of the child's performance. Let me specify some of the manoeuvres Wood, Ross and I observed in a study of mothers teaching their 3-to-5-year-olds how to assemble a set of interlocking blocks to make an intricate pyramid.

1. *Modelling*. The mother typically models not only the final pyramid by constructing it slowly and with conspicuous marking, but also the sub-assemblies that she recognizes the child needs to create the constituents. She does this only after she has achieved the child's concentrated attention.

2. *Cueing*. Once the child has achieved a means–end routine of any kind, she cues him with respect to the opportunities for using it so that it may reach successful conclusion.

3. *Scaffolding*. She systematically reduces the number of degrees of freedom that must be controlled by the child in carrying out parts of the task – as in helping him guide blocks into place when he is attempting to put them into the assembly. She also, by way of diffuse scaffolding,

protects him from distraction by limiting the site in which the task occurs, and by ritualizing it. I shall talk of this shortly in the context of language acquisition as 'format construction', a means of limiting the complexity of tasks to situations where the child is able to carry out tasks and to evaluate feedback off his own bat.

4. *Raising the ante.* It is characteristic of most mothers we have observed that once the child has mastered one component of the task, they find ways of challenging him to incorporate it into a more complex routine for achievement of a more remote end. It may often have the nature of teasing rather than teaching (challenging the child, as one mother put it, to 'make the ultimate effort'). But its function is certainly benign and it is a feature of variation in mother–infant interaction that saves the child from being bored out of action by a series of confirming reinforcements when he already knows that he already knows.

5. *Instruction.* And final irony: when the child already knows how to do it and can indeed account for what he's doing, at that stage the mother starts using verbal instruction successfully and seriously. (There is plenty of talk before that, but it is not 'serious'.) Verbal instruction appears only when the child is able to encode his acts in joint reference with the interlocutor, his mother.

The conclusion to which I am forced is that the mother is operating as if the child had intentions in mind, as if he were trying to deploy means to its realization, as if he were out to correct errors, as if he had a finished task in mind – but that he is not quite able to put it all together in a fashion to suit him or his mother. She imposes regularity on the task, takes account of his channel capacity for information processing, and keeps him activated by managing to keep full effectance just out of reach. I can come to one of two conclusions. Either the mother is a victim of common sense and does not really understand action, else she would put her charge into a Skinner box and devise a schedule of reinforcement for his operant responses. Or she is behaving appropriately toward an immature member of the species who does in fact operate along the lines of intentional action I originally proposed.

(Let me confess at this point that the original view, presented as 'taken for granted', may remind you of some things you may have read in the literature – like Von Holst and Mittelstaedt (1950), Bernstein (1967) and Miller, Galanter and Pribram (1960). That should not deter you.)

Now language acquisition. This is not the occasion to go deeply into the question of the functions that language fulfils and the means whereby conventionalized devices or procedures are developed and used for their fulfilment. I do not want to be engaged directly in this issue at this point; enough only to say that something of the order of speech-act theory and the Gricean cycle (Grice 1957) plus some set of controlling maxims to regulate presuppositions are for me an essential aspect of any linguistic theory and particularly of one that hopes to make contact with work on acquisition. What I would like to do is take first the case of the child learning to label, and then to move on to the child mastering requestive forms, as an illustration of my points.

Consider an infant learning to label objects. Anat Ninio and I (Ninio and Bruner 1978) observed Richard in his home every two weeks from his eighth month until he was two years old, video-taping his actions so that we could study them later. In this instance, he and his mother are 'reading' the pictures in a book. Before this kind of learning begins, certain things already have been established. Richard has learned about pointing as a pure indicating act, marking unusual or unexpected objects rather than things wanted immediately. He has also learned to understand that sounds refer in some singular way to objects or events. Richard and his mother, moreover, have long since established well-regulated turn-taking routines, which probably were developing as early as his third or fourth month. And finally, Richard has learned that books are to be looked at, not eaten or torn; that objects depicted are to be responded to in a particular way and with sounds in a pattern of dialogue.

For the mother's part, she (like all mothers we have observed) drastically limits her speech and maintains a steady regularity. In her dialogues with Richard in 'book-reading' she uses four types of speech in a strikingly fixed order. First, to get his attention, she says, 'Look'. Second, with a distinctly rising inflection, she asks, 'What's that?'. Third, she gives the picture a label, 'It's an X'. And finally, in response to his actions, she says, 'That's right'.

In each case, a single verbal token accounts for from nearly half to more than 90 % of the instances. The way Richard's mother uses the four speech constituents is closely linked to what her son says or does. When she varies her response, it is with good reason. If Richard responds, his mother replies, and if he initiates a cycle by pointing and vocalizing, then she responds even more often.

Her fine tuning is fine indeed. For example, if after her query Richard labels the picture, she will virtually always skip the label and jump to the response, 'Yes'. Like the other mothers we have studied, she is following ordinary polite rules for adult dialogue.

As Roger Brown has described the baby talk of adults, it appears to be an imitative version of how babies talk. Brown (1977) says: 'Babies already talk like babies, so what is the earthly use of parents doing the same? Surely it is a parent's job to teach the adult language.' (p. 18.) He resolves the dilemma by noting, 'What I think adults are chiefly trying to do, when they use [baby talk] with children, is to communicate, to understand and to be understood, to keep two minds focussed on the same topic.' (p. 19.) Although I agree with Brown, I would like to point out that the content and intonation of the talk is baby talk, but the dialogue pattern is adult.

To ensure that two minds are indeed focussed on a common topic the mother develops a technique for showing her baby what feature a label refers to by making 90 % of her labels refer to whole objects. Since half of the remainder of her speech is made up of proper names that also stand for the whole, she seems to create few difficulties, supposing that the child also responds to whole objects and not to their features.

The mother's (often quite unconscious) approach is exquisitely tuned. When the child responds to her 'Look!' by looking, she follows immediately with a query. When the child responds to the query with a gesture or a smile, she supplies a label. But as soon as the child shows the ability to vocalize in a way that might indicate a label, she raises the ante. She withholds the label and repeats the query until the child vocalizes, then she gives the label.

Later, when the child has learned to respond with shorter vocalizations that correspond to words, she no longer accepts an indifferent vocalization. When the child begins producing a recognizable, constant label for an object, she holds out for it. Finally, the child produces appropriate words at the appropriate place in the dialogue. Even then the mother remains tuned to the developing pattern, helping her child recognize labels and make them increasingly accurate. For example, she develops two ways of asking, 'What's that?'. One, with a falling intonation, inquires about those words for which she believes her child already knows the label; the other, with a rising intonation, marks words that are new.

Even in the simple labelling game, mother and child are well into making the distinction between the given and the new. It is of more than passing interest that the old or established labels are the ones around which the mother will shortly be elaborating comments and questions for new information:

Mother: What's that? [with falling intonation]
Child: Fishy.
Mother: Yes, and see him swimming?

After the mother assumes her child has acquired a particular label, she generally drops the attention-getting 'Look!' when they turn to the routine. In these petty particulars of language, the mother gives useful cues about the structures of their native tongue. She provides cues based not simply on her knowledge of the language but also on her continually changing knowledge of the child's ability to grasp particular distinctions, forms or rules. The child is sensitized to certain constraints in the structure of their dialogue and does not seem to be directly imitating her. I say this because there is not much difference in the likelihood of a child's repeating a label after hearing it, whether the mother has imitated the child's label, simply said 'Yes', or only laughed approvingly. In each case, the child repeats the label about half the time, about the same rate as with *no* reply from the mother. Moreover, the child is eight times more likely to produce a label in response to 'What's that?' than to the mother's uttering the label.

I do not mean to claim that children cannot or do not use imitation in acquiring language. Language must be partly based on imitation, but though the child may be imitating another, language learning involves solving problems by communicating in a dialogue. The child seems to be trying to get through to the mother just as hard as she is trying to reach her child.

Dialogue occurs in a context. When children first learn to communicate, it is always in highly concrete situations, as when mother or child calls attention to an object, asking for the aid or participation of the other. Formally conceived, the format of communication involves an intention, a set of procedures, and a goal. In this sense, the formats of language acquisition are much like the tasks described by Wood, Bruner and Ross (1976).

A second major function of speech is requesting something of another person. Collaborators and I (Bruner, Roy and Ratner, in press) have been studying its development during the first two years of life. Requesting requires an indication that you want *something* and *what* it is you want. In the earliest procedures used by children it is difficult to separate the two. First the child vocalizes with a characteristic intonation pattern while reaching eagerly for the desired nearby object – which is most often held by the mother. As in virtually all early exchanges, it is the mother's task to interpret, and she works at it in a surprisingly subtle way. During our analyses of Richard when he was from 8 to 24 months old and Jonathan when he was 8 to 18 months old, we noticed that their mothers frequently seemed to be teasing them or withholding obviously desired objects. Closer inspection indicated that it was not teasing at all. They were trying to get the infants to reach for what they wanted and to 'say something' (as one mother urged her son), pressing them to make their intentions clearer. When the two children requested nearby objects, the mothers were more likely to ask 'Do you really want it?' than 'Do you want the X?'. The mother's first step is pragmatic, to get the child to signal that he wants the object.

Children make three types of requests, reflecting increasing sophistication in matters that have nothing to do with language. The first kind that emerges is directed at obtaining nearby, visible objects; this later expands to include distant or absent objects where the contextual understanding of words like *'you/me'*, *'this/that'* and *'here/there'* is crucial. The second kind of request is directed at obtaining support for an action that is already in progress, and the third kind is used to persuade the mother to share some activity or experience.

When children first begin to request objects, they typically direct their attention and their reach entirely toward the object, opening and closing their fists, accompanied by a 'standard', stereotyped call with characteristic intonation pattern. As this request expands, between 10 and 15 months, an observer immediately notes two changes. In reaching for distant objects, a child no longer looks solely at the desired object, but shifts his glance back and forth between the object and his mother. His call pattern also changes. It becomes more prolonged, or its rise and fall in intonation is repeated, and it is more insistent.

When consistent word forms appeared, they were initially idiosyncratic labels for objects, gradually becoming standard nouns that indicated the desired objects. The children also began initiating and ending their requests with smiles. The development of this pattern is paced by the child's knowledge, which is shared with the mother, of where things are located and of her willingness to fetch them if properly asked. Once the child begins requesting distant and absent objects, the mother has an opportunity to require that the desired object be specified – her emphasis shifts from the pragmatic to the referential. Other conditions begin to be imposed: the request, for example, must be 'legitimate' and 'appropriate', the object essential, 'timetable' conditions must be honoured – and when the request is not granted, the child is expected to understand and accept the mother's verbal reasons.

Requests for joint activity contrast with object requests. I think they can be called precursors to invitation. They amount to the child asking the adult to share in an activity or an experience – to look out of the window into the garden together, to play Ride-a-cock-horse, to read together. They are the most playlike form of request, and in consequence they generate a considerable amount of language of considerable complexity. It is in this format that the issues of agency and share (or turn) emerge and produce important linguistic changes. Most of these requests are for activities that are quite ritualized and predictable. There tend to be rounds and turns, and no specific outcome is required. The activity itself is rewarding. In this setting the child first deals with share and turn by adopting such forms of linguistic marking as *more* and *again*. These appear during joint role enactment and migrate rapidly into formats involving requests for distant objects.

It is also in joint role enactment that the baby's first consistent words appear and, beginning at 18 months, word combinations begin to explode. *More X* (with a noun) appears, and also combinations like *down slide, Mummy ride, Mummy read, Eileen do*. Indeed, it is in these settings that full-blown ingratiatives appear in appropriate positions, as in prefacing a request with *nice Mummy*. Ingratiatives serve to assure that the other continues to act as a means to the achievement of intention.

After the children were 17 months old, the mothers we studied began to demand that they adhere more strictly to turn-taking and role-respecting. The demand can be made most easily when they are doing something together, for that is where the conditions for sharing are most clearly defined and least likely, since playful, to overstrain the child's capacity to wait for a turn. But the sharp increase in agency as a topic in their dialogue reflects as well the emergence of a difference in their wishes. The mother may want the child to execute the act requested of her, and the child may have views contrary to his mother's about agency. In addition, the child's requests for support more often lead to negotiation between the pair than is the case when the clarity of the roles in their joint activity makes acceptance and refusal easier. A recurrent trend in development during the child's first year is the shifting of agency in all manner of exchanges from mother to infant. Even at 9 to 12 months, Richard gradually began taking the lead in give-and-take games (Bruner 1978), and peekaboo games follow a similar pattern (Ratner and Bruner 1978). In book-reading too, Richard's transition was quite rapid. Role-shifting is very much part of the child's sense of script, and I believe it is typical of the kind of 'real world' experience that makes it so astonishingly easy for children to master soon afterwards the deictic shifts, those contextual changes in the meaning of words that are essential to understanding the language. The prelinguistic communicative framework established in their dialogue by mother and child provides the setting for the child's acquisition of this language function. His problem solving in acquiring the deictic function is a *social* task: to find the procedure that will produce results, just as his prelinguistic communicative effort produced results, and the results needed can be interpreted in relation to role interactions.

The last type of request, the request for supportive action, has a very special property. It is tightly bound to the nature of the action in which the child is involved. To ask others for help in support of their own action, children need at least two forms of knowledge. One of them represents the course of action and involves a goal and a set of means for getting to it. The second requirement is some grasp of what has been called the arguments of action (Parisi and Antinucci 1976): who does it, with what instrument, at what place, to whom, on what object, etc. Once children have mastered these, they have a rudimentary understanding of the concepts that will later be encountered in case grammar (cf. Fillmore 1968).

The degree to which a child comes to understand the structure of tasks is the degree to which his requests for support in carrying them out become more differentiated. These requests do not appear with any marked frequency until he is 17 or 18 months old and consist of bringing the 'work' or the 'action' or the entire task to an adult: a music box to be rewound, or two objects that have to be joined together. In time, a child is able to do better than that. He may bring a tool to an adult or direct the adult's hand or pat the goal (the chair on which he wants up). He is selecting and highlighting relevant features of the action, though not in a fashion that depends on what the adult is doing. Finally at about the age of two, with the development of adequate words to refer to particular aspects of the action, the child enters a new phase: he requests action by guiding it successively. The pacemaker of the verbal output is progress in the task itself.

Let me give an instance of this successive guidance system. Richard, it transpires, wishes to persuade his mother to open a cupboard so that he can get something out; she is seated (and very pregnant). Successively, he voices the following requests:

Mummy, Mummy; Mummy come . . . Up, up; up . . . Cupboard . . .
Up cupboard, up cupboard, up cupboard; up . . . Get up . . .
Cupboard, cupboard . . . Cupboard-up, cupboard-up, cupboard-up
. . . Telephone . . . Mummy . . . Mummy get out telephone.

His mother objects and asks him what it is he wants after each of the first
two requests. She is trying to get him to set forth his request in some
'readable' order before she starts to respond – to give a reason in terms
of the goal of the action. Richard, meanwhile, achieves something
approaching a request in sentence form by organizing his successive
utterances in a fashion that seems to be guided by his conception of the
needed steps in the action. The initial grammar of the long string of
task-related requests is, then, a kind of temporal grammar based on an
understanding not only of the actions required, but also of the order in
which these actions must be executed. This bit of child language is an
interpersonal script based on a young child's knowledge of what is
needed to reach the goal in the real world; it is the matrix in which
language develops.

Requesting, I think, serves as an ideal model for what we have been
discussing as our general theme. Its very form in language and in the
context of its appropriacy depends upon the formulating and the
transmitting of intentions and, by its very nature, it forces what at the
outset I referred to as explicit, reportable intentions. It is no curiosa that
the mother, before the lesson of request is over, insists that the child,
almost like a student of the philosophical Miss Anscombe (1957), should
make clear (or be prepared, at least, to make clear) what it is that he has
in mind in launching on a line of behaviour that requires that another
enter in to help change his state of the world, to paraphrase Hintikka
(1974).

One final point. Intentions involving more than a single person in
their execution are the stuff of which social life is composed. Social
psychologists refer to their bringing together as a negotiatory process. It
is indeed negotiatory, but the negotiation requires a context or format
or, as some prefer, a scenario in order for the two or more sets of
intentions to be meshed smoothly. Much of earlier developmental
psychology stressed that children were egocentric, and by implication
could not enter into scenarios in a way that made it possible for them to
see the role of the other. When one observes the conversation of
4-year-olds (as Nelson and Gruendel (1977) have), it becomes clear that
much of what has been taken for egocentrism is simply a failure on the
part of the child to grasp the nature of the scenario. They report that

4-year-olds who may show egocentrism in the standard, adultocentric tasks used in Geneva can nonetheless bring off dialogues over a toy telephone as follows:

Gay: Hi.

Dan: Hi.

Gay: How are you?

Dan: Fine.

Gay: Who am I speaking to?

Dan: Daniel. This is your Daddy. I need to speak to you.

Gay: All right.

Dan: When I come home tonight we're gonna have . . . peanut butter and jelly sandwich . . . uh . . . at dinner time.

Gay Uhmmm. Where're we going at dinner time?

Dan: Nowhere, but we're just gonna have dinner at 11 o'clock.

Gay: Well, I made a plan of going out tonight.

Dan: Well, that's what we're gonna do.

Gay: We're going out.

Dan: The plan, it's gonna be, that's gonna be, we're going to McDonald's.

Gay: Yeah, we're going to McDonald's. And ah, ah, ah, what they have for dinner tonight is hamburger.

Dan: Hamburger is coming. OK. Well, goodbye.

Gay: Bye.

To return to my preliminary remarks, there are three alternative views that can be entertained as to why we ever considered that the organization of action was other than I have described it here. One is that at the 'natural' or biological level, the 'machine language' of the system is in fact as it has been described by exponents of a model of 'trial-and-error-cum-reinforcement'. I think it can be said that the arguments of Von Holst and Mittelstaedt (1950) and of Miller, Galanter and Pribram (1960) score strongly against this view by demonstrating that at the molecular level as well there must be something 'intentional' present that makes possible the generating of a subsequent correction term. The second view is that the socialization process 'shapes' human action into its highly intentional form. This is doubtless true, in the sense that ever higher-level intentional systems are called for by adults in their interaction with children. Nonetheless, what is most crucial is that human young have the capacity to respond to such 'goading' by adults in the society. The third view holds that intentional activity in man is 're-quired' by the nature of the 'social–technical' system into which man enters. The social–technical system of human society can be conceived of as a treasury of 'prosthetic devices' in the form of means for achieving ends. The evolution of the species is such as to have shaped man's action patterns into an ever more intention-directed, means-sensitive, corrective form. It is likely that older views of action result from a spirit of reductionism that believed the 'true' nature of man could best be explained by using a phylogenetically primitive model that ignored man's evolution into a tool- and symbol-user.

Let me end where I started. The evidence of child–adult interaction argues strongly, I claim, that human behaviour is organized under the control of intentions much as I have described the process. The folk wisdom of a species bringing its young into the social and physical envelope of the species' econiche, human culture, argues much more strongly in that direction than at first seemed to be the case when, unfortunately, we based our inferences about action on models of learning, motivation, and behaviour that were remote from the pattern of conduct that one observes man actually indulging in.

References

Anscombe, G. E. M. (1957) *Intention*. Blackwell, Oxford.
Bernstein, N. A. (1967) *The coordination and regulation of movement*. Pergamon, Oxford.
Brown, R. (1977) Introduction to C. E. Snow and C. A. Ferguson (eds.), *Talking to children: language input and acquisition*. Cambridge University Press, Cambridge.
Bruner, J. S. (1978) 'Learning how to do things with words.' In J. S. Bruner and A. Garton (eds.), *Human development* (Wolfson Lectures 1976). Oxford Univerity Press, Oxford.
Chomsky, N. (1965) *Aspects of the theory of syntax*. Massachusetts Institute of Technology Press, Cambridge, Mass.
Fillmore, C. J. (1968) 'The case for case.' In E. Bach and R. Harms (eds.), *Universals in linguistic theory*. Holt, New York.
Garvey, C. (1974) 'Some properties of social play.' *Merrill-Palmer Quarterly* **20**, 163–80.
Grice, H. P. (1957) 'Meaning'. *Philosophical Review* **66**, 377–88.
Hintikka, J. (1974) 'Questions about questions.' In M. K. Munitz and P. K. Unger (eds.), *Semantics and philosophy*. New York University Press, New York.
Kenny, A. (1975) *Will, freedom and power*. Blackwell, Oxford.
Lyons, J. (1970) *Chomsky*. Fontana, London.
Miller, G. A., E. Galanter and K. H. Pribram (1960) *Plans and the structure of behavior*. Holt, New York.
Nelson, K. and J. Gruendel (1977) 'At morning it's lunch time: a scriptal view of children's dialogue.' Paper presented at the Conference on Dialogue,

Language Development and Dialectical Research, University of Michigan, Ann Arbor, December 1977.

Ninio, A. and J. S. Bruner (1978) 'The achievement and antecedents of labelling.' *Journal of Child Language* **5**, 1–15.

Parisi, D. and F. Antinucci (1976) *Essentials of grammar*. Academic Press, New York.

Ratner, N. K. and J. S. Bruner (1978) 'Games, social exchange and the acquisition of language.' *Journal of Child Language* **5**, 391–401.

Shatz, M. and R. Gelman (1973) 'The development of communication skills: modifications in the speech of young children as a function of listener.' *Monographs of the Society for Research in Child Development* **38**, no. 152.

Von Holst, E. and H. Mittelstaedt (1950) 'Das Reafferenzprinzip.' *Naturwissenschaften* **37**, 464–76.

Wood, D., J. S. Bruner and G. Ross (1976) 'The role of tutoring in problem solving.' *Journal of Child Psychology and Psychiatry* **17**, 89–100.

Behaviour, action and act in relation to strategies and decision-making

V. REYNOLDS

1. Definitions

The matter of definition is always at the heart of discussions in the field of animal behaviour or human action. In my case I have followed the usage of the sociologist Weber as translated in Parsons and Henderson (Weber 1947). Weber distinguished clearly between the physical, potentially observable part, which he refers to as behaviour (*Verhalten*), and the ideational, unobservable part, which he refers to as meaning (*Sinn*). The combination of the two, that is what an animal or human being does in its totality, he refers to as action (*Handeln*). Putting these together, we can say the following. If we describe what people or animals do without enquiring into their subjective reasons and/or interpretations, we are talking about their behaviour. If we study these subjective aspects of what they do, the reasons and ideas underlying and guiding it, then we are concerned with the world of meaning. If we concern ourselves both with what people are overtly and objectively seen to do or not to do *and* the reasons for their so doing or not doing which relate to the world of meaning and understanding, we then describe action. All this is well expressed by Max Weber in his book *Wirtschaft und Gesellschaft*. I have adopted these definitions because I have found them useful in comparing animal behaviour with human action. The reasons for preferring the term *behaviour* for animals and *action* for humans will be discussed briefly in the following section.

Before passing on to that, however, I should like to mention one aspect of the interpretation of human action, which was not made clear in the first edition of my book *The biology of human action*, but which I feel is probably necessary for a full understanding of action. This is the inclusion of a new element which has been called by Harré and Secord (1972) the *act*. *Act* is used by Harré and Secord to refer to action in its

329

social context. We therefore need to think of action in terms of firstly the *behaviour* which is the part we can see and describe, secondly the *meaning* which is the part we cannot see but can in fact obtain information about by asking the subject why he did something, and thirdly *act*, or that perspective or part of what a person does which is intimately connected with the social situation in which he performs and represents the place or effect of the action in that situation. For instance we can see a *behaviour*, a hand movement say, as a meaningful gesture, that is as an intended *action, and interpret it as an act* of protest. These three words between them should, I think, suffice for giving us the necessary tools for a roughly adequate form of description of the things people do, i.e. their actions. Actual descriptions will, of course, call for a specific vocabulary of which these terms specify the necessary genera.

There remain certain difficult problems, notably that of moral autonomy. This is considered problematic because it seems to call for yet another dimension, the evaluative, over and above that of *act*. Thus an act of protest could be evaluated differently by the actor, who might feel it was the right thing to do, his friends, who might consider it rash or foolhardy, and the surrounding community, for whom it might be wrong or even illegal.

But first we need a clearer understanding of normative action structure; after that we can remedy deficiencies in the model being used.

2. Language

The important, indeed crucial, intervening variable between the animal dimension and the human dimension in the field of communication is the extent to which, in the case of man, language and culture transform the world from its natural condition into a condition which may be considered natural by the humans concerned in it, but is in fact cultural. Language in particular is seen in this analysis as a transforming device entered into more or less voluntarily by the child during his socialization in collaboration with his mother, other members of his family, his childhood peers, and other significant people in his experience during his childhood, and later imposed by the full force of social variables he will encounter at school and in everyday life. This transformation of the world is mastered by the individual as he matures. This mastery of the techniques of transformation of meanings is essential if the person is to have a successful adjustment to life in his or her society.

Techniques and conventions for the assignment of meanings vary from one culture to another and this variation is proof that we have here a symbolic and arbitrary set of representations; not only do languages differ from each other, but the categories into which languages divide up the social and non-social universe, including the self, vary also in innumerable different directions. Indeed, it is almost impossible without deep and prolonged study for a person in one culture to be able to comprehend the dimensions of another which is significantly different. Whole areas of emphasis in one culture may lack such emphasis in another. For instance, sex may be heavily tabooed in one culture and not at all so in another. Competition, the root of much of ordinary Western life, is in some cultures frowned upon, while others do not consider competition an important matter and particularly do not elevate it to the ultimate moral good. Mary Douglas has considered these matters in her books and refers to the unknown elements in our interaction with our cultures as implicit meanings. Until such implicit meanings are rendered explicit (and it is for social anthropologists and social psychologists to do this) they are at best dimly perceived by the people concerned.

For present purposes, the important point is that this entire system of communication based on a set of conceptions which are culturally mediated is believed to be absent from the animal world by a number of students in philosophy, psychology and sociology. In the case of animals, and this is why the word *behaviour* is used to describe their interactions, we consider that the mode of communication consists of the transmission of signals which themselves convey the meaning, that is by the effects they produce. These signals come in a variety of forms, visual, auditory, olfactory, tactile. Each species has a system of signals and each individual displays at any given point in time or over any period a certain number of signals from the species' system. The signals given by one member of the group to another member of the group may well differ from those received from that other member. This case would describe a situation in which one animal is dominant over another: the dominant animal gives threatening and aggressive signals, the sub-ordinate animal gives signals of appeasement and fear. Between them they make a communicative network such that the two animals are held together in a certain kind of relationship. If enough animals join in this kind of signalling game, we can speak of a hierarchy or social structure.

Structures are thus built up of relationships, and relationships are created and maintained by signals. The signals themselves, and hence the relationship, and finally the structure can ultimately be reduced by careful analysis to descriptions of the behaviour of the animals themselves. As to the question of whether the animals have any underlying cognitive representations or mental intentions, whether they are aware of their relationships or of the social structure in which they live, these issues are exceedingly difficult to formulate and investigate scientifically, and have so far yielded much fruitless work and poor scientific results.

3. Primate studies

I should now like to look at some of the studies which I made of rhesus monkeys many years ago, in order to illustrate on an empirical basis the kind of problems that arise in this field of study with regard to animal behaviour and the problem of underlying representations, especially the representation of alternative behaviours, the possibility of which would introduce an element of deliberation into the genesis of animal behaviour. In the study of a colony of rhesus monkeys which I made after graduating in social and physical anthropology, I was concerned with a description of the social life of some 15 monkeys living together in a large enclosure. I decided to adopt the ethological method – that is to describe the behaviour I could see the animals using in terms of the signals or bits of behaviour they were displaying towards each other. I used ordinary English language because of its richness, with occasional use of terms having a specific meaning in primate ethology. In all I found a total of 73 different units of behaviour which seemed to make up the bulk of the monkeys' behaviour patterns. I was at the time largely unaware of the differences that arise when different individuals describe monkey behaviour.

Subsequent studies of the work of other primatologists who have watched rhesus monkeys have convinced me that different ethologists see different behaviours in their monkeys and it is still unclear to me whether this is a result of the monkeys' behaviour actually being different, or whether it is a result of the primatologist cutting up the behaviour of the monkeys in different ways: most likely it is a combination of both. We should therefore probably talk of a *catalogue* of behaviour items. However the case may be, what we see when we observe a colony of rhesus monkeys over a period of time of six months or one year is a number of animals engaging in very complex social interactions with one another in which they form alliances, antagonisms, sexual relationships, and friendships based on grooming behaviour; usually, too, one or other of the animals is socially isolated from the rest of the group, often being a subject of universal attack, even by monkeys much smaller and younger than itself. Overall, one can describe the structure of such a primate group and even represent it graphically.

From this kind of analysis one can ask questions about whether the monkeys have any underlying conception either of themselves and their place in the group, or of the nature of the group itself and its structure. Certain events that took place during my own observational studies made it appear superficially as if the monkeys *had* such conceptions. However, I was trying to explain behaviour without recourse to such allegedly unscientific and undemonstrable or untestable notions as representations in the mind of the monkey. I wanted to see if behaviour could be explained without recourse to these and I believe that very largely it can.

I shall give details shortly, but in the meantime, I feel that here again we must make the strongest contrast with the situation that prevails in human interactions in normal human social groups. Because of the ability of humans to represent the relationships, to designate roles, to envisage structures and to work with a self-concept within these structures, the whole system of controls of human behaviour derives from an understanding of the reconstructed world in the mind of the human being, rather than directly from the interplay with other members of the group. Every aspect of the interaction between human beings in normal social life has to be considered with respect to two things: first, to the actor's conceptual scheme which exists in abstract in his own mind, and second, to the collectively located *'representations sociales'*, but not to reality in any form of natural phenomenon external to the person himself. It is largely for this reason that we need a different kind of analysis for the understanding of human social action from the kind of analysis that will, in most cases, suffice for non-human primates. Please note that this is not to deny the existence of intentions or other internal representations in the mind of the monkey or other animal. I believe that such intentions and some form of awareness of a more complex kind, wholly unobservable, *do* exist in the minds of monkeys and other social animals. However, we have yet to discover how to think in these terms scientifically. When we do, it may lead to great insights and we should certainly continue all possible means to this end.

4. The self

The concept of self I use in the present paper is derived largely from the work of G. H. Mead and E. Goffman and the sociology of Berger and Luckmann. To these perspectives, I think we ought to add an organic basis and this will be discussed next. In order to derive such a concept of the self, we must begin with a genetically unique life-agent, during whose ontogeny there is the integration of cultural schemes, personal strategies and so on, into a coherent whole. This integration is never complete; the self is never perfectly formed. Mead in particular was concerned in his analysis of the relationship between the 'I' and the 'me' to show how there was constant interaction between the element of the self that comes from within, the 'I', grounded in the cybernetic capacities of the organic element I have referred to above, and the 'me' which is the self as seen in terms of the cultural and immediate social environment, a reflection of my personification by others.

This interaction produces an ongoing dialectic in terms of which the individual sees his project and even his life, and in terms of which he develops strategies of action which lead to his performance of the various activities which constitute his life. At all stages, choices are made. Man is essentially a choosing animal, and it is again within the possibilities for a man to choose *any* course of action of which he is aware and which he feels motivated to pursue. Man is essentially free in the sense of Jean-Paul Sartre and can, if he wants, disobey social constraints or norms, and disregard the rules which society presents to him. He can also disobey the rules or tendencies which are presented to him through his organic being. For example, if he wishes, he can refrain from sexual activity, refuse to reproduce and if need be, choose death by starvation or asphyxiation rather than life. Such freedom is not available to any other species, in which the forces coming from within and resulting from evolutionary tendencies lead to a much greater heritable component in the behaviour and reduce consequently the extent of freedom of the individual. Thus we can expect and do find a greater similarity in the behaviour of the monkeys and apes in different parts of their ranges, or in captive groups, than we find in the case of humans living in different parts of the world in different cultures.

It does seem fair to speak of species-characteristic behaviour for animals, whereas it does not seem particularly useful or appropriate to speak in such terms for humans, except with regard to one very limited perspective of human communication, namely that aspect of it which is concerned with non-verbal communication. Even here the recent work on gestural options and the cultural differentiation of gaze conventions throws some doubts on this.

A final point in this section: the fact that man tends to see himself as constrained by social reality, the so-called reification of social structures and norms, should not confuse us any more than it has done sociologists such as Marx about the reality of such structures. In the case of man, social structures and social interactions are largely the outcome of representations devised in the last analysis by man himself and perpetuated by man himself though how free is a person brought up in a particular society is not clear. To this extent man can free himself from these norms and structures, and can change them in any number of ways. They will of course have a certain inertia and their guardian institutions may be very strong in safeguarding themselves, having if need be recourse to socially approved violence and even to the elimination of individuals trying to reconstruct the social world. This should not be taken, however, for any kind of reality of those structures themselves, comparable to physical reality.

5. Transmission mechanisms

In this section I treat briefly of the way in which social life is transmitted from one generation to the next. I wish to contrast the process in animals with that in man. In a way this is to repeat the old and well-known distinction between what anthropologists such as Kroeber called organic and superorganic evolution. In the case of organic evolution or organic transmission from generation to generation, the process is essentially one in which the information about both morphological and behavioural aspects of life is transmitted down the generations through the genes. This does not mean that the genes are responsible for all aspects of morphology, growth patterns and behaviour. This is not the case. There is an entire and complex range of processes based on genetic instructions by which growth processes take place and it is always in conjunction with the prevailing environment that the growth and learning and maturation and behaviour and social structures arise in the course of life. Nevertheless the organic transmission process is the most important process for the conveying of behavioural information and thus for the transmission of animal societies from generation to generation.

By contrast, in the case of man, a superorganic, or if you prefer, non-organic process takes precedence in the field of action and society.

This marks something of a discontinuity with animal society, although this discontinuity can be and is constantly challenged. For the moment, however, let me emphasize the discontinuity. The method of transmission is the oral and verbal transmission of the representations referred to above. This takes place by word of mouth and by other cultural devices such as written documents, so that the individual in a human society gains his awareness and understanding of appropriate reality through his interaction with others during his lifetime. He does not have instructions on this matter provided to him by his genetic endowment. His genes do not program the way in which he will eventually occupy a place in the social structure, nor any features of that structure itself. Naturally, he *is* provided with genetic instructions, and genetic instructions to a greater or lesser extent (always in a particular environment) control his growth processes, and abilities to accept or even to understand the representations of social action and social reality. Thus he could not possibly grasp these without a complex brain and such a brain is provided organically. We have as yet, however, no evidence directly concerning the structure of this brain which would lead us to assume that certain kinds of social reality are causally influenced by that structure. In this respect the greatest contrast exists between man and animals. In animals we must assume that a large neural component is concerned with the causation of social behaviours, social responses and hence relationships and social structures. Again we know that in the case of animals, especially higher animals, the environment is very influential in shaping these neural constraints. We know how powerful learning is in animal species. However, we do not have reason to think that learning goes so far as to bring about a complete reconstruction of social reality in the cases of animals, whereas we do have good reason to think this is the case in man.

The reason it is very important to make one's position clear with regard to transmission mechanisms is that there is currently a trend towards the explanation of human social behaviour and social organization in terms that derive ultimately from the organic processes of evolution. I refer, of course, to the misunderstanding of human nature, human society and human affairs proposed by such writers as Edward Wilson in relation to the general field of sociobiology. It is entirely possible that man may have been programmed for countless generations to have an increasingly versatile brain but however versatile the brain, it is nevertheless impossible to explain aspects of social life in terms of organic factors and ultimately gene transmission if we are correct in assuming that such features are determined by man-made and culturally transmitted inventions.

There are two objections that can be raised against the above. First, what about the flexibility of social arrangements, for example in macaques or langurs, which show different kinds of relationships and structures from group to group? Second, what about all the evidence for culture in non-human species? Are these not sufficient to force us to give up any clear dichotomy between animals and man?

Taking the first problem, the flexibility of non-human primate social schemes, this can best be explained using the model of animal society already referred to, namely the formation of relationships from behaviour and of social structure from relationships. The essential point is that there is a *variety* of relationships that can be derived from a given set of behaviours, depending on how the latter are combined. And again there is a variety of social structures that can be constructed from a number of relationships. Between them, these two indeterminacies enable animals to develop solutions to the environmental problems they face, and hence to produce flexible social solutions to these.

Regarding the second problem, of animal cultures, there is an essential difference between these and the cultures of man. The difference is expressed by Lévi-Strauss when he says 'rules have their own life'. By this he means, as he explains, that the existence of social structures and rules of social life in human societies is not dependent on people's *actions*, which are often in default of, or even in breach of, what the rules propose. Thus the marriage rules of an Aborigine tribe may call for marriage between a man and his father's father's brother's son's daughter, but a man may actually marry someone else. This does not alter the rules in the least. Such is not the case in animal cultures: if the 'rules' or activities of animal cultures are not put into practice they are lost.

In either case, therefore, the dichotomy between animals and man with regard to culture is upheld.

6. Alternative strategies and their representation in the mind of animals

Here I want to discuss briefly the situation as I observed it in the rhesus monkeys referred to earlier in this paper and show how the problem I posed there can be made into the subject of an interesting analysis of the similarities and differences between humans and animals. The colony I observed had a dominant male, Henry, his consort, Anne, and a series of other females which included Malvolia and Blondie. Malvolia was subordinate to Anne, and Blondie was subordinate to both Anne and Malvolia.

My observations were as follows: as a result of a certain amount of fighting in the colony, Anne received severe injuries and had to be removed from the colony. This left the dominant male Henry without a consort; it also left the female hierarchy without its most dominant and most aggressive element. Malvolia, next in the hierarchy, changed her behaviour when this happened. She became much more overtly interested in Henry, following him around, attempting to groom him and sit with him. At the same time she became much more aggressive to other members of the group, especially other females including Blondie. Henry, however, responded negatively to Malvolia's behaviour. He moved away from her, he threatened her, he chased her and bit her. At the same time he followed Blondie and made efforts to groom her but she was very frightened at first. In due course of time, Malvolia began to lose confidence in her ability to stay with Henry and be consort; in other words, observationally I saw her groom him less frequently, and approach him more circumspectly than she had done at first. She also became less aggressive to other females including Blondie, while Blondie moved closer to Henry and eventually formed a link with him. At this point, Malvolia became subordinate to Blondie and gave up her efforts to groom and engage in other kinds of activity with Henry.

So much for the observation: now for the interpretation. It seems to me there are two ways of interpreting this set of events; on the one hand we can see it all in terms of Malvolia's realization that Henry was now without a consort, her realization that she was next in line, and her efforts to become the consort of the dominant male. We could treat her as having a more or less full understanding of everything that was happening and we could make good sense in our own terms of what I have just described. In the case of Blondie, we could say she was initially frightened of Henry and that subsequently as a result of his advances she became clearer in her mind that he wanted her to be his consort and eventually she herself came to think that she could become his consort, lost her fear and eventually formed a link with him and began to dominate Malvolia. All this would involve a series of conceptual understandings in the minds of the monkeys, and we have no way of being sure whether such conceptions are or are not taking place.

However, there is another way of understanding the behaviour concerned. We could instead make no assumptions whatever about mental events in the minds of the monkeys. We could say that Malvolia had, prior to Anne's death, inhibited her approach tendencies to Henry, and with the disappearance of Anne, this inhibition disappeared. She then exhibited overtly behaviours that had previously been repressed. These approach behaviours to the dominant were not reinforced positively, but were progressively, often painfully, punished. As a result of this punishment she desisted from such behaviours. In the case of her action towards other females, we could again point out that whereas previously her aggressiveness to other females was inhibited because of the presence of Anne, who was herself concerned with such aggression, in the absence of Anne her aggressiveness to other females was disinhibited and therefore become overt. Likewise in the case of the changes observed in the behaviour of Blondie, we could describe the events in terms of progressive changes in overt behaviour resulting from a change in the punishment-and-reward schedule operating in the social context. All of this would not deny the existence of detailed cognitive representations, or of intentions, but would be an effort to describe the ongoing flow of behaviour and the changes which took place without reference to such representations. Instead the explanation would rely on the reception of signals from monkey to monkey and responses to those signals in terms of the species characteristic repertoire found in rhesus monkeys, together with a 'binding' set of constructs referring to latent structures (e.g. aggressiveness, punishment).

The question is, what criteria should be used for determining which of the two kinds of explanation is the correct one, rather than which one is the most scientific. Science is concerned with the observable, with testing, with verification and falsification, and sometimes, where appropriate with experiment but above all with explanation. In the case of mental activity, simple testing procedures seem out of the question in such a complex situation as the one just described. Should we then prefer a more theoretical explanation as one would in the physical sciences, for instance introducing molecules to explain the behaviour of gases? How do we make progress in resolving this issue? The answer is as yet unclear. I should simply like to make one point. There is currently emerging a science of decision-making which seems capable of making helpful suggestions about how both cognitive mechanisms and other fields in which alternative behaviours get resolved could be analysed. The term decision-making can be related both to organic problems and non-organic or superorganic problems including mental phenomena in either category, depending on whether one sees them as neural events or events to do with cognitive representations in the mind. For instance, in the field of animal behaviour there are now a number of studies which analyse the actual behaviours adopted by animals, whether insects or fishes, birds or mammals, in terms of strategies for survival. These strategies for survival can be related to the genes them-selves as for example has been done in Dawkin's book *'The selfish gene'*. In such an analysis, genes themselves work together with other genes in an organism to produce, eventually, via the whole long causal chain from amino acids through protein synthesis to physiologic-al structures, the behaviour strategies that have long-term survival prospects for the genes. Genes go on from generation to generation, individuals do not. Thus it is natural that, over the course of the generations, those genes that in some way predispose animals to make decisions and adopt strategies that will lead to those genes being transmitted will survive while others will die out. Thus we can say that a kind of decision-making occurs in the process of organic transmission, and that this process too has to be incorporated into any general theory of alternatives, or theory of choosing, as applied to the laws governing animal behaviour.

In the case of man, because of all that has been said so far, we cannot put the matter of decision-making in genetic terms. If we want to ascertain how decisions are made in the field of human action, we need to have recourse to a different level of theoretical analysis, which has been discussed earlier in this paper. In that discussion I emphasized freedom to choose and consequently the existence of 'projects' as one of the characteristics of man. Nevertheless, we can end by seeing quite clearly that man, too, has to survive in the organic sense if human society and all its traditions are to survive. Where physical survival is no longer possible, as has happened in the case of so many human groups, cultures and civilizations in the past, then the entire superorganic world dies with those people. The big question is, can we say that super-organic decision-making, and strategies resulting from this, are influen-tial in determining the survival of the organic world by which men themselves reproduce and continue down the generations? Work must continue on this problem. These are a series of leads. Writers such as the anthropologist W. Durham emphasize that cultures practise selective retention of features that promote survival. If they did not, they would disappear and, in many cases, have disappeared. Thus to some extent only those cultures that are conducive to physical viability go on through time and are with us now. It is in respect of the relationship between the process of decision-making in human society and the continuance of man's physical existence that some of the most difficult problems for this branch of study continue to challenge us.

References

Berger, P. L. and T. Luckmann (1967) *The social construction of reality*. Penguin, Harmondsworth.

Dawkins, R. (1976) *The selfish gene*. Oxford University Press, Oxford.

Douglas, M. (1975) *Implicit meanings. Essays on anthropology*. Routledge & Kegan Paul, London.

Durham, W. H. (1978) 'The coevolution of human biology and culture.' In N. Blurton-Jones and V. Reynolds (eds.), *Human behaviour and adaption*. Taylor & Francis, London.

Goffman, E. (1956) *The presentation of self in everyday life*. University of Edinburgh publication, Edinburgh.

Harré, R. and P. F. Secord (1972) *The explanation of social behaviour*. Blackwell, Oxford.

Kroeber, A. L. (1952) *The nature of culture*. University of Chicago Press, Chicago.

Lévi-Strauss, C. (1968) Comment on p. 211. in R. B. Lee and I. DeVore (eds.), *Man the hunter*. Aldine, Chicago.

Mead, G. H. (1934) *Mind, self and society*. University of Chicago Press, Chicago.

Reynolds, V. (1980) *The biology of human action*, 2nd edn. W. H. Freeman, Oxford.

Sartre, J.-P. (1948) *Existentialism and humanism*. Methuen, London.

Weber, M. (1947) *The theory of social and economic organisation*. Free Press, London.

Wilson, E. O. (1978). *On human nature*. Harvard University Press, Cambridge, Mass.

The primate constructional system: the theory and description of instrumental object use in humans and chimpanzees

PETER C. REYNOLDS

1. Some properties of goal-directed action

Although the concept of the *behaviour pattern* has become a standard technique in the description of primate behaviour, such an atomistic approach is in many respects a serious distortion of the complexities of primate action. Primates do have a repertory of innate and relatively stereotyped behaviours, as this approach implies, but they are normally integrated into goal-directed sequences in which the consequences of action are both anticipated and attended to. In the present context, a *goal* can be defined as the intended effect of an action. This definition presupposes (1) the ability to mentally represent the consequences of action prior to the execution of the action itself, (2) the ability to compare the actual consequences to the anticipated consequences, and (3) the ability to alter subsequent action on the basis of experience with prior executions. Goal-directed action requires a functional characterization of behaviour which interrelates observed behaviour, observed effects, and hypothetical intended effects. Contrary to the positivist philosophy which has been so pervasive in Anglo-American psychology, there is nothing methodologically suspect in postulating hypothetical intended effects in the naturalistic description of behaviour (Pribram, in press). Such hypothetical intended consequences are only postulated when there is sufficient behavioural evidence to justify them, and empirical criteria for such interpretations can be specified.

In the study of goal-directed action, the concept of a BLOCK is crucial to naturalistic description (Charlesworth 1979). In a well-integrated skill which is executed without mishap, there are few behavioural grounds for subdividing the action into constituent units or for inferring the subgoals of these constituents. However, when a goal-directed action encounters BLOCKS, which prevent the action from continuing,

343

coping behaviours occur which either provide an alternate pathway to the same goal or attempt to remove the BLOCK. Unlike the fixed-action patterns described by Lorenz (1973), which can run-off without attention to their effects, the assessment of consequences is basic to goal-directed action. A BLOCK can therefore be defined as an unintended consequence or an unanticipated condition which interrupts a sequence of goal-directed acts. A BLOCK should be distinguished from a *loop*, which is a repetition of actions instrumental to the same goal, each of which is incremental to the final effect, such as the repetitive hammering of a nail. The distinction between a repetitive loop and a BLOCK is an empirical one, cued by *behavioural indicators of BLOCKS* observable in the record of behaviour.

Behavioural indicators of BLOCKS are systematically related to novel events. In the case of instrumental play, such as children digging in a sand-pit, it is frequently observed that a novel event may lead to a repetition of the behaviour which induced the event, even if the ongoing action sequence is permanently interrupted. (It is this propensity to 'follow up' novel consequences which gives instrumental play the 'sequential flexibility' which has been reported for play generally.) On other occasions, steps may be taken to reinstate the external situation before the unexpected event intervened. In the case of loading sand into a bucket, for example, in which the child's arm is bumped by another, spoiling his aim, the entire sequence may be repeated from the beginning. The attempt to *reinstate* the situation which occurred before an interrupting event is one indicator of a BLOCK. Another indicator is the attempt to *circumvent* the BLOCK: to perform an action sequence which has the same effect that the original action would have had had it been allowed to continue in an uninterrupted manner. These coping behaviours which deal with BLOCKS are no different in principle from other kinds of instrumental action, so there is not necessarily any morphological distinction between an instrumental action and a coping behaviour. The distinction can only be made by reference to the relationships among behaviours. Reinstatement is usually followed by a *resumption* of the activity which had been interrupted, whereas circumvention is usually followed by the act which would normally follow even if the BLOCK and circumvention had not occurred.

As with BLOCKS, there are also behavioural indicators of goals. One of the most important is that of *terminal consequence – the event which results in the termination of an action sequence without any subsequent reinstatement, circumvention, or resumption.* To take a simple example, we infer that the goal of 'hammering a nail into the wall' is operative when the action terminates after the underside of the nail head makes contact with the wall surface. We infer that 'bending the nail' is a BLOCK when 'hammering' is interrupted in order to straighten the bent nail, and when hammering resumes once the nail is straightened. However, 'bending the nail' could just as easily be a goal in other circumstances, and nail-straightening events would then be BLOCKS. The same actions might be involved in all of these cases, but the ordering in relation to BLOCKS, coping behaviours, terminal consequences, and goals differs under the varying conditions. For this reason, characterizations of behaviour which rely primarily on sequential ordering of morphological- ly defined behavioural units, such as pretransformational linguistics or most of ethology, are bound to fail because they take insufficient notice of the functional differences implied by sequential reordering.

Purely statistical definitions of sequence are equally suspect for these models look for the organization of behaviour in the deviation from randomness instead of in the systematic relationship between intended action and observable effect. Although classical ethologists recognized that behaviour was structured, as in Tinbergen's hierarchical model of instinct (Tinbergen 1950), this observation has been slighted by nearly two decades of atomistic ethograms in which the connection between one behaviour and another was simply probabilistic. Irrespective of whether these ethograms are apt descriptions of non-primate be- haviour, they are poor descriptions of primate skills because they imply that the transition from one behavioural element to the next is a matter of probability and not the product of an assessment of consequences and the intelligent production of alternatives. Although empirical records of behavioural sequences can be *described* by transition probabilities, such descriptions cannot provide an explanation of what is in most need of explanation: the production of novel alternatives not previously per- formed and the prediction of consequences not yet seen. Since such models give no scope to intelligence in the production of observed behaviour, they slight exactly those aspects of behaviour which are most characteristic of the higher primates. As such, they are poor theories of primate behaviour, irrespective of their superficial rigour.

Although some ethologists have recognized the limitations of the animal construed as a 'probabilistic behaviour generator', and have reintroduced the concept of behavioural structure in the form of hierarchical relations among behavioural elements (Dawkins 1976), such models still do not come to terms with the fact that hierarchical control is only one organizing principle of primate skill. Goal-directed actions are not only organized into chains-of-command but are also organized by the principle of subsystem autonomy. The programs of goal-directed action would be better characterized by McCollough and Minsky's term of *heterarchy*, in which relatively autonomous goal-directed *modules* interact to perform complex sequences, and any module can assume *top-level control* when certain *entry conditions* are met (Minsky 1975). In a heterarchical model, which shares features with Leyhausen's *relative hierarchy of moods* (1973), the location of behavioural units in the hierarchy of control is not fixed but is relative to the goal of the module which is temporarily in top-level control. The dual organizing principles of chain-of-command and subsystem autonomy can provide a framework for the empirical description of goal-directed action in higher primates.

2. Introduction to programmatic description

Formal models of goal-directed behaviour have existed for several decades in the computer sciences (Schank and Colby 1973, Bobrow and Collins 1975, Minsky 1975, Winston 1975, Anderson 1976), and the naturalistic description of such behaviour in primates can benefit from the application of such models, as a number of authors have suggested (Miller, Galanter and Pribram 1960). However, the application of computer methods is not as straightforward as might be supposed. Although many approaches to behaviour, both in linguistics and in ethology, have characterized behavioural sequences by the hypothetical program which generates them, the properties of primate goal-directed action indicate that a more radical strategy is called for. If goal-directed action has as one of its defining features the recombination of behavioural units into different instrumental action sequences, then it cannot be defined by the program for any single empirical action sequence or even by a class of such programs. Rather it is necessary to characterize the hypothetical 'programming language' which allows such recombinations to be 'written' in the first place. As implied by Chomsky's critique of pretransformational linguistics (1959), the primary strategy of a scientific 'grammar of action' is not a delineation of the programs which generate particular sequences of goal-directed action but the delineation of a hypothetical programming language which is rich enough to encode the differences among the various instrumental programs which can be empirically observed. The advantage of this approach is that it allows a theory of goal-directed action which is more general than the skill repertory which exists at any particular time in any particular population. Since there is also no reason to restrict a programming language of primate action to only those operations which can be performed by existing computers, a hypothetical programming language, modelled on computer language but not limited by them, can be used to encode the relationships among behavioural events *as if* they were expressions in a programming language, irrespective of whether such expressions are in fact executable by computers.

A hypothetical programming language has a number of advantages over natural language in the description of behaviour. Although verbal descriptions are readily understood and communicated, semantic theory suggests that a great deal of linguistic comprehension rests on shared knowledge which is tapped by the verbal message. Consequently, verbal descriptions of simple actions are unlikely to reveal the constancies of primate action which such common knowledge assumes. Yet it is precisely such intuitive knowledge which a theory of skill must clarify. Also, although formal descriptions can always be rephrased in natural language, the appropriate phrasing is often not apparent until after the behaviour has been analysed using a formal notation. Moreover, because language is non-iconic, the same term can be applied to skills differing greatly in complexity, whereas a formal language can be designed to mirror the complexity of the action in the complexity of the description. Although movement notations preserve the complexity of action in the form of the description (e.g. Hutchinson 1973, Benesh and Benesh 1977), they are inspired by the discrete and linear form of musical and linguistic notations. Constructional action involving the manipulation of objects is better represented by a notation which encodes images as easily as symbols and which can incorporate the interrelationships among actions performed at different times. Formal notations also provide increased precision in terminology, and most importantly, force the observer to attend to empirical detail which is ignored by more ambiguous coding systems. The formal notations of logic and linguistics share these advantages, but they were designed to encode the relationships among sequential symbols, whereas in constructional action, simultaneity is as important as sequential ordering. A formal notation for constructional action should (1) allow for the easy encoding of images into the description, (2) mirror the complexity of the action in the complexity of the description, (3) be capable of expressing complex temporal relationships among action components, (4) take cognizance of the high 'connectivity' among the components of goal-directed acts, (5) make it easy to express recursive and self-organizing properties, and (6) ideally, should be perceived as visual Gestalts by the right cerebral hemisphere rather than read linearly by the left.

Table 1 (see p. 351) illustrates a notation designed with these properties in mind. It is inspired by the computer programming language LISP (Siklossy 1976), and it consists of nine hypothetical operations, called *DAEDALUS functions*, which operate upon images to produce transformed images as outputs. As Bruner has pointed out (1973), the diversity of human skills may be reflective of the great number of 'arguments' to which basic operations are applied rather than represent any great diversity in the set of operations itself. In a similar way, differences among constructional skills are expressed as differences in the way the nine DAEDALUS functions are combined, both with each other and with different physical objects. In a simple analogy, if the DAEDALUS functions are thought of as beads which come in nine different colours, a wide variety of skills can be expressed by the repetitions and combinations into which these beads can be arranged in reference to an open set of physical objects and body parts. However, since each function is a distinct operation, some combinations of operations are counterintuitive, and these have been excluded by rules of combination called DAEDALUS syntax (see Appendix 1). One or more DAEDALUS functions combined in accordance with the rules of DAEDALUS syntax is called a *DAEDALUS expression*. When a DAEDALUS expression is written as an encoding of an empirically observable, goal-directed act, the expression is called the *DAEDALUS description* of the act.

DAEDALUS notation is designed to represent *constructional activity* involving the manipulation and arrangement of objects. It cannot be used to represent all aspects of goal-directed action, nor can it deal with all types of action with equal facility. Constructional activity is itself a composite system which cuts across motor, perceptual, and conceptual processes. DAEDALUS notation is designed to operate at the interface between the perceptual exemplification of visualizable concepts on one hand and motor acts guided by perceptual and conceptual information in iconic form on the other. The empirical applicability of DAEDALUS notation will diminish as activities approach the purely conceptual, in which non-iconic relational information is manipulated, the purely motor, in which parameters of force, angle, and speed are most pertinent, or the purely perceptual, in which sensory information is processed with little overt activity. However, DAEDALUS notation is useful in describing goal-directed action which involves images and their transformations, and it is especially applicable to characterizing the *differences* among similar skills. Since DAEDALUS programs operate with images, they are especially well suited for representing the interrelationships among images preserved in ciné film and video records of behaviour. Such records, henceforth called *iconic documents*, preserve a series of two-dimensional images which represent past movements in three-dimensional space. If such a succession of images is considered to be the product of a program written in DAEDALUS notation, then the document can be described by the hypothetical DAEDALUS program which generates it.

3. DAEDALUS descriptions

A DAEDALUS description is created by assigning the images on the iconic document to the DAEDALUS functions which are hypothesized to generate them. The use of film and video is basic to the writing of DAEDALUS descriptions because goal-directed action is simply too rapid to be adequately recorded in any other way. In the approach taken here, *the two-dimensional image on the iconic document is theorized to be an historical record of one or more DAEDALUS function evaluations, and the description of a goal-directed act is the hypothetical DAEDALUS program which could account for this particular history.* For example, in a picture of a right hand holding a cup, it is hypothesized that this image was produced by the function GRIP operating on the arguments 'cup' and 'right hand'. A DAEDALUS description of an iconic document is a DAEDALUS expression which could account for the sequence of images seen on the film. The DAEDALUS functions, however, are not necessarily unitary psychological mechanisms. They are *functional characterizations* of goal-directed constructional action expressed in the medium of images and their transformations.

There are only nine DAEDALUS functions, and they are best understood as hypothetical integrated circuits, each of which performs a distinct function. Complex sequences of images can be generated by interconnecting these nine basic units. Each function operates upon its input images to produce a transformed image which is available to other DAEDALUS functions as specified by the syntax. For example, the DAEDALUS function GRIP takes two obligatory arguments and one optional argument. The first argument must be the target of the GRIP function and the second argument must be a body part which can serve as a gripper – a hand, a foot, or the mouth. The function then *evaluates* to an image of the specified body part gripping the specified target. The image which is made available to other DAEDALUS functions is called the *value* of the function. The inputs and outputs of DAEDALUS functions are to be thought of as either three-dimensional images or as data structures which are convertible into three-dimensional images, even though two-dimensional representations must be used on the printed page. The image which is recorded on the iconic document is an epiphenomenon of those DAEDALUS functions which produce behaviour in the course of evaluation – and only GRIP and AIMCON necessarily produce *observable behavioural correlates.* However, all DAEDALUS functions produce a value upon evaluation which can be used by other functions – even if the value is NIL. Since eye movements are necessary for visual perception, FOCUS also usually produces overt behavioural correlates as well, but these acts are only accessible with special equipment. The various DAEDALUS functions, their arguments, their hypothetical operations, their pictographic representation, and their values are listed in Table 1. Table 1 is largely self-explanatory, but a few general aspects of the notation can be mentioned. The DAEDALUS functions are named – GRIP, AIMCON, etc – but each has a pictographic equivalent which is used in the actual DAEDALUS descriptions. Each argument is represented in the pictograph by a numbered *terminal,* and DAEDALUS functions are connected together by drawing a line from the output terminal of one pictograph to the input terminal of another. The output terminal is always the bottom-most line on the pictograph, with the exception of the BLOCK function, in which terminal 2 is also an output. The 'interpretation' given an input is determined completely by the number of the terminal. Terminal 1 of GRIP, for example, is always interpreted as a target, and terminal 2 as the body part which is to perform the gripping. A pictographic DAEDALUS program is also technically a *graph* as well as program, and rather than attempting verbally to read these graphs it is far easier to imagine the designated inputs, imagine their transformation by the function, and then imagine this transformed image as the input to the next operation. Also, the output of a DAEDALUS function can be used by any number of other functions simultaneously, but only one argument of an input terminal can be active during any single evaluation. All of the DAEDALUS functions except BLOCK have only a single output. BLOCK, which can recognize when BLOCK occurs in its argument, can be used to shunt

Table 1. *DAEDALUS functions*

Pictograph	Function name	Number and name of arguments	Effect of function	Evaluation
	AIMCON	2 1. effector 2. target	Moves effector into contact with target	Value is an image of the state of the aimed movement
	BLOCK	1 1. main	Evaluation is at output 3 if the arguments do not BLOCK and output 2 otherwise	Value is either BLOCK of the argument BLOCKS or the value of the main argument otherwise
	FOCUS	2 1. domain 2. concept	Locates an exemplar of the concept in the domain	Value is an image of the exemplar
	GRIP	2 or 3 1. target 2. gripper 3. isomer	Moves the gripper so that the target is gripped in the orientation specified by the isomer and makes the target into a body part	Value is an image of the gripper gripping the target
	OFF	1 1. module or module address or OFF function	Inhibits the module specified by the argument	No value or NIL
	ON	1 1. module	Creates a module and stores it at the top of the module list	Value is the value of its argument
	SEQ	any number 1 . . . *n* steps	Evaluates each argument in turn as specified by the sequence	Value is the value of step being executed or the step before a BLOCK. When all steps are evaluated, value is NIL
	SIBYL	2 1. domain 2. concept	Maps a simulated image of a concept onto real perceptual content of a domain	Value is an image of the region of the domain that embodies the simulated image
	TERRA	2 1. supportee 2. support	Tests if the second argument can physically support the first argument	Value is an image of the support system with any intervening material connections

program control from 'main program' to 'coping behaviour' and back again. With the exception of SEQ (SEQUENCE), and OFF, all DAEDALUS functions produce a three-dimensional image (or a potentially iconic data structure) as a value. SEQ and OFF, which do not always produce images on final evaluation, are called *NIL-value functions* and are constrained by the syntax from being used as arguments in situations which presuppose images. It should also be noted that DAEDALUS programs are written in highly nested form, inspired by the computer programming language LISP, so that an image may be transformed by a succession of functions 'wired in series'. In these cases, a function cannot evaluate until the function used as an argument has evaluated – and so on through the nested sequence. Such nestings should be distinguished from the function SEQ which simply evaluates each of its arguments sequentially. The top level of a DAEDALUS program is represented by the SEQ function (called *control sequence*) which programs the series of operations to be performed. However, since DAEDALUS functions can BLOCK if unexpected situations are encountered, program control can be shunted to some coping behaviour by a BLOCK function which is watching the controlling sequence. Hence, a succession of images on the iconic document may represent different top-level control functions within the same connected graph. In a similar fashion, a particular DAEDALUS expression may be represented by a sequence of frames on the iconic document. All of the film frames which represent the same evaluation of an expression are termed the *image span* of the evaluation. For example, an object may be held in the hand for an entire film, and in this case, the entire film is the image span of a single GRIP function, even though other functions may have shorter image spans within the same film. A single film frame can therefore participate in the image spans of multiple DAEDALUS functions which are operative simultaneously. The function ON can be used to 'modularize' DAEDALUS expressions so they remain tonically active until turned off by an OFF function. Modules also perform other functions, and the exact interpretation of ON is determined by the DAEDALUS function used as its argument. Since modules also produce an output, they too can use each other as arguments. It is important to remember that since DAEDALUS programs operate with images, information must first be converted to iconic data structures, and this is done with FOCUS, which can exemplify concepts with iconic perceptual data in any sensory modality. FOCUS can also be used to further differentiate images which are produced by other DAEDALUS functions – as if the output of a prior function were external perceptual information which can be conceptually analysed. The characteristics of DAEDALUS notation are best conveyed by the description of actual iconic documents through frame-by-frame analysis (*microanalysis*) of multiple examples of the same act (see Kendon (in press) for discussion of microanalytic technique).

4. The movements of ladder-building

In a 16-mm film (document Chimp-8-78), Emil Menzel has preserved a number of examples of ladder-building activity by colony-housed chimpanzees described by him in a previous publication (Menzel 1972); and he has made this film available for DAEDALUS description (see Table 2 and Appendix 2). In the most highly developed form of ladder-building, the chimpanzee finds a pole of appropriate length, strength, and straightness, carries it in proximity to the catwalk which circles the compound, positions one end on the ground and places the other end in contact with the catwalk, tests the pole for rigidity, climbs the pole to the top of the catwalk, hauls the pole up behind him by a hand-over-hand pull, repositions the pole on the catwalk, aims the top to a tree which has been electrified on the lower trunk, and climbs the pole to the tree without triggering the electric wires.

Although this verbal description is economical and readily understandable, any comparative study of primate goal-directed object use should encode behaviour so that similarities and differences are revealed. The economy of language can in fact work against this goal. Beck (1975) has summarized the kinds of object use which occur naturalistically among non-human primates, but it is not apparent from the different English words 'throwing', 'hitting', 'probing', 'stripping off leaves', 'raking', 'placing', etc that all of these activities are alternative implementations of contact between an external target and an object held in the hand. Moreover, they are all about the same level of structural complexity: a FOCUS function to find the manipulandum, an ON to remember it, an ON GRIP to hold it, another FOCUS to differentiate one part of the GRIP complex, an AIMCON to move that part to a target, a FOCUS to find the target, and a SEQ function to interrelate these components. The differences among these activities are minor. 'Throw' differs from the others in that an OFF GRIP implements the object contact, and the AIMCON in a throw, instead of moving the gripped object to the external target, moves it to a 'ready point' for the start of the throw. 'Dropping' an object is done with OFF GRIP and a different AIMCON. 'Placing' one object on another requires a TERRA if the object is to stay there, combined with an OFF GRIP, as in throwing. Using a rake requires a second (nested) FOCUS function to locate the *back* of the target and (in humans) an ON AIMCON to maintain contact. A 'probing' action requires an ON SEQ to recycle the 'contact operation'. 'Hitting' has to do with the effect of the AIMCON on the target and the power of the act. 'Stripping off leaves' is a repetitive sequence in which the target (the leaf) is GRIPped and the AIMCONed until the leaf is no longer supported by the stick, that is until TERRA BLOCKs 'Stripping off leaves' and 'connecting two sticks' are more complex than the other activities because they ordinarily require two simultaneous GRIPs, each gripping a different target. Using a crushed leaf as a sponge, is sophisticated on the conceptual level (where DAEDALUS is inapplicable), but it is simple behaviourally. From the perspective of DAEDALUS notation, the naturalistic tool-using activities of non-human primates are nearly all permutations of short programs containing about a dozen to twenty DAEDALUS functions which interrelate a gripped object to a target which may itself be gripped. DAEDALUS expressions can always be rephrased in natural language, but this fact is deceptive since the appropriate phrasing is often not obvious until after the analysis is done. For example, the term 'ladder building' obviously denotes some sophisticated form of constructional activity using objects, whereas 'climbing' sounds like a form of locomotor activity which can be conveniently ignored by students of higher mental processes. After examining the movements of chimpanzee ladder-building, however, such a line between 'locomotion' and 'cognitive ability' is by no means so easy to draw. Ladder-building is not only a coping behaviour to BLOCKed climbing, and using a ladder requires climbing, but aspects of the constructional activity of making a ladder appear to be fragments of locomotor activity. Moreover, if we expand the comparative range with examples of human action, constructional activity can also be used to perform the locomotor function of climbing. Such interrelationships are not obvious from their non-iconic descriptions.

Although neurophysiologists have long been interested in the neural programs underlying locomotion, a DAEDALUS description does not attempt to duplicate such analyses. Simple functional categories, such as contact placing of a single foot, are mediated by extremely complicated neural mechanisms, and such physiological models must be investigated by physiological techniques (Carlsöö 1972). Rather, DAEDALUS notation is designed to express the functional interrelationships among observed movements and inferred goals while begging the physiologists' question of how such processes are encoded in the nervous system. Such a description can nonetheless be useful in comparing functional activities to each other and in categorizing the evolutionary and ontogenetic development of primate goal-directed action. In a DAEDALUS description of locomotion, the movements preserved on the film are encoded as AIMCON functions which move the body parts in reference to the goals of supporting the body weight and advancing the body. The support goal is represented by the DAEDALUS function TERRA (Latin for 'earth') which finds whether its second argument physically supports its first argument, and it evaluates to an image of the supports, the supported objects, and their material connections. The locomotor goal of advancing the body is defined as the transition from the place where one is now (called *locus*) to the place where one wants to get (called *neolocus*), but no attempt is made to define the procedures by which these locations are chosen in the first place. Although different kinds of locomotion also differ in such parameters as speed and tempo, these characterizations are beyond the semantic powers of DAEDALUS. Rather, DAEDALUS defines *climbing* as *locomotion* in *which alternating GRIPs are used to implement TERRA and to advance the body from locus to neolocus.*

From an evolutionary perspective climbing requires the integration of GRIP into locomotor movements, and this preadapts climbing for constructional functions which involve the manipulation of substrates. By this definition, brachiation is also a form of climbing, since it uses GRIP in locomotion, but it differs from conventional climbing in that the feet are not involved. In all types of climbing, GRIP provides support (TERRA) for the body so that locomotion can be implemented. Also, neolocus is a complex goal which must be defined as the intended direction of motion; otherwise there is no way of distinguishing slips which cause a downward movement of the body from actual cases of climbing down. The intended direction of motion can itself be defined as a constant relationship between movement and the axis of the body.

In describing movements, DAEDALUS notation uses the concepts of *content* and *domain*. Each body part is assumed to exist within a region of space defined by its range of possible movement relative to a joint. The body part is thought of as 'perceptual content' which can be moved within this region, called its *domain*, by the DAEDALUS function AIMCON, which moves an effector towards a target. Rather than attempting to specify movements in terms of a Cartesian coordinate system, DAEDALUS uses a 'subjective' space which defines movements relative to a normal position for each body part. For discussion purposes, DAEDALUS domains are considered to be spherical, even though for many body parts, they would be irregularly shaped solids due to the anatomical constraints of the range of possible movements. DAEDALUS domains are also considered to be divided into *domain sectors* by sagittal, horizontal, and frontal planes, which yield hemispheres corresponding to top v. bottom, front v. back, and left v. right; and these are *always* defined relative to the actor, with the joint serving as a window into the front of the domain. These three reference planes DAEDALUS shares with comparative anatomy, but it is not necessary to define such planes for each body part. Virtually any kind of reference system which is convenient can be set up by a DAEDALUS program which imagines body parts to be in particular positions relative to normal position and imagines the domain planes of other body parts to be in alignment with them. The function SIBYL, which simulates iconic content, allows such imaginary transpositions to be defined. In addition, specific parts of a domain can be addressed by nesting FOCUS functions with 'front', 'back', 'left', 'right', etc as arguments. Also, it is possible to address the real-world area which lies between the outer edge of a domain and the content of a domain. This area, called the *nimbus* because it surrounds the content like a halo, is useful for directing activity to a location near an object or next to an object. The body, called *soma*, is also 'perceptual content' in its own domain and can be moved about by aimed movements. However, the long axis of the body also defines two hemispheres which are called *cephalo* and *caudal* to avoid the ambiguity of the terms 'front' and 'back' when used in reference to both quadrupedal and bipedal postures. These body reference planes have neurological support in the three planes of the vestibular system and in primate righting reflexes which bring the head and body to normal verticals (Peiper 1963).

The characterization of movement in terms of aimed movements of body parts within their domains is supported by the play behaviour of primates. Many play activities appear to be systematic explorations of the range of aimed movement. For example, in a videotape of 3- and 4-year-old children at an Australian preschool (document Preschool-10-77-Imitation), one girl (alias Jeff) performs a number of movements which are imitated imperfectly by a smaller girl (alias Mutt). Jeff makes eight jumps in place simultaneously with six claps of the hands, and Mutt apparently attempts the same sequence but produces four jumps with one clap; also, Mutt's clap is given while the feet are on the ground, whereas Jeff gives her claps in the air. These differences do not necessarily reflect differences in intention but could be explained equally well as differences in performance, such as a slower execution time in the younger child. Since playful jumping in place and clapping are not obviously implementing any higher-order goal, nor are they oriented to any external objects, they must be described as movements if they are to be described in DAEDALUS at all. The actions can be described as either rotations of body parts within their own domains or as *black-box procedures*, such as 'flexion at the knee', which are incorporated into the description but left undefined in DAEDALUS notation. Such *movement stratum* descriptions are often required for primate play, and further examples would be a boy systematically rotating his arms through various positions (Preschool-10-77-Imitation) or a chimpanzee turning somersaults (Chimp-8-78).

However, in constructional activities where one object or body part is moved relative to another, it is not the movement which is important but the *effect produced by the movement* (cf. Pribram's concept of an action, in Pribram 1971). In these cases, the movements can be considered as implementations of specific goals which cannot themselves be described in movement terms. Consequently, the relevant operations are specified as AIMCON functions which move effectors toward targets, and these expressions can be regarded as requests to the motor system to implement the specified action with the relevant movements. Such implementations are known to be in repertory because their movements are preserved on the film! Although all DAEDALUS descriptions of action can in principle be carried down to the movement stratum, analogous to articulatory phonetics in linguistics, it is generally more convenient to define movements by their film or video image. This is done by incorporating pointers to a specific image span of a specific iconic document into the DAEDALUS description of the action. In the discussion of chimpanzee ladder-building, the movements which implement the action can thus be assumed because the goal-directed action itself has been inferred from the examination of iconic records of the movements involved.

Figure 1 illustrates a primate climbing a tree and a partial DAEDALUS description of climbing activity. The program uses SEQ functions to produce alternating GRIPs and a SEQ module to cycle the sequence indefinitely. It is assumed that GRIP has access to AIMCON so that

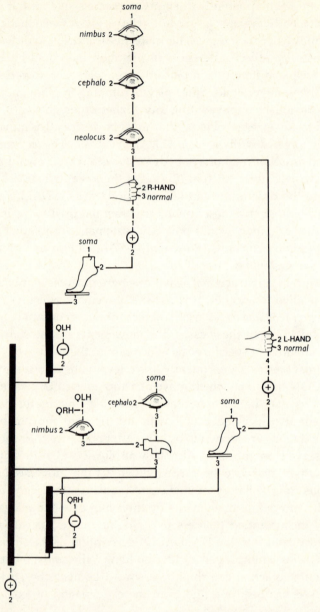

Fig. 1. A chimpanzee climbing a tree and a DAEDALUS description of the behaviour. Climbing is defined as a repeating sequence of alternating hand grips that are instrumental to both advance of the body (soma) and support of the body

aiming is performed automatically. The support function is monitored by TERRA, and locomotion is defined relative to a supporting substrate in the nimbus of the cephalo hemisphere of the body domain. The nested functions in the description make it easy to encode the *entry conditions* of action, since a BLOCK in any nested function will BLOCK any others which use it as a value. The ON in ON GRIP is required by DAEDALUS syntax, since GRIP is tonic by definition. Although a complete description of climbing would also specify the placing of the other limbs, the present research is not concerned with locomotion *per se* but with those aspects of it which appear to function in constructional activity. In this respect, the program in Fig. 1 demonstrates very well Bruner's contention that the flexibility of skill resides to large extent in the capacity to run the same program with different arguments, and it

Fig. 2. Chimpanzee pulling up a pole hand-over-hand

also demonstrates the reversibility of sensorimotor skills emphasized by Piaget. Comparative examination of the episodes of Chimp-8-78 indicates that the arm movements of climbing *down* a tree are the same movements which are used to haul *up* a pole hand-over-hand (Fig. 2). Additional support for this generalization is provided by several dozen examples of humans hauling up water from a well observed by the author during a field study in Papua New Guinea (video-tapes Beroi-2 and Beroi-3). The simplicity of DAEDALUS notation is conveyed by the fact that both *climbing down, climbing up,* and *hand-over-hand pulling* can be derived from each other by *argument switches.* For example, the program for *climbing up,* as shown in Fig. 1, can be converted into a program for *climbing down* by replacing cephalo by caudal in both places at which it occurs. *Hand-over-hand pulling* can be derived from Fig. 1 by

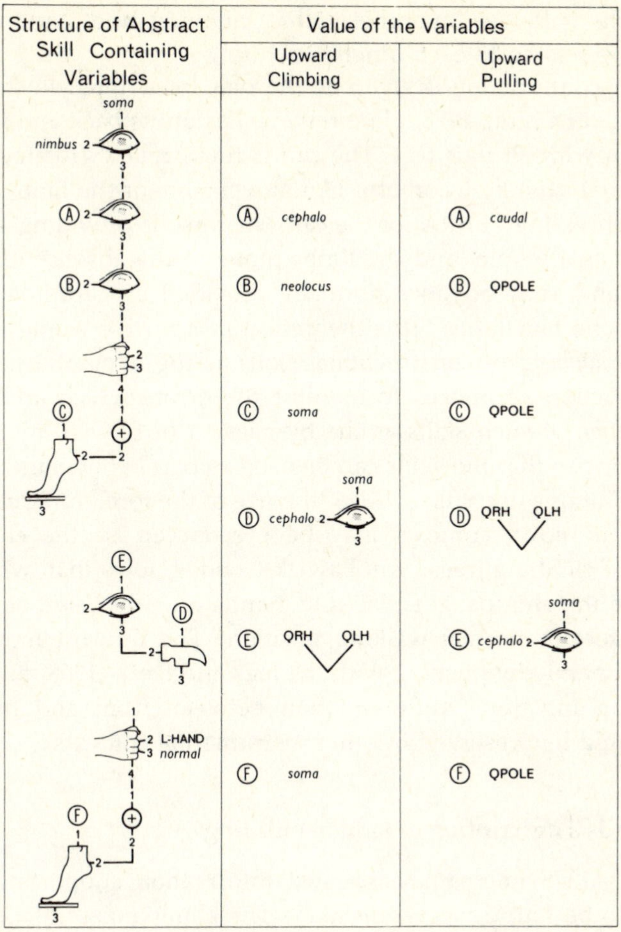

Structure of Abstract Skill Containing Variables	Value of the Variables	
	Upward Climbing	Upward Pulling
(A) cephalo	(A) caudal
(B) neolocus	(B) QPOLE
(C) soma	(C) QPOLE
(D) cephalo 2	(D) QRH QLH
(E) QRH QLH	(E) cephalo 2
(F) soma	(F) QPOLE

Fig. 3. The leftmost column shows a structural 'backbone' which is common to both upward climbing and upward pulling of a pole. The circled letters indicate places on the 'backbone' where substitutions of one argument for another will transform climbing into pulling or vice versa. Columns 2 and 3 show the arguments that define climbing and pulling respectively. The circled letters are variables that can take different values. Sets of related skills can be defined by a table that specifies the values for each member of the set

making the changes summarized in Fig. 3. In this diagram, *variable arguments* are placed at substitution points, converting an empirical description of a single skill into an abstract description of multiple skills, and the values of these variables are shown for upward climbing and upward pulling. The major difference between these two skills is that soma is supported by the gripped pole in climbing; whereas in hauling, the gripped pole is supported by soma. This means–end reversal is compatible with the hypothesis that climbing and hand-over-hand pulling are related to each other structurally.

Further confirmation is given by the play behaviour which occurs in episode 27 of Chimp-8-78. Here the ape lies on its back and supports a coffee can with all four feet. The can is then 'rolled' (rotated about its longitudinal axis) by locomotor-like movements of the limbs. Here the feet are providing TERRA for the can, the torso is providing TERRA for the body as a whole, and the limbs move in the absence of the body support and body advance normally provided by coordinated movements of the four limbs. This theoretical perspective would regard the initial *development* of constructional skills as the integration of BLOCK into the action sequences to monitor the errors which arise and the *generalization* of such skills as the by-passing of BLOCK by secondary connections so that the skills can be used as part behaviours with some entry conditions unfulfilled. Also, the use of the forelimb component of climbing in novel contexts may be preadapted by the chimpanzee method of climbing trees. Van Lawick-Goodall notes that 'when climbing a tree the chimpanzee places its hands on either side of the trunk with its feet in normal walking position. The upward movement is achieved mainly by pushing with the legs and feet.' (1968, p. 177.) This suggests a functional differentiation between front and hind limbs which could be preserved in other instrumental contexts.

5. Towards a description of ladder-building

In DAEDALUS microanalysis, most information supporting inferred goals is to be found in the mistakes. The chimpanzees of Chimp-8-78 make a number of errors which are useful in delimiting the significant operations of ladder-building. In episode 3, the pole starts to slip as the animal begins to climb from the catwalk to the tree. The pole then falls to the ground below the catwalk as the chimpanzee retains its grip on the former bottom end. The skill then recycles at this point to hand-over-hand pull-up, and it is a good example of *repetition of an act* until the goal is completed. This evaluation is interpreted in DAEDALUS as the only act whose entry condition is neither BLOCKed nor fulfilled. This inference of the intended goal is supplemented by other behavioural indicators: the *gaze direction* is toward the top of the pole when it is being positioned a second time, suggesting that the operation which had previously failed is now being attended to. However, when the bottom of the pole starts to slip, the chimpanzee looks down to the base of the ladder. From such examples it is inferred that the positioning of the top and bottom of the pole are separate operations, each of which is regarded as a TERRA function that takes the pole as an argument. In a successful positioning, the pole remains in place when the chimpanzee is no longer holding it. Conversely, the absence of a TERRA function can be recognized in cases where the animal simply plants one end of the pole on the ground and climbs up it before it falls over, as in episode 15. In many cases, the gaze is toward the location where the anticipated effect is expected to appear. In episode 3 the chimpanzee does not watch the top of the pole as it moves towards the tree but the place on the tree where the pole is heading. *Emotional expression* is also a behavioural cue to a BLOCKed or completed goal. In episode 16, the chimpanzee attempted to position the top of the pole before positioning the bottom, and the episode ends with the animal fear-grimacing intensely at its would-be ladder. In DAEDALUS notation, the correct temporal ordering between top and bottom positioning would be expressed by a SEQ function. The *test conditions* of a completed goal may also have behavioural indicators. For example, in episode 8, the chimpanzee twice tests the positioned ladder by cautiously placing its weight on the pole and then stepping back. Ethologically speaking, these are intention movements of climbing with ambivalence; but as they are also likely to provide information for TERRA, they are conceptualized as under its control. Similarly, the entry conditions of a particular skill, such as a pole of the right length and strength, may have behavioural manifestations. In episode 24, for example, the ape first selects one pole, drops it, and then selects another, even though the exact criteria used here are unknown. The *active reinstatement of entry conditions* after a BLOCK is also a good indicator of a goal. In episode 3, when the pole starts to slip as the chimpanzee begins to climb it, the animal climbs back down (using the caudally directed hand alternation already noted) and repositions the ladder. Cases such as this indicate that TERRA is modularized and actively monitoring the pole. Similarly, the necessity for postulating goals or terminal consequences is indicated by examples of repetitions of single acts until a particular effect is observed. In episode 5, for example, the first AIMCON of the pole toward the tree misses the tree entirely. The pole is then moved back to initial position and the AIMCON is executed again. Three executions were attempted before the pole was put in contact with the tree, but DAEDALUS would regard these as three attempts to evaluate the same AIMCON function, not as three separate operations.

It is only by examining multiple examples of similar acts, particularly those that exhibit errors or BLOCKs, that sufficient behavioural evidence can be gathered for the inference of goal-directedness. However, in this respect, the inference of goal and intentionality is no different in practice from any other branch of empirical science, in which generalizations are also supported by multiple examples. Moreover, the inference of goal-directedness utilizes a wide range of behavioural indicators, including (1) reinstatement of entry conditions through repetition of a prior act in the sequence, (2) creation of a terminal consequence through repetition of the present act, (3) circumvention of a BLOCK through substitution of another act which produces a related consequence, (4) gaze direction toward anticipated consequences, (5) emotional reactions to consequences, and (6) *anticipatory movements* which are acts appropriate to an external effect but which are given before that effect has taken place, as when a chimpanzee begins to climb the ladder before it is fully in position. Taking all of these lines of evidence together, the inference of goal-directedness in behaviour does not appear to be epistemologically weaker than many other kinds of scientific inference which have been generally accepted. The formal analysis of skills, by allowing the constituent operations to become more precisely characterized, can further refine the inference of goal-directedness and intentionality.

The microanalysis of Chimp-8-78 indicates that the most complex examples of ladder building require the following hypothetical operations:

(1) pole selection, including length, strength, straightness and portability
(2) location of the pole relative to the catwalk; the pole must either reach to the catwalk or be transported to another location where it will reach
(3) gripping the pole
(4) positioning the bottom of the pole so that it both supports one's body weight and also allows the top end to be supported
(5) positioning the top of the pole, which must be the opposite end of the same pole as in step (3)
(6) climbing to catwalk
(7) hand-over-hand pulling of the pole to the catwalk; the body has to be repositioned in a sitting posture (an entry condition), and
(8) steps (4) to (7) are repeated with a different target.

In addition to this strategy of ladder-building, there is also a variant (episodes 19 and 24) which uses a *pole-vaulting* action to make the initial contact with the catwalk. Since the pole-vaulting variant has been filmed without interruption, the total duration of the ladder-building skill can be timed. Assuming 24 frames per second as the film speed, then the pole-vaulting variant seen in episode 19 takes only 11.5 seconds from selecting the pole to reaching the tree. In episode 24, the duration of the skill, from selecting the pole to placing the top of the pole on the tree (at which point the animal paused), is only 7 seconds. Nonetheless, a DAEDALUS description, which encodes all of the operations just reviewed, is quite complex, as shown in Fig. 4. In order to clarify this diagram, functionally important parts are numbered for explication purposes.

Ladder-building is considered to be a coping behaviour to blocked climbing, and control would be transferred to the program in Fig. 4 by a BLOCK function in some calling program. The ladder-building would be entered through its control sequence function, to which lines 12–15 and 20–21 connect. Since the SEQ functions evaluate their arguments from the top down, the skill begins with the first argument of the control sequence (line 12), which is another SEQ function containing ladder-building proper. The entry conditions to ladder-building (line 1) require a pole with certain physical properties, expressed as nested FOCUS functions, and a pole is located if one does not already exist in memory as an exemplar module (QPOLE). The ordering of the FOCUS functions here is arbitrary, but humans often indicate entry condition priorities by behavioural tests bound to the FOCUSes, as when a pole is bent to test its strength and resilience. In DAEDALUS, such tests would be represented as coping behaviours to BLOCKs in the exemplification of entry conditions.

Once a suitable pole is found, the exemplar module is used as a target for a GRIP. A two-hand GRIP requires two separate GRIP functions, since DAEDALUS syntax specifies a single body part as a gripper argument. It is assumed that a GRIP with hand or foot is always on its own side of the midline of the body unless specifically countermanded. Such *default values*, as built-in assumptions are called in computer science, can be defined in DAEDALUS notation at the beginning of each program. However, the GRIP on the pole is further complicated by the fact that the hands must contact the pole toward the middle of the pole itself. To deal with this, a further default value is introduced, namely, that the centre of an object is used as a target unless specifically countermanded. These default values, since they are already assumed, are not encoded in Fig. 4. However, there is a further complexity to the

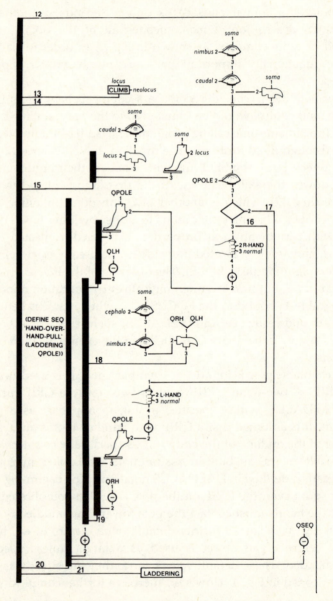

Fig. 4. The DAEDALUS description of chimpanzee ladder-building which generates the empirical sequence of instrumental action seen in the film Chimp–8–78

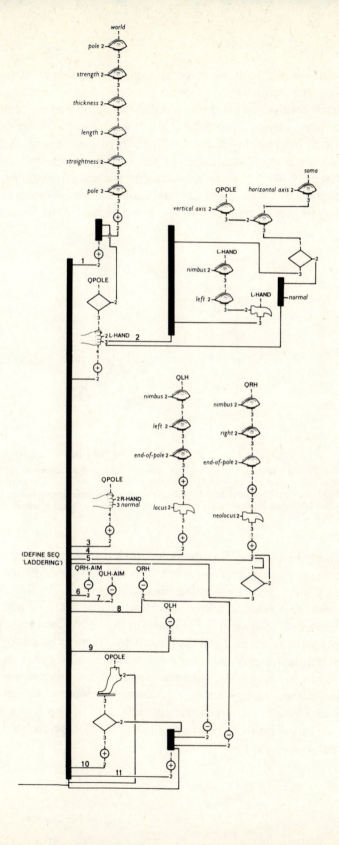

GRIP which is explicitly encoded as the third argument of the GRIP functions. The combination of hand plus object can exist in different geometrical configurations, provided that the object has an internal axis of asymmetry – that is, provided it is not superimposable on its mirror image in all orientations (Gardner 1969). Such geometrical variants of the same hand–object combination are called *isomers*, and the third argument of GRIP specifies the isomeric variant. An isomer can be defined either by an image of the final configuration or by the DAEDA-LUS program which generates it. Fig. 5 shows the isomer actually used

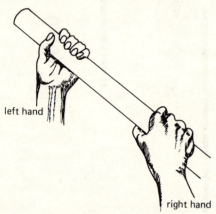

left hand

right hand

Fig. 5. The configuration of 'gripper plus object' can exist in different geometrical orientations, called *isomers*, depending upon the initial orientation of the gripper to the object. The above isomer is used by chimpanzees to grasp the pole during ladder building. Note that the left hand must be rotated to the left before the grip takes place

by the chimpanzee in holding the pole, and it can be created by rotating the left hand from normal position into the left hemisphere of the left-hand domain before executing the GRIP, as shown by line 2 of Fig. 4. However, this rotation is only necessary when the long axis of the pole is horizontal relative to the long axis of the body. Consequently, the hand rotation preserved on the film can be taken as evidence for an entry condition for pole-axis–soma-axis alignment. In other cases the *normal* placing of the hands, with one on each side of the pole, will give the same isomer. Consequently, the isomer is represented as a conditional expression, in which the rotation only occurs if the vertical (long) axis of the pole can be exemplified in the domain defined by the horizontal axis of the body.

The placement of the hands on the pole also provides a simple definition of the top and bottom of the pole. Since the domain sections or hemispheres of each body part are defined relative to normal position of the body part, in an anatomical sense, rather than relative to current position, the two ends of the pole are necessarily in the left hemisphere of the left-hand domain and the right hemisphere of the right-hand domain. These values can be used to exemplify the two ends of the pole if they are remembered and actively monitored with exemplar modules. This is done in lines 4 and 5 (Fig. 4), where a particular region of a particular hand domain is located, and the end-of-pole exemplifiable in that region is remembered with ON FOCUS. For convenience, modules are automatically assigned names in DAEDALUS. Exemplar modules take the letter Q followed by the second argument of the antepenultimate FOCUS function, if there is one, followed by the second argument of the penultimate FOCUS function. Thus the left end of the pole is automatically named QLEFT-END-OF-POLE and the right end QRIGHT-END-OF-POLE (cf. Fig. 4). If multiple concept exemplars could be given the same name by this procedure, then the duplicates are stored on a list with the first one created called Q-, the second one- etc. The GRIPs are also automatically named in DAEDALUS as Q followed by the second argument (the gripper). Thus QRHAND could be used as a value in a DAEDALUS description, but its value would change whenever a new object was gripped. Such module names can be used internally in DAEDALUS programs instead of connecting lines, but their values will change as some modules are turned OFF and others take their place. Lines 6 and 7 show AIMCON modules used as arguments by name.

Once the ends of the pole are distinguished, it would seem a simple matter to direct them with AIMCON and TERRA functions to their proper targets: the pole is positioned on the ground and aimed toward the catwalk and then positioned on the catwalk and aimed toward the tree. However, this characterization of the targets as 'catwalk' and 'tree' lacks generality, for a new target must be enumerated each time the ladder is used and no prediction is made about possible future uses of the skill. In such a case, an abstract characterization in terms of functional properties is more useful, and the target of ladder-building is best defined as a *supporting object which can be reached by a pole in the absence of an existing substrate for climbing*. This definition encompasses both the tree and the catwalk; it predicts possible future targets of chimpanzee ladder-building; and it allows for incremental approach to a distant target by building multiple ladders through a succession of targets. However, even this abstract definition is not sufficient because the description of locomotion always requires at least two points in space: the location where one is and the location where one is heading. This is also true of ladder-building, in which the two ends of the ladder must be positioned relative to two different locations, termed locus and neolocus for 'place' and 'new place'. These spatial locations are functionally distinct from their support capability, as can be seen by a comparison of pole-vaulting to ladder-building. Both skills require that one end of the pole be positioned at locus and that the pole support the body (TERRA soma pole), but ladder-building also requires that neolocus support the opposite end of the pole. However, the ladder is more than such concatenated positionings of pole ends because neither end of the pole can support the ladder by itself: they must support the ladder together. The 'ladder' is a new functional relationship created by coordinated actions which cannot be produced by those same actions in sequence. Consequently, *ladder-building is distinct from pole-vaulting in a fundamental way, even though there are no constituents of ladder-building which are not also in pole-vaulting.* Moreover, the coordination of multiple pole-end positionings cannot be represented as a sequence of acts, because the support of one end of the pole requires the support of the other end of the pole. This situation raises insuperable obstacles for notations of primate action which presuppose purely sequential symbol strings or atomistic behaviour patterns, but it is amenable to a notation like DAEDALUS in which operations can be joined in relationships of simultaneous recursiveness: ladder-positioning has access to the SEQ of which it is a component.

The act of creating a ladder is shown in lines 4 and 5 of Fig. 4, in which AIMCON modules aim each end of the pole to supporting substrates in locus and neolocus. This illustrates the use of AIMCON as a request to the motor system: no movements are encoded in the description, but since GRIP makes an object into a body part, a FOCUSed part of a gripped object, such as one end of the pole, is also a body part and can be used as an effector in an AIMCON function – an assumption whose justification is provided by films of primates doing exactly that. This AIMCON portion of the ladder program is shared with pole-vaulting, but unlike pole-vaulting, which requires rapid climbing up the pole before it falls over, these components are integrated in a SEQ which also requires that the entire pole be supported before locomotion takes place. This is represented by a 'hands off' test in lines 6 to 10 which tests whether the action of the AIMCONs can produce a pole which is supported in the absence of GRIP. The second argument of TERRA (line 10) in this case is the SEQ function of which TERRA is a part. Since TERRA evaluates to the image of supported anᴶ supporting objects, including their physical connectedness, it can be used to access the composite objects created through sequences of acts. The notation allows functions to be used recursively, so that a ladder is defined as the sequence of behavioural/object interactions which support a pole on both ends. If TERRA BLOCKs, then the 'hands off' test is negated by OFFing the OFFs (ON OFF is undefined in DAEDALUS), and the entire SEQ is reactivated (line 11). Since line 11 is a module which can only evaluate in the event of failure, the SEQ exits at line 12.

Climbing, which is left undefined, is encoded as a black-box procedure (line 13), followed by turning around (line 14) and sitting down (line 15). The hand-over-hand pulling component, discussed above, is given in line 20, and it exits when there is no more pole to be exemplified in the caudal region of the body domain. It can be regarded as a coping behaviour to a BLOCKed QPOLE at neolocus. At 21 the ladder-building occurs for a second time. Fig. 4 also illustrates a meta-DAEDALUS function, DEFINE, which can be incorporated into the graphs to make them easier to write. DEFINE takes the first pictographic argument of the designated type to the right and assigns it the name given in quotation marks. Thus 12 is defined as LADDERING, and it is called as a defined procedure in 21. Similarly, 20 is defined as HAND-OVER-HAND-PULL which assumes the QPOLE of LADDERING as an entry condition.

6. The comparative study of getting higher

The DAEDALUS description of Chimp-8-78 reveals that ladder-building is a form of coping behaviour to BLOCKed climbing, and most of the component acts and concepts are themselves components of normal climbing behaviour: the alternating GRIPs of hand-over-hand pulling, the discrimination of substrates in the cephalo and caudal regions of soma, the testing of physical support through TERRA, the advancing of the pole through the use of the hands, the selection of physical objects by properties relevant to supporting the weight of the body, and judgements of relative strength, length, and distance. Even with locomotion left undefined, the structure of the skill in Fig. 4 is nonetheless complex, and DAEDALUS provides two quantitative measures of this complexity. One measure, the *static DAEDALUS number*, is simply the number of separate functions (or nodes) in the connected graph. The other measure, the *dynamic DAEDALUS number*, is the number of times each function is evaluated empirically – that is, the number of times each pathway is traversed (with modules counting as one evaluation each time they are turned ON). The static number provides a measure of the complexity of an act, while the dynamic number provides a measure of activity level. Concatenated ladder-building, for example, is not statically more complex than a single ladder because it only requires repetitive execution of the same program. Nonetheless, concatenated ladder-building would have a higher dynamic number. Since it is likely that different species of primates will differ in the complexity of their constructional activities, these measures may prove useful in comparative description.

Chimpanzee ladder-building is of particular interest comparatively because it provides one of the most complex examples of non-human primate constructional activity ever reported and one of the most complex ever to develop without human intervention. As Beck's survey indicates, object use and manipulation are common in Old World primates, but genuine examples of *construction in which matter is transformed or new object configurations created through intentional action* are relatively rare. Frequent and complex constructional action is a human speciality among primates, and DAEDALUS notation by forcing attention to detail, reveals some of the species-specific aspects of human object use. The similarities and differences are best conveyed by examining human activities which have features in common with climbing and ladder-building in chimpanzees.

Strictly speaking, chimpanzees do not make ladders but position them. Nonetheless, this is a constructional process because it involves mechanical inference and intentional action which result in enduring alterations in the configuration of material objects. The chimpanzee's use of ladders appears to be fully comparable to human use, and much of their play with ladders is also comparable to human play. During observation in an Australian preschool, some of my students obtained a video-tape (document Preschool-10-77-Imitation) which contains about twenty minutes of ladder play by 3- and 4-year-old children. Fig. 6 shows a number of actions performed with these child-sized ladders. They are all isomers of two-hands–ladder GRIPs, and, as in chimpanzees, they are closely integrated with locomotion to produce dragging, pushing, and carrying. Some of these behaviours also occur in Chimp-8-

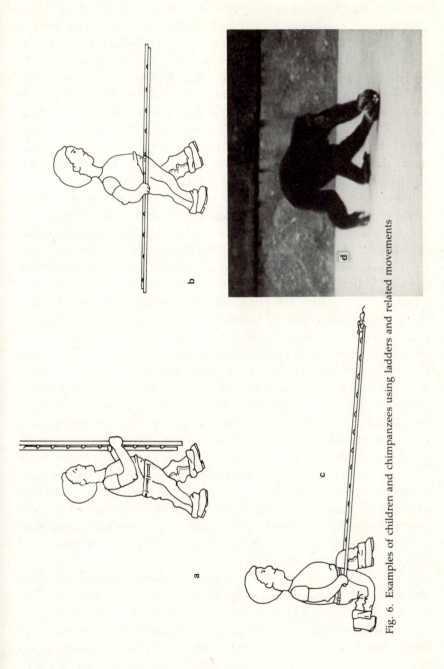

Fig. 6. Examples of children and chimpanzees using ladders and related movements

78, but with a coffee can instead of a pole, as shown in Fig. 6d. However, the children seem to pay close attention to the internal axes of symmetry of the ladders, so that the body and the ladder are symmetrically aligned. This is especially clear in Fig. 6b, where the child gets inside the ladder and aligns the front–back axis of the body to the longitudinal axis of the ladder before picking it up.

The climbing movements of humans and chimpanzees appear to be very similar, but the climbing of manufactured ladders is more comparable to walking up stairs than it is to climbing poles. For this reason, some examples of human tree-climbing were obtained and examined in detail. In many parts of the world, particularly in the tropics, tree-climbing is a normal part of human subsistence activity.

In some human cases, however, the locomotor component of climbing does not simply take place on a constructed substrate like a ladder but the constructional process is interlocked with the climbing movements themselves. Rock-climbing with pitons hammered into the rock wall before every advance is one example of this, and a more utilitarian form is to be found in a film by Timothy Asch and Napoleon Chagnon, *Climbing the peach palm*. This film, taken among the Yanomamo Indians of Venezuela (Chagnon 1977) illustrates the use of a climbing-frame to gain access to the fruits of the *rasha* palm. This tree has long thorns growing from the trunk in an ascending spiral, and it cannot be climbed by normal methods. The Indians use two climbing-frames constructed in position on the trunk with the aid of poles and thongs. Each frame is formed like an × by crossing two poles and looping a thong around both the poles and the tree. When a man's weight is placed on both arms of one × on one side of the tree, the arms adjacent to the trunk grasp the trunk like calipers. The man supports his weight on one frame while advancing the other frame up the trunk with his hands. Then he shifts his body to the advanced frame and repeats the process (Fig. 7). TERRA and advance are also the goals in this form of climbing, but the advance is implemented by first moving the frame with one's hands and then moving the body, while the TERRA is implemented with a mechanical GRIP, using the concept of calipers.

Where subsistence activities require it, humans become very good tree-climbers, but the locomotor act is closely integrated with constructional activities in a way that is characteristically human. Climbing is both used to implement constructional activities (the Roti case discussed below) and constructional activities are used to implement climbing (the Yanomamo case). Like apes, humans also climb for fun, but the play

Fig. 7. Yanomamo Indian using climbing-frame

behaviour involving climbing also has a uniquely human character. In Western preschools the imitative and pretend aspects of social play are very noticeable, and similar phenomena occur in very different cultural contexts, among children who are as agile in the trees as chimpanzees. Fig. 8 shows an illustration of a scene of a video-tape record (Batek-9), taken by the author among nomadic hunter–gatherers on the Malay Peninsula (Schebesta 1928). These children, who appeared to be about 5 to 9 years of age, were 20 feet (6 metres) up in a grove of thick bamboos. The movements appear comparable to chimpanzee climbing play, but the game had a strong pretend aspect. The children told the observer they were monkeys, and they all howled in unison in imitation of *Presbytis* spp. (*melanocephalos?*). One child had a strip of cloth hanging from his waist, which was probably a 'tail'.

7. The primate constructional system

If the goal of a notational system is to clarify distinctions which might not be so obvious or encodable in another idiom, then DAEDALUS

Fig. 8. Batek children pretending to be monkeys

notation satisfies this criterion by forcing attention to the logical structure of constructional activity. Microanalysis comparison of ladder-
building in chimpanzees to tree-climbing in humans, both purposeful
and playful, indicates that primate constructional activity cannot be
characterized by catalogues of behaviour patterns, for such an approach

totally ignores the productive aspects of constructional skill. Moreover, DAEDALUS microanalysis also questions the utility of behaviouristic definitions of tool use, such as Beck's, which equate tools with material objects. Rather, an approach to tool use based on the principles of computer modelling of cognitive phenomena would see the material tool as only one external manifestation of complex mental programs using a wide variety of perceptual, conceptual, and motor processes which presuppose goal-directedness and intentionality. A tool is not an object but a mental program which can interrelate that object with others to implement anticipated external effects. Tools, in other words, are as much mental as material, and *their description is not a photograph of the material object itself but an empirically verifiable characterization of the mental knowledge and behavioural programs which allow the object to be produced and used*. This approach indicates that the differences between the most complex constructional activities seen in apes and the simplest constructional activities seen in humans are profound. Although humans and apes share similar locomotor programs, presumably homologous, human constructional activity always occurs as part of a network of constructional skills which ramify through hundreds and thousands of object types.

The species-specific aspects of human constructional and locomotor skill are even clearer in an example from the island of Roti in eastern Indonesia. On Roti, palm trees are regularly climbed to obtain palm juice, and Timothy Asch and James Fox recently filmed examples of this technology (unedited footage, document Roti-79). In this film, the movements can also be explained as the implementation of TERRA and advance, in which alternating GRIPs play an important part. However, this climbing component is integrated into a complex technology (Fox 1977) which reveals very clearly the enormous difference in the constructional repertory of normal human subsistence and the most sophisticated ape performances. In the Roti document, the man first attaches baskets, a knife, and a spoon to his belt before ascending the tree. The baskets are hand-folded into shape, using large leaves, to make a watertight container for the juice. In pouring the juice from the collection basket to his transport container, a *multitarget GRIP* is created by the left hand, in which the spoon is propped against the side of the basket to make a spout or lip for the container to facilitate pouring. This whole configuration is then used as an effector to pour the juice into a container held by the right hand. Fig. 9 shows the DAEDALUS description and resulting juxtaposition of objects in the Rotinese exam-

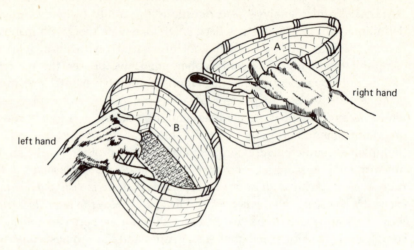

Fig. 9. Drawing of a Rotinese pour

ple, based on a simulated performance by a right-handed person in the laboratory. Line 1 shows the isomer for a spoon, which requires two AIMCON operations because it has two axes of symmetry. The spoon is then gripped by the right hand, and this complex is then used as the argument for a second GRIP on a basket, shown in line 2, which also has an isomer. The 'right side of the rim of the right side of the concave surface of the spoon' is then contacted to the 'left side of the rim of the left side of the basket held in the same hand' and maintained there (see points 2 to 3). The spoon must also be aligned to the horizontal axis of the basket (points 3 to 4). The liquid in the basket is aimed to the bowl of the spoon, and the liquid in the spoon is aimed to a second basket (Q'BASKET) held in the left hand (points 4 to 5). Q'BASKET must itself be gripped with an isomer, aligned to the absolute horizontal, and moved underneath the left half of QBASKET (line 6). These multiple object parts are necessary because behaviour in other contexts shows that these distinctions are used.

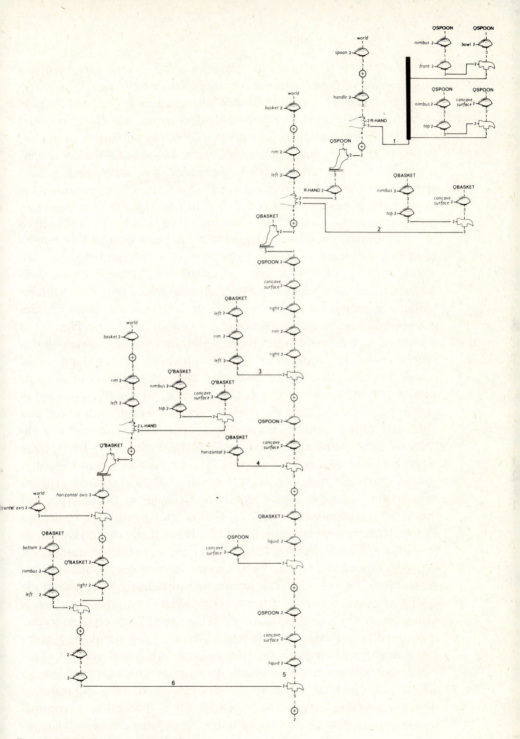

Fig. 10. DAEDALUS description of pour

It is instructive to compare this program, which is only a fragment of a much longer sequence, to the chimpanzee ladder-building shown in Fig. 4. The high level of nesting in the Rotinese example appears to be typical of humans, judging from other iconic documents not discussed here, and the right hand alone four nested AIMCON modules, up to five nested FOCUS functions per domain, and two nested GRIPs. Moreover, the argument structure is extremely complex, with all of the functions above point 5 in Fig. 9 serving as an effector relative to all the functions above point 6, which serve as a target. In fact, there is more structure present simultaneously in the right hand of the Rotinese pour than in all of LADDERING performed sequentially. A good deal of this human complexity appears to be necessitated by the differentiated tool-kit, which includes not only a variety of different tool types, but also tools manufactured with multiple axes of internal asymmetry due to differentiated functional regions. However, tool-kits such as these presuppose certain cognitive capacities, and the difference between Figs. 4 and 9 suggest that primatologists might fruitfully look for human–simian differences in (1) the depth of nested expressions, (2) the alignment of objects to planes in external spaces, (3) the differentiation of isomeric variants, (4) the presence of multitarget GRIPs, (5) the differentiation of perceptual domains using the domain section concepts such as left and right, and (6) the simultaneous nesting of operations performed sequentially in apes. Also, as pointed out elsewhere (Reynolds 1981), there is also evidence for a major discontinuity in primate tool-using capacities between humans and apes: the construction of many human artifacts requires the control of motor activity by an image of the final product that is being produced by the skill. That is, motor activity is controlled by simulated perceptual content that is only gradually created empirically (Holloway 1969, Bordes 1971). In carving a particular design, for example, one cannot access the design through perception because the design does not yet exist. Yet the artisan must clearly be accessing the design in order to impose it upon his material. This process, which is distinct from the 'foresight' involved in the exemplification of concepts, is encoded with DAEDALUS function SIBYL, which simulates perceptual content and maps it on to empirical perceptual content. Eye-movement studies may eventually provide behavioural evidence of SIBYL, but at present, its justification is to be found in the imposition of form on formless material in which an act is directed to perceptual regions whose distinctive features only emerge later in time. In all cases of chimpanzee construction known to me, empirical perceptual features are potentially observable in the iconic control of action; that is, the action is describable by FOCUS, and SIBYL is not needed. The pretend aspect of play in children, including their constructional play, is also suggestive of an active process of imagination which interrelates simulated and perceived content. The SIBYL function is likely to be an evolutionary emergent which is specific to hominids and datable archaeologically to the appearance of shaped tools. If this hypothesis proves to be correct, then human constructional action not only has a structural complexity and a social connectivity without parallel in the animal world, but it also requires the phylogenetic differentiation of an additional DAEDALUS function that is lacking in apes.

Table 2. *Synopsis of film Chimp-8-78*

Episode	Foot meter	Summary of contents
1	0–12	Hand-over-hand pull and ladder-positioning
2	12	Partial positioning of ladder
3	13–40	Hand-over-hand pull, ladder-positioning, and climbing; failure to secure top
4	40–58	Jumping and climbing
5	58–85	Ladder-positioning and climbing
6	85.5	Somersaults
7	85.5–93	Ladder-positioning and climbing
8	100–124	Hand-over-hand pull, ladder-positioning, incipient climbing
9	124–133	Climbing ladder and tree
10	133–139	Tree-climbing
11	139–151	Running
12	151–153	Display and jump to tree
13	153–161	In tree
14	162–205	Failed attempt to position ladder
15	205–214	Pole-vaulting and climbing pole but failing to hold on to it when reaching top
16	214–243	Failure to position bottom of pole before top
17	243–256	Two chimpanzees gripping same pole in play
18	256–263	Running
19	269–275	From pole selection to climbing into tree
20	275–312	Several apes with pole and climbing the pole
21	312–318	Ladder-positioning; second ape holds pole as first one climbs; third ape holds while second climbs
22	322–324	Climbing and swinging
23	324–336	Climbing down tree
24	336–341	From pole selection to positioning pole on tree, with incipient climbing, full climb into tree
25	341–357	Multiple climbing up pole
26	357–370	Climbing up pole
27	347–473	Play with coffee can and tug-of-war with pole
28	479–555	Chimpanzees competing for pole to get access to observation platform; some positioning and incipient climbing (16 incomplete ladders)
29	555–578	Same (3 incomplete ladders)
30	578–580	Holding pole

In addition to these putative differences in cognitive ability, there are also great social differences in the constructional activities of humans and apes. Not only is the human tool-kit more differentiated and more complicated in its use, but there is an open-endedness to the DAEDA-LUS descriptions of all human constructional acts. For even the simplest technologies known to anthropology, the description of one technical task requires the description of a host of other constructions and procedures, and these are partially performed by others. While all behaviours, even in chimpanzees, are ultimately interconnected, as revealed by studies of intra-animal behavioural transitions, humans are apparently unique among mammals in that constructions made by others are similarly interconnected in complex webs of functional contextualization. The use of one ladder by several apes, described by Menzel, is one of the few examples among non-human primates of the social use of a construction made by others of its species. On any transition to a human level of technology, this situation must become the norm. However, since human constructional activity has a social matrix, even individuals acting alone can still be performing socially co-operative tool use; and definitions of social co-operation cannot be restricted to only those cases in which multiple individuals are jointly performing a task. Since *technology*, in a human sense of that term, presupposes a social infrastructure for even individual performances, theories of the ape–hominid transition which attempt to derive 'co-operative tool use' from 'tool use' have placed the cart before the horse. Since intentional action is frequently co-operative and socially regulated in non-human primates, it makes more sense to derive co-operation from social interactions where it already exists than from object-using programs where it does not. Consequently, a theory of the evolution of human technology should place less emphasis on differences in the tool-using capacities between humans and apes (important as these are) but ask instead how emergent tool-using capacities become integrated into the domain of intentional social action.

Appendix 1. Notes on DAEDALUS syntax

An earlier version of DAEDALUS notation has been defined in Backus Normal Form, a notation used for defining the syntax of programming languages (Reynolds 1980). A definition of the present version will eventually be made available to interested persons. In brief, GRIP requires a hand, foot, or mouth as a 'gripper' (second argument), whereas AIMCON can take any 'effector' as its first argument. An effector is any body part, any GRIP module, any FOCUSed part of a GRIP module or body part, any AIMCON function or module, or any FOCUSed part of an AIMCON function or module. All functions can be modularized with ON except for OFF, since 'ON OFF' is undefined, and only ON or OFF functions can be an argument of OFF. The *targets* of GRIP and AIMCON and the domains of FOCUS and SIBYL must be either FOCUS functions, FOCUS modules, or body parts. TERRA can have SEQ functions, SEQ modules, FOCUS functions, FOCUS modules, or body parts as its arguments. BLOCK can have any DAEDALUS expression as an argument. The 'concept' arguments of FOCUS and SIBYL can be any DAEDALUS expression (except OFF) or any word serving as a concept name. Any DAEDALUS expression can also be an argument of SEQ or the *isomer* argument of GRIP.

Recent versions of DAEDALUS use 13 basic operations and simplified syntax making for easier reading.

Appendix 2. Technical data on iconic documents and DAEDALUS descriptions

Chimp-8-78 is a copy of 16-mm colour film taken by Professor Emil Menzel of the State University of New York. It was taken at the Delta Regional Primate Center in Covington, Louisiana, and the author wishes to thank Emil Menzel for the opportunity to examine this material. The film was analysed with aid of a Steenbeck editing machine.

All of the video-tapes were recorded on a Sony Portapack ½″ black-and-white video tape-recorder 3420-CE and video camera AVC-3420-CE. They were analysed with the aid of a Sony editing machine 3670-CA and a Data Systems Design video frame-number generator. All video equipment conforms to Australian (Western European) video standard of 25 frames per second and 625 scanning lines per frame.

The video-tapes discussed were collected by the author or under his supervision at three locations: Preschool-10-77-Imitation at the Australian National University Preschool among 3- and 4-year-old children in a playground; Batek-9 among a hunting and gathering aboriginal group studied by Kirk and Karen Endicott in Kelantan State, West Malaysia; and Beroi-2 and Beroi-3 at a village of Ganei-speaking horticulturalists in Madang Province, Papua New Guinea, studied by Sacha Josephides. I wish to thank the staff of the A.N.U. Preschool, Kirk and Karen Endicott, and Sacha Josephides for their valuable assistance in collecting this material.

The film *Climbing the peach palm* is a 16-mm colour film by Timothy Asch and Napoleon Chagnon, available commercially through Documentary Educational Resources, 5 Bridge Street, Watertown, Massachusetts, U.S.A. The Rotinese material is unedited 16-mm colour footage provided by Timothy Asch.

The DAEDALUS symbols were drawn by Pam Millwood of the Department of Geography, School of General Studies, the Australian National University, and Jane Goodrum provided valuable technical advice on their design. The symbols are photoreduced on to 3M Company translucent stripping film and transferred to 3M Company type 465 transfer tape. They are then transferred one at a time with a stylus to the DAEDALUS graph, which in turn is photoreduced as a unit. The photographs were all taken by the author with a Nikkormat 35-mm camera. The chimpanzee and Yanomamo photos were made from single 16-mm film frames with the aid of an Illuitran slide duplicator. Pam Millwood prepared the graphs and composite figures, and Ann Buller provided invaluable assistance in the preparation of the manuscript.

The collection of the Malaysian material was supported by a small grant from the United States National Institute of Mental Health. The Laboratory of Human Ethology and Ethnographic Film of the Department of Anthropology, A.N.U., provided the facilities for the research described here.

Present affiliation of author: Peter C. Reynolds is presently preparing a monograph on the relationship between language and tool use through the courtesy of a grant from the Harry Frank Guggenheim Foundation.

References

Anderson, J. (1976) *Language, memory and thought.* Lawrence Erlbaum, Hillsdale, N.J.

Beck, B. (1975) 'Primate tool behaviour.' In R. H. Tuttle (ed.), *Socioecology and psychology of primates.* Mouton, The Hague.

Benesh, R. and J. Benesh (1977) 'The Benesh movement notation.' In J. Blacking (ed.), *The anthropology of the body. ASA Monograph, no. 15.* Academic Press, London.

Bobrow, D. G. and A. Collins (eds.) (1975) *Representation and understanding: studies in cognitive science.* Academic Press, London.

Bordes, F. (1971) 'Physical evolution and technological evolution in man: a parallelism.' *World Archaeology* **3**, 1–5.

Bruner, J. S. (1973) 'Organization of early skilled action.' *Child Development* **44**, 1–11.

Carlsöö, S. (1972) *How man moves* (trans. William P. Michael). Heinemann, London.

Chagnon, N. (1977) *Yanomamo: the fierce people*, 2nd edn. Holt, New York.

Charlesworth, W. R. (1979) 'Ethology: understanding the other half of intelligence.' In M. von Cranach *et al.* (eds.), *Human ethology: claims and limits of a new discipline.* Cambridge University Press, Cambridge.

Chomsky, N. (1959) 'Review of B. F. Skinner's *Verbal behavior.*' *Language* **35**, 26–58.

Dawkins, R. (1976) 'Hierarchical organisation: a candidate principle for ethology.' In P. P. G. Bateson and R. A. Hinde (eds.), *Growing points in ethology.* Cambridge University Press, Cambridge.

Fox, J. (1977) *Harvest of the palm: ecological change in eastern Indonesia.* Harvard University Press, Cambridge, Mass.

Gardner, M. (1969) *The ambidextrous universe: left, right, and the fall of parity.* New American Library, New York.

Holloway, R. L., Jr (1969) 'Culture: a *human* domain.' *Current Anthropology* **10**, 395–412.

Hutchinson, A. (1973) *Labanotation: the system of the analyzing and recording movement*. Theatre Art Book, New York.

Kendon, A. (In press) 'Some theoretical and methodological aspects of the use of film in the study of social interaction.' In G. P. Ginsburg (ed.), *Emerging strategies in social psychological research*. Wiley, London.

Lawick-Goodall, J. van (1968) *The behaviour of chimpanzees*. Animal Behaviour Monographs, no. 1.

Leyhausen, P. (1973) 'On the function of the relative hierarchy of moods (as exemplified by the phylogenetic and ontogenetic development of prey-catching in carnivores).' In K. Lorenz and P. Leyhausen (eds.), *Motivation of human and animal behavior: an ethological view*. Van Nostrand Reinhold, New York.

Lorenz, K. (1973) 'The comparative study of behavior.' In K. Lorenz and P. Leyhausen (eds.), *Motivation of human and animal behavior: an ethological view*. Van Nostrand Reinhold, New York.

Menzel, E. W., Jr (1972) 'Spontaneous invention of ladders in a group of young chimpanzees.' *Folia Primatologica* **17**, 87–106.

Miller, G. A., E. Galanter and K. H. Pribram (1960) *Plans and the structure of behavior*. Holt, New York.

Minsky, M. (1975) 'A framework for representing knowledge.' In Henry Winston (ed.), *The psychology of computer vision*. McGraw-Hill, New York.

Peiper, A. (1963) *Cerebral function in infancy and childhood* (trans. Benedict Nagler and Hilde Nagler). Consultants Bureau, New York.

Pribram, K. H. (1971) *Languages of the brain*. Prentice-Hall, Englewood Cliffs, N.J.

— (In press) *Behaviorism, phenomenology, and holism in psychology: a scientific analysis*. Symposium on the Nature of Consciousness, American Psychological Association, Toronto, 1978.

Reynolds, P. C. (1980) 'The programmatic description of simple technologies.' *Journal of Human Movement Studies* **6**, 38–74.

— (1981) *On the evolution of human behavior*. University of California Press, Berkeley and Los Angeles.

Schank, R. C., and K. M. Colby (eds.) (1973) *Computer models of thought and language*. W. H. Freeman, San Francisco.

Schebesta, P. (1928) *Among the forest dwarfs of Malaya* (trans. Arthur Chambers). Hutchinson, London.

Siklossy, L. (1976) *Let's talk LISP*. Prentice-Hall, Englewood Cliffs, N.J.

Tinbergen, N. (1950) 'The hierarchical organization of the nervous mechanisms underlying instinctive behaviour.' In *Physiological mechanisms in animal behaviour*. Symposia of the Society for Experimental Biology, no. 4. Academic Press, New York.

Winston, P. H. (ed.) (1975) *The psychology of computer vision*. McGraw-Hill, New York.

Editors' Epilogue

This volume has become much larger than originally intended; and although a thorough comparison of the viewpoints presented in the various chapters, and a profound discussion of the multitude of emerging problems, would demand a comprehensive concluding chapter, we restrict ourselves to a few remarks. This may be justified, since the chapters' introduction, and especially our considerations in Chapter 1 are already a synopsis.

A complex of theory, method and tentative empirical findings, such as that presented in this work, has to find its justification at several different levels and on several different axes. The methods that derive from the need to test the power of the theoretical concepts to inspire empirical hypotheses must show that the concepts are indeed substantiated, in some plausible way. Even in the material here presented it is plain that the dual hypothesis, that actions are to be understood in terms of the intersection of actors' intentions and interactors' interpretations, and that they are the product of a specific kind of cognitive process are well substantiated. Just what kind is prescribed by the general theory of action which requires that there be some system of means–end structures, which come into being through the joint process of goal-setting and rule-selection. In both the studies of skilled motor performance and skilled social performance (Chapters 2 and 3) there are clear empirical demonstrations of key aspects of the general theory. Hacker, Kaminsky and von Cranach and Kalbermatten demonstrate that there are means–ends cognitions and Marsh shows that competent actors have a presentation of the usable rules.

Von Cranach and Kalbermatten's examples also indicate, that means–end cognitions can be rule-determined themselves. The tension between the means–end and the rules viewpoints constitutes the first pervading theme of discussion of cognitive action-steering factors, and the integra-

387

tion of these two viewpoints remains one of the most urgent tasks for research. This theme is complemented by two other topics, the question of how the conscious quality of action is related to cognition, its appearance and function; and the problem of the interrelation of the structures of social and individual knowledge (see especially Luckmann and Kreckel), which forms the basis of all action-related cognitions.

But at another level of justification there must be some consideration of temporal axes. If the general theory enables one effectively to study adult performance, it should also suggest developmental problems. How is that mode of action genesis established in the individual, and how was it established in the species? The latter requires comparative studies of action genesis ideally across the whole primate family. P. Reynolds has shown the similarities and contrasts between man and chimpanzee, but only with respect to instrumental object use. The next step would be to follow up such anecdotes as Jane Goodall's description of Mike's innovations in the expressive, symbolic use of objects, in order to explore comparative hypotheses about social cognitions. In looking at developmental problems on an individual basis Bruner has shown how complex is the process by which action schemata are laid down. A fairly well-defined research programme opens out from his position, again naturally branching into the study of motoric, practical action schemata and the study of social, expressive schemata. The importance of metonymic uses of material things in the expressive order suggests that the study of the coordination of these developmental processes and stages would repay very detailed study.

Let us now turn to some of the particular problems of the chapters, which also give rise to general considerations. There are three main conclusions which we can draw from Chapter 2; they concern the basic action model, the need for descriptive research and the necessity to develop new methods. Not only these three articles (Hacker, Kaminsky, and von Cranach and Kalbermatten), but also other papers in the book (e.g. Bruner, Peter Reynolds) show that there exists in fact a well-developed and consistent, although still restricted, common theoretical nucleus: the model of the two-dimensional (temporal and hierarchical) organization of action, governed by mental representations and regulated by feedback cycles (as has been developed in Marxist psychology of labour activity and industrial psychology; e.g. Hacker). Note that this is as much a mode of the organization of motor performance as of its interaction with the steering cognitions which provide directedness and control, and that it allows for the introduction of different degrees of conscious awareness. This model is so general in application, so flexible and by now so well sustained by research outside and inside the laboratory, that it can be considered a solid starting point.

The paper by von Cranach and Kalbermatten, an attempt to demonstrate the social nature of GDA, illustrates how additional concepts can be integrated into this model to develop a more general action theory. These are just core concepts of a rule or grammar approach, so that we could seriously question whether there still remains need and room for a *separate* 'grammar of action'. Certainly, we should not just relate 'expressive action' to the rule approach and 'practical action' to the means–end approach. Perhaps we should apply, as a next step, the two-dimensional organization model to purely expressive acts. From this kind of research, an integrated theory could develop which would differ from the labour-activity concept by considering social cognitions as regulative factors in action organization; and from a conservative rule approach by transforming the concept of rule from a prescription which is externally determined and given *a priori* to an actor's cognition which constantly emerges in the interplay between intentions and the representations of society. This would be quite in line with some of the ideas presented in Chapter 3 by Clarke and Brenner.

Our second general conclusion is that any further development of action theory, in whatever direction it should lead, demands a broader inductive basis; we therefore need many more descriptive studies from various areas of social life. These should aim at different kinds of action performed by different kinds of actors in different cultural contexts, and should shed light on the interplay of variables as well of behaviour organization as of cognition and social meaning, as they occur in natural situations. Before further contrasting elaborated models, it is essential to know what people actually do when they are free to choose, not just what scientists think they should do.

A prerequisite of such endeavour (and this is our third conclusion) is the development of adequate methods, in addition to the existing ones. Since, in comparison to their evaluation, the collection of data has been neglected, the primary need is the development of descriptive methods; first attempts have already been presented in some of the studies. Equally useful might be the development of analytical and inferential methods which are not based on inadequate probabilistic assumptions.

We have already discussed some of the problems of a rule approach. If we consider the contributions of Clarke, Brenner and Marsh together and in their own right, some fairly strong conclusions emerge. Clarke shows that if action analysis is to be faithful to the material to be analysed then action must be thought of as structures emerging in time, rather than as atomic events contingently connected. Brenner demonstrates that there is a penumbra of important types of cases where the structure must be considered not only to be emerging but to be evolving in time. So if, as Marsh has demonstrated, the hypothetical rule systems which are assumed to control the emergence of such structures are actually researchable objects, Brenner's observation opens up a further research dimension. There are various possibilities to explain the evolution of a structure in real time. It might be that the rule system engaged in its production is itself evolving, but it might be that the appearance of novelty of structure may be due to the interaction of several existing rule systems, which though themselves stable, interact in novel ways. Some of Brenner's own research tends to suggest the latter.

But there is another and more tantalizing conclusion that follows from Clarke's observation that none of the existing mathematical systems used in the analysis of the nearest analogue to episode structure, namely linguistic structure, can be transferred to the social realm. The mathematics for systematic, abstract representation of the form of social action structures does not yet exist. Quite clearly we are being offered a research target of some magnitude. Some preliminary work is already under way in Oxford on remedying this deficit. If one looks at the problem of structure with some analogue of Saussure's distinction between paradigmatic and syntagmatic order in mind, certain further analogies suggest themselves. In a Saussurean analysis every item that actually occurs in a real-time structure, the syntagm, is to be considered as a choice from a repertoire of possible items that might, under certain meaning-preserving constraints, have appeared at that point. The paradigmatic dimension then consists of a vector whose elements are possible alternatives to what actually was produced, and whose structure represents the relative probabilities of that alternative appearing in that type of structure. The set of such vectors is a matrix of possibilities, labelled with probabilities. At each moment in real time the actual choice modifies the probabilities of the next choice, that is reorders the elements of the next vector (or column of the total matrix). The mathematics for this kind of operation are already well developed in quantum mechanics. Whether this effort is successful or not, it remains clear that a major research dimension has now opened up.

The contributions by Luckmann and Kreckel fit together as theoretical analysis and empirical verification. There are stocks of knowledge differentiated as Luckmann suggests. The further study of the means by which such stocks are used, by people such as Kreckel's family members, has already been adumbrated in the contributions by von Cranach, Hacker and Kaminsky. All that is required to include the use of a local stock of knowledge in the social context is no more than a turning of investigative attention to cases of social action. So a very obvious enlargement of the existing research possibilities opens out from there.

Luckmann has emphasized both in his chapter and in other places how important it is to think of the common stock of knowledge as differentiated. The same thought must surely apply to the restricted stock that constitutes a family's social conventions. There is social order within a family, and there are likely to be differentiations in the degree to which different members are taken to be authoritative on what is an authentic item of knowledge. The research so far has concentrated on showing what the family have in common in contrast to outsiders. But it is clearly also worth studying how that material is internally organized and differentiated. Finally, it would be intriguing to investigate how and to what degree this social organization of knowledge is reflected in the individual actor's mind.

The idea that action and knowledge should be seen in relation to various temporal dimensions, such as history and autobiography, suggests some further dimensions of research. Insofar as the psychology of the people of an epoch is a function of what they believe themselves to be and how they believe action should be organized and indeed controlled, the idea of a historically conditioned psychology appears. Some fragmentary efforts have been made to study these matters, but much remains to be done. The autobiographical point has been much emphasized by J.-P. de Waele in his pioneering studies of the way people can be assisted to formulate very detailed accounts of their own life-courses. So far his studies have been restricted to a narrow slice of time and place, but a great deal of interest must lie in pursuing that kind of study, with an eye to the growing stock of knowledge.

Such a view seems to presuppose a concept of the life-long development of action; but this is as yet far out of reach, since today we command just a few insights into the development of action in small infants. In Chapter 2, we have presented these together with discussions of the phylogenetic development of action, since the two topics have a number of problems in common. The three papers in Chapter 5 stress the general importance of the action concept for the understanding of early socialization processes of non-human primate behaviour. These papers bring problems to our attention which we cannot afford to overlook. First the authors emphasize the social nature of action; but Bruner's and Vernon Reynolds's reports make it very obvious that the organization of action is very much related to affect and emotion. Second, all these papers agree on the fact that an action definition suited for non-human primates and small infants must do without the character of conscious awareness. *Consciousness and emotion* are the two main topics left for discussion; we can treat these topics separately, but also try to bring them together into a more coherent statement of the problem.

As to *consciousness*, we have presented some reasons why it constitutes an important concept in the analysis of adult action (von Cranach, this volume, section 5.2.1). Let us add that the conscious nature of action-related cognitions *relates action to society*: the *societal* (and that is more than just *social*) character of GDA depends on the actor's conscious control of his own behaviour. Animals' actions are social, but not societal; and infants and children, insofar as they lack conscious action control, are not self-reliant members of society in regard to their actions, but share their fate with their related adults. (Thus the relations of action psychology to other disciplines, like law, come into our view.) Therefore it is crucial in socialization research to investigate the development of conscious control; and the study of its forms, distributions and functions remains an important task of action psychology in general.

Consciousness, to define it in a very general way, is selective awareness of our own state. Thus, it is a *self-monitoring device*, as these are useful for the operation of complex information-processing systems. The attention theorem proposed by von Cranach (this volume) predicts that as far as action is concerned, consciousness reflects the points of difficulty, where something is at stake. We should not overlook that *emotion* probably serves a very similar function. At least some modern theories of emotion (e.g. Lazarus) tend to maintain that emotion indicates to the organism, in a more general way, his stance in affairs where it matters; and affect, its more aroused form, tells the organism that something of greater importance, an existential problem, is at stake. From the phylogenetic point of view, emotion may be an older self-monitoring device which is present in higher animals; but as far as we can say these have no awareness; they may feel, but certainly do not reflect upon their emotions. Man possesses a double self-monitoring outfit, the system of emotions and that of conscious cognitions; and, what makes it even more complicated, the former is mirrored in the latter, so that a *self-reflection of emotion* can occur: we do not only feel our emotions, but reflect them as our own state in our conscious cognitions.

After these preliminaries, let us come to our point: in consequence of its proposed functional analogy to conscious cognitions, emotion must be assumed to serve important action-related functions too; and its reflection in conscious cognitions must result in an organizing and regulating impact on the details of performance in action. In fact, intuitively and from experiences from other disciplines (like psycho-pathology and psychotherapy) we do know that this is the case; but in GDA research, to our knowledge, directed studies of these processes have never been performed. Such research would be of highest import-ance for our field, and would also promote our understanding of emotion in general.

At this point, the reader may feel entitled to expect an excursus into the problems of emotion's sibling, motivation. Since this concept has hardly been treated in this book (nor at the conference), we shall not go into the matter here. It may be sufficient to state that in order to be of use for the study of GDA, motivation should not be treated as a gross variable operating before and at the basis of behaviour, but (just like emotion) in its detailed consequences for the sequential and hierarchical organization of action. Nor should we forget that all these labels, cognition, motivation, and emotion, reflect as much the scientist's intellectual approach as the organism's true structure.

To conclude, these considerations again show that action research is related to many problems in the social sciences; small wonder with a concept which is so central a category in the social sciences.

Subject index

Note: page numbers in bold type refer to a major discussion of the topic; those in italic refer to a diagram or table.

Name index